MARK, MUTUALITY, AND MENTAL HEALTH

Society of Biblical Literature

Semeia Studies

Gerald O. West, General Editor

Editorial Board
Pablo Andiñach
Fiona Black
Denise K. Buell
Gay L. Byron
Steed V. Davidson
Jennifer L. Koosed
Monica Jyotsna Melanchthon
Yak-Hwee Tan

Number 79
Volume Editor: Gerald O. West

MARK, MUTUALITY, AND MENTAL HEALTH

ENCOUNTERS WITH JESUS

By
Simon Mainwaring

SBL Press
Atlanta

Copyright © 2014 by SBL Press

All rights reserved. No part of this work may be reproduced or transmitted in any form or by any means, electronic or mechanical, including photocopying and recording, or by means of any information storage or retrieval system, except as may be expressly permitted by the 1976 Copyright Act or in writing from the publisher. Requests for permission should be addressed in writing to the Rights and Permissions Office, SBL Press, 825 Houston Mill Road, Atlanta, GA 30329 USA.

Library of Congress Cataloging-in-Publication Data

Mainwaring, Simon.
　Mark, mutuality, and mental health : encounters with Jesus / Simon Mainwaring.
　　　p. cm. — (Society of Biblical Literature. Semeia studies ; number 79)
　Includes bibliographical references and indexes.
　ISBN 978-1-58983-984-7 (paper binding : alk. paper) — ISBN 978-1-58983-986-1 (electronic format) — ISBN 978-1-58983-985-4 (hardcover binding : alk. paper)
　1. Bible. Mark—Criticism, interpretation, etc. 2. Bible. Mark—Postcolonial criticism. 3. Mental health—Biblical teaching. 4. Power (Christian theology)—Biblical teaching. I. Title.
　BS2585.52.M27 2014
　226.3'06—dc23   2014010038

Printed on acid-free, recycled paper conforming to
ANSI/NISO Z39.48-1992 (R1997) and ISO 9706:1994
standards for paper permanence.

All things are twofold, one opposite the other,
and he has made nothing incomplete.
One confirms the good things of the other,
and who can have enough of beholding his glory?

Sirach 42:24–25 RSV

Contents

Foreword..ix
Acknowledgments..xi
Abbreviations xiii

Introduction 1

1. Relational Dynamics of Poor Mental Health:
   Assessing Existing Paradigms..15
   1.1. Relational Dynamics and Mental Health:
        Tracing the Contours of Context   15
   1.2. Liberation Hermeneutics and Poor Mental Health:
        Resistive Theologies at the Margins   21
   1.3. Foucault: Power and Poor Mental Health   32
   1.4. Conclusion   40

2. Mutuality: A Postcolonial Praxis for the Relational Dynamics
   of Poor Mental Health 43
   2.1. Beyond Mutuality as an Aspiration: Mutuality as a Praxis   43
   2.2. Postcolonial Praxes: Cocreating Third Space   51
   2.3. Mutuality as a Postcolonial Praxis of Resistance
        and Transformation   58
   2.4. Conclusion   61

3. Dialogue and Difference: Mutuality and
   Biblical Hermeneutics...63
   3.1. Postcolonial Biblical Criticism: Strands of
        Hermeneutical Interest   63
   3.2. Difference in Colonial Relational Dynamics:
        Renegotiating the Jesus Encounter in Mark   67
   3.3. Reading with Difference: Dialogical Biblical Criticism   71

	3.4. Mutuality and Mark: A Method for Reading with Persons with Poor Mental Health	78
	3.5. Conclusion	87
4.	Identity, Labels, and Resistance: Mark 3:1–6 and 3:19b–35	89
	4.1. Mark 3:1–6	89
	4.2. Mark 3:19b–35	109
	4.3. Conclusion	127
5.	Negotiating Marginal Agency: Mark 5:21–43 and 7:24–30	129
	5.1. Mark 5:21–43	129
	5.2. Mark 7:24–30	149
	5.3. Conclusion	164
6.	Dialogue and Mutuality: Mark 5:1–20 and 15:1–5	167
	6.1. Mark 5:1–20	167
	6.2. Mark 15:1–5	185
	6.3. Conclusion	201
7.	Mutuality and Mark: Reflections Textual and Contextual	203
	7.1. Mutuality As a Postcolonial Praxis: Qualities and Efficacies within Textual Relational Dynamics	203
	7.2. Mutuality and Mark: Hermeneutical Achievements and Limitations	212

Appendix: Reading Group Transcripts 223

Bibliography 315

Index of Ancient Sources 345
Index of Modern Authors 349
Index of Subjects 355

Foreword

Our custom in Semeia Studies is to allocate a member from the editorial board to work alongside the author or editor of the project submitted. As the General Editor of Semeia Studies, I usually try to identify someone from the board who would resonate with the project and offer support to the author or editor. In this case, I allocated myself!

Semeia Studies assigns itself the task of trawling the edges of the discipline(s) of biblical studies, in search of projects that push and transgress the boundaries and that offer innovative sites of interpretation and methods for interpretation. My own work inhabits not only the margins of the discipline(s) but also the margins of society. So Simon Mainwaring's project was of immediate interest.

Those of us who do our biblical studies in "the south" or "third world" are always drawn to colleagues in "the north" or "first world" who do their work on the margins of their world. We have little choice in working on the margins. Our communities summon us from our academies and demand that we deploy our resources with them as they struggle to forge redemption from a text that matters in their contexts. Fewer of our northern colleagues, inhabiting either the (tenuous but tenacious) empires of old in Europe or the newer empire of "America," seem to be summoned as we have been, so we pay attention when we witness such a summons.

Simon Mainwaring has been summoned by those who suffer poor mental health, and he has responded, coming alongside those on this margin and offering his resources to read with them. Mainwaring carefully locates himself among these marginalized people who reside in the cracks of empire. He also carefully locates himself among the experience and scholarship of those who have made similar choices. His detailed engagement with our work is a significant contribution of his book, bringing together as he does a range of diverse voices and sites of social location. Equally significant is how he constructs his own place within this work, as mindful of those he does his readings among as his academic dialogue partners.

The late Per Frostin argued many years ago now that liberation biblical and theological hermeneutics was distinctive in two related respects. First, social relations were seen as the primary site of doing theology; second, within the domain of social relations, a preferential option was made for the poor and marginalized. This commitment is more than an ethical choice; solidarity with the poor and marginalized has consequences for the perception of social reality; it is an epistemological necessity in the struggle for liberation.[1] Early forms of liberation theology did not recognize what Marcella Althaus-Reid refers to as the "indecent" margins of the margins.[2] Mainwaring has, and in doing so he serves us all, acknowledging the dignity of these people, allowing their readings of Mark to summon us to our own rereadings.

Itumeleng Mosala reminds us that only eyes shaped by marginalization can see particular dimensions of both context and biblical text.[3] This is why we must read with them. Until they have spoken, we cannot know what these texts (that matter in certain contexts) might mean. Mainwaring's work, and those he reads with, offers us resources both old and new.

Gerald O. West

---

1. Per Frostin, *Liberation Theology in Tanzania and South Africa: A First World Interpretation* (Lund: Lund University Press, 1988), 6–7.

2. Marcella Althaus-Reid, *Indecent Theology: Theological Perversions in Sex, Gender and Politics* (London: Routledge, 2000).

3. Itumeleng J. Mosala, "The Use of the Bible in Black Theology," in *The Unquestionable Right to Be Free: Essays in Black Theology* (ed. Itumeleng J. Mosala and Buti Tlhagale; Johannesburg: Skotaville, 1986),196.

Acknowledgments

I am grateful to R. S. Sugirtharajah for all of the guidance that he has offered; to those who have dialogued with me through the process of producing this work, particularly Barbara Allison-Bryan, Tyler Watson, and Hans Patton; and to all the group readers without whom this project would not have been possible. I dedicate this work to my wife, Monica, for all of the hours, early, late, and in between, that she listened, encouraged, debated, and looked after our family for the both of us.

Abbreviations

Bib	*Biblica*
BNTC	Black's New Testament Commentaries
BTB	*Biblical Theology Bulletin*
ExpTim	*Expository Times*
JBL	*Journal of Biblical Literature*
JSNT	*Journal for the Study of the New Testament*
JSNTSup	Journal for the Study of the New Testament: Supplement Series
NovT	*Novum Testamentum*
NRSV	New Revised Standard Version
NTS	*New Testament Studies*
RSV	Revised Standard Version
SBLDS	Society of Biblical Literature Dissertation Series
SemeiaSt	Semeia Studies
SJT	*Scottish Journal of Theology*
SNTSMS	Society for New Testament Studies Monograph Series
ZNW	*Zeitschrift für die neutestamentliche Wissenschaft*

Introduction

A woman paces from pew to pew around the church. She is shouting, "I don't know what to do, tell me what to do." She has been in and out of our lives for the past several days, homeless and destitute, struggling to hold onto a coherent thought and often displaying rapid mood swings. She has come early for the Alcoholics Anonymous group that meets in an upper room of the church building as one of hundreds of men and women that the church welcomes every week as they find their way back from the abyss on the strength of a community of witnesses to their journey of pain and hope. I stand with her, then we sit. We pray. She goes. And then, ten minutes after her AA meeting begins, I see her leave by the back alleyway door with a fresh cup of coffee in her hand.

Conversations matter. Connections matter. How people relate to one another matters. The above vignette describes one of many relational encounters that have served for me as a motivation to undertake the work that follows. It has been via conversations such as these that I have found both a passion and an intellectual interest emerge for how people relate to persons with poor mental health.[1] Even in this age of inclusion, of antidiscrimination legislation,[2] and of altered nomenclature,[3] fear and

---

1. I have chosen to use the term "poor mental health" rather than "mental illness" in respect for the many readers with whom I have worked through the course of this project. That is, in sharing texts with readers who experience poor mental health of differing forms, I have noticed a common resistance to labeling such as "mad," "crazy," or "lunatic," which to some of the readers has suggested a radical and perhaps even insurmountable alterity. By contrast, the term "poor mental health," while still being a label of sorts, is at least an attempt to describe a lived reality rather than an attempt to categorize persons as essentially different.

2. See, for instance, the Disability Discrimination Acts (1995, 2005) and the Mental Health Act (1983) in the U.K. and Mental Health Parity Act (1996) and Americans with Disabilities Act (1990) in the U.S.

3. For instance, "differently abled" rather than "disabled" and "developmentally challenged" and "mental distress' rather than mentally retarded and mental illness.

stereotypical representation of poor mental health and the denigration of persons with poor mental health are still commonplace in North Atlantic societies.[4]

This work is interested in the societal contexts of those who suffer poor mental health, and in particular the relational dynamics of those contexts, namely how identity, agency, and dialogue are negotiated in personal encounters. I am interested in these relational dynamics not merely for their own sake, but in how these contextual dynamics of relating might correlate with the relational dynamics narrated in the stories of ancient biblical texts, and then in turn how the reading of those texts might offer insights for those contextual dynamics.

This pattern of context to text and back to context is a well-worn path in biblical studies, and I will locate this particular work within that milieu in the pages that follow. It suffices to say here that this work seeks to serve as a heuristic, such that interested readers might better understand the dynamics of relational power that pervade encounters with persons with poor mental health. As a biblical scholar who is embedded not in the academy but in the contexts about which I write—working with those who struggle with the societal consequences of suffering with poor mental health on a daily basis[5]—this work is intended to offer an incitement for those who wish to engage with it to reassess how they relate to such persons. There are no models or prescriptions for behavior offered here. Rather, textual encounters are offered as vehicles for contextual reflection, and I hope that whoever the readers of this work might end up being, their views, both of the texts in question and of the contexts under consideration, might at least be enriched if not incrementally altered. In a sense,

---

4. I have chosen to utilize "North Atlantic," referring to North American and European societies, rather than alternatives such as "more developed," "First World," or "Western" societies. I have done so mindful of critiques both of the notion of development as an acceptable delineation of nations in an era of globalization that has problematized such delineations, and of the notion of what constitutes "the West." Given my interest in postcolonial studies, avoiding the use of "Western" is particularly significant. For instance, Benny Liew has offered a critique of the notion of "Western" as a kind of "cultural territorialism that 'fossilizes' different cultures in distinctly separate and definable spaces'; an endeavor proven "untenable in the light of history" (Liew 1999, 24).

5. Currently, my social location for this work is in a beach community in San Diego, California, working with a homeless population among whom mental health challenges while hard to quantify are self-evidently high and significant.

then, I hope that every reader of this work will end up being a contextual biblical theologian, such that through the interpretation of the relational dynamics narrated in ancient biblical stories the current pattern of relational dynamics vis-à-vis poor mental health, as much as they diminish human value, might be resisted and perhaps even begin to be reimagined and in doing so be incrementally transformed. Indeed, if all reading is a political act it is certainly my hope that this book will not prove to be an exception to that rule.

Given its interest in text and context, this is a project that is broad in its range of interdisciplinary interests. Chapter 1 begins by laying out the background for this contextual biblical study by offering a description of what I argue to be the societal location of the relational dynamics of persons with poor mental health in contemporary North Atlantic societies. Following that fundamental contextual premise, and wishing to locate my own contextual biblical work within biblical and theological paradigms that have considered the societal location of poor mental health, I present an analysis of liberation hermeneutics.[6] While offering much to biblical hermeneutics and praxis in its wider appreciation of structural power and its call to prophetic pastoral praxis, I argue that liberation hermeneutics' fundamental flaws of textual selectivity, theological predeterminedness, and a limited analysis of power relations, severely constrict it as a paradigm for context and for its textual analysis of relational dynamics. Indeed, the most central critique of liberation hermeneutics is that inherent in the paradigm is the notion of progress from bondage to freedom in the motif of liberation from the margins. Such a motif is offered in the end, both to the reading of texts and to the praxes of contexts, as an aspiration or teleology without any significant suggestion as to how such a struggle for freedom might occur other than it should.

Thus, taking on liberation hermeneutics' interest in relational power yet also recognizing the deficit that I argue to exist in this paradigm with

---

6. Throughout the book I refer to liberation hermeneutics as one whole collection of different forms of biblical criticism. While I do assess in ch. 1 the various ways in which this form of biblical criticism and theology has evolved since its Latin American inception, I assess its use as a way of thinking about the relational dynamics of poor mental health as reasonably unified. Thus the singular grammatical form being used here is not to suggest that liberation hermeneutics in all of its complexities and variations is homogenous; rather it is to suggest that its use by theologians who have been interested in poor mental health has been most closely tied to its earliest form focusing on the motif of "liberation from the margins."

regard to its ability to articulate how power structures might be resisted, I then turn to a paradigm outside biblical criticism: the work of Michel Foucault and his analysis of discourse on "madness/unreason." Making clear that he sees power not only as oppressive but also productive, I argue that Foucault's work offers some of the conceptual tools that might enable an analysis of how struggles for power might be had not beyond "the margins," but within them as struggles for power in relationship. That is, the focus that Foucault's work offers is how struggles are had within oppressive power dynamics, thus resisting the move away from oppression that liberation hermeneutics tends to focus on. Thus I argue that despite some significant critiques that have been made of Foucault's understanding of agency inherent in his concepts of discourse and power, his work points to the possibility of power in relation and counterdiscourse. Thus the core benefit of a Foucauldian analysis of the relational dynamics of poor mental health is the incitement to reimagine such hegemonic relational dynamics.

Building on the insights of both liberation hermeneutics and Foucault, in chapter 2 I introduce mutuality as the core concept of this work. I argue that it is the Foucauldian analysis of relational dynamics operating within hegemonic societal power structures that prompts the exploration of mutuality as a way of conceiving of power within relational encounters. I also maintain that my analysis will be based primarily on the study of textual relational encounters rather than theological concepts or textual motifs. That is, unlike liberation hermeneutics, my own approach to reading biblical texts as a way of thinking about the real life relational dynamics of poor mental health will not explore texts for overarching themes, or theological frameworks, rather it will closely read encounters in texts as they occur between individual characters to see how the praxis of mutuality operates in those encounters.

In setting up this textual study, I assess the uses of mutuality as it has emerged in three paradigms: mental health literature, feminist theologies, and theologies of disability. Within mental health literature the use of mutuality is diverse, and I argue that as a consequence the concept retains a nebulous quality and holds very little explanatory power in terms of how the aspiration for mutuality might be attained or negotiated within relational dynamics. In this regard, theologies of disability are seen to be more descriptive of the tensions that the praxis of mutuality inhabits within relational dynamics, such as Nancy Eiesland's work, which stresses the ambiguity of embodiment, such that relational dynamics are seen as the negotiation of a single space of difference and sameness. Thus Eiesland's work, despite utilizing the liberation paradigm, largely evades the binaristic oppressor/oppressed nature of that conceptual frame and invites a consideration of mutuality as the ambiguous exchange of relational dynamics. A similar appreciation of ambiguity is explored in the feminist theology of Carter Heyward and her use of mutuality as a core component of right relating that is inherent as a potential in encounters between persons. Heyward argues that the power to transform hegemonic power structures is not a power that needs to be given to persons; rather it is a power already present.

While Eiesland and Heyward's notions of mutuality as ambiguous, and the inherent power in relating, are significant conceptual developments, what I argue to be absent from these explorations is the strategic element that a praxis-oriented approach to mutuality requires. In the end, the work of these thinkers still leaves the explanatory power of the concept of mutuality at a loss, and is still more aspirational than it is descriptive of how power is reimagined. In search of a more strategically inclined understanding of mutuality, I then seek to locate the concept within the paradigm of postcolonial criticism in the work of Homi Bhabha in particular. What I take from Bhabha's work for the exploration of mutuality as a postcolonial praxis is twofold. First, with his own strategic elements of postcolonial praxes in mind—hybridity, mimicry, sly civility, and so on—mutuality can be situated as one strategy among several. That is, when textual relational dynamics are explored, mutuality should not be considered as a praxis that operates in isolation, but as one that interacts with other praxes influencing their effectiveness and vice versa, as well as merging with them to form a composite postcolonial praxis. Second, and responding to the critique of Bhabha's work that it seems to limit the notion of resistive agency to struggles for survival within hegemonic discourse, I argue that what Bhabha's *Third Space* agency offers my exploration of mutuality is the notion of postcolonial praxis operating more at a liminal level, or in appreciation of James C. Scott's work, at a hidden level of relational encounter. Thus, via Bhabha, mutuality might be conceived of as a postcolonial praxis that exercises incremental and supplemental agency within the structures of power.

I also argue, somewhat as an extension of Bhabha's work, that as a postcolonial praxis, mutuality might be seen to push at the boundaries of postcolonial thought as a strategy not only for reactive survival within power structures but also for the transformation of those structures. Thus, while wishing to explore mutuality as a strategic praxis, I also seek to retain its aspirational qualities as held to be significant by the theologies of Eiesland and Heyward. Pulling these various strands together, then, I conclude chapter 2 by presenting my own understanding of mutuality as a strategic praxis of resistance and transformation that will be considered as a praxis for contemporary contexts through the reading of ancient biblical texts.

It is to this act of reading that I then turn in chapter 3. The texts used in this contextual biblical study are all taken from the Gospel of Mark. I selected Mark due to its potential as a text rich in points of tension between the different characters in the stories narrated. The six pericopae selected within Mark all narrate encounters had by Jesus and other characters and were chosen for their interest in the relational dynamics between Jesus and those characters: Jesus, "the Pharisees," and the man with the withered hand in the synagogue (3:1–6); Jesus, his family, and "the scribes" (3:19b–35); Jesus and the demon-possessed man among the tombs (5:1–20); Jesus, Jairus, and the woman with hemorrhages (5:21–43); Jesus and the Syrophoenician woman (7:24–30); and Jesus before Pilate (15:1–5). The hermeneutic utilized in reading these texts draws on the impetus of mutuality as the core concept of this work and postcolonial criticism as the core paradigm for its exploration. I explore the potential of postcolonial biblical criticism as a hermeneutic for reading via an outline of the broad clusters of this hermeneutic in general, and then via an assessment of how postcolonial criticism has been applied to Mark in particular. The potential of postcolonial biblical criticism in general is that it stands as a hermeneutic spacious enough for multiple questions and multiple answers to be offered of texts, generating multiple interpretive perspectives. This has been seen in a number of different ways, with some forms of postcolonial biblical criticism interrogating ancient texts for their colonial contexts, others attempting to uncover the so-called hidden or at least submerged voices within texts, and still others exploring the potential interlocution offered by extrabiblical literature. As well as these, there is the strand that is of most interest to this work, that seeks to utilize the insights of postcolonial criticism as offering heuristics for the reading of texts. The potential of this particular hermeneutical strand applied to Mark has been used to question the notion of agency in the reading of that gospel. I analyze Benny Liew's questioning of the predominance of an over-romanticized interpretation of Jesus and his argument that suggests that Jesus mimics rather than contests colonial power structures. As a contrast, I consider Simon Samuel's suggestion that the postcolonial lens renders a more fluid and ambiguous Jesus whose agency is not always easy to place. Arguing along the lines of Samuel's stress on the fluidity and ambiguity of agency in Mark, I propose my own model for how the characters in Mark might be seen to engage in a contested space of agency, wherein power is negotiated between characters and is not the sole reserve of some at the exclusion of others.

With this conceptual alignment within postcolonial biblical studies in place, the fundamental gap in this milieu that I argue this work wishes to fill is the one that I take to be present in Gayatri Spivak's paradigmatic shaping question: "Can the subaltern speak?" (Spivak 1995). Spivak wishes to problematize the notion that the oppressed, if given the chance, "know and can speak of their conditions" (25). She argues that in this searching out of previously unheard voices, the "rendering of the individual" is lost to a rendering of the structures that the individual finds herself in and has been hidden by (28). That is, Spivak's critique is that the search for particular histories and voices of oppressed persons is subsumed in the analysis of the structure of power and knowledge that has led to the oppression of the oppressed in the first place. What Spivak's argument brings to the fore is a crucial distinction between the consciousness of the intellectual who encounters "the subaltern" in textual analysis and the subaltern herself/himself. That is, the insurgent voice is, according to Spivak, uttered from an "irretrievable consciousness" (28). For, as the voice of the "other" is heard it is transcribed into a *grammar* that is not its own. And so the voice of the oppressed in the dialect of the academy is not one that ever speaks of itself.

However, one of the searing ironies of postcolonial criticism's concern for the voice of the "other" is the absence of the subaltern's voice in postcolonial academic writing.[7] Furthermore, the vocabulary of the postcolonial

---

7. A similar argument has been put forward by Rieger with regards to liberation theology's interest with "the margins" as a paradigmatic marker of theological inquiry. Rieger argues for "creating broader alliances with people at the margins" and the need for a "connection to the margins" with theology articulated "from the perspective of the subaltern" (see Rieger 2004, 211–15). However, while Rieger argues that "we" should give up our conventional assumptions, his own exploration of the possibility of "creating broader alliances" still looks to fall within the dichotomous paradigm of classic liberation theology, utilizing statements such as, "truth thus conceived can only be perceived from the margins." Left unanswered by such a stance are questions as to how different "truths" might interrelate, and in his own essentializing of "the margins" as a site of hermeneutical privilege there is no sense that there might be struggles within

genre is oftentimes so dense and jargonized that it is hard to imagine many who are not in "the know" of the postcolonial lingua franca being able to engage in a dialogue with postcolonial critique without first having to learn another grammar. It is here that the irony lies: not just that postcolonial criticism is at times an inaccessible and overintellectualized form of academic parlance, but that it inhabits a practice of exclusion.

In response to Spivak's assertion that the subaltern cannot speak in the textual expressions of the academy, this work seeks to directly address the absence of subaltern voices within postcolonial biblical criticism by inviting them to the table of textual interpretation. This is not at all to dismiss the profound challenge that both assessing the social location of and engaging with so-called subalterns in the reading of texts poses. What it is aimed at doing, though, is to open the somewhat closed-off system of postcolonial criticism to other voices, keeping in mind that this endeavor will be an imperfect expansion of this hermeneutical frame, yet an expansion all the same.

With this aim in mind, the second strand of concern in developing the reading strategy is how the core concept of mutuality and the paradigm of postcolonial biblical criticism might be applied to the field of dialogical hermeneutics. Tracing the development of the field, particularly with the work of Gerald West, I explore how the dialogical approach to contextually interested biblical studies offers much in its engagement with the so-called ordinary reader, thus breaking the isolation of biblical studies from the interlocution of those who are often socially disconnected from the contexts of such ordinary readers. What dialogical hermeneutics contain, then, is the potential to have room for difference.

That said, while this potential for having room for difference is there in dialogical hermeneutics, I argue that the reality has proved harder to achieve. Central to this has been the role of the reading facilitator as an "interested reader" and the way in which this facilitator retains the right to arbitrate difference when interpreting texts with others. I argue that this distinction between so-called ordinary and trained reader proves to be unhelpful and propose instead a more flat model for reading wherein no arbitration of difference is offered. Laying out my own reading strategy, then, I describe how the relational dynamics of textual narratives are explored in a succession of prepared and spontaneous questions. True to

---

marginal spaces for discursive voice; multiple levels of power, and voice, and "truth." Indeed, it is exactly this multiplicity of struggle that I seek to explore.

the affinity that dialogical biblical criticism shares with reader-response criticism,[8] the questions posed of Mark treat the pericopae being studied as stories. Therefore, fundamentally, an in-front-of-the-text approach is taken toward this Gospel with questions framed so as to probe the relational dynamics between characters in the texts via questions that ask group readers to explore both the actions and the imagined thoughts and feelings of those characters. Within such questions, the relation of texts to both the contexts of readers and their experiences of poor mental health in society is explored.

Drawing on this reading strategy, the middle chapters of the book turn directly to the text. Via an analysis of six encounters with Jesus and focusing on the relational dynamics of these encounters, I explore the major themes of identity, agency, and dialogue, the three aspects of relational dynamics that I argued in chapter 1 to bear the marks of hegemonic forms of relating. This analysis is designed such that the insights of biblical scholars are placed alongside the insights of reading groups. Building upon the emphases that group readers provide, and placing those emphases in relation to scholars' insights, I then work through each pericope assessing the core thesis that mutuality is an effective postcolonial praxis of resistance and transformation.

Thus there are three sets of voices in this work's dialogical method. The first set of voices are those of biblical scholars, samples of whose interpretations are touched on across a diverse range of biblical criticisms inasmuch as they focus on the relational dynamics of the texts in question. This sampling approach is followed in order to look for interpretive tendencies and patterns across a range of scholarship, rather than go into depth in any one form of biblical scholarship. Furthermore, what is pursued is not a dialectical model with differing interpretations analyzed in such a way as to sublate the difference other interpretations present, leading to some sort of synthesis for reading. Rather, a dialogical approach is pursued that

---

8. The sort of dialogical reading that my own work represents can be seen to directly respond to Hans Robert Jauss's critique of this form of biblical criticism as stated by George Aichele et al.: "As long as biblical reader-response critics concentrate on the implied reader and narratee *in* the biblical texts, they will continue to neglect the reception *of* biblical texts by flesh-and-blood readers" (1995, 36). A similar critique is leveled against ideology criticism, which, similar to my own work, is interested in the dynamics of power that texts inhabit; yet ideology criticism remains at the level of theory and "rarely listens to ordinary readers" (de Wit et al. 2000, 31).

views competing interpretive voices as creative of openings for reading pushing at the limits of stated framings of the text.[9]

The second set of voices is made up of those with whom I shared interactive Bible studies in four settings in the metropolitan Boston area of Massachusetts. The readership of these studies was rich and varied. What I shall call Reading Group One was based at a day treatment center for seniors with poor mental health. Reading Group Two formed at a drop-in center for working-age adults with poor mental health. Reading Group Three was based at a residence where persons who experience various forms of poor mental health live in community while holding down professional jobs and courses of study during the day. Reading Group Four was based at a residential project that offered its residents help with substance abuse along with problems with poor mental health.[10]

In each of these settings, the populations of the reading groups were varied across ethnic, socioeconomic, and gender lines, and it was rare that one week's group members were the same as the next. Difference was also present in terms of the readers varied faith perspectives: from those who forefronted a Christian faith, to those who explicitly viewed the Markan texts strictly as stories. The multiple subject locations of the group readers rendered a rich array of interpretations that I placed in "dialogue" with the interpretations of the first set of conversation partners, from the academy, in such a way as to expand views of text and context retaining difference within the tensive openings readings offered.

It is here, at these points of tensive opening, that I chose to add the third voice: my own. There is no attempt for me to present the interpretations that follow as the work of a somehow neutral and objective arbitra-

---

9. What my approach offers to the competing scholarly and group reader interpretations is a response in part to de Wit's challenge that given the voluminous quantity of "popular readings of the Bible" collected to date, especially in the Southern Hemisphere, and the relative scarcity of systematic research done on it, there is a need to produce some sort of "theoretical framework" or "coding system" for those readings (see de Wit et al. 2004, 16). De Wit's response is to propose a new form of "empirical hermeneutics" (41) wherein his project's products are placed side by side and analyzed almost as scientific data. My own approach is also to place reading products side by side but in a way that does not only seek to describe the patterns that emerge, but also to question them, probe the points of emphasis and tension and then consider avenues that such a contrapuntal association suggests.

10. The exact identity of these locations and groups is not given in a desire to protect the confidentiality of group participants.

tor of interpretive difference. Not only does the dialogical hermeneutic I have employed preclude such notions of arbitration and objectivity, it sees them as profoundly limiting. My own interpretive voice, then, is a subjective and socially located part of this dialogical exchange. Particularly, this includes my "subject location" of being an English man, educated in the academy of biblical scholarship, ordained in the Anglican Church, with little direct personal experience of marginalization along lines of socioeconomic disadvantage, ethnic background, sexual orientation, gender, or seasons of poor mental health.[11] At another level, there is my experience more indirectly via relationships with persons in my own life, and indeed via transitory relationships with readers and people I meet through my work as a parish priest, of the hegemonic societal reality (as well as the psychological and spiritual reality) of being designated as other in the discourses of mental health.

With this reading strategy in place, the six pericopae under consideration were divided into three pairs, each taking up a chapter of the book. In chapter 4 the first pair considers the question of identity and how acts of labeling and exclusion pose threats to the abilities of characters to self-identify in the narrative of the texts. In the first pericope (Mark 3:1–6) I consider the strategies of relating that are employed by Jesus and a man with a withered hand to reimagine notions of identity and agency. On one hand, I argue that the agency narrated in 3:1–6 is an instance of mutuality and hybridity acting as praxes both of resistive survival and of relational as well as physical transformation. On the other hand, the consequences that readers imagined there might be for such spectacular acts of resistance are severe, suggested by the plot to "destroy" Jesus (3:6) narrated at the end of the pericope.

By contrast, the strategy of ambiguity that I argue to be at the heart of Jesus' response to charges in 3:19b–35 that he has lost his mind and his theological credentials (3:21–22), while an act of resistive survival on the part of Jesus, appears to be less able to bring about any sort of transformation either to that relational dynamic or to ones that follow it in the text. What emerges from these two pericopae that focus on identity, then, is

---

11. Although it is not insignificant that I have experienced on several occasions shorter periods of poor mental health, which although never leading to hospitalization, medication, or the complete debilitation of functioning, have been times of depression that make me able to empathize a little with those who have experienced more acute episodes or seasons.

a conclusion that the praxis of mutuality is one that operates transiently within relational dynamics. That is, what I argue to be the transformative impact of the praxis of mutuality, in its operation with other postcolonial praxes, is that it occurs as a momentary reimagining of power structures, not as their overcoming.

In chapter 5 the second pair of pericopae consider how gender and ethnicity further complicate the dynamics of power in the exercise of agency in colonial relational dynamics. The first pericope considers the contrasting strategies of agency practiced by Jairus, a prominent synagogue leader, and a woman who has been suffering from hemorrhages for twelve years (5:21–43). Both of these individuals seek healing and go about it in different ways: one exercising agency in the open, publicly attempting to negotiate a healing for his daughter; the other exercising a surreptitious agency, reaching out for the corner of Jesus' clothing, attempting to take healing unnoticed. What I argue female agency in this pericope reveals is the necessarily supplemental and incremental struggle for power that the power differential between genders within colonial relational dynamics demands. Thus the praxis of mutuality in this pericope between male and female is limited within the thin space of colonial discourses on gender and agency. Contrary to some feminist re-readings of this pericope, then, I argue that reciprocity is not in the end gained for the females in this encounter; rather it is because of reciprocity's denial that the necessarily supplemental agency of the woman with hemorrhages is exercised in the way that it is.

In the second pericope of the pair (7:24–30) the gradations of power and gender are further complicated by the impact of ethnicity. That is, within an ethnically charged exchange of words between Jesus and a Syrophoenician woman, where Jesus appears to throw insults as well as metaphorical food, the agency of a doubly othered woman emerges along the Bhabhian lines of mimicry. Thus, arguing again differently from certain feminist rereadings of this text, I suggest that that there is not mutual transformation in this story; rather, what is seen is mimetic agency that renegotiates the terms of the relational dynamics of power present between Jesus and the woman. Furthermore, I argue that there is no textual sense in postulating that Jesus has been transformed in this pericope anymore than the woman has; rather, what emerges from 7:24–30 is the ambivalent agency of Jesus, whose indeterminacy precludes definitive conclusions being reached about the nature of transformation in the story.

In chapter 6 the final pair considers the question of dialogue and its potential as an emancipatory tool that is seen both to lead to the opening up of new possibilities for life and to its closing down. The first pericope, 5:1–20, explores the potential of dialogue as an emancipatory tool in the encounter between Jesus and a man who lives among the tombs. In exploring the thicker description of the alterity of the man that group readers offer, I argue that the engagement between the man and Jesus is a central element of the story. The significance of this engagement, though, is not seen as the healing that the man receives at the hand of Jesus; rather it is the potential it opens up for the man to articulate his own talent for survival and his own way to healing. Furthermore, the significance of the commission of the man to go back to those who had chained him in the first place is argued to be paramount to an understanding of the postcolonial reimagining of these colonial relational dynamics, with 5:1–20 presented less as an act of miraculous healing and more as a recovery story enabled by dialogical engagement.

By contrast, the efficacy of dialogue in the final pericope, Jesus' so-called trial before Pilate in 15:1–5, appears to be at a loss from the outset, with Jesus' silence in that exchange taken by several interpreters as a sign of a passive acceptance of victimhood. Arguing along a different trajectory via the emphases of group readers, I suggest that Jesus does not passively acquiesce to his fate, but rather chooses to dialogically engage Pilate, rather paradoxically, through the employment of a strategy of silence. I explore the potential of this composite praxis of silence and mutuality as a way of opening up the thin space of the relational dynamics Jesus is faced with for others to enter into mutual relating. While in the end I argue that as a praxis that seeks to resist external hegemonic power this strategy fails, its significance lies as a strategy of internal resistance that allows for a mutuality with the self to emerge when all other hopes for mutual relation are seemingly lost.

Chapter 7 brings this work back to its stated contextual concerns by assessing how much mutuality has operated as an effective form of resistive and transformative postcolonial praxis in the textual interpretations that the previous chapters have practiced. Specifically, I assess the efficacy of the praxis of mutuality as it operates within the structures of hegemonic relational dynamics. I also explore mutuality's operation delineated by gender, by open and hidden agency, as well as its operation complementary to other postcolonial praxes and as supplemental to hegemonic power.

Along with this, I close with an exploration of some of the perceived benefits and limitations of the hermeneutical model pursued.

I hope that readers of this work might include those who live with, relate to, care for, advocate for, or take an interest in persons with poor mental health and discourses on mental health. Similarly, I hope that this work might be of interest to those whose work is to offer criticism of ancient texts and the reading of such texts, and in particular I hope that those whose own work leads them to dialogue with others might find the hermeneutic and insights of this particular attempt at dialogical biblical interpretation a source of interest. Yet more than anything else I hope that this work is able to engage those who struggle for transformed relating in the everyday encounters of persons with poor mental health and so might offer some encouragement not only to continue in that struggle but to engage critically with the issues such struggles raise. Indeed, if there is one ethical imperative that the political act of reading calls for, it is that conversation continues to go on, and that participants continue to be found, engaged, and, one hopes, even changed.

1
Relational Dynamics of Poor Mental Health: Assessing Existing Paradigms

In this first chapter I offer three analyses. First, I analyze the relational dynamics of poor mental health in twenty-first-century North Atlantic societies in terms of perceptions of identity, representations of agency, and dialogical encounters. Second, I analyze how contextual biblical criticism has attempted to respond to these relational dynamics. Specifically, I explore how liberation hermeneutics is used to talk about poor mental health in particular, and how in general as a form of contextual biblical criticism it is both fruitful yet limited. Third, and with this critique of liberation hermeneutics in mind, I turn to the work of Michel Foucault, considering how through a Foucauldian analysis of context an alternative conceptual frame for the relational dynamics of poor mental health might emerge that is more subtly power-aware and more centrally relational. Aligning with a Foucauldian analysis of relational dynamics as operating within hegemonic societal power structures, I then conclude the chapter by suggesting the benefits of exploring an alternative concept to liberation hermeneutics' "liberation from the margins," which leads the discussion on to chapter 2.

1.1. Relational Dynamics and Mental Health: Tracing the Contours of Context

I begin this chapter's exploration of the societal location of poor mental health with an anecdote from the reading group Bible studies that form the heart of this book. The anecdote touches on questions of identity, agency, and dialogue, the three fundamental concerns of this work with regard to how people with poor mental health are related to in contemporary societies:

> C: I think very often, more a feeling or knowing and a willingness and desire to take responsibility of judging. In my own view mental health

professionals as a group can be judgmental to greater extents than some others.

B: Because they have some knowledge that they didn't give up. People who go into the field want to help with "diagnosis." I think that when a person decides to devote their life to that kind of thing. ...

C: They have issues ... (laughs).

B: I think they'll encounter some arguing, some hostility even, and also the nature of the idea of a psychological illness is a very significant collection of beliefs. Persons with issues have different labels, reasons why their judgment might be this way, they might feel like they are not being reasonable or normal.

C: It's hard not to feel patronized and it's tough not to feel stymied.

A: And not to blame individuals who go into the field because it's part of how it is taught.

B: It's a problem of great complexity. People read too much into things.

C: You think misdiagnosis—label—say, schizophrenic, and you really aren't one.

A: I think it is a name of something. It is useful when someone like us walks into an office. There may be a whole lot of reasons why our judgment might be off.

C: And we might feel inferior to the person.

B: You can feel invalidated.

C: It's difficult, you always know it is a professional argument. It's really tough, learning how to live with it and in the midst of it. I can be paranoid.

B: It's almost like a caste system of your brain. Technically I can't judge my teachers.

C: They take us back.

A: That can be one really positive aspect, you can be forgiven because they understand you're dealing with a lot.

B: I don't want you to say that I can't judge them, it's just you don't have the same education as they do.

A: I think there's healthy judgments.

C: Sometimes judgments are off. Sometimes they see things you are not seeing.[1]

What should be made of instances of relating as the opening encounter of this chapter describes? That is, are feelings of being "patronized," "stymied," and being made to feel inferior and invalidated peculiar to this particular

---

1. Excerpt from Reading Group Three, April 3, 2006, commenting on Mark 3:1–6. Letters denote the different participants and relate in no way to true names or identities.

group of individuals, or do their experiences reflect a wider societal picture? Furthermore, if such a picture of relating is more than anecdotal, how might such relating be resisted and begin to be transformed?

It is my contention in this chapter that the anecdote above does indeed reflect to a significant degree North Atlantic societal relational dynamics as they pertain to poor mental health. That is, despite the supposed progress of the past thirty or so years in the area of "mental health reform," relational dynamics between persons with poor mental health and others are still had in spaces wherein the voices of persons with poor mental health are often reduced to the sounds of their illness (Foucault 2001, 237–38, 250–51). I will substantiate this assertion by considering three main facets of relational context that influence the formation of acts of relating: representations of identity, perceptions of agency, and acts of dialogue.

In terms of the representations of identity, one of the most significant contributors to shaping the relational dynamics in encounters with persons with poor mental health is stigma. Two kinds of stigma are identified in research: public stigma as the general population's reaction and attitude to persons with poor mental health, and self-stigma as the prejudice that such persons turn on themselves (Corrigan and Watson 2002, 16). Both types of stigma are understood to have three components: stereotype, prejudice, and discrimination (ibid.). For instance, while people who hold certain stereotypes might not agree on whether they are valid, prejudice acts both to endorse negative stereotypes (e.g., "persons with mental illness are violent") and to generate negative emotional reactions (e.g., "they all scare me") as a result (Hilton and von Hippel 1996).

In a number of studies from North Atlantic societies, a stigma about mental health is found to be widely endorsed by the general public.[2] One of the most effective vehicles for public stigma is the media. One study finds that Americans identified mass media as the source from which they get most of their knowledge about "mental illness" such that persons with poor mental health were depicted as objects of ridicule, as people fundamentally different from others, as violent, criminal, and dangerous, and were often referred to via slang or other disrespectful words (Wahl 2003, 3). Indeed, such media representation of persons with poor mental health, both in films and in print, tends to emphasize three major themes:

---

2. In the United States: Link 1987; Phelan et al. 2000; Rabkin 1974; Roman et al. 1981. In Europe: Bhugra 1989; Brockington et al. 1993; Hamre et al. 1994; Madianos et al. 1987.

persons with poor mental health are homicidal and should be feared; they have childlike perceptions of the world and should be marveled at; they are responsible for their illness and therefore have weak characters (Hyler et al. 1991). Via the representation of mental health in the media it is found that often, regardless of the specific symptoms or behaviors observed, people tend to respond to those with psychiatric labels on the basis of the label by recalling images and stereotypes the particular label in question conjures up (Wahl 2003, xiv). This is even found to operate in health-care settings.[3]

Representation, then, is seen to influence how dialogical exchanges are formed. Such a limiting of dialogue is also seen in the representation of mental health in everyday dialogical exchanges via perceptions of language and agency. Sander Gilman suggests that the designation of language as *bizarre* is a means of demarcating the normal and the pathological: "Thus we use the stereotype of the bizarre language of the schizophrenic as a means of defining our own sanity" (1988, 243). Furthermore, she argues that it is the realization of the "banality of madness" that is most formative in the representation of poor mental health. The line between the well and unwell, the sane and insane, begins to shift when the picture of the "mad-dog killer" is replaced by persons "just like us," and so "the mentally ill" have to be different in order to reassert the demarcation (243). Gilman's thesis is that there is a need in society to represent mental health absolutely and that this totalizing tendency therefore precludes those designated as stigmatized from entering the conversation: "one does not even have to wait for the insane to speak. The mentally ill are instantly recognizable" (48).

The power of public stigma, labels, and the resultant limiting of dialogue with persons with poor mental health is significant. It is not surprising, then, given such findings, that when interviewed such persons speak

---

3. For instance, in an experiment where eight pseudo-patients (who were considered to be in good mental health at the time) self-admitted into different hospitals and were subsequently given a psychiatric label, it was found that there was nothing "normal" that the pseudo-patients could do to overcome the label designated to them. Rather, all behavior was interpreted to confirm the label, including the notes the pseudo-patients made recording the behavior of staff toward other patients and themselves. Perhaps most interestingly no questions were ever asked of the pseudo-patients as to what they were writing, and the consequent medical notes revealed that their writing was interpreted almost universally across the experiment as evidence of their symptomatic behavior. See Rosenhan 1996, 70–75.

of the self-stigma and of the debilitation of agency—the "embarrassment, shame, and discouragement"—experienced in reaction to the real and perceived responses of the public toward them (Gilman 1988, xiv). Such self-stigma might even develop into acts of stigmatizing, labeling, and relating between persons with poor mental health.[4]

The impact of such public stigmas and the media's propagation of such stigmas' influence is postulated to act not only on an individual level in terms of self-stigma; it is also seen to operate at a more structural level where the agency of persons with poor mental health is presumed to be limited. In the United Kingdom, discrimination against persons with poor mental health is reported in a number of areas. The British newspaper *The Guardian* reported on June 25, 2005: "People with mental health problems face discrimination from financial providers and retailers." The report went on to quote the U.K.–based advocacy and advice charity *Citizens Advice*, which reported that 85 percent of its clients' claims against payment protection insurance policies fail in cases of "mental illness." In U.S. studies, such perceptions of agency find discrimination to take a number of forms: withholding help, avoidance, coercive treatment, and segregated institutionalization (Socall and Holtgraves 1992). More than half of respondents in a U.S. survey said they would be unwilling to spend an evening socializing with, work next to, or have a family member marry a person "with mental illness" (Martin et al. 2000).

Even within health-care systems, prejudice may lead to the withholding of help or the replacement of health-care provisions with services provided by the criminal justice system (Corrigan 2000). Indeed, within health-care systems that provide for people with special needs, health services continue to grow as scientists define more and more "defects." Consequently, as more and more people view themselves as increasingly "defective," the demand for treatment and therapy also increases (ibid., 431).

The significant aspect to appreciate about the potency of stigma, labeling, and language's impact on persons with poor mental health, and the ways in which these factors help to construct the praxis of relating with such persons, is that these factors do not operate in isolation: socioeconomic,

---

4. For instance, take this reflection of an individual user of a mental health drop-in in the United Kingdom: "It's a funny sub-culture. ... There's a certain amount of mockery in it as if they say, 'Come on, take your tablets!' That kind of thing. ... There's a strange sort of sub-culture where they say, 'You haven't got a job have you? How did you get a job? You're a mental patient'" ("Jeffrey" in Barham and Hayward 1996, 234).

cultural, political, and gender issues, among others, come into play. For instance, a study that focuses specifically on schizophrenia found that individuals from lower socioeconomic groups have an earlier age of first presentation and longer periods of untreated illness. Furthermore, individuals "with schizophrenia" are overrepresented in the homeless population, among migrants, those in prison (indeed, other research has found that 66 percent of the remand population in the United Kingdom is thought to have some sort of mental health problem, compared to 39 percent of the sentenced population; Bird 1998, 1), and people who generally find it difficult to generate social capital (Kelly 2005). One may argue that these factors, combined with the societal reality of public stigma and its hegemonic impact on some individuals, constitute a "structural violence" that not only impairs access to psychiatric and social services but also amplifies the impact of individuals' symptoms (ibid., 721). Indeed, another study asserts that the structural impact of stigma and labeling alone might be the single biggest cause of an episode of poor mental health leading to a "career" as a "mentally ill person," such that the label outlives the internal reality of the condition (Scheff 1996).

Sadly, such structural and systemic existential violence has also been attested at the more immediate societal level of family and friends. A study commissioned by the United Kingdom's Mental Health Foundation found that the most common sources of discrimination cited by respondents were from those closest to them, such as family and friends. People interviewed stated that the stigma and discrimination experienced in relation to mental health made acceptance by others a vital element of their survival and frequently proved to be a means of self-acceptance (Wright and De Ponte 2000, 1). One respondent described the pervasive subtlety of discrimination that limited opportunities for real dialogue: "Always being asked if the way I'm feeling is due to my mental health problems. Not allowed to express emotions good or bad like 'normal people'" (2).

Despite the endless potential for counteranecdotes and statistical analyses, and indeed, despite the significant advances in community care, public awareness, and positive if rather idiosyncratic media representations of poor mental health (e.g., in the film *A Beautiful Mind*), this brief sketch of the North Atlantic relational dynamics of persons with poor mental health is one within which such persons are at a considerable disadvantage. This is not to say, however, that positive and life-giving relationships and acts of relating do not exist in North Atlantic societies. The point is that there exists a way of perceiving and representing poor mental health that is still dominant enough to draw the conclusion that, for many, the state of the relational dynamics of encounters with persons with poor mental health has the potential to leave such individuals at a considerable social and specifically relational disadvantage. Furthermore, as I shall argue later in this chapter, it is not that persons in society in their interactions with persons with poor mental health are unable to resist such perceptions and representations; rather it is that the impact of such relational dynamics needs to be recognized if it is going to be resisted.

With this analysis of the relational dynamics of poor mental health in place, the next step for this work as a piece of contextual biblical studies is to consider the sort of responses that have been made to this contextual reality in order to assess which aspects of these responses might be useful for this work. The predominant paradigm within biblical studies that has been used in this regard is liberation hermeneutics. Specifically, I will focus on pastoral theology and biblical hermeneutics, and how both draw from the insights of liberation theology; this is an endeavor that will prove to be both fruitful and limiting.

1.2. Liberation Hermeneutics and Poor Mental Health: Resistive Theologies at the Margins

Liberation came to the fore of theological concern in the 1970s following the publication of Gustavo Gutiérrez's *Theology of Liberation,* which defined liberation as the release from "all that limits and keeps human beings from self-fulfillment, and from all impediments to the exercise of freedom" (1988, 18). From this starting point, Gutiérrez and his successors delineated three levels of liberation: personal, sociopolitical, and spiritual (Gutiérrez 2007, 26). Within the context of global Christian theology, it represented a counterdiscourse to the individual-focused theologies that predominated at the time. That is, it was a hermeneutic that took societal contexts seriously and chose to resist their oppressive forms by opting to speak out of a more structurally power-aware theological imagination.

This seemingly holistic approach has attracted a number of pastoral theologians who argue for the theological paradigm shift that liberation hermeneutics represents.[5] For instance, Stephen Pattison asserts that pas-

---

5. See Pattison 1994; Swinton 1999; and on related topics see Morris 2006; Eiesland 1994.

toral care and theology in North Atlantic societies have largely been too myopic in scope, too narrowly focused on the individual etiology of poor mental health, and too little focused on wider social and political aspects (1994, 5). It follows that, from this limited paradigm, theology is unable to offer a fully critical reflection and "liberating praxis" to the lived societal reality of persons with poor mental health (6).

Liberation hermeneutics made an impact similar to the conceptual shifts made in the areas of ecclesiology and biblical interpretation[6] when applied to mental health. It views the person from a broader perspective: not only as a psychological and intellectual individual being, but also as a political and societally embedded one. Also, the paradigm shift calls for a form of pastoral care that looks beyond the counseling room and individual, private encounter out to the public encounter of mental health in the world, characterizing such a theology as committed, prophetic, and praxis-led. For instance, one of the praxis-led responses made by pastoral theologians is to embrace an ethic of friendship that seeks to recenter the marginal displacement of persons with poor mental health, perceiving this praxis as a core ministry of the church (Swinton 2005, 72).

With the broader area of disability studies in mind, the adoption of the liberation paradigm by theologians and practitioners interested in mental health represents an alignment with the move away from the so-called medical model of disability wherein disability is fundamentally perceived as a loss of function or ability and is thus seen primarily as a medical or biological condition (McCloughry and Morris 2002; Mitchell and Snyder 1997). The adoption of liberation hermeneutics, then, reflects the move in

---

6. The impact of liberation theology has moved far beyond its initial scope as a protest and challenge to so-called North Atlantic based theologies to challenge theology that it considered to be "no longer relevant" in the face of widespread oppression (see, e.g., Torres and Fabella 1978, 269: "We reject as irrelevant an academic type of theology that is divorced from action"). Not only did liberation theology inspire and unite the various theological responses of people in Latin America in terms of praxis, including many such as Oscar Romero who were martyred for their outspoken commitment to such praxis; it also inspired similar and further developed theological movements in thought and praxis globally, often biblically based and thus significantly reorienting biblical studies toward politically situated reader-response strategies, making an impact in much of Africa and south and east Asia. See, e.g., Mosala 1989; Sugirtharajah 2006b. Moreover, the impact of liberation theologies has been felt beyond the developing world, influencing the emergence of various contextual theologies and their concomitant methodologies. See, e.g., L. Green 1987.

disability studies to the minority or social group model, which contends that the notion of disability is not primarily bodily or biological but is socially constructed via physical and attitudinal barriers created within society that serve to "marginalize, segregate, devalue, and discriminate against people with disabilities."[7]

In terms of mental health specifically, liberation hermeneutics raises a central question: Does pastoral theology and praxis with persons with poor mental health recognize the situation of the oppression of such people and attempt to "set the captive free," or does it tend to be blind to, or even collude with, the forces of oppression? For Pattison, pastoral theology and praxis stand accused of complicity in a systemic and epistemic "violence" against some of the most vulnerable in society, including those with poor mental health. In his words, such "theological praxis needs liberating" in order to commit itself adequately to the cause of the oppressed.[8]

Such an approach recognizes that the societal location of those in need of pastoral care, such as persons with poor mental health, is embedded beyond the pathology of an individual alone. It argues that public pastoral ministry has to be committed to struggling with the social pathology of societies, recognizing that the individualization of mental health denies the societal causality of socioeconomic displacement in many incidences of individual poor mental health. Pastoral care that recognizes the causality of social pathology aligns with Pattison's argument that "factors affecting the diagnosis, care, and situation of mentally ill people … are profoundly influenced and shaped by the socio-economic practices, values, and assumptions associated with the present capitalist social order" (1994, 94). Put even more strongly is Larry Graham's position that the network of care for persons with poor mental health at the microcosmic, individual level is rendered necessary and organizes itself largely in response to a mas-

---

7. Toensing 2007, 134. The social model of disability is identified as part of the social constructionist approach, which has closely aligned its struggle within society as the struggle for civil rights for persons with disabilities. See Reinders 2008, 59.

8. "The suspicion was formulated that pastoral care might have social and political implications of which it is ignorant, and which lead it to unwittingly side with the powerful over against the oppressed" (Pattison 1994, 261). One such instance of a "liberated theological praxis" comes from the work of Ignacio Martín-Baró (1994), writing from both a Latin American perspective and as a psychologist and theologian, noteworthy not only for his public commitment to the cause of the mental health of the people, which in the end cost him his life, but also for his emphasis on a psychology *of* the oppressed rather than *for* the oppressed.

sive network of oppression and violence at the macrocosmic level (1992, 16). The classic pastoral care tasks of healing, sustaining, guiding, and reconciling are thus to be expanded to include "prophetic efforts toward emancipatory liberation, justice-seeking, public advocacy, and ecological partnership" (20).

Described in what have become recognizable paradigmatic terms—preferential struggle, capitalist social order, emancipatory liberation—liberation hermeneutics encourages biblical criticism to be aware of the "hidden dynamics of power" (Swinton 1999, 25) that interpersonal encounters inhabit. In terms of mental health in its societally embedded relational context, this structurally power-aware imagination tends toward a conception of societies in the spatial terms of centers and margins such that persons with poor mental health are considered silenced, hidden, and displaced as people at the margins. Indeed, they are persons who are spoken of and for. The margin for much of liberation hermeneutics is considered as an exclusionary site—a place for persons that is other to the power that creates it: a place outside, at the outskirts of dwelling, beyond the city wall. Indeed, these are the images of theological and pastoral imagination that have inspired the heroic work of many who have ministered among the world's most desperate, and from these notions numerous biblical readings have been generated from places of exclusion.[9] The fundamental movement inherent in much of liberation hermeneutics with regard to marginal relational dynamics, then, is one from oppression to liberation. The margins have become the mission grounds, onto which it is not the colonizing North Atlantic theologian who brings the Bible to the natives, but rather the liberation theologian who speaks of the God of that very Bible coming to "set the captives free." God is the liberator from oppression; Jesus is his revolutionary.

The significance of such a paradigmatic framing for theological articulation and biblical interpretation with regard to mental health is great indeed. In the reading of biblical narratives this paradigm has reconfigured the interpretive landscape such that individual relational encounters of persons in those narratives are no longer only seen in individualized terms (e.g., of Savior and saved), or in limited historical critical groupings (e.g., Galilean charismatic and Jewish/Gentile representative). Rather, via

---

9. See Ateek 1995; L. Green 1987; McGovern 1993; Morris 2006; Mosala 1989; Rowland and Vincent 2001; Masoga 2002; Plaatjie 2001; Schüssler Fiorenza 1989; Sibeko and Haddad 1997; Tolbert 1995; Weems 1993; West 1994; 1999a; 2007b.

the expansive horizons of liberation hermeneutics, relational encounters are framed in their imagined societal contexts along socioeconomic, cultural, and political trajectories, both in terms of how biblical critics assert texts to have been produced and in terms of how they have been received.

This move toward a societally aware biblical imagination offers much to contextual hermeneutics. However, as well as offering much, this particular form of liberation hermeneutics as it has been applied to mental health also limits interpretive possibilities particularly in relation to its framing of context within a center-margin paradigm. First, the very nomenclature of liberation hermeneutics contains a certain binaristic character, even in the titles of books on the subject,[10] which leaves it rife with opposites: liberation as opposed to oppression, the preferential option for the poor (and so not for the rich), God on the side of the poor, the hermeneutical advantage of the poor, opting for the margins, and so on. To conceive of margins via such binaristic nomenclature might highlight the plight of those who have been subjugated in the history of mental health, but it also limits the scope of the hermeneutic to speak incisively about the nature and quality of such power differentials. *Poor, oppressed*, and *marginalized* become "sloganistic typologies": generalized metaphors without the necessary and particular descriptive power that might allow the paradigm to be able to assess the dynamic flow of power relations other than in terms of oppressor and oppressed.[11]

This binaristic notion of the margins in liberation hermeneutics also has consequences for how it makes use of biblical texts—a significant feature for this book as a work of contextual biblical criticism. Take for instance the use of the biblical motif of the exodus. As a biblical motif the exodus is commonly used in the Hebrew Bible as a way of introducing the theme of liberation (as well as the theme of punishment) in biblical texts (e.g., Amos 2:10; Hos 11:1; Ezek 20:6; Jer 7:25). Because of this, liberation hermeneutics utilizes the exodus motif in attempts to theologically justify a commitment to the liberation of the oppressed in society. For example, in a study of the exodus motif in the Hebrew Bible, George Pixley and Clodovis Boff hold that the exodus account clearly shows that "justice means taking sides with the oppressed. ... The Yahweh of the exodus takes the part of the oppressed" (2006, 209).

---

10. See, e.g., L. Green 1987; Rieger 2001; West 1999a.

11. Indeed, Marcella Althaus-Reid has argued that any theology concerned with issues of wealth and poverty "needs to consider more the incoherence of oppression and its multiple dimensions rather than its commonalities" (2000, 168).

However, the use of the exodus motif within liberation hermeneutics is often too selective. This point is well illustrated by Robert Warrior's analysis of the exodus motif from the perspective of Native American history (2006). Whereas for much liberationist biblical interpretation use of the exodus motif has begun with Exod 3:7–10 ("I have observed the misery of my people who are in Egypt …") and ended with the liberation from that bondage in Egypt, a Native American reading focuses on the plight of the Canaanites, the people who already lived in the land. Within the Hebrew Bible, these are the people who are to be destroyed (e.g., Exod 23:31b–33; Deut 7:1–2). Warrior's concern is that this reading is too selective: that while the leading into the land was a redemptive moment for some, for others it was "a violation of innocent peoples' rights to land and self-determination" (240). The problem with reading for liberation in these texts is that it rests on a binary interpretation wherein one attends only to those texts and parts of texts that can support the notion of liberation as a movement from bondage to freedom.

It is not hard to see how such selectivity in the use of biblical texts to generate a theology of liberation might be equally limiting with regard to mental health. For instance, David Pailin offers a critique of liberation hermeneutics within the broader field of disability studies when applied to intellectual disabilities in particular. One critique is that the "claim to self-representation as the necessary condition of liberating action" cannot be applied to persons who have intellectual disabilities and who largely need to be represented by others.[12] Presenting the societal location of mental health in the dichotomous terms of oppressor-oppressed does not allow for a proper consideration of the complexity of that societal location. What of the families of those with poor mental health? What of the myriad of health-care workers and other professionals? What of other patients, pastors, and society at large? Surely resistance to levels of repression might take on a multiplicity of different forms, perhaps even operational at the same time. There may be open "siding with the oppressed" by certain health-care workers, family members, and of course patients themselves. At other times, though, there may be more submerged resistance.[13] If all of

---

12. See Pailin 1992, 20–22. He offers two further critiques. One is that a liberation theology of disability is in danger of further segregating persons with disabilities by promoting a subculture within society (24–25). The other is that disabled persons cannot be liberated from their disabilities (27).

13. Indeed, more broadly, it has been a critique of liberation hermeneutics that it

these complexly intertwined agents are to be placed onto either one or the other side of a binaristic power framework, then several opportunities for a more nuanced analysis of relational dynamics are lost.[14] Of course, the fundamental caveat in the oppressor-oppressed paradigm is that not all relational dynamics that involve mental health are oppressive.

Another significant feature of liberation hermeneutics' conception of the margins is in how the assumed movement from the margins to the center has generated somewhat predetermined theological reflections. Textually, it is an implied assumption that ultimately texts from the Bible are texts that speak of liberation *because* they are biblical texts, and this is in the end a theological assumption. For instance, according to Carlos Mesters, "it is as if the word of God were hidden within history, within their struggles. When they discover it, it is big news" (1993, 11). And what "bigger news" than to discover that the struggles of the "common people" are also the struggles of the God who brought his people out of Egypt? The exodus of the Israelites becomes the exodus of the Brazilian "common

---

has not managed to reflect the more nuanced and "differentiated character of liberatory practice" (M. Taylor, 2004, 45–46).

14. It should be noted that Pattison's dialogue between mental health and liberation theology does to an extent recognize the gradations of power at work in societal and institutional structures. For instance, while Pattison recognizes that patients with poor mental health are "the most impotent group" within hospital services, he also argues that junior nurses are "also relatively powerless," while doctors are "relatively powerful" (1997, 226). Similarly, he recognizes that within such groupings (as essentialized as they are) there are also gradations of power, citing elderly patients as victims of abuse and neglect "in the back wards of the old psychiatric hospitals" (261–62). However, the drawback with Pattison's application of liberation theology is that he is unable to offer his own societal analysis adequately nuanced tools for a study of such power differentials, both politically and theologically, due to it being tied to a binaristic and theologically limiting paradigm. Indeed, his own proposal that persons committed to pastoral care should utilize an "unfinished" model for social and political action (a model that advocates both short-term reform and long-term change "in the totality of the order" without opting for one at the expense of the other) and should make a "concrete option for the oppressed in the mental health sector" highlights the ambiguity of pastoral praxis when faced with decisions about aligning with or against hospital care, care in the community, or a hybrid of both (229–38). It is clear that Pattison's desire for a more discerning and nuanced pastoral praxis, where there are "no cut and dried answers to these complex questions" (238), is not adequately supported by the theological paradigm he has chosen to use.

people" because this God is a God who struggles with the oppressed.[15] Taken alongside the challenge Renita Weems (1993) articulates in an essay concerned with rereading the struggle of women in biblical texts, that the marginalized reader must use "whatever means necessary" to recover the voice of the oppressed within biblical texts, liberation can be said to be a hermeneutical given because it is taken as a theological given.

The problem here is that the more that one reads God as necessarily siding with the poor and oppressed, the less one uncovers any inherent ambiguity in the text. The textual reality is that the Bible presents liberation not in isolation but in tension with oppression, endorsing both freedom and slavery: God does not always side with the poor; sometimes he commands their annihilation (e.g., those already in the land, although presented biblically as "mightier" than the Hebrews [Deut 7:1], can hardly all be rich). Thus the very concept of "the poor" is not only to an extent overesteemed in the hermeneutical and theological privilege liberation hermeneutics gives them, it is also a homogenized and essentialized category that is not sensitive to gradations of poverty either in texts or in contexts.[16] As Marcella Althaus-Reid argues, liberation hermeneutics and its conception of the margins is a paradigm that continues to obey "certain masters" that regulated available strategies for freedom, even "pre-emptying the notion of freedom in itself" (1998, 268).

Overall there are some considerable problems with liberation hermeneutics as it is applied to the relational dynamics of mental health. As mentioned, it practices a binaristic approach to the public and structural societal reality of mental health: of oppressor and oppressed. Such an approach is thus limited to generating essentialized and predetermined theological interpretations of biblical texts whereby theological reflection is limited to a paradigm that remains somewhat tied to its own archetype.

---

15. Such predeterminedness is not restricted to the exodus narrative. For instance, a study that reads the Bible with members of a north Brazilian community's women's association contains this theological prolegomenon in the form of the instruction of the facilitator of the study: "In the beginning of our meeting, I made a short introduction to the anointing story in the Gospels, helping the women to remember what they knew well: that Jesus had lived persecuted because of his option of the poor" (Ottermann 2007, 104).

16. For instance, "the poor" as an essentialized concept presents such persons as having an essential nature, and thus neglects the gradations of poverty, as well as the differential components of it along lines of gender, ethnicity, and religion.

Biblical texts are thus read too selectively, and the contextual gradations of power and resistance are not able to be appreciated.

Along with these particular limitations, two broader issues are also problematic: one, the inherent notion of progress in the liberation paradigm; and two, its inability to capture the relational aspects of so-called marginal struggles. In terms of the first issue of progress, then, what the liberation paradigm calls for is a movement from the periphery to the center, from the slavery of Egypt to the liberation of the entry into the land of promise. Applied to the relational dynamics of mental health in North Atlantic societies sketched out in the previous section, progress as liberation might look like the breaking of stigma and stereotype, and the realigning of representations and perceptions of others concerning mental health from societally marginalizing forms of relational exchange to societally centering ones.

On one level, in terms of seeking to align biblical studies to the world around it, this inherent notion of progress in liberation hermeneutics is consonant with other theological approaches to context that seek not to individualize or apoliticize biblical interpretation. Indeed, some contend that if theological conviction and pastoral care are to move beyond an "ambulance ministry" and its accompanying theology, then the political and the spiritual must retain their inseparability (Leech 1999, 94). Political and spiritual liberation, then, must remain a goal of theological enterprise. My own work is not intended in any way to suggest that striving for social change is somehow to be avoided in the relational dynamics of mental health. However, the problem that I wish to highlight with the liberation hermeneutics paradigm and its inherent momentum toward progress is its lack of explanatory power. That is, it is unable to say much about *how* such a movement from the periphery to the center might take place other than that it *should* take place.[17]

I do not make this criticism of liberation hermeneutics expecting biblical hermeneutics to mandate social transformation. The shortcoming of liberation hermeneutics is that this notion of progress from the margins to the center is poorly resourced to articulate the intricate structures of power that pervade acts of relating. This very issue of power leads directly into the second major shortcoming of liberation hermeneutics:

---

17. More recent work within liberation hermeneutics has recognized some of these criticisms and has seen the need to analyze agency in a more nuanced way "in the counterpressures that are formed when we get in touch with the repressions of life" and in "day-to-day forms of resistance" (Rieger 2004, 217–18).

there is little appreciation of the relational within the paradigm. The inherent binarism of liberation hermeneutics renders its analysis incapable of moving beyond dichotomous conceptions of power, and so the negotiation of power differentials is similarly constrained. Power is confined in analysis to a coercive and binaristic influence that is read into and out of biblical texts. Thus the focus on relational dynamics that I pursue is not able to be adequately addressed within such a framework.

Before moving on from the "classic" form of early liberation theology that various pastoral theologians use in offering theological reflections on the contexts of mental health, I think it is worth noting that the various forms of liberation hermeneutics have not remained static, and the pastoral theological insights above do not reflect the considerable evolution of what is now a global paradigm. For as well as having migrated from its Latin American roots to inform black theologies of liberation (Antonio 2007), feminist theologies (Grey 2007), and then "third world" feminist critiques of the same (Vuola 2002), and other identity-specific theologies spanning Africa (Walshe 1987) and Asia (Wielenga 2007), the original paradigm has also evolved, offering a more nuanced critique of certain aspects of its earlier forms. For instance, one significant development has been the emergence of the exile over the exodus as a biblical motif for liberationist theological reflection, where God might be seen as one who does not provide reconciliation for victims of oppression but remains hidden in the exilic experience of poverty.[18]

However, while it is the case that the more recent work on liberation theology attempts to address some of the critiques of binaristic conceptions of identity and power, somewhat predetermined biblical theologies, and an inherent tie to the notion of progress,[19] it has not been possible for the global paradigm to wrestle free from its fundamentally dichotomous nature. For instance, while Ivan Petrella's 2005 collection of Latin Ameri-

---

18. See Yoder (1990, 287–88) on the necessity for the incorporation of the exile into liberation hermeneutics' use of biblical motifs.

19. Some of the more significant events in recent liberation theology on a global scale have been the World Forums on Liberation and Theology held first in Brazil in 2005 and then in Kenya in 2007, with over three hundred participants, predominantly from Africa, reflecting the still vibrant and now global scale of the liberation theology movement interested in issues such as global north and south economic divides, "ecological debt," poverty and slavery, fundamentalism and modernity, and globalization (see Althaus-Reid et al. 2007).

can liberation theologies reveals more nuanced appreciations of such key concepts as "the poor,"[20] "the margins,"[21] and the "overestimation" of the exodus motif "to enact liberation in history," offering instead the crucified God as a paradoxical "defeated-liberator" (Sung 2005, 11), the strong association with God's preferential option for the poor remains.[22] Thus, even if this notion of "the poor" has been more thoroughly contextualized than its earlier theological manifestations, it is this theological teleology that means that for my own explorations of power and relating via the reading of biblical texts I will seek alternative hermeneutical paradigms.

Overall, then, while liberation hermeneutics proves to be fruitful in its foregrounding of structural power for the description of contextual relational dynamics of poor mental health via textual interpretation, it is the binaristic and progress-led descriptions of contexts and interpretations of texts that leave it limited. In the effort to assess existing paradigms, I will turn now to a conceptual framework from outside biblical studies, namely the work of Michel Foucault. With the emphasis on the centrality of power that liberation hermeneutics offers, in the next section I explore through Foucault's work how the relational dynamics described in the first section of this chapter need not be viewed in binaristic terms but as experiences that congregate around a struggle for power in relationship. Furthermore, I contend that it is with a more nuanced appreciation of these power differentials that contextual biblical studies is able to speak meaningfully and incisively to the relational dynamics of mental health.

---

20. This is not a homogenous category but must be complicated by issues of gender, ethnicity, and sexuality; see Maldonado-Torres 2005, 55.

21. For instance, Silvia Regina de Lima Silva has argued that "Afrodescendant" women challenge liberation theology, "questioning and deconstructing the patriarchal theology that in Latin America and the Caribbean has assumed a male, white, and elitest face, fostering an ethnocentric, class-based, macho theology" (2005, 68); thus "the lives and experiences of black women are a new theological locus, from the margins of the margins" (70).

22. The determination of liberation theologies to remain grounded in this preferential option for the poor is clearly understandable given the obvious global disparities that such a theology has articulated. Thus, for the liberation theologian, it is crucial to recognize that binarisms do exist and poverty is real. See Petrella 2008.

1.3. Foucault: Power and Poor Mental Health

Foucault frames the struggle for power within the notion of discourse, that is, the notion that when knowing is exercised over a state of affairs, or over persons, this act of describing reality is also somewhat a production of that reality. At the core of Foucault's arguments concerning mental health is that discourse emerges on the social landscape, not as the emergence of truth—and particularly not as the emergence of the truth about persons with poor mental health—but as the emergence of power. What Foucault means by this can be elucidated by turning to two key concepts of his work: *genealogy* and *archaeology*.

Foucault's understanding of *genealogy*, based partly on Nietzsche's use of the term, is a rejection of linear history: in contradistinction to the search for origins and universal structures of knowledge, there is no unity or teleology to events, no "timeless and essential secret" behind history at the origin of things but a discontinuity (Foucault 1998, 371–72). That is, he seeks to point to the ways in which North Atlantic societies have organized what counts and what does not count as knowledge of mental health, and within this organization of knowledge what counts as reasonable and as unreasonable in society.

To demonstrate this it is worth briefly sketching Foucault's genealogy of mental health in *Madness and Civilization* and how it relates to his other central concept: archaeology. Essentially Foucault holds that a set of rules of formation determine what can be stated at a particular time about a particular category, such as poor mental health, which also dictate how such a statement of knowledge is related to other statements of knowledge. He calls these the rules of discursive formation and describes these rules as "the archaeology of knowledge" (2002, 155). Archaeology is not an attempt to define thoughts, or representations, or images concealed or revealed in discourses; rather it is an attempt to describe "those discourses themselves … as practices obeying certain rules" (138).

The first traces of such a formation of discourse on mental health that Foucault outlines are in the seventeenth and eighteenth centuries, which saw the "great confinement" of persons with poor mental health. Not only did this signal a hiding of poor mental health; according to Foucault, this new world of confinement also created a neutralizing space wherein autonomy was forsaken in a predetermined social milieu. First, autonomy was lost in a predetermined exchange of the provision of food and water for the physical constraint of confinement (Foucault 2001, 45). Second, autonomy was lost in an even more profound way, as Foucault contends in his earlier work *Mental Illness and Psychology*: "Madness, which for so long had been overt and unrestricted, which had for so long been present on the horizon, disappeared. It entered a phase of silence from which it was not to emerge for a long time; it was deprived of its language; and although one continued to speak of it, it became impossible for it to speak of itself" (1976, 68).

Foucault also asserts that this loss of autonomy in being confined was often combined with an inability to work in an age when the failure to produce labor was akin to moral laxity. Thus developed the notion of poor mental health as a problem, as a social and moral deficit (1976, 59). Aligning with Foucault's analysis, Roy Porter, in his historical survey of the social location of poor mental health, demonstrates how in the latter half of the eighteenth century the emergence of the specialist public asylum saw certain antisocial behaviors—traditionally labeled as sins, vices, and crimes—being labeled as "madness" by magistrates who began to fill asylums with political opponents and criminals (2002, 122). Foucault contends that this signaled a new relationship between persons with poor mental health and the criminal: "Madness forged a relationship with moral and social guilt that it is still perhaps not ready to break" (1976, 68).

By the eighteenth century, as well as being confined, persons with poor mental health were beginning to be associated with hegemonic stereotypes. The emergence and power of the stereotype was further and profoundly compounded by the nineteenth-century rise of science and the concomitant emergence of psychiatry. Porter has argued that among other things this led to the wider classification of poor mental health, the positing of neurological etiologies of symptoms, and the general development of phrenology and its assertion that the seat of "the mind" is the brain, and therefore that there is a physical substrate to insanity (2002, 147). Foucault goes on to state that these developments led to a focus on the designation of "madness" as a disease and on persons with poor mental health as objects of scientific study—knowable, able to be captured by the knowing subject, the scientist; and literally, bodies of evidence proving the veracity of scientific diagnosis, prognosis, and regimes of treatment. From this separating out of "madness" as an object of science, "mental illness" was born; and, as Foucault contends, nascent psychiatry was able to posit that the only truth available to "madness" was the one that sought to reduce it; thus psychiatry's domain of diagnosis and cure was born (Foucault 2001, 188). The diagnosis-cure paradigm, emerging with the advent of the nineteenth century's asylum system, thus broke from the practice of physical restraint of persons with poor mental health, seeing mental reform as the only way to a cure for "mental illness" (Porter 2002, 104).

Foucault's point, therefore, is that this paradigm shift of "mental reform" meant that even though the asylum saw the end of chaining up persons with poor mental health, the loss of autonomy witnessed in the confinement of the eighteenth century only deepened in the nineteenth century, extending into the modern period. Indeed, he argues that a process of objectification was deepened as the restored visibility of "mental illness" to the eyes of reason led not to the renewal of the "stammered" dialogue of reason with persons with poor mental health but to the seemingly totalizing occupation of communicative space by the voice of reason, making persons with poor mental health even more deeply known objects: "All the rest is reduced to silence … the silence of mental disease, as it would develop in the asylum, would always only be of the order of observation and classification. It would not be dialogue" (Foucault 2001, 59). "Delivered from his chains, he is now chained by silence" (248).

Foucault contends that this objectification along a diagnosis-cure axis most emerged via the advent of the medical expert, not because that person truly knew "mental illness," but because within the social world of the asylum, the expert could isolate and master it. The doctor's power enabled him to produce the reality of "mental illness" characterized by the ability to reproduce behavioral phenomena completely accessible to scientific study (1997d, 44). Foucault sums up this colonizing of persons with poor mental health in his description of the encounter between the asylum patient of the nineteenth century and the doctor: "Now the combat was always decided beforehand, madness' defeat inscribed in advance in the concrete situation where madman and the man of reason meet. The absence of constraint in the nineteenth-century asylum is not madness liberated, but madness long since mastered" (2001, 239).

Where then does Foucault's genealogy of the discourses of "madness" lead? One can argue that Foucault presents a picture of power relations that have emerged as expressions of various rules of discursive formation—rules about what constituted "madness" and rules about the societal location of persons with poor mental health. Such rules led to confinement and concomitant losses of autonomy and associations with criminality. Stereotyping of mental health became another feature that marked out persons for difference. The rise of science and its paradigm of diagnosis and cure further compounded this objectification, as the designation of medical labels led to an attenuation of power and the ability for persons with poor mental health to speak for themselves. Furthermore, what Foucault demonstrates is that as these rules of formation of discourses on mental health interacted with other discourses' rules of formation (e.g., science, penal codes, the individual), the result was a deepening of this marginal condition rather than a movement toward some sort of Enlightenment notion of progress or "humane" representations and encounters with persons with poor mental health.

While Foucault's work offers much to reflect on the social location of mental health in general, and its focus on relational power in particular, we must address three fundamental critiques of Foucault before we can take up his insights as paradigmatic markers for this work. The first critique relates to the accuracy of his historical analysis. Foucault's presentation of the societal location of persons with poor mental health as liminal and somewhat predetermined may not truly reflect the societal forces shaping that location during the periods in question. That is, Foucault's work may lack what is normatively considered to be historical accuracy. For instance, some think that Foucault's work in *Madness and Civilization* relies too heavily on the French context and that his analysis is overgeneralized (Porter 2002, 93). For example, with the exception of France, the seventeenth century did not witness a surge of institutionalization. It was different in different countries. In Russia state-organized institutions for the insane did not appear until the 1850s, and if people were confined it was mostly in monasteries (ibid.). Similarly, some have asserted that the asylum developed in England during a period when the emergence of capitalism and the processes of urbanization saw an associated decreased tolerance of bizarre or inappropriate behavior (Scull 1993, 217). The argument follows that the growth of the asylum had more to do with the drive to construct a productive society than to mark out "others" for difference.[23]

---

23. Other arguments, though, have aligned more with Foucault's stress on the normalizing dynamic that he argues to have been at the heart of the growth of the asylum, with such institutions providing a symbolic as well as a practical means of securing and isolating parts of ourselves that are "wild, dangerous and out of control." See Shoenberg 1980. A related critique of Foucault's work in terms of its historiographical standing has been that his genealogical work relies too heavily on "minor texts" and "obscure artifacts" (see Fendler 2004, 450, for a framing of the limits of this kind of critique). However, the same feature of selectivity has been highlighted from a different vantage point, with Foucault being celebrated for practicing such a form of

However, the historical accuracy critique misses the point of Foucault's work as genealogy. Rather than offering a description of historical progression, Foucault's point is to offer analyses of the power dynamics embodied in encounters with persons with poor mental health that speak as much to the present as they do to the past. As Richard Bernstein (1994) points out, representation of historical facts or events is not the goal of genealogy; it is not an example of didactics, rather it is a "rhetoric of disruption," which, as Lynn Fendler notes, models a kind of thinking that questions received wisdom and aims to incite attention to the present (2004, 450). The targets of genealogical critique, according to Fendler, are those assumptions in the present that serve to "sort people unjustly," undermining the supposed naturalness of such assumptions (451). Therefore, she argues, the effectiveness of Foucault's work is not found in the accuracy of his presentation of knowledge as such, but in the effectiveness of his argument to incite a questioning of how we perceive knowledge (450). Furthermore, as David Hoy states, "Foucault paints the picture of a totally normalized society, not because he believes our present society is one, but because he hopes we will find the picture frightening" (1986, 14).

As a study of the past that attempts to incite a questioning of the present, Foucault's work offers a potential reframing of the societally structured relational dynamics present in encountering persons with poor mental health: perceptions of identity via stigma and stereotype; representations of agency via the media, language, and labeling; and limits set on dialogical exchanges with persons with poor mental health as legitimate and capable partners in relational exchange. Furthermore, in terms of contextual biblical hermeneutics, while liberation hermeneutics offers a paradigm that depicts power as dichotomous and its resistance characterized as the progression out of slavery and into freedom, Foucault's work brings the question of power to the forefront in quite a different way.

For Foucault, power in the relational dynamics of mental health is not the power of knowing subjects over known objects. Or, put within the paradigmatic nomenclature of liberation hermeneutics, it is not that power is somehow held by the oppressors over the oppressed, such that challenging power would be a process of progressing away from states of oppression, or moving out of the margins and into the center of power. For Foucault

---

historiography, because in doing so he has called attention to hitherto marginalized voices and narratives. For an overview see Goldstein 1994.

the working of power in society is within discourse, and so power is more diffuse and relational than binaristic and only oppositional.

However, the potential for Foucault's work to open up a more relationally subtle appreciation of power has to be set in relief to the second key critique of Foucault that I wish to address: he underestimates the potential of individual agency. This critique has often been based on Foucault's perceived overstating of the dominance of discourse over individuals. For instance, Foucault examines "whether the subjects responsible for scientific discourses are not determined in their situation, their function, their perceptive capacity, and their practical possibilities by conditions that dominate and even overwhelm them."[24] That is, Foucault may be read to suggest that power relations between human subjects are less to do with the agency of the individual who has the appearance of having power, and more to do with the structures of power that form discourses on poor mental health.

However, if Foucault is read this way, a significant problem arises: if all subjects are "overwhelmed" by the pervasiveness of discourse, Foucault's notion of power appears to leave the question of the resistance and the transformation of hegemonic relational dynamics—a possibility that liberation hermeneutics argues strongly for—at a loss. Indeed, Foucault's genealogy of confining, estranging, objectifying, and silencing all might lead one into thinking that those who were being marked out for otherness complied with such designating without any resistance or protest. Therefore, the pervasiveness of power within the dynamics of relational encounters could be interpreted to mean that persons are viewed as passive agents, simply formed by the power structures of discourse (see Dews 1987, 161). Some contend that Foucault would thus be read as being too reductionistic and one-dimensional in his appreciation of power to allow for a critical appreciation of human agency (McCarthy 1994, 272) and would present a view of agency wherein the structures of power actively oppress while persons are subjected to the operation of that power in a

---

24. What Foucault is questioning here is the high view of the human subject that gives an absolute priority to the observing subject as being able to somehow reflect upon an essential human phenomenology. He cannot accept the notion of the knowing subject placing "its own point of view at the origin of all historicity—which, in short, leads to a transcendental consciousness. ... Historical analysis of scientific discourse should, in the last resort, be subject, not to a theory of the knowing subject, but rather to a theory of discursive practice" (1970, xiv).

silent form of acquiescence. This question of agency and resistance has been a critique of Foucault, most famously proposed by Jürgen Habermas, who maintains that there is an inherent functionalism to Foucault's work such that everything, including individual identity and agency, is a function of power (1990, 253).

There is, however, a central problem with this sort of critique of Foucault. If one is to read Foucault in such a way, then power remains only an imposing force operating as a limit on human agency. The crucial element that this misses is that for Foucault, as Dan Butin points out, power is to be understood not as a force per se, but as a relation (2003); and it is not conceived of only in negative terms, not solely a force of oppression or restriction. As Foucault states, "We must cease once and for all to describe the effects of power in negative terms: it 'excludes,' it 'represses,' it 'censors,' it 'abstracts,' it 'masks,' it 'conceals.' In fact, power produces reality; it produces domains of objects and rituals of truth" (1991, 194). Functionalism is avoided in Foucault's work by the simple fact that he conceives of power dynamics as acted out in a space that is always open to renegotiation: "These power relations are thus mobile, reversible, and unstable. It should also be noted that power relations are possible insofar as the subjects are free" (1997a, 292).

Contrary to critiques of Foucault that he reduces the potential for agency in discourse, I believe that Foucault's notion of power in discourse can be read to open up the potential for agency *within* hegemonic relational dynamics; resistance is inherent within the relations of power, not absented by them. For Foucault such resistance belongs to those who are capable of seizing "the rules" of discourse and struggle to dominate chance events.[25] That is, the ideological functioning of a science should be tackled as a discursive formation at the locus of the generative power of those discourses—the discursive rules of formation—and should be challenged point by point (2002, 205). So, for persons with poor mental health, Foucault does not advocate a program for the dismantling of institutional psychiatry, but rather suggests a way of viewing the communicative space between patient and doctor, between "mad" and "sane," between any two people in such a way that allows that space to be freed, to be reimagined, not according to a new and stable set of parameters but on a continually ad

---

25. Indeed, he argues for the destruction of the "asylum space" in our contemporary asylum society by transferring power to the patient to produce his/her own truth of his/her poor mental health (1997d, 47).

hoc basis in an agonistic relationship "which is at the same time reciprocal incitation and struggle" (1982, 222). Such a view of renegotiating relational context stresses the strategic aspect of the encounter, moving from the seeming sense of predeterminedness of Foucault's discursive rules of formation to encounters continuously configured and reconfigured.

Centrally, then, Foucault's work suggests that resistive and transformative struggles with hegemonic relational dynamics inherently involve acts of reimagination. It is this incitement to reimagine societal landscapes that is crucial to appreciate in Foucault's contribution to my presentation here of the relational dynamics of persons with poor mental health. Power does not belong to one group or individual. Rather, as Bo Isenberg argues, power is always in the midst of relational dynamics, always situational (1991, 301). Indeed, as Foucault himself states, power is a product of relational dynamics and so is always up for grabs: "a power relationship can only be articulated on the basis of two elements that are each indispensable if it is really to be a power relationship: that 'the other' (the one over whom power is exercised) be thoroughly recognized and maintained to the very end as a person who acts" (1982, 220).

However, if one emphasis that might be taken from Foucault is that persons can be seen as those who act within power dynamics—wherein power might be produced in acts of reimagining discourse—the final critique of Foucault to address is offered by Fendler. She contends that Foucault's work is too apolitical to sustain such acts of reimagination in its failure to take stances on issues or offer frameworks for political engagement (2004, 450), or as Isenberg put it in Habermas's terms, for "communicative action" (1991, 305). Hence one can argue that little scope is provided in his work for the heuristic of reimagining to be drawn forth.

While this looks like a valid critique of Foucault, where it falls down is in its misreading of what genealogy is. That is, as David Owen explains, genealogy cannot be expected to legislate agency and autonomy "for us"; it can only exemplify its commitment to it (1995, 492). Indeed, it is here that Foucault's work provides both a new notion of political engagement with those who have been "disempowered" in society and a damning critique of liberation hermeneutics' treatment of poor mental health. For, while in the liberation paradigm the so-called marginalization of the oppressed presupposes the need to empower those whose voices are obscured at the margins, one can argue that Foucault's work reveals that the liberation paradigm will ultimately reinforce an essential and asymmetric relationship between those who are regarded as autonomous and those who are regarded as dependent (see Cruikshank 1999). Genealogy, on the other hand, seeks to rethink the notion of political agency, contending that all subject agents can exercise autonomy in the reimagining of discourse.

While I would contend that it is not the case that Foucault's work lacks political engagement, one can argue that it is still left unclear in Foucault's treatment of human agency and resistance *how* relational dynamics might be reimagined when in Foucault's genealogy, despite the presentation of the productivity of power, the agency of the human subject is set within discourses that are too "overwhelming" and within power networks that are too complex and pervasive. The central problem, then, is that while Foucault can be read as offering incitement to reimagine relational dynamics, the praxis of resistive agency may still look elusive.

The fundamental problem that remains with Foucault's work, as Edward Said asserts, is that what is missing is the presence of counter-discourses.[26] That is, there is an absence in Foucault's work of the "different claims" on discourse that are already being articulated in the societal relational dynamics of persons with poor mental health (Connolly 1985, 368). For some, Foucault's genealogy leaves little room for listening to such voices or for facilitating such a process of communication with such voices (Bauman 1987, 5). In terms of my own interests in this book, Foucault does not offer attentiveness to the ways in which persons with poor mental health already do struggle to produce power in the reimagining of their relational dynamics. So, while Foucault is interested in the local manifestation of political struggle, he is not interested in its person-by-person manifestation. Put another way, there is no engaging with the political subjects of discourse; and with this limitation to his work, there is no possibility for the reimagining of discourse to be explored as such—there is only the implicit suggestion that it should be.

1.4. Conclusion

I have assessed two key paradigms of thought for how they offer a conceptual framework for biblical criticism to offer textual insights into the relational dynamics of poor mental health. Liberation hermeneutics offers a strong emphasis on the central importance of power and the central

---

26. "There is, I believe, a salutary virtue in testimonials by members of those groups asserting their right of self-representation within the total economy of discourses" (Said 1986, 153).

notion that individuals with poor mental health are to be understood not as isolated individuals but as persons who act within a social structure that in ways can be oppressive to them. In terms of how one might respond to such patterns of oppression, the core emphasis of liberation hermeneutics is the biblical mandate to resist oppressive social structures, moving toward liberation from that which binds.

That said, it is the limiting nature of liberation hermeneutics' treatment of power—both contextual and textual—that calls for a more nuanced appreciation of relational power, found in the work of Foucault. He presents power as both a repressive and a productive reality. Indeed, it is this relational core to Foucault's argument that power might not be seen as purely coercive but also productive of resistance that is a key element for the potential use of Foucault's work in the exploration of the relational dynamics of context and texts. Indeed, the central point of Foucault's work in terms of my own interest in the relational dynamics of poor mental health is the potential of subjects to exercise an agency that reimagines relational dynamics.

Preferring Foucault's social philosophy over liberation paradigm's biblical theology, in chapter 2 I will explore the potential of mutuality as an alternative concept to "liberation from the margins" that will draw from a Foucauldian appreciation of relational power.

2
MUTUALITY: A POSTCOLONIAL PRAXIS FOR THE RELATIONAL DYNAMICS OF POOR MENTAL HEALTH

In the course of this chapter I explore the use of mutuality within various conceptual frameworks as a preparation for understanding mutuality specifically as a postcolonial praxis. In doing so, I will draw on mutuality's presence both in the worlds of mental health literature and of theology, particularly Nancy Eiesland's theology of disability and Carter Heyward's theology of mutual relation. Seeking a more strategic understanding of mutuality as a praxis, I turn to the work of postcolonial thinker Homi Bhabha, and from a critique and analysis of Bhabha I conclude the chapter by offering my own development of the concept of mutuality as it applies to the textual analysis of relational dynamics.

2.1. BEYOND MUTUALITY AS AN ASPIRATION: MUTUALITY AS A PRAXIS

The centrality of societal power in liberation hermeneutics and in Foucault's work, the concept of power as relational, and the incitement in his work to reimagine hegemonic power dynamics are the core features of the previous chapter that I carry into this one. Moreover, in parsing the significance of these two paradigms, one of the key insights that I think Foucault offers over liberation hermeneutics is the assertion that individuals can exercise agency in the reimagination of discourse. In other words, the "disempowered" of the liberation paradigm do not need to be empowered by some source external to them; they already have the potential for counterdiscourse.

That said, the fundamental drawback that has been pointed to in Foucault's work is a lack of attention to the practice of actual counterdiscourses. Thus, while retaining the power and relationally aware imagination of these two paradigms, and this notion of agency as the power to reimagine discourse, I propose in this chapter a way of analyzing relational dynamics that directly addresses this perceived deficiency in Foucault's work and that focuses on counterdiscourses. I wish to focus the analysis of the relational dynamics on the level of individual encounters as a way of speaking about the possibility of counterdiscourse. Moreover, I am interested in how individual encounters are negotiated within the structures of hegemonic power without having to look toward a necessary teleology of liberation from that hegemony. Therefore, I wish to explore the moment-by-moment instances of resistive agency and thus move from the theoretical analysis of relational dynamics to the praxes of relating and ask what these praxes might say of the nature of resistive agency.

The specific praxis of resistive agency that I am interested in exploring is *mutuality*. Exactly what "mutuality" is understood to be varies somewhat according to the discipline making use of it. Understanding mutuality as a praxis rather than as a theoretical concept or a philosophical ideal, I will study how it emerges within relational dynamics. Indeed, there is a Foucauldian premise to viewing mutuality as a praxis that speaks to a confidence that the reimagination of hegemonic discourse does indeed exist in the form of counterdiscourses.

This praxis-led approach means that defining what is meant by mutuality will be difficult to specify as mutuality emerges in encounters between persons in multiple forms. For instance, some explorations of mutuality in action focus on it as a praxis centering on the importance of relationship, such as analyses of classroom dynamics or methodologies of pedagogy that emphasize mutuality as the shared process of knowledge assimilation within dialogue (see Wallace and Ewald 2000). Similarly, the missiology of the World Council of Churches emphasizes the role of the local church in enabling a "mutuality in mission" to emerge that is aware of the intercultural nature of mutual relationship and agency (Ionita 1997). Other explorations of mutuality focus on its appreciation of difference, such as in ecclesiologies where a trinitarian model of church is proposed as one that therefore has room for differences within church membership and identity (Jinkins 2003), and in the ecumenical movement where "mutual accountability" is promoted in the pursuit of consensus over majority rule, seeking to emphasize interdependence as a way of remodeling ecumenism.[1]

---

1. See Apostola 1998. It is interesting that one common thread in the application of mutuality to relational dynamics, whether pedagogical or ecclesiological, is that room should be made for difference as persons are encountered in society. Such a feature makes mutuality as applied in these varied milieus markedly different from

With such a broad appeal, as a concept "mutuality" has retained a nebulous quality, loosely related to a wide range of attempts to take "the other" into account. It has served both as an aspiration and as a methodology. It is also clear that mutuality as a concept used within multiple areas of concern has fallen foul of being used to form various catchphrases such as "intercultural mutuality" (Ionita 1997) and "mutual accountability" (Apostola 1998). The danger is that mutuality might be taken as an idea and a praxis whose impact is lost to a combination of ubiquity and vagueness. Given this wide variety of its usage, I will focus on how mutuality has been understood in three paradigms: the study of poor mental health in society, Nancy Eiesland's theology of disability, and Carter Heyward's theology of mutual relation.

In mental health literature, when mutuality is considered from the lived perspective of persons who have experienced poor mental health, the concept is understood as "the experience of real or symbolic shared commonalities of visions, goals, sentiments, or characteristics, including shared acceptance of difference" (Hagerty et al. 1993, 294). It is understood fundamentally as an experience between persons where there is room for difference, and so by nature this understanding retains a degree of idiosyncrasy. Similarly, "shaping" mutuality between nurses and family caregivers of mental health patients focuses care on mutual partnership and understanding, which is able to allow all involved to accept different perspectives and changing attitudes (Jeon 2004). Furthermore, such mutual partnerships as models of caregiving push at the limits of what is normatively perceived as the demarcation between caregiver and care-receiver wherein mutuality in praxis is seen as a blurring of certain client-caregiver boundaries such that identities and boundaries are set in a process of continual negotiation (McAllister 2004, 28). Indeed, Robert Watson states that "at the right moments" what is most therapeutic in psychotherapy is a real relationship between two people characterized by "mutuality, reciprocity, and intersubjectivity" (2007, 67). Furthermore, this state of "mutual surrender" is one wherein the other is truly recognized, wherein a tension is maintained between recognition of the other and self-assertion, such that the tendency to collapse the relational space shared or perhaps even constructed in this act of mutual recognition is resisted (ibid.).[2]

---

its application in economic theory, where a homogeneity of interests is considered a prerequisite for economic success. See Deakin et al. 2008.

2. Watson goes on to note how the struggle for intersubjective mutual recogni-

Similarly, mutuality is explored as a theme in recovery from seasons of poor mental health in terms of the relational encounters between persons. For instance, by sharing experiences of survival and recovery, women have been able to give up shame, self-blame, and isolation as well as enter into reciprocal relationships that can have a prolonged power to heal (Fearday and Cape 2004, 262). Indeed, mutuality is described as the "background music" in women's experience of mental health such that its relative presence or absence is found to be a significant contributor to well-being, affecting how women perceive their lives and relationships.[3] Also, within the area of recovery literature, mutuality is considered in Aristotelian terms as the recognition of the healing potential of "noble friendship" (Aristotle 1962, 33). Mutuality occurs for Aristotle in the moral moment of taking up the good of the other as our own (224), and it is in such a praxis that the "profound healing" potential of mutuality is experienced (Stocker 2001, 166). Conversely, "nonmutuality" is "the source from which oppression springs" (168).

What emerges from this assessment of some of the uses of mutuality in mental health literature is a series of aspirations: mutuality should mean having room for difference, being open to crossing interpersonal boundaries, valuing reciprocation, interdependence, shared experience, and accountability. Thus, with the contextual picture of relating that I describe in chapter 1 in mind, one might understand mutuality as an aspirational praxis that seeks the transformation of hegemonic relational dynamics. However, for such aspirations to become practical realities an awareness of power and its complexities is called for.

If we draw from the wider field of disability, while in the case of the care of disabled babies "narrowly conceived interpretations of normality" can be challenged by "embracing alternative narratives" of the care of those babies, what exactly does it take to embrace an alternative narrative (Fisher 2007)? Is it a question of merely listening to, or is it more taking account of those narratives and allowing them to reshape medical care? Or is it even a question of having those alternative narratives provide a redefinition of medically modeled diagnosis? Certainly, from a Foucauldian point

---

tion is reflected in the life of God in the Trinity: a pattern of relationship without the motive of power over the other (72).

3. Hedelin and Jonsson 2003. Indeed, the significance of mutuality in the lives of women in particular has been widely studied and postulated to be a core indicator of mental health. See, e.g., the survey in Sperberg and Stabb 1998, 224–25.

of view, without an incisive grasp of how the discourses of medical power and societal behaviors toward disabled babies and children might work across various social settings, the efficacy of "embracing alternative narratives" stands little chance of reimagining the power it seeks to alternate.

With its highly aspirational focus, one of the aspects of relational dynamics that mutuality in mental health literature fails to consider fully is the inherent ambiguity that relational encounters inhabit. It is in this regard that the second paradigm, Nancy Eiesland's theology of disability, offers more insight into the workings of mutuality as an embodied praxis. Within the discipline of theologies of disability, she seeks to explore the potential of mutual relation along the axis of the inherent ambiguity that such relating embodies when encountering disability. She argues that mutuality evades the binaristic oppressor/oppressed paradigm and invites theological reflection and with it, praxis, beyond the categorizing and essentializing of the disabled body as if it were an ontological category of its own, and into an ambiguous space (1994, 116). Moreover, she holds that the disabled person is not to be viewed as a person enslaved to a picture of normalcy for which they should strive, but is already fully human, highly ambiguous, and imbued with the endless potential for relational mutuality (48). Hence, and rather ironically, given her stated interest in liberation hermeneutics, such an emphasis on the ambiguity of the embodied encounter with disability resists the teleological temptation to move beyond difference and toward, somehow, its liberation.

This is so because for Eiesland the encounter with disability is not the recognition of "the other"—not the recognition of an essentially different being—but the recognition of difference and sameness at the same time. Embodiment, as Eiesland argues, is a profoundly ambiguous reality (95). The self and the other are faced with a somewhat messier relational reality than the dichotomous liberation paradigm suggests; with this emphasis on the ambiguity of mutuality, relational dynamics look less and less like two sides of a dichotomous exclusion and more and more like the negotiation of shared relational dynamics. Thus, within such a paradigmatic understanding of relating, a desire is contained to remain in dialogue with difference.

This emphasis to remain in dialogue with difference is exactly where I believe mutuality differs most significantly from the notion of liberation from the margins. At the margins, there is no space for the difference of marginalized persons to be renegotiated with the center. Within classic liberation hermeneutics there is only the exodus movement out of the peripheral location (the margins) to the imagined center. Mutuality on the other hand is a relational dynamic that does not suggest a place where the other is excluded but rather the struggle wherein difference is renegotiated within shared relational spaces. There is no movement from-to; or put another way, there is no sublation of difference—there is an attempt to work with difference rather than try to progress past it.

In framing an understanding of the praxis of mutuality, what we can take from Eiesland's theology of disability is an appreciation that this praxis is one that pauses within the relational encounter to perceive and be perceived by the ambiguous difference of embodiment. However, one might also say that this is as far as this framing of the praxis of mutuality goes: it is suggestive but not explanatory. That is, exactly how sameness and difference are negotiated within relational dynamics remains something of an enigma in Eiesland's theology. It is hard to see a strategic appreciation of mutuality here; it remains largely aspirational.

Given this critique, the third paradigm that I consider in framing my understanding of mutuality as a praxis—feminist theologies—offers the concept of mutuality a more robust description of its potential to be a power-aware praxis. There are multiple applications of the notion of mutuality within feminist theologies, from those who explore the role of mutuality and violence (Fortune 1995), to those who explore feminist ethical considerations of economics (Robb 1995, 156–59), and to those who explore the role of mutuality in sexual ethics,[4] including theological analyses of prostitution.[5]

What feminist theologies offer to the consideration of power dynamics in relational encounters is an appreciation of how as a relational concept mutuality is often subordinated to other ethical norms. For instance, feminist theologians critique the notion of sacrifice for the mutual good of all as a praxis that only perpetuates a hierarchical framework wherein some persons end up being more mutual than others. According to Joseph Marchal, when mutuality is paired with sacrifice this tends to result in an uneven distribution of sacrifice such that women in particular suffer a disproportionate deficit in true mutuality in the cause of the mutual good of

---

4. See Ellison 1996, 30–58; Harrison 1983; Gudorf 1994, 24–50; Jordan 2002, 163–68.

5. Karen Peterson-Iyer (1998) has argued that the feminist moral norm of "right relationship" as mutuality/reciprocity, which requires relationships to be characterized by nonsubjection and equal regard, should be applied to the institutional practice of prostitution.

all (2005, 17-6). What feminist theologians attempt to do is to deconstruct models of mutuality that have been subjugating in effect even though liberating in their rhetoric.

One of the most significant feminist thinkers in this regard has been Carter Heyward, whose work brings contextual acts of relating into an incisive theological dialogue with the notion of mutuality. For Heyward, mutuality involves being in right relations with the other, respecting that other's integrity, and moving beyond sexist, racist, and heterosexist modes of relating (1989). At the same time, she sees *relation* as a term with significant theological overtones: "the radical connectedness of all reality, in which all parts of the whole are mutually interactive" (1999, 61). This notion of connectedness has profound implications for her doctrine of God such that "God" is "the movement that connects us all" (ibid.); God is not only in the "relationality" between us, God is our power in mutual relation, "the Spirit celebrating mutuality" (65). From this theological standpoint, Heyward wishes to stress the move beyond a mere interpersonal understanding or even a communal understanding of mutuality, to a cosmic one that sees mutuality as the "creative basis" of all life and all parts of reality. Mutuality, then, becomes both the enlivening Spirit of relation and the moral work of all creatures (62).

The notion of "beginning in relation" is not only the fundamental unit of Heyward's work, it is also where mutuality is most significant in terms of its existential depth. Specifically, the notion that "the experience of relation is fundamental and constitutive of human being" (1982, 1) points to a radical understanding of agency, power, and ambiguity. In terms of agency, she believes that "simply because we are human, we are able to be co-creative agents of redemption" (2). Power in relation is a power that "we choose to claim or not" (3). Mutuality, for Heyward, is the presupposition of our existential state. We are to have confidence not only in its possibility but in the reality of its power (44).

Heyward's conception of mutuality as a praxis is Foucauldian in its notion of individual agency having the potential to reimagine hegemonic discourse. In terms of the biblical motifs of liberation hermeneutics, it is a move away from the notion of persons with poor mental health as disenfranchised and disempowered subalterns of society. Heyward's is a picture of power presupposed already to exist. To speak of mutuality is to speak of power that is inherent, power that should be taken for granted.

Picking up the theme of ambiguity again, Heyward's concept of power is not only a fundamental of human existence and being, it is also highly unpredictable. This unpredictability is suggested in her emphasis of the Markan use of δύναμις (e.g., 6:2b, καὶ αἱ δυνάμεις τοιαῦται διὰ τῶν χειρῶν αὐτοῦ γινόμεναι (NRSV: "What deeds of power are being done by his hands") to refer to instances of Jesus' use of power in the Gospel. Heyward argues that δύναμις is not power that is held or possessed by one individual or another in a binarism of oppressor-oppressed. Rather, it is a power that is always "a dynamic exchange between and among persons" (1982, 47), and a power that may be experienced by others as "raw power, spontaneous, uncontrollable, and often fearful" (41). This differs from ἐξουσία (e.g., Mark 11:28, ἐν ποίᾳ ἐξουσίᾳ ταῦτα ποιεῖς; ἢ τίς σοι ἔδωκεν τὴν ἐξουσίαν ταύτην ἵνα ταῦτα ποιῇς; (NRSV: "By what authority are you doing these things? Who gave you this authority to do them?"), which, Heyward argues, is hierarchical and socially licensed (ibid.). For her, δύναμις is a power underneath the authoritative order of external power, a power of sometimes hidden resistance; yet at other times it is a highly provocative and explicit demonstration of power. Indeed, from a Foucauldian perspective, Heyward sees Jesus as a figure who seeks to "re-image" power, to "give *exousia* to relational *dunamis*" (42).

Such a power-in-relation is not only unpredictable and in ways subversive to received expressions and recognitions of power, it is also ambiguous to the point where persons in relational encounters share a permeable space of potential transformation. Persons are not only "immersed in [the] ambiguity, tension, [and] shifting foci" (159) of the other but are open also to the possibility of ambiguity in the self. Encounters of relational power are truly mutual encounters, where each person is affected by the relational power of the other. For Heyward, this is as true of God as it is for us: "with us, by us, through us, God lives, God becomes, God changes" (9). What she is saying here about power relations is that mutuality requires persons to be always open to change: "a dynamic relational dance in which each nurtures and is nurtured by the other in her time of need" (1979, 156).

Overall, then, with Heyward's descriptions of the praxis of mutuality as δύναμις, the reciprocal negotiation of power between persons, and with the fluid and ambiguous impacts of such relational dynamics, this particular framing of the praxis of mutuality offers much to the theological imagination for reading biblical texts and rethinking relational contexts. To see power as inherent in relational dynamics is to see it in the Foucauldian sense: always up for grabs. Furthermore, Heyward's notion of power as relation adds to the consideration of the relational encounters of biblical characters and subsequently to how these textual encounters might speak to contextual relational dynamics of persons with poor mental health. It offers an expanded view of such individuals whose agency in texts and contexts should not be easily dismissed. Indeed, Heyward's theology of relating points to the potentially transformative aspect of the praxis of mutuality.

Moreover, in terms of the fundamental deficit of explanatory power as to how resistive agency might operate within networks of relational dynamics that I have noted in both liberation hermeneutics and in Eiesland's theology of disability, Heyward's work offers some movement forward with her notion of the praxis of mutuality as sometimes hidden and sometimes public and highly provocative. That said, due to Heyward's description of δύναμις as an uncontrollable and spontaneous power, the hope of being able to describe how such an agency of resistance might operate is somewhat mitigated by its unpredictability. Thus, even with the notions taken from Eiesland and Heyward's work that have understood mutuality as a praxis as centering on the ambiguity of embodiment, the appreciation of difference, the spontaneity of sometimes hidden and sometimes open shows of power, in the end, what remains fundamentally lacking is a fuller appreciation of the strategic element to relational encounters. I would argue that such a strategic focus is necessary for this work's hope of utilizing mutuality as a heuristic for the relational dynamics of poor mental health. In other words, unless the textual analysis of relational dynamics is robust in its power awareness, any reflections that one might offer from text to context will be limited in value.

Therefore, in order to explore mutuality more robustly as a praxis, I now turn to a final and more strategic paradigm: postcolonial criticism. While in many ways postcolonial criticism reflects much of the sort of boundary-defying mutuality described above, it also enables a more incisive analysis of the strategies of agency and resistance of the praxis of mutuality, which I believe opens the way for both an aspirational and a strategic conception of mutuality.

2.2. Postcolonial Praxes: Cocreating Third Space

In broad terms there have been two approaches toward defining postcolonial criticism. One approach has retained the hyphen, with *post-colonial* used to refer to a temporal and a sociopsychological reality (Segovia 2000a, 12). Such a term refers to struggles set within geopolitical contexts of colonial rule such as the French in Algeria or the British in

India. Within such contexts, "post-colonial struggles" might be defined as struggles for liberation after the achievement of political independence (Young 2001, 11). The other approach uses the term *postcolonial* (without the hyphen) and signifies a discourse of reactive resistance articulated by the "colonized" who critically interrogate dominant knowledge systems (Sugirtharajah 2002, 23). That is, its concern is to trace the relations between center and periphery, and to rearticulate conceptions of those relations (Segovia 1999, 103). Moreover, as Robert Young states, postcolonial criticism attempts to undo the ideological heritage of colonized forms of knowledge via a "decentring of intellectual sovereignty" hitherto held by one group over another (2001, 65). In this second paradigm, relational dynamics are traced in struggles for power in contexts that are "colonizing" as they result in the subjugation of knowledge and persons.[6]

It is this nonterritorial conception of postcolonial criticism that I utilize here in the reimagination of the relational dynamics of poor mental health in contemporary North Atlantic societies through the reading of biblical texts. Within this postcolonial paradigm, while "diasporic or intercultural" postcolonial thinkers such as Segovia,[7] and "transcultural" ones such as Spivak and Bhabha,[8] speak of border-crossing in global, colonized, and/or transcultural terms, I am interested in the transgressive boundary crossings of shared relational encounters. That is, I am interested in exploring the ways in which the rearticulation of identity, the exercise of agency, and the practice of dialogue might push at the boundaries of relational dynamics constructed under hegemonic discourse. Thus the postcolonial nature of praxis that I am interested in exploring is the praxis that renegotiates relational dynamics in the Foucauldian attempt to reinscribe the rules of the formation of hegemonic discourse. And so, with particular reference to the praxis of mutuality, what I am now interested in exploring is how this second form of postcolonial criticism might offer a strategically robust paradigm to complement the aspirational conceptions of mutuality explored earlier in this chapter.

---

6. Stephen Moore has listed a number of "interrelated relia" that fall within the "orbit" of the second form of postcolonial thought, including imperialism, Orientalism, universalism, resistance, assimilation, creolization, colonial mimicry, hybridity, and the subaltern marginalization among others, all "intersected by the ubiquitous determinants of language, gender, race, ethnicity, and class" (2006b, 9).

7. See Samuel 2007, 21–22, for the designation of Segovia's work as such.

8. Ibid., 26, for the same designation.

2. MUTUALITY: A POSTCOLONIAL PRAXIS

To frame the praxis of mutuality, I have chosen the work of Homi Bhabha because of its strategic edge. At first sight, Bhabha's conception of relational encounters is similar to Heyward's notion of power as relation, in that Bhabha views relational dynamics as occurring in spaces within which and upon which agents act, as well as spaces that act upon them in the occurrence of the operation of what Bhabha calls a *third space* (1994, 37). This third space is not neutral; it is a space wherein identity and agency are malleable such that human subjects in relational encounters are open to self-change. However, Bhabha's work speaks from a different place than Heyward's work: the experience and agency of the colonized person, which he characterizes as resistive survival (Moore-Gilbert 2000, 452), a praxis of "dealing with or living with and through contradiction and then using that process for social agency."[9] It is not, then, the commonality of the encounter that Bhabha emphasizes—it is the difference.

For Bhabha, relational encounters occur at a site of a negotiation between persons termed a "space of translation." This space exists at the boundary between persons, and "from [it] something begins its presencing" (Bhabha 1994, 5). That something, for Bhabha, is repetition. As with Heyward's description of relational power as an existential constitutive element of power in relation, Bhabha wishes to foreground the issue of power and authority and explore the dynamics of its operation within relational dynamics in a different subversive way. In this regard, the notion of repetition demonstrates how the colonial or subjugating presence of the so-called knowing subject is not authoritative, but undermined in the very act of its enunciation: "The colonial presence is always ambivalent, split between its appearance as original and authoritative and its articulation as repetition and difference" (107–8).

What Bhabha is describing here is that this relational third space, wherein power is negotiated, is a space that does not leave the subjecthood of persons engaging in the relational encounter the same from beginning to end. The voice of one is echoed; the gaze of the other is returned. And what is returned to the other person is both the same, a repetition, and different. It is this very repetition that makes the relational encounter in the shared between space one that prevents the so-called knowing subject from having the power "to signify, to negate, to initiate historical desire, to establish its

---

9. Bhabha 1995, 80. Elsewhere, Bhabha describes this agency of survival as "vernacular cosmopolitanism" wherein individuals learn how to translate between and across cultures in order to survive. See Bhabha and Comaroff 2002, 24.

own institutional and oppositional discourse" (1994, 31). What is present in this space is the struggle with what is known in postcolonial parlance as *hybridity*,[10] wherein encounters occur and leave a "resistant trace," a "stain" of the subject being encountered as a sign of resistance (49). In other words, encounters in third space hybridize those who encounter within it.[11]

A specific example of this sort of resistance can be seen in Bhabha's essay "Signs Taken for Wonders," wherein he describes a missionary's attempt to convert a group of villagers outside Delhi, subverted in the renegotiation of the terms of conversion by the villagers (1994, 102–22). Facing the "authoritative gaze" of the missionary, the villagers resist conversion on the grounds that the word of God came to them from the mouth of a meat eater, not a vegetarian (118). The villagers, in their demand for a "vegetarian Bible," reimagine the rules of colonial discourse, thus estranging the basis of its authority, and in this act of resistance "the dominated" effectually "contaminated" the dominant discourse with their own suppressed knowledge (Kapoor 2003, 564).

For Bhabha, it is this "splitting," this space that opens up within and between one and the other, that leads to the possibility of resistance. Bhabha sees this form of resistance as a form of subversion that is incremental and often liminal, wherein the "small differences" and "slight alterations and displacements" become "often the most significant elements in a process of subversion and transformation" (1995, 82). They are significant because these slight alterations produce "supplemental positions" that highlight the incommensurability of the colonial project of knowing "the colonized" (Kapoor 2003, 564). Such supplemental agencies described through Bhabha's *Location of Culture* (1994) include praxes such as hybridity, mimicry, ambiguity, and sly civility.

---

10. Hybridity is a central concept in postcolonial thought, understood as the "interdependence of persons in the dialogical relational encounter and the mutual construction of their subjectivities" (Ashcroft et al. 2000, 118).

11. Bhabha's notion of sharing space and resistance within it is very different, then, from the form of resistance that, at the conceptual level at least, liberation hermeneutics argues for. That is, the hybridity of the third space is not a generalized, global category that dehistoricizes and delocalizes encounters. To the contrary, it is a notion that seeks to emphasize the local and particular nature of power relations and resistance. Bhabha's rendering of relational "space" is similar then to the discourse analysis of Foucault, who argues that "only the historical contents allow us to rediscover the ruptural effects of conflict and struggle that the order imposed by functionalist or systematising thought is designed to mask" (1980, 82).

2. MUTUALITY: A POSTCOLONIAL PRAXIS

The question remains whether "slight alterations" are enough of a strategic edge for such postcolonial praxes to be effective. One of the most significant critiques of Bhabha's work is that it lacks political efficacy. In other words, his insights are somewhat disconnected from lived reality. Some critics focus on political realities and the weakness of third-space resistive praxes in their relation to the "material exclusions, repressions, and subjugations" of lived contexts (Goldberg 2000, 82), questioning whether while hybridity might be a "critical aspect of subversion," it might not be a "sufficient agent of colonial failure" (McClintock 1995, 66–67). A related line of critique is that Bhabha's notion of hybridity conflates the psychic identities of the "colonizer and the colonized" while discounting the "crucial material differences" between them (JanMohamed 1985). The same sort of critique is made in relation to how gender (Holmlund 1991) and class (Moore-Gilbert 2000, 460) might complicate Bhabha's models of identity and cultural interaction. Indeed, for Bhabha, apart from some anecdotal reflections in *The Location of Culture*, most notably in the essay "Signs Taken for Wonders," there is little evidence of how effective hybridity is as a resistive product of colonial milieus (see Moore-Gilbert 2000, 459). These critiques are significant, and they focus on the challenge that much postcolonial criticism is susceptible to: its rhetorical engagement with colonialism is in danger of not being able to relate to the lived experiences of colonialism as material, political, and embodied.

However, to dismiss Bhabha's work here for its lack of political efficacy would be not to recognize the strategic element of his work. For, while one might argue that Bhabha's work does not address the embodied political realities of power, differentials of class, gender, and economic disparity, one can equally retort that it is the strategic nature of repetition and mimicry, hybridity, and sly civility—what might be termed third-space praxes—that is most suited to these embodied realities. The strategic nature of these praxes is that they are not praxes of open defiance but strategies employed under the guise of colonial rule.

James Scott's work on hidden transcripts of resistance is informative here. He argues that in the interests of safety and success, the dominated have tended to prefer to disguise resistance within the "public transcripts" of domination (1990, 86).[12] The possibility of knowing how effective such

---

12. The specific proposition that Scott wishes to put forward is that subordinate groups have "learned to clothe their resistance and defiance in ritualisms of subordi-

hidden resistance might be, therefore, is limited by the nature of the public transcript of the dominant and the need of the dominated not to call attention to any signs of resistance (89). Thus, as Scott points out, "unless one can penetrate the official transcript of both subordinates and elites, a reading of the social evidence will almost always represent a confirmation of the status quo in hegemonic terms" (90). That said, a number of studies explore the use of "hidden" forms of resistance in a diverse range of settings that might offer some corroboration of the sort of agency Bhabha's work describes.[13]

Bhabha's third-space strategies of resistance might in truth be highly effective even if they do not appear to be evident. Indeed, if the "hidden transcript" is "a critique of power spoken behind the back of the dominant" (Scott 1990, xii), then one would not expect such strategies to be easily recognizable as having political efficacy. It is at this more submerged and even hidden level of resistive praxis that Bhabha's third-space postcolonial imagination operates.

However, an even more serious critique for Bhabha's thought is that it appears only to conceive of agency within the premise of hegemony and subjection. Some have contended that there is no question in Bhabha's paradigm of challenging authority "from outside" colonial discourse, or as Benita Parry has put it, "no alternative texts are supposed to have been written."[14] That is, with Heyward's notion of power as relation in mind, there is no innate or preexistent δύναμις from which agency might be expressed. This seeming limiting of agency within the premise of hegemony not only limits the role of the "colonized" to that of a reactive counter to prevailing discourse and never producers of discourse in their own right; it also seems to limit the imaginative scope of third-space praxes in reimagining postcolonial space into being.

Bhabha's notion of agency can be seen as merely a reduction of the voices counter to the dominant discourse to the level of "sly civility."[15] If

---

nation that serve both to disguise their purposes and to provide them with a ready route of retreat that may soften the consequences of a possible failure" (1990, 96).

13. See, e.g., Rahman 2001, 42–44; Loew 1997; Nations et al. 1997; Levi 1999.

14. Parry 1995, 43. She quotes Frantz Fanon (1967, 231) to point out that postcolonial discourse has not taken up the challenge of taking up an oppositional discourse: "I am not a prisoner of history; it is only by going beyond the historical, instrumental hypothesis that I will initiate the cycle of my freedom."

15. Furthermore, widening the scope of this critique beyond Bhabha alone and

such a limit is extrapolated to the relational dynamics of poor mental health, there is a sense that Bhabha's work encourages an archetype of "colonialism": discourses of mental health that minimize the identity, agency, and dialogical voice of persons with poor mental health. The problem with such a limiting view of relational dynamics is that while indeed they are embedded in hegemony, if the agency practiced within them is only to be viewed as a reactive survival, then the potential operation of mutuality as a more positive and even transformative praxis, as suggested by the work of Eiesland and Heyward, is seemingly precluded.

Yet the question that is being begged here is whether Bhabha's notion of liminal postcolonial praxis does preclude a more hopeful notion of praxis. For, while Bhabha leaves it unclear whether resistive agency can be consciously programmatic or purposive (see Moore-Gilbert 1997, 38), his work still has something of an invitational element to it. Persons, albeit perceived only to operate within hegemonic discourse, are invited by virtue of their colonial hybridity to a postcolonial praxis of resistance that is open to the possibility of self-change and structural transformation, if at an incremental rate.

Indeed, specific to those who consider the potential impact of Bhabha's work within the field of psychiatry, this invitational element is described as an opportunity for "psychiatric others" to "sing their world into existence" (Fox 1999, 130), to become "ontological architects" who "create, shape and 'hold' space for healing" (J. Watson 1999, 257). Identity, agency, and dialogue are in a sense always in a process of becoming (Wilkin 2001, 119), and in this becoming, looking for "new, better, more interesting, more fruitful ways of speaking" (Rorty 1980, 360). Bhabha's third space, then, is interpreted as a space of becoming, of transformation (Goldberg 2000, 83), a mode of articulation in a productive space capable of "engendering new possibility" (Meredith 1998, 3). Moreover, once persons in relational encounters enter into such a third space, Bhabha himself has argued that "we're in a different space, we're making different presumptions and mobilizing emergent, unanticipated forms of historical agency" (1995, 83).

---

to postcolonial thinkers in general, some have argued that the postcolonial critique neglects the significance of precolonial thought and agency. See Vaughan 1994, 5. In terms of postcolonial biblical criticism, R.S. Sugirtharajah is one of the few thinkers who is alert to this caveat and attempts to draw attention in the postcolonial paradigm to texts, interpretations, and praxes that predate colonialism. See, e.g., Sugirtharajah 2001.

Referencing Bhabha's more recent work on migration that speaks of "postcolonial contramodernity" (1997) as a description of the colonized migrant within dominant culture both interrogating and hybridizing that culture's current narratives of self-representation and self-legitimation (Moore-Gilbert 2000, 460), I would like to highlight his work of agency beyond only a resistive survival in the face of hegemony. In this more recent work, while retaining his predilection for the incommensurability of migrant and dominant cultures,[16] Bhabha does stress that the relationship between the two is not entirely antagonistic. That is, within the ambivalence of the meeting of cultures in the migrant experience there is some measure of desire, such that migrant and native "both are in some ways mutually in need of each other" (Moore-Gilbert 2000, 461). This notion of mutual need is also discernible in how Bhabha describes his own notion of hybridity in third space, not as an identity as such but as an identification. That is, hybridity is a "process of identifying with and through another object, an object of otherness," in such a way that each bears the feelings and practices of the other (Bhabha 1990, 211).

To summarize the points of Bhabha's work: the third space is a space of becoming and of transformation that engenders new possibility and unanticipated forms of historical agency wherein each is in mutual need of the other, bearing the feelings and practices of the other. Bhabha's own notions of resistive agency are hybrid. On one hand, Bhabha's work seems to limit the notion of resistive agency to relate to struggles for survival within the power interstices of hegemonic discourse. On the other hand, Bhabha invites more than being tied to this archetype. It is this invitation to more that contributes to my own conception of mutuality as a postcolonial praxis, utilized throughout the rest of this work, as both resistive and potentially transformational.

2.3. Mutuality as a Postcolonial Praxis of Resistance and Transformation

Mutuality is a concept that to an extent evades definition. In the several paradigms considered, it emerges variously as a praxis focused on relationship, having room for difference, valuing interdependence, transgressive

---

16. One of the defining features of Bhabha's collection of essays, *The Location of Culture* (1994).

of interpersonal boundaries, valuing the potential of reciprocity, ambiguity, connectedness, and relational power between persons that is open to change in the self and in the other.

Drawing from the strategic elements of Bhabha and the aspirational elements of Heyward and Eiesland, I define mutuality as a postcolonial praxis that resists and potentially transforms hegemonic relational dynamics via the renegotiation of perceptions of identity, representations of agency, and instances of dialogical exchange. This praxis serves as a reminder that those whom Gayatri Spivak has called the othered (1995, 24) agents of colonial power are also persons who have legitimate identity, agency, and dialogical potential.

I take two key strategic elements from Bhabha's presentation of such praxes for the analysis of mutuality. The first is that mutuality is somewhat submerged or supplemental to colonial power. That is, as I argued in relation to James Scott's work, the exercise of mutuality as a postcolonial praxis might reasonably be assumed to be more hidden within the hegemonic structuring of relational dynamics rather than in outright opposition to them. That said, the theological imagination of Carter Heyward, specifically her conception of the praxis of mutuality as sometimes hidden yet sometimes openly provocative, should also be kept in mind. The aspirational element to mutuality needs to be retained within its composite nature as a postcolonial praxis of resistance and transformation. Within relational encounters I posit here there are occasions when open and defiant agency is risked in the renegotiation of relational space by the othered person.

The second strategic element of Bhabha's work is that one can assume that through the lens of postcolonial criticism mutuality will emerge as one praxis in operation among several. That is, I expect that postcolonial praxes of hybridity, mimicry, ambiguity, sly civility, and other such incremental and supplemental forms of agency will be present and interact with the praxis of mutuality. It is here that the crucial distinction between mutuality and other postcolonial praxes described herein is made clear. The critical expansion that mutuality as a praxis offers to postcolonial criticism is to move it from the conception of agency within colonial spaces as only reactive survival operating under the assumption of hegemonic relational dynamics toward a more positive and hopeful praxis.

I view mutuality as a postcolonial praxis as a way of not only viewing relational exchanges as struggles for survival but also of reimagining them. Viewing the role of agency through such a praxis is to see persons entering these relational encounters resistively imagining as if a different "set of rules" for discursive formation existed. Therefore, the struggle for relational dynamics is no longer seen as only the struggle over colonial spaces, but also in the Foucauldian sense as the reimagining of those spaces as postcolonial ones. Reading postcolonial agency as both an agency of resistive survival *and* as an aspirational transformation is to radically reimagine relational dynamics *within* the reality of discourse and power. Indeed, returning to how mutuality might be seen to interact with other postcolonial praxes, I posit that it is this aspirational element to mutuality that might make other postcolonial praxes more effective as resistive praxes. This is not to suggest that the praxis of mutuality will somehow enable the postcolonial agent to move past hegemonic power struggles; rather I postulate that the fundamental benefit of the praxis of mutuality is its ability to enable the renegotiation of the terms of hegemonic discourse as they occur.

While a person might be understood to practice mutuality unilaterally by reasserting their rights to identification, agency, and dialogue, the full form of the praxis of mutuality is multilateral in nature with an inherent reach toward and inclusion of the other. That is, both the self and the other are recognized as mutual partners in the relational encounter, in a form of relating wherein each has room for the difference that the other embodies.

The praxis of mutuality understood as a renegotiation of power may not suddenly transform relations between persons; rather, in the Bhabhian sense, the praxis of mutuality may be an incremental one that enables the transformation of relational dynamics only gradually. Thus, in reading the relational dynamics of encounters within biblical texts, I am not approaching the texts with a teleological hope that this praxis will be seen to be an agent of colonial collapse or even of relational reconciliation. Rather, I am approaching the textual presence of the praxis of mutuality with an open mind as to how effective such a praxis will prove to be in each case.

In presenting the significance of mutuality as a praxis of resistance and transformation and basing this presentation on an appreciation of the aspirational potential of Bhabha's work, I think it is worth noting that Bhabha himself is wary of placing an ethics and agency of survival within the "uplifting, tall stories" of progress and liberalism's celebration of cultural diversity. Bhabha's concern is that this celebratory move is in danger of losing agencies of survival within a discourse that reifies the teleology of the normative principles of such a liberalized society (Bhabha and Comaroff 2002, 31). While wishing to take heed of that warning, and recognizing this critique's similarity to critiques I offered of liberation hermeneutics in chapter 1, I also wish to contend with Bhabha that only speaking of agency as survival runs the risk of losing sight of the potential for an aspirational agency of transformation. I believe that in seeking to emphasize the possibility of a third-space agency of both resistive survival and aspirational transformation, I take up something of Bhabha's own hopefulness, as stated in one of his more recent interviews, that our own twenty-first-century transmigrational milieu is one of "emergent peoples entering that transitional movement that might lead them to a difficult, yet necessary, freedom" (46).

2.4. Conclusion

It is in being hopeful in my view of hegemonic relational dynamics that I wish to approach the last and most significant feature of my exploration of mutuality as a postcolonial praxis of resistance and transformation: the group readers who have known what it is to experience hegemonic relational encounters in their own lives. The final phase, then, in setting the stage for this work of contextual biblical criticism is to establish a reading method that will most suitably enable a close reading of relational dynamics as I have described them in this chapter. Thus reading strategies ideally will reflect room for difference, ambiguity, and agonisms of power in the analyses of the relational dynamics between characters in the texts. With this in mind, I explore in the next chapter the possibility of mutuality as a heuristic for reading. I will argue that mutuality can be used to influence not only how the text might be approached theoretically, but that it may also be used to influence who might count as readers and interlocutors of the text. With the notion of mutuality at the forefront of a discussion of biblical hermeneutics, in chapter 3 I present the possibility of reading biblical texts with others as a way of listening to, for, and with the voices of persons with poor mental health whose readership I seek in this work both to learn from and to question.

3
Dialogue and Difference:
Mutuality and Biblical Hermeneutics

This chapter seeks to explore a hermeneutical approach for this work as a piece of contextual biblical criticism drawing from two specific foci of biblical criticism and to relate these foci to the concept of mutuality. First, I explore postcolonial biblical criticism, and specifically how the application of the more theory-driven strand of this form of biblical criticism relates to my approach to the Gospel of Mark and to the concept of mutuality. Second, I explore dialogical biblical criticism, and in particular consider how the power dynamics inherent in the relationship between facilitator and readers correspond to the concept of mutuality. At the end of the chapter, in light of a critical analysis of both postcolonial and dialogical biblical hermeneutics, I present the particularities of my own hermeneutic.

3.1. Postcolonial Biblical Criticism: Strands of Hermeneutical Interest

In chapter 2 I explored the core concept of mutuality as a postcolonial praxis and defined mutuality as the praxis of resisting and potentially transforming hegemonic relational dynamics via the renegotiation of perceptions of identity, representations of agency, and instances of dialogical exchange. Taking this core concept of mutuality into this chapter's exploration of reading method, I first consider how mutuality's location within the broad milieu of postcolonial criticism relates to my use of postcolonial biblical criticism as a way of preparing to apply mutuality to the relational dynamics of texts.

A number of predominant strands of postcolonial biblical criticism have been identified in biblical studies. The first is described by R. S. Sugirtharajah as being interested in the colonial contexts of the production of biblical texts, with postcolonial critiques of those texts leading to a revaluation of colonial ideology, stigmatization, and negative portrayals embedded in content, plot, and characterization. This form of postcolonial biblical criticism also attempts to "resurrect lost voices" that have been distorted or silenced in the canonized text (Sugirtharajah 1999b, 4). Stephen Moore has suggested that this strand might better be labeled "empire studies," with its sustained focus on empire in the interpretations such scholars offer of texts.[1]

A second strand has an interest in "the once-colonised to produce knowledge of their own" (Sugirtharajah 1999b, 4). In other words, as well as having a deconstructionist tendency, postcolonial biblical criticism emphasizes the reconstruction or rereading of texts, attempting to remain sensitive to various subaltern elements hitherto submerged in those texts. Moore argues that this strand of postcolonial hermeneutical interest emanates to an extent from more recent liberation hermeneutics that might be grouped together as contextual or vernacular hermeneutics, focusing on "recovering, reasserting, and reinscribing identities, cultures and traditions" (2006b, 14–15). Also related to these approaches is a strand that Simon Samuel has labeled as a "diasporic intercultural model" that recognizes the plurality of readers and readings of texts.[2]

A third strand, interested in the reception of colonial texts, has been pioneered largely by the evolving work of Sugirtharajah. As one of the protagonists of the evolution of postcolonial biblical criticism, he has been something of a moving target in biblical studies—with Moore's clustering of postcolonial biblical criticism identifying him as a leading proponent of contextual or identity-specific interpretation (2006b, 14–17), and Samuel identifying him as a leading proponent of the "resistance/recuperative" model[3]—one can certainly also argue that Sugirtharajah has been more interested in recent years in probing the reception history of colonial texts during colonial times, both from a biblical and an extrabiblical perspective (e.g., 2003, 2008b, 2009). Additionally, he has encouraged an expansion of

---

1. Moore contends that Richard Horsley is the leading figure in this particular cluster; see Moore 2006b, 17–19.

2. Samuel identifies Fernando Segovia as the leading figure in such work (2007, 21–26).

3. Samuel cites the evolution of the work of Sugirtharajah as exemplary of this approach in its interest in "oppositional reading practices" and Said's contrapuntal mode of reading (2007, 17–21). See also Sugirtharajah 2008a.

postcolonial biblical criticism to include studies of the canonization and translation of biblical texts (see, e.g., 2006, 255–90; 2005).

A fourth strand has an interest in extrabiblical postcolonial studies. For some, this has meant pushing at the boundaries of what does and what does not constitute "biblical" studies. For instance, Kwok Pui-lan contends that to read the Bible in Asia requires a dialectical reading between two worlds—the "biblical" and the "nonbiblical."[4] This dialectical model of interpretation attempts to shift the emphasis from one scripture to many scriptures, and from one religious narrative to many possible narratives. While this does open up hermeneutical space for reading within biblical texts, space is also opened up exterior to the biblical text in a set of tensions between biblical and other texts. Put another way, it would seem that this sort of creation of hermeneutical space in biblical studies makes it possible and permissible for almost any questions to be asked of and subsequently almost any answers to be given in the interpretation of the Bible, and indeed beyond the Bible. It is a reading strategy that does not seek to privilege participatory space such that only those who fall within certain confessional or ideological boundaries might be "allowed" to interrogate texts and their readings. Rather, the potential that postcolonial criticism promises is one of a highly participatory, mutual space of textual engagement.

A fifth strand is also interested in extrabiblical sources, this time from within the more theoretical milieu of postcolonial criticism, drawing on the insights of thinkers such as Bhabha, Spivak, and Said. Moore has described this as an "intensely interdisciplinary" and "theory-fluent" mode of postcolonial biblical criticism, citing the work of Ronald Boer and Tat-siong Benny Liew, to name a couple of its proponents (Moore 2006b, 21). Such an approach to biblical texts does not begin with a set of epistemological starting points, such as with liberation hermeneutics' commitment to the poor and the oppressed and their liberation through the liberator-God.[5] Rather, it wishes to open up biblical reading freed from

---

4. Kwok 1995. This approach, she argues, means that certain boundaries within biblical studies are transgressed. First, sacrality: the Bible is not sacred alone, but one text among others. Second, canonicity: the Bible is not to be conceived of as a closed system, but is both inclusive and repressive of truth, and subject to expansion via cultural rereading. See the discussion by Segovia 2000b, 76–78.

5. See Torres and Fabella 1978, 269. That said, Catherine Keller et al. contend that the engagement of postcolonial criticism in theological reflection is "incoherent out-

the trajectories of orthodoxy and theological givens.[6] The starting point for such postcolonial readings is not epistemological but enunciative. That is, reading biblical texts is not to begin under the guidance of a set of pedagogical principles; rather reading is performative, an event in the present moment. There is a certain Foucauldian aspect to this approach to reading that recognizes the need for critiques of power inscribed in the text, as well as in the dominant history of its interpretation, to problematize and interrogate dominant discourses of texts. It is a reading that is open to the irreducibly infinite possibilities of multiple readings and readers.

While each of these five strands of postcolonial biblical criticism has its merits, it is the first two and the last that I draw on here. The first two strands are significant in their emphases on both the attempt to "resurrect lost voices" and on "the once-colonised producing knowledge of their own" (Sugirtharajah 1999b, 4). My interest in drawing from these strands does not lie in the behind-the-text concerns that have occupied much postcolonial biblical criticism in terms of the colonial contexts of the production of texts. Rather, I am interested in the reading of texts as stories set within colonial contexts. My exploration of the Gospel of Mark, therefore, seeks out so-called lost voices in texts in terms of characters in the stories narrated. Later on in this chapter I will examine ways in which postcolonial biblical criticism, in as far as it has been applied to Mark, has been limited in its analysis of the relational dynamics of individual-to-individual encounters, the key interest of this work.

Beyond this, I am also interested in expanding the frame of postcolonial biblical criticism in terms of gathering readers with poor mental health not normally counted as interlocutors of such texts within this paradigm. To make this move to expand the scope of postcolonial biblical

---

side of the effects of liberation theology," because it was liberation theology that made theologians conscious that the church is political by default, not by intention (2004, 5). Similarly, Sugirtharajah's critique of postmodernism states that its "lack of a theory of resistance" and failure to take into account "liberation as an emancipatory metastory" points to the fact that postcolonial criticism must maintain its link to liberation theology (1999a, 15).

6. Indeed, Moore has argued that a defining feature of postcolonial biblical criticism "as distinct from (although by no means in opposition to) 'liberationist' biblical exegesis, is a willingness to press a biblical text at precisely those points at which its ideology falls prey to ambivalence, incoherence, and self-subversion—not least where its message of emancipation subtly mutates into oppression" (2006a, 197).

criticism, I explore later on in this chapter how the insights of dialogical biblical criticism might apply to this interest to read with such persons.

My interest in postcolonial biblical criticism also lies in the final strand outlined above that focuses on both its interdisciplinary and its theoretical tendencies. In the next section, I will critique the treatment of relational dynamics that I assess to be present in Markan postcolonial biblical scholarship, and then state how I seek to utilize the conceptual paradigm of postcolonial thinkers such as Homi Bhabha as a way of paying closer attention to the struggles for power that the pericopae in question narrate.

3.2. Difference in Colonial Relational Dynamics: Renegotiating the Jesus Encounter in Mark

My fundamental interest in Mark is to explore individual textual encounters in terms of the relational dynamics between characters, seeing the text as a space of narrative struggle for voice and power. In focusing interpretation on the space between Jesus and other characters, I seek to foreground the role of the so-called minor characters in Mark by exploring six relational encounters: Jesus, "the Pharisees," and the man with the withered hand in the synagogue (3:1–6); Jesus, his family, and "the scribes" (3:19b–35); Jesus and the demon-possessed man among the tombs (5:1–20); Jesus, Jairus, and the woman with hemorrhages (5:21–43); Jesus and the Syrophoenician woman (7:24–30); and Jesus before Pilate (15:1–5). In analyzing these pericopae through a postcolonial lens, I recognize the significance of the colonial context of Roman rule of these stories as the sociocultural backdrop of the various characters involved. In doing so, I am interested in what Liew has called the "construction of colonial subjects" in Mark (1999, 33). That is, I am interested in studying how subjects acting within hegemonic relational dynamics in the Gospel exercise agency as colonial subjects, as persons subject to colonial discourse. That said, a brief sketch of postcolonial readings of Mark will reveal how I wish to analyze colonial subjecthood rather differently from much postcolonial scholarship to date.

Much postcolonial and similarly inclined interpretation of Mark has tended to emphasize the ideological underpinnings of the text's supposed production. For instance, Ched Myers (1988) argues that Mark rejects the imperial hegemony of Rome and the temple's exploitative alignment with it, advocating an egalitarianism by way of binding the strong colonial man (Caesar) via an ethic of nonviolence. Similar views—that Mark advocates an anticolonial ideology—can be found in the work of a number of scholars: Herman Waetjen (1989), via a Marxist analysis of the text, argues that Mark calls for a partisan questioning of the sociopolitical structures of the society of the day in Roman occupied Syria for a community of Gentile peasants; Richard Horsley (1998, 158) proposes that Mark is providing an alternative reading of history to the Rome-centered historiography of the day (although other postcolonial scholars have questioned the extent of Mark's anticolonial ideology);[7] and Robert Hamerton-Kelly (1994) maintains that Mark challenges violent ideology and praxis via the text's narration of the resurrection, which signifies that despite his violent death, Jesus' way offers the possibility of a new community characterized by love and inclusion.

However, these largely anticolonial readings of Mark are susceptible to criticism. For instance, Samuel has highlighted how such interpretations tend to romanticize and homogenize "the subaltern subject Jesus" (2007, 82). The fundamental problem for such readings of Mark is that Jesus tends to be essentialized, one way or another. Indeed, such is the theological significance of Jesus in the history of interpretation that as a character it is almost impossible not to see more of Jesus than the text alone presents.

For instance, arguing not for Jesus as a "subaltern subject" but for Jesus as an authority figure, Liew posits that Jesus in Mark—as a character inscribed with an absolute authority as God's son and heir—replaces one colonial authority with another, ultimate authority (2006, 209).[8] Furthermore, rather than being a liberatory move, Liew maintains that this represents a sharp binarism between insiders and outsiders, based on those who look favorably on Jesus' authority, teaching, and actions—in short, those who accept him—and those who do not. Arguing, then, for a Markan "politics of parousia," Liew (213) presents Jesus in rather stark

---

7. Moore has suggested that in comparison to "Mark's near-contemporary cousin," the book of Revelation, the Gospel lacks the "snarling, fang-baring hostility toward the Roman state" (2006, 197). Indeed, Moore argues that "Mark's anti-imperial invective really only extends to the local elites" (199). Liew has also problematized the notion of Mark as an anticolonial authority text with particular attention paid to Jesus' authoritative role in the Parousia (13:24–27), portrayed in the Gospel with Jesus' "ultimate show of force (and authority) … [that] will right all wrongs with the annihilation of the 'wicked'" (1999, 107).

8. Liew contends that Mark is an ambivalent text. That is, it includes both critiques of the existing colonial order and "traces of colonial mimicry that reinscribe colonial domination," or in other words, a procolonial ideology (2006, 215).

terms where his reappearance in power and judgment (8:38–9:1; 12:9–11, 36; 13:1–2, 26; 14:61–62) in the Parousia will bring about a realignment of sociopolitical power and the full establishment of God's reign.

At the heart of Liew's argument is the issue of power. He asserts (214) that Mark makes Jesus' teachings inseparable from his miracles, with his power to perform miracles resident in Jesus' authority, and Jesus' authority resident in his status as God's beloved and heir (1:9–11; 9:2–8; 12:6; 15:39). This authority demands the submission of everything and also the annihilation, ultimately in the Parousia, of all those who do not submit. Mark then defeats power with more power and so offers an ideology (and with it a theology), which is no different to the ideology of the hegemony of colonial rule (215).

However, from a Foucauldian perspective, the significant problem with Liew's argument is that he only appears to conceive of power in oppressive terms. That is, Liew's Markan Jesus is the absolute authoritative knowing subject of the Gospel. Therefore, in the force of his own rhetoric, Liew almost leaves no room for resistance in the face of such power. What is missing, then, is the notion that Foucault's analysis of power foregrounds: power is both repressive and productive, and furthermore, power is expressed in relationship with the "other." It is the irreducible difference of the other that Liew's reading of Mark oversteps, and so, while he contends that it is Jesus who reduces the role of minor characters to that of "sidekicks," and in the case of the disciples in particular, to "gophers" and "loyal satellites" (212), I would maintain that Liew himself is somewhat complicit in that act of reduction. Indeed, Liew asserts that with Mark's "grim view of human agency" (1999, 115), where "human beings remain objects instead of subjects of agency" (123), in the Gospel "human agency for change is futile" (119).[9] Such a reading underestimates the potential of colonial subjects for resistance, particularly, as Samuel highlights, in critiquing Liew's notion of colonial mimicry in Mark. Colonial power is not only duplicated in the praxis of mimicry, it is also disrupted (Samuel 2007, 84).

My own approach to the Gospel of Mark seeks to resist excessive readings of Jesus, and to probe the text for agency exercised in shared relational encounters. In doing so, I align with Samuel's problematizing of the ten-

---

9. Liew goes on to argue that as constructed colonial subjects in Mark, such characters "are limited in their choices as well as their abilities to bring about positive socio-political change" (1999, 132).

dency to present Jesus in a monolithic way—in postcolonial criticism, for instance, Jesus is presented largely either as pro- or anticolonial[10]—preferring instead with Samuel to see him, and other characters around him, as a hybrid blend of both antagonism against and affiliation with colonial discourse.[11] Indeed, Samuel sees Mark as a whole as a postcolonial discourse that reflects the longings of a subjugated community for a "strategic space between Roman colonial and the relatively dominant Jewish ... discourses of power," and that this longing is presented through an "indeterminate and fluid picture" of Jesus (2007, 153).

My own interest is in analyzing the characters in Mark as they encounter one another in a story set in the colonial times of Jesus' own day. This analysis probes the complex relational dynamics between Jesus and others, and moves beyond the interpretation of the characters Jesus encounters as necessarily subordinated to his supposed superlative status as the one who ushers in the reign of God (Mann 1986, 242), or as an absolute authority (Liew 2006, 212). Rather, such so-called minor characters are examined as potential cocreators of the narrative outcomes being analyzed; and, with the praxis of mutuality as presented in chapter 2 in mind, I consider such characters afresh as agents of the renegotiation of the complex of relational dynamics found in hegemonic social orders. In the pericopae that I explore, therefore, being made well (3:5), being made clean (5:1–20; 7:29), being healed (5:34), and being brought back from the dead (5:41–42) are not events set within a framework where the transformation that takes place in those encounters is only passively received; rather it occurs in sharing a common relational space.

To see relational dynamics as taking place in a common relational space does not mean that my interpretations of Mark begin with an expectation that the praxis of mutuality will be somehow present in the text a priori. That is, unlike the preoccupation of liberation hermeneutics with the textual movement from contexts of oppression to contexts of liberation, I seek to probe acts of relating as they are; in other words, the praxis

---

10. Indeed, according to Samuel, "the very fact that one can construct such contrasting portraits out of Mark suggests that the portrait of Jesus in Mark is much more complex, i.e., the Markan portrait of Jesus is both pro- and anti-colonial in nature" (2007, 156).

11. Samuel describes this as a combination of "strategic essentialism and transcultural hybridity" (2007, 128; cf. also 86).

of mutuality might be abundantly present in a particular text or it might be almost completely absent.

Thus, in alignment with Samuel in seeing "the postcolonial" as a spatial category—as a "cultural discursive space in between" (2007, 158)—I analyze the relating that takes place between characters in biblical texts and move beyond stereotyped, or typecast, interpretations of identity and agency, and ask what might emerge if reading remains attentive to the power dynamics of relating. Thus from the colonial landscape of Jesus' encounters with others I assess if postcolonial strategies of relating are present. Specifically, as I stated in chapter 2, I want to place the praxis of mutuality alongside other postcolonial praxes—hybridity, ambiguity, mimicry, sly civility, and so on—as agencies of hegemonic disruption and to ask whether mutuality might operate as both a resistive and a transformational praxis.

With this relationship to postcolonial biblical criticism in place, the second focus that I wish to explore within biblical criticism as it relates to mutuality is the milieu of dialogical biblical criticism. Here I ask how the praxis of mutuality might serve as a heuristic to the construction of a reading space with those who have experienced poor mental health. In utilizing mutuality in such a way, I am extending the application of this concept into the practical mechanics of how reading with others might be carried out. Furthermore, in engaging the interlocution of group readers who have firsthand experience of the societal location of poor mental health, I am grounding my exploration of biblical texts within that societal reality.

3.3. Reading with Difference: Dialogical Biblical Criticism

The notion of biblical criticism as a dialogue within groups of readers located outside the academy remains a peripheral form of biblical interpretation facilitated by scholars in the academies of the Northern and Western Hemispheres.[12] However, this is less the case elsewhere. In Latin America, a key forerunner to the present forms of reading in dialogue is Ernesto Cardenal's Nicaraguan study of reading the Gospels in Solentin-

---

12. Note that "biblical criticism as dialogue" is distinct from but not unlike Kwok Pui-lan's notion of the "dialogical imagination," which seeks to open up the biblical world and its interpretation to new dialogue partners outside the normative circle of hermeneutic concern, such as other cultural and religious voices. See Kwok 1995, 12–13.

ame with local villagers (1976–1982). Also key are the multiple *comunidade ecclesial de base* (CEB), which consisted of local gatherings of Catholics engaging in Bible studies, led by lay and ordained "pastoral agents," inspired by the Second General Conference of Latin American Bishops in Medellin in 1968 (itself inspired by the spirit of Vatican II [1962–1965]), which accorded the "Christian base community" formal ecclesial status (Dawson 2007, 145). The significant dialogical feature of both the Solentiname and the CEB models is that texts are read aloud and then those gathered reflect on the text and how the text speaks to and from the contexts of daily life, thus leading to an engagement in key community issues within the classic liberation paradigm's praxis-led hermeneutical circle (147).[13] Although having faced some considerable challenges from the Vatican since its height in the 1980s, when over a hundred thousand CEBs existed in Brazil (152), the work begun four decades ago is still vibrant today with organizations such as the Brazilian Centro de Estudos Biblicos galvanizing local dialogical projects.[14]

In Africa, where much of the most prominent dialogical reading work is done today (although there is similar work being done in other contexts too),[15] a key proponent of this method is Gerald West, who argues that at the heart of reading together is a relationship between the "trained/socially engaged biblical scholar" and the "ordinary individual reader" (1999b, 37). West sought to explore this relationship following his frustration that the actual voices of "the poor" are rarely heard despite their apparent hermeneutical privilege in liberation theologies,[16] a mark of distinction that

---

13. Gerald West argues that the fundamental praxis-led model of See-Judge-Act present in current South African dialogical reading also has its roots in the work of Joseph Cardijn, who worked among factory workers in 1930s Belgium (2006, 138).

14. See http://www.cebi.org.br. West argues that CEB dialogical readings have tended to rely on scholarly sociohistorical reconstructions of biblical texts, although reading methods have apparently diversified lately. It was a move away from this model, which West felt was overly reliant on the trained biblical reader, that characterized the work of the Ujamaa Centre (2006, 139–40).

15. For instance, in the United States see Ekblad 2003; in the United Kingdom see Lees 2007b; in the United States Vincent Wimbush leads work in Los Angeles looking at the role of scriptures in the cultural contexts of Los Angeles (see The Institute for Signifying Scriptures website at http://iss.cgu.edu/about/index.htm); and, globally see de Wit et al. 2004. See also the more recent publication by de Wit and West 2008.

16. West 2004b, 173. This frustration led to the establishment of the Institute for the Study of the Bible, South Africa, in 1990 (later formed into the Ujamaa Centre for

West claims delineates the earlier Latin American liberation theologies and their African counterparts (2006, 137). In developing this relationship, West uses a "participatory research" or "action research" methodology (1991, 91). This sort of methodology is committed to begin the act of reading from the needs and experiences of communities of "poor and oppressed" people, using the interpretive categories of such participants to shape interpretation (92). Within this framework three further commitments of contextual Bible study are delineated. First, a commitment to read the Bible in community, equally valuing the contributions of so-called trained and untrained readers. Second, a commitment to read the Bible critically. And third, a commitment to individual and social transformation through Bible study (94–95).

West's stated desire is to read with others. However, he argues that as soon as the biblical scholar speaks of the readings, strategies, and resources of the so-called ordinary reader, the vernacular hermeneutics that he advocates and practices cease to be vernacular. What he argues for, therefore, is a reading *with*, not a reading *for*. The dialogical hermeneutic West proposes, then, is highly relational and is about the sharing of reading spaces with those who previously have so often been the objects of academic production now acting as subjects and coproducers of biblical interpretation.

This "contextual Bible study"[17] paradigm has a number of advantages. First, with the unpredictability of the interlocution that multiple readers bring, overly selective interrogations of texts are less likely. Furthermore, many have found that multiple readers bring multiple confessional and other ideologically positioned perspectives to texts, thus decentering the tendency for academically produced interpretations to remain only at an imagined objective distance from socially located interpretive positions. Second, dialogical biblical criticism naturally and necessarily draws on an individual level of analysis, and thus in the sharing of interpretive space particular voices are given the option to be heard. Third, for West the practice of being embedded in the action-reflection cycle of the liberation

---

Biblical and Theological Community Development and Research; online: http://www.sorat.ukzn.ac.za/ujamaa/default.htm), modeled to an extent on the Brazilian Centro de Estudos Biblicos (see http://www.cebi.org.br).

17. This is the term most recently used by West et al. (2007) to describe the dialogical hermeneutic he has been developing over the past decade or more.

paradigm allows reading to be oriented toward praxis in the communities of readers.[18]

In terms of the contextual concerns specific to this work, dialogical biblical criticism has the advantage of opening up the way for persons with poor mental health to be directly engaged in acts of interpretation of texts and contexts. This allows biblical studies to enter a conversation with context as it truly is, as it is experienced. Whatever the nature of such experience is, the lived reality of poor mental health in contemporary society is not assumed to be known by the biblical scholar; rather in a dialogical space there is openness for lived experiences to be offered as interpretive lenses for the reading of texts and the analyses of contexts.

On the face of it then, dialogical biblical criticism has the potential to retain difference within the act of reading. That is, when different readers offer varied and perhaps contradictory interpretations of texts, interpretive space is opened up for those different interpretations to be placed side by side in an agonistic tension. Indeed, such a practice might be seen as a critical pedagogy, which, as Anneliese Kramer-Dahl maintains, opens up space for the marginalized "to give voice to their experience and to develop a critical analysis of oppressive social systems in order to transform them" (1996, 242; cited in Lees 2007b, 85).

However, the drawback of much dialogical biblical criticism practiced to date is that in the face of such interpretive tension, difference has often not been retained but instead resolved by the arbitration of the so-called trained biblical scholar. This is discernible in West's own work when the terms of the reading relationship are examined more closely. West's use of "scholar" and "ordinary,"[19] a differentiation he also delineates as "critical" and "precritical," already betrays a certain predeterminedness about the

---

18. West 2007c, 1. A further advantage has been argued for by Janet Lees with regard to her work with communities in the United Kingdom where biblical texts in worship are remembered by congregants of churches rather than read. Lees found this remembering of texts in the form of dialogue to have significant advantages for participants who struggle with various communication impairments (2007b, 74).

19. West's recent work recognizes the problematical nature of the term *ordinary reader* with his acknowledgment of a comment made by Gerald Sheppard in Toronto in 2002 that "all ordinary readers are actually 'extraordinary' readers" (2007c, 4). A simple alternative is proposed by Katharine Doob Sakenfeld, who suggests that *academic* and *nonacademic* might be a more suitable delineation, recognizing that even with such labels there is a continuum between the two (2008, 5). The notion of a continuum would suit West's own work with facilitators through the Contextual Bible

reading relationship he is describing. Before readings can begin, expertise has already been located and normalized in the form of the trained biblical theologian. The local and particular expertise of the readers who will read with the biblical theologian are denied the mantle of expert or scholar.[20] This is so even in the most careful dialogical reading, simply because the "ordinary reader" is denied the voice of arbitration. Indeed, West states that "ordinary readers have little choice in how they read the Bible," not having been trained in the critical modes of reading that characterize biblical scholarship.[21]

West's response to the problem of difference has left a tension at the heart of his project as it has developed through the years. While West argues that the contribution of the trained reader to the reading process should be limited to "constantly encouraging and facilitating ordinary readers to read the text carefully and closely" (1994, 161), managing conflict, and keeping the Bible study "moving toward the conclusion" (West et al. 2007, 12–13), the facilitator, described as "just one voice" in the study, is a voice that is loaded with a certain amount of predetermined knowledge and power that ultimately still shapes the reading process. West is aware that this tension exists in his work between a "colonised consciousness" and a "critical consciousness" (1991, 100). On one hand, he argues that it should be recognized what centuries of colonization have done to the consciousness of the "poor" and "oppressed" (yet the same attention is not given to what centuries of colonizing have done to the consciousness of the colonizers). On the other hand, West maintains that it must be rec-

---

Studies with the Ujamaa Centre, where there is a diversity of embeddedness in the academy among the facilitators (West et al. 2007).

20. Indeed, some contend that the characterization of the "poor" and "oppressed" as "ordinary readers" and scholars as "critical readers" implies that material poverty necessarily reflects intellectual poverty (Hinga 1996, 284). John Riches also challenges the sharp distinction between ordinary and critical readers, arguing that those who are not academically trained should not necessarily be assumed to be entirely lacking in techniques of biblical interpretation (1996, 186). On another front, Stephen Jennings offers the critique that the term *ordinary reader* is problematical because "it tends to elide various categories of persons who are not necessarily the same" (2007, 49).

21. West 1991, 90. Some also contend that the formulation of the untrained-versus-trained distinction is based on an uncritical acceptance of the "ideologies, choices and commitments inherent in the 'training' of the so-called trained" (Plaatjie 2001, 119).

ognized that even with this history of subjugated knowledge, the "poor" and "oppressed" do offer a critical consciousness, albeit "different from those with which we are familiar" (ibid.). Although the evolution of West's work has attempted to address this tension by refining and flattening the relationship between facilitator and readers, focusing on questions rather than answers (West et al. 2007, 25), the teleological presence of liberation as a marker of biblical interpretation continues to draw this process back to reserving the facilitator's role as the ultimate arbitrator of theological exploration and the provider of answers.

Beyond West's paradigm-shaping contribution to dialogical biblical criticism, one method that has emerged more recently has been pioneered by Hans de Wit and the Free University of Amsterdam project, reading John 4. This project paired over one hundred twenty partner groups across the globe in twenty-two different countries seeking to address whether intercultural reading of biblical texts might result in "a new method of reading the Bible and communicating faith that is a catalyst for new, trans-border dialogue and identity formation" (2004b, 4). The reading method consists of groups reading texts communally and then sending the reports of their readings to their partners somewhere else in the world in exchange for that group's reading report, thus enabling both groups to see the text through the eyes of another group's interpretation. A third phase consists of each group responding to the reading report of the partner group (5).

One of the fundamental methodological premises and stated values of the project was that the "ordinary Bible readers" were the owners of the project: "the group had the power" (5). However, as with West's work, one of the key critiques of the project in terms of how it shapes reading with others is how interpretive differences are dealt with. One of the key aspects of de Wit's project is that the reading groups should "strive for consensus" (14); yet it is never made entirely clear why such a goal should exist. Indeed, while de Wit states that "all possible and impossible connotations of texts have a vote in spontaneous understanding" (14), he also makes clear that as "an interpretive community we need to come to grips with the differences; we have to resolve the tensions that arise" (30). This stated need for a resolution of tensions reveals a basic assumption governing the project—that "God's liberating action is also especially directed toward" the "poor and sacrificed ones" (18)—thus leading to a theological teleology that lies at the heart of the conversation between trained and "ordinary" readers.

What is missing from the forms of dialogical biblical criticism that have been explored above is what is central to my presentation of mutuality as a postcolonial praxis of renegotiation. For, if the terms of this renegotiation and the scope of so-called ordinary readers are limited in advance of acts of reading together, then the fuller potential of dialogue is lost. Moreover, this critique of the trained biblical scholar acting as an arbitrator of reading difference within the act of reading is particularly ironic for readers who have experienced the societal location of poor mental health where being spoken for and having their interpretations of reality judged by others is commonplace, as I argued to be the case in chapter 1.

The question remains, then, how dialogical biblical criticism still might be able to engage with voices different from those with which academic production is familiar without sublating that difference in that very act of engagement. In other words, the hope here is for a methodology, as Louis Jonker argues for, that can embrace the "communality" of having interpretive room for multiple and contradictory voices (both of texts and interpreters), and that can thus resist the potential for dialogical hermeneutics to collapse into self-reflection (2007, 484).

One way forward is to consider what it means for the untrained readers who articulate difference into the interlocution of texts to produce their own knowledge of those texts. In this vein, another South African voice, Alpheus Masoga, argues that it is time for the "periphery" (those "marginalized" and "oppressed" in the South African context) "to occupy its own space without the interference of the center" (2002, 101). Although maintaining a highly binaristic perspective, Masoga's challenge that the "periphery" might occupy its own space might require biblical scholars to withdraw the voice of arbitration or validation and enter into a genuine dialogue. This is not the same as biblical scholars having nothing to say about texts and contexts and thus becoming merely mediums for others' thoughts to be communicated in academic forums they might not otherwise have access to; rather it is to think of a starting point[22] for acts of reading that foregrounds "cognitive dissonance"[23] as a potentially rich resource for reading rather than a problem for it.

---

22. This would not be, however, Masoga's pedagogical sort of starting point: his dialogical Bible study begins with an introductory session that demonstrates how "Jesus was interested in the renewal of the complete person and community" (2002, 106).

23. Sibeko and Haddad 1997, 91. Such dissonance might involve a confrontation

The reading method that I wish to pursue, therefore, is a blend of postcolonial and dialogical biblical criticism. I wish to open up a postcolonial-type reading space in dialogue with other readers so that the method might generate a reading whose interpretations are unpredictable and free, as much as possible, from the prevailing corrective discourse of the biblical scholar in the role of facilitator. In other words, in reading with others there is the potential to begin reading from the assumption of difference.

3.4. Mutuality and Mark: A Method for Reading with Persons with Poor Mental Health

The fundamental shift that I am proposing with regard to normative forms of postcolonial biblical criticism is to focus not only on the interpretation of texts but also on the act of reading itself and the space wherein that reading takes place. The hermeneutic that I wish to propose is a dialogical form of postcolonial biblical criticism that is informed in numerous ways by the praxis of mutuality. Thus the postcolonial aspect of this reading method is not only in its focus on the colonial contexts of texts but also in its construction of the reading space for group reading such that it might have room for mutuality in the negotiation of interpretive difference.[24] That is, mutuality informed this work's method of dialogical postcolonial biblical criticism in creating a dialogical space for reading wherein each reader is influenced by the voice of the other in a movement that has the potential to displace the other protagonist to some degree, yet does not disavow their presence or their voice.

---

with the dominant theology of a group or of an individual on the part of the facilitator. See Ekblad 2004, 139.

24. Difference is presumed from the outset of a dialogical reading project such as this because in terms of the contextual realities under question, there is no knowing subject location from which to be expert or trained, no universal or essential subject position to "read from." Persons with poor mental health elide the categories placed on them simply because of the infinite particularity of their subjecthood. As Dorothee Wilhelm argues regarding the related context of disability: "I own all information about me, and no one is allowed to take definition-power over my life or appropriate me, or make me a thing. Without a reciprocal coming together, we will remain invisible to each other. Your images of normalcy or of me actually cloud your vision. What you see when you meet me are your fears, your hurts. We are all broken in some fashion. Let us mediate our brokenness" (1999, 436).

The Bible studies were carried out across four locations in the metropolitan area of Boston, usually over consecutive weeks. A typical reading group session for the Bible studies would begin with an invitation to anyone in the setting who might want to join to come to a designated meeting place. Each setting presented different challenges in this regard. In Reading Group One, which was based at a day center for seniors with poor mental health, the participants were already largely stationary in a large meeting room. Here the challenge was to encourage participation from those in the room without leaving others who did not want to be part of the studies feeling excluded. Reading Group Two, which met at a drop-in center for working-age adults with poor mental health, was much more transient. Here participants had a number of other activities that they might be engaged in at the time of the Bible studies, and so this particular group, unlike the first, changed in its membership from week to week. Reading Group Three, based at a small private residence, held the Bible studies in their common living room, and participants either took part or went to their own bedrooms. Due to the number and availability of residents, these reading groups were sometimes small. Reading Group Four had the most regularity in terms of attendees; based at a large residential project at the heart of Boston, the members of this group were heavily scheduled, and so my weekly Bible studies were easily accommodated.

Once groups were gathered, I welcomed everyone to the group and described how our time together would be spent. I described how everyone's contribution was valuable, and asked that everyone respect each person's entitlement to his or her point of view. I shared a little about myself and said that I had come to explore a story from the Bible with them and how it might relate to their experience of mental health.

The first way that mutuality acted as a heuristic for the formation of the method of this work was that each participant's interpretations were received without qualification or validation of veracity. It was made clear that I would not be offering any kind of final summation or correction to any particular comment either during or at the end of the session,[25] and

---

25. To practice a facilitation style where no arbitration of reading differences is offered is to attempt to retain agonistic tensions within the reading process rather than attenuate them in any way. A corollary of this approach is that it places my methodology more within what has been described as a weak view of "ideological hegemony," wherein it is assumed that "marginalized" readers are "already aware of their agency"; and unlike the assumption of the position of "strong ideological hegemony," they

so rather than encouraging coming to definitive conclusions about right or wrong interpretations of texts, the difference of multiple interpretations was retained in the practice of group reading in the hope of opening up space for more to be said about texts.[26] People were encouraged to speak of their experiences, yet at the same time these experiences entered into a mutual space of interpretive negotiation in the shared act of reading.

In terms of the historical background of the texts, my approach to the Bible studies represented a different reading stance from the "contextual Bible study" methodologies described earlier in this chapter where through an interplay between contextual and textual questions the facilitator offers certain behind-the-text aspects of the potential historical locations of texts (West et al. 2007, 9). Within my own work with group readers, I made a conscious decision not to engage in such a practice in an effort to avoid a greater reading distance being formed between facilitator and readers by establishing myself as the "trained expert" in the room in contrast to the group readers. Consequently, each pericope that was used for the Bible studies was presented as a "story" that both facilitator and reading group members would be oriented to approach as such. In essence, then, my own approach to the text as facilitator was to follow a reader-response hermeneutic that treats the text at the level of a narrative whose dynamics should be attended to primarily in their own right rather than with a concern for behind-the-text features or other features of theological significance.

That said, within the reading space it was clear that each group and participant would naturally bring their particular subject location to the reading of the text. Bernard Lategan points out that it cannot be assumed that the relationship between facilitator and readers can simply be formed

---

do not need assistance by "the organic intellectual" to "recognize the contradictions inherent in the hegemony of the dominant sectors" (West 2004a, 216). However, while my decision not to arbitrate reading differences might place this work in the weak ideological hegemony "camp," it does not necessarily follow that I subscribe to the notion that the readers I encountered were always aware of inherent contradictions in the way West describes them. That said, I do believe that the group readings did reveal a freedom to interpret texts both in ways that collude with dominant interpretations, sustaining the interests of the powerful or dominant in the stories, and in ways that subvert such interpretive tendencies.

26. Retaining such difference is what has been called the "hermeneutical spiral." Different from the hermeneutical circle, the notion of a spiral is intended to convey a process of reading with others that detects previously overlooked "aspects of meaning" or "blind spots," thus allowing for "new discoveries to be made" (Kahl 2007, 149–50).

given that a series of "other contrasts" inhabit the reading space such as "theoretical/empirical," "dominated/dominant," "male/female," and so on (1996, 244). Within the reading groups that I engaged with, both groups as a whole as well as individuals within groups tended to exhibit certain distinctive orientations to the text. For instance, Reading Group Four, at a large faith-based "rescue mission," tended to coalesce around more faith-based interpretations of texts; by contrast, Reading Group Three, at a small residential setting, tended to offer a more critical stance toward the text and Jesus' actions within it.

Beyond specific group dynamics, it was clear that all the readers brought into their own particular participation in the act of reading a set of paradigmatic and ideological assumptions not only about the texts, but also about themselves, other readers, and society around them. Questions were needed, therefore, that would continually upset and unhinge any particular dominance of voices or knowledge. Indeed, heeding Leela Gandhi's warning about the danger that so-called subjugated, colonized, and unheard voices are assumed (by virtue simply of being the voices of the "periphery") to be able to articulate interpretations infused with subversive counterdiscourses of hegemony (1998, 154), the role of the facilitator in returning readers to the text at hand was key.

Following the introduction to the session, papers were handed out with the day's passage and a set of questions. As the facilitator, I then read aloud the passage slowly and paused for a time of silent reflection. I then read the passage again or asked a participant to do so. Unless one of the participants made some sort of response to the reading of the passage—in which case, I would ask the participant to say more about her or his insight—the session would typically continue with the first of the questions. These questions, which I formulated beforehand and used as a pool to draw from, attempted to probe textual relational dynamics via an exploration of the potential thoughts, feelings, and motivations of characters in those texts; the outcomes of those dynamics; and significantly, pointers to readers' lived contexts of poor mental health that might be found in the text.

Focusing on the relational dynamics of texts with group readers is an approach that takes the introspective tradition of reader-response criticism (Fowler 1991) and applies it to actual readers. Indeed, it has been a critique of reader-response criticism that the reader in that particular hermeneutic has remained only at the level of abstraction or within the imagination of the biblical scholar. What my own reading method advocates is a move beyond this shortfall and to shift biblical interpretation from what is characterized as a bipolar relationship between text and biblical scholar to a multipolar one incorporating multiple readers where not only is the relationship between readers and texts probed, but the interpretive relationship between readers is probed as well (Kessler 2004, 453–56).

The questions that I prepared beforehand were selected verse by verse and sought to probe the relational dynamics of the encounters that the text narrates, with particular attention to the minor characters as well as to Jesus. An example of such a series of questions is given below (the complete transcripts of each of the reading group sessions can be found in the appendix at the end of the book) for the reading of Jesus' encounter with a man who had a "withered hand" in Mark 3:1–6:

Verse 1

> Who was this man "with a withered hand"?
> What might it feel like to be him?
> Where is he to be found and how is he to be recognized?
> What do we learn about this man?
> Where are his friends?
> What do you think he is doing in the synagogue?

Verse 2

> Who are "they"?
> What do they know about Jesus?
> What does Jesus know about them?
> Why do you think "they" are watching Jesus?

Verse 3

> "Come forward." What does this sound like to you? A command? A request?
> Has anyone asked for help?
> What is the "man with the withered hand" coming forward for?
> Where was he? Can you picture where he might have been? Was he hidden?
> Have you ever been asked to "come forward"?
> Who asked you?
> What did it feel like?

Along with the pool of preselected questions, new questions were asked either by myself or by group readers as the readings occurred,[27] a product, I would suggest, of the attempt to create a more flat reading relationship between facilitator and group readers.[28] I would ask additional questions, sometimes in succession, or follow up questions that were asked by group members as the reading process dictated. If there was particular interest being generated in a certain direction, then I would facilitate the Bible study to move that way until the interest seemed to wane.

There were also some practical reasons why such a combination of both prepared and arising questions was pursued as a reading strategy mostly to do with keeping readers engaged and focused on the task at hand, and in some cases keeping them awake.[29] The ability of groups to stay focused on the text in question, on the task of reading in general, or even on the processing and production of language altogether, varied greatly. Some individuals were very fluent and the sessions flowed beautifully. Others deviated or hesitated, and in some cases participants drifted in and out of consciousness through the proceedings. With regard to the reading populations engaged with, if I had settled on a methodology that had presented the text before the readers and simply asked them to "say what they saw," I believe that responses would have been severely attenuated. Because I wished to create a reading environment that remained open, I made clear from the outset that people would be free to stay or leave or come back again as they chose. All readers came voluntarily.

Maintaining a flow of questions was part of the reading strategy not only for practical reasons; it was also part of an attempt to engage readers in as incisive and interrogative a manner as possible. In other words, I was interested in probing what readers think about texts and why they think in the ways that they do. What this facilitation style represents, then, is a blend of what Alma Lanser-van der Velde describes as the task-oriented

---

27. This openness to the generation of new questions is what Riches sees as the paradigm shift that dialogical reading has the potential to open up, with so-called ordinary readers opening up the possibility of new avenues of thought in a dialogue with the academy (1996, 186).

28. The attempt to strike a balance between a facilitation style that has no real leadership and one where leading questions can potentially stifle the process is a familiar challenge for those who practice dialogical reading. See Anum 2004, 176.

29. West notes that in the attempt to read the text carefully and closely, most "ordinary readers" found the task very difficult (1991, 97).

style, which closely follows the prepared questions and steers the reading process, giving the facilitator a central role, and the relationship-oriented style, which creates space for individual members to "put a meaning to the text" (2004, 300); and, I would add, "put meaning" to the one another as group readers and facilitator.

In pursuing such a blended approach, as the facilitator I chose to engage with the interpretations of group readers. When I was asked to comment on others' opinions, I did not remain silent but stated that "this was one way of looking at it." Likewise, when participants were curious about what I thought personally, I would offer my own view but would also point to a number of opinions, often drawing reflectively on interpretations already offered by other group participants.[30] No reading strategy and no facilitator can claim to be without shortcomings; and while attempting to keep the dialogue as open as possible, I am sure that my own view of texts and questions about texts had an effect on the other readers. By not offering introductory sessions, or the intermittent offering of historical details, or the interjection of corrective judgments, I hope that my own effect on others was not so overwhelming to be significantly more influential than the other readers' influences.

Thus the act of reading dialogically not only includes the dynamic input of the reading group members, but also the input of the facilitator as an interrogator of those questions and answers. Indeed, this element of mutual questioning of the insights of readers and facilitator is one of the most significant ways in which the praxis of mutuality shapes this project's reading method. However, in order to proceed with a facilitation style that sought to probe the answers given by readers[31] it was necessary to create what West describes as a "safe interpretive site" for reading (2004a).[32] Such

---

30. West describes this facilitation style in relation to Bob Ekblad's work as a dialogical form of facilitation that he sees to be distinctive within the larger field of reading with groups (2004a, 217). Reading in dialogue has also been termed as "conversational biblical hermeneutics" such that in this spirit of openness both facilitators and readers are faced with their "truths" being "continually challenged and changed" by the conversation (Masoga 2000, i).

31. This is an important facet of Ekblad's reading with prison groups; see West 2004a, 220.

32. Indeed, as West quotes, James Scott has argued that "a fundamental requirement for marginalized sectors to speak in their own voices, rather than strategically mimicking the discourse of the dominant culture, is a safe site" (West 2004a, 227; Scott 1990, 113–15).

a site is characterized by the continued practice of the affirmation of readers' input,[33] an acceptance of shifting the focus of reading when readers seek to do so, then dovetailing back to the questions or the text at hand more directly (216); and prior to all of this, embedding to some extent in the life of the reading group outside the reading experience.[34]

In sum, described above is the endeavor to create a reading relationship that seeks to have each reading perspective enlarge the scope of the other. However, such an approach to group reading generates a central question in dialogical hermeneutics of how much untrained and trained readers' perspectives can relate to one another. Hans Snoek asks whether a fruitful discussion between "intuitive" and "schooled" readings is really possible. That is, because the role of the facilitator is not always clear, he questions how "naïve readings" can make a contribution to biblical scholarship (2004, 305). Answering his own question, Snoek suggests that it is the tension between scholars and group readers' perspectives that might offer "points of contact for a fruitful dialogue" (308).

It is exactly this sort of approach that I pursue in the middle chapters of this work, following the distinctive format that I have chosen. That is, I have intentionally juxtaposed three strands of interpretation: biblical scholarship, group readers, and my own interpretations. Thus, informed by mutuality as a postcolonial praxis of the negotiation of difference, I have chosen to organize my analysis in such a way that the insights of biblical scholars and the group readers are placed side by side in separate sections to allow for the distinctiveness of each to be seen, and then in a third section I ask where the new emphases of group readers[35] might push at the boundaries of how particular texts are interpreted. In assessing the reading products of scholarly and group readers, I have sought to retain and probe the agonistic tensions between readings rather than to resolve differences.

---

33. A key component of my own style and that of Ekblad; see West 2004a, 217.

34. This was central to my own experience as a facilitator in the various reading sites I worked at. At one I attended worship, at another I ate lunch and socialized with members, some of whom joined reading groups and some of whom did not; and at another I forged a link with the community through a common friend.

35. Probing the emphases of "ordinary readers" is also advocated by Nestor Miguez, who suggests that working with such interpretations might enable the biblical scholar to "construct new meanings" of texts and as well as the contexts of those readers (2004, 347).

I approach biblical scholarship by sampling a range of interpretations of the particular pericope in question, with a specific focus on the ways in which scholars interpret the relational dynamics of the encounters narrated. Thus I have not chosen to concentrate on one form of biblical criticism alone or to confine this sampling only to postcolonial biblical criticism. Rather, I have decided to assess a range of scholarship that tends to consider the relational dynamics of the narratives in question in order to highlight various patterns and tendencies in these interpretations of identity, agency, and dialogue in six Markan texts. Consequently, I tend to refer to a particular range of scholarship in the chapters that follow: reader-response criticism,[36] sociorhetorical criticism,[37] sociopolitical criticism,[38] postcolonial biblical criticism,[39] feminist biblical criticism,[40] and dialogical biblical criticism;[41] alongside a range of commentaries on Mark.[42]

In terms of group readers' interpretations, I seek to remain true to the dialogical method of this work. That is, as I have stated in this chapter, in the practice of dialogical biblical hermeneutics I offer no correctives to what may be deemed to be wayward interpretations, nor do I offer arbitrations of competing or contradictory interpretations between different readers. I do not do so, not only because there would be a dishonesty to maintaining the absence of critiques in the midst of dialogical Bible study only to offer critique later on, but also because I wish to explore the reading group interpretations for what they are: not the work of trained biblical scholars, but insights that offer fresh emphases and contextually informed ways into reading ancient texts. Therefore, I present the reading group interpretations as they coalesce across the different reading groups. Thus, in the chapters that follow, I explore these emphases, which are sometimes

---

36. For example, Fowler 1991; Heil 1992; van Iersel 1998; Yee 1995.
37. For example, Camery-Hoggatt 1992; Witherington 2001.
38. For example, Belo 1981; Horsley 2001; Myers 1988; Oakman 1988; Cárdenas Pallares 1986; Theissen 1991; Waetjen 1989.
39. For example, Liew 2006; Moore 2006a; Perkinson 1996; Samuel 2007; Sugirtharajah 1999b; 2006a.
40. For example, Cotter 2001; Haber 2003; Kinukawa 2004; Plaatjie 2001; Ringe 2001.
41. For example, Avotri 2000; Cardenal 1976–1982.
42. For example, Anderson 1976; Broadhead 2001; Brooks 1991; Deibert 1999; Gundry 1993; Hare 1996; Hiebert 1994; Hooker 1991; Juel 1999; Mann 1986; Marcus 2000; Painter 1997.

contradictory, as far as they pertain to questions of identity, agency, and dialogue, and mutuality.

By drawing from group readers' perspectives across the different groups by theme or emphasis, one loses some of the distinctiveness of individual reading groups and individual readers. Keenly aware of Dorothee Wilhelm's denial that others might have "definition-power over my life or appropriate me, or make me a thing" (1999, 436), there is an inevitability to the process of working with group readers for the purposes of academic work that a degree of appropriation takes place. The challenge facing biblical scholars who seek to engage readers within shared acts of reading is how to incorporate the insights of those readers while attempting to honor their particularity. While the entirety of the reading group interpretations can be found in the appendix at the end of this book, what is not found there are the tone and tenor of the group readers themselves. In the end, dialogical reading reaches its glass ceiling and Spivak's haunting question—can the subaltern speak? (1988)—remains as significant and troubling as ever.

That said, if works like this one can remain platforms for dialogue that begin mutual conversation rather than end it, then the engagement of so-called ordinary readers is an important task for biblical studies that faces significant but not insurmountable challenges. Indeed, at the heart of the hope of this work is that this is not an endeavor that seeks to speak for those who live with poor mental health—it is one that seeks to speak with them, and others, albeit in a limited way.

3.5. Conclusion

There are two postcolonial tendencies in the approach to the text that I propose here that are influenced by the concept of mutuality. The first tendency, which focuses on the text itself, seeks to see the relational dynamics narrated in texts as a mutual space of participation, wherein characters share a struggle for discursive voice and power. Furthermore, this hermeneutic seeks to conceptualize "the postcolonial" spatially, focusing reading on mutuality as a praxis of resistance and transformation that may or may not be exercised in textual relational encounters. That is, alongside other postcolonial praxes, mutuality will be explored within relational dynamics of texts that might resist and seek to transform and thus be antagonistic to a colonial ordering of power, as well as those dynamics that might collude with such hegemonic power.

The second postcolonial tendency also seeks to dialogue with difference, this time in terms of the act of reading itself. In this chapter I explored various forms of dialogical hermeneutics and critiqued the influence of the liberation paradigm on such hermeneutics. I argued that this tendency led to the retention of a theological teleology that results in facilitators unduly guiding reading toward liberative interpretive conclusions, thus limiting the potential for actual interpretive differences within reading groups to be explored. Following this, then, I proposed that a postcolonial dialogical reading space, informed on multiple levels by mutuality, might have room to read with difference, arguing that this represented an attempt to nurture a more "flat" reading relationship between readers and facilitator.

Some have argued that biblical studies needs "a clamour of diverse voices" to allow "whispered voices" to be heard as well as "loud confident ones" (J. Campbell 2003, 43). In some ways then, the act of reading itself is a postcolonial response to the contextual hegemonic landscape of poor mental health I described in chapter 1. I hope the elided theological voices of readers with poor mental health might read Mark in the light of their own experiences of power and knowing. The extent to which they do will be considered in the chapters that follow.

4
IDENTITY, LABELS, AND RESISTANCE: MARK 3:1–6 AND 3:19B–35

The first pair of encounters—Jesus in a synagogue with a man who has a withered hand (3:1-6), and Jesus with his family and some scribes (3:19b-35)—examines the question of identity and how both "the man with a withered hand" in the first pericope and Jesus in the second face radical challenges to their ability to self-identify. In the first pericope, identity is recovered; and with it the relational dynamics that had previously designated the "other" for difference are transformed. In the case of the man in 3:1-6, difference as a mark of hegemonic identity—withered—is resisted and indeed transformed in its repetition. That is, in the action of choosing to come into the middle and stretch out his hand, the man reimagines hybridity into the mark of hegemonic identity previously inscribed as disabled. The praxis of mutuality is thus exercised in the opting for the hybrid emphasis of the difference the withered hand symbolizes.
In the second pericope, Jesus faces an attack on his identity, this time with acts of labeling—mad and/or bad—that attempt to mark him out for difference. Here I am interested in how Jesus resists the two acts of labeling that seek to impose identities upon him. I suggest that rather than successfully reinscribing his identity along binaristic and therefore supposedly clearly delineated lines, as many scholars do, Jesus responds with reactive discourse couched in ambiguous terms that evade the praxis of mutuality in its full form of resistive and transformative agency.

4.1. MARK 3:1–6

1 Again he entered the synagogue, and a man was there who had a withered hand. 2 They watched him to see whether he would cure him on the sabbath, so that they might accuse him. 3 And he said to the man who had the withered hand, "Come forward." 4 Then he said to them, "Is it lawful to do good or to do harm on the sabbath, to save life or to kill?" But they were silent. 5 He looked at them with anger; he was

grieved at their hardness of heart and said to the man, "Stretch out your hand." He stretched it out, and his hand was restored. 6 The Pharisees went out and immediately conspired with the Herodians against him, how to destroy him.[1]

4.1.1. Introduction: Jesus and the Man with the Withered/Divine Hand

The tendency for biblical scholars to rely too heavily on stereotype in the reading of identity and relating in Mark 3:1–6 leads to a limited analysis of the relational dynamics discernible in the text. I wish to reconsider the relational dynamics of 3:1–6 via the suggestions and emphases that group readers offer in their interpretations of this text. Specifically, their interpretations suggest that this pericope narrates not only the story of an argument between Jesus and some Pharisees, and not only the story of a man whose hand was restored to normal function following the invitation of Jesus to stretch that hand out, but also the story of an invitation to choose to step out of a life-denying relational dynamic and into the praxis of mutuality. It is this emphasis on the potential of mutuality as a praxis of renegotiating relational dynamics that offers much to the interpretation of this pericope in its expansion of the frame of the text. It is not only Jesus and some Pharisees who bring forth questions of identity and agency in the pericope, it is also the unnamed man who says nothing, yet whose choice to act reconfigures the relational dynamics he experiences in the synagogue and perhaps beyond.

4.1.2. Reading Mark in 2-D: Stereotype and the Interpretation of Relational Dynamics—Scholars' Perspectives

Much biblical scholarship considers a question posed by Jesus in 3:4 to lie at the heart of 3:1–6: "Is it lawful to do good or to do harm on the sabbath, to save life or to kill?" Furthermore, a great deal of attention is paid to what emanates from this question about Jesus and about the mysterious "they" who are watching him (3:2). For instance, some think that Jesus implicitly contrasts his own act of healing—doing good, saving life—to the supposed hostile activity of his opponents, who are "doing evil" by trying to find a way to destroy him (Rawlinson 1949, 35–37). Others believe that

---

1. All of the pericopae are taken from the NRSV. I chose this particular translation due to its use as the standard text in academic biblical studies.

4. IDENTITY, LABELS, AND RESISTANCE

the question in 3:4 and the pericope overall express a general principle that the failure of the Pharisees, and with them the Herodians, to do good on the Sabbath is tantamount to doing evil, hence resulting in the pericope having a polemical function (V. Taylor 1966, 222). My core critique of such views of this text is that they tend to interpret the text's relational dynamics more upon a binary construction of difference that has relied on the operation of stereotypical views of the identities of those involved in the story rather than on a close reading of the text alone.

One can see the operation of stereotype in interpretations of the three primary agents in the text: the Pharisees, Jesus, and the man with a withered hand. The Pharisees are commonly held to be the "they" of "they watched him" (3:2),[2] although the Pharisees are not named explicitly until verse 6. The language of some scholars immediately betrays an ideological edge to their reading of the text's relational dynamics. For instance, Lamar Williamson states that the language in 3:2 "conjures up the image of figures lurking at a discreet distance," and later compounds this negative and oppositional image with his comment on 3:4: "their silence is poisonous" (1983, 74–75). Likewise, Bas van Iersel characterizes the Pharisees in his reading of 3:1–6 as "criminals and murderers," with Jesus' actions serving to "expose the stubbornness of their criminal mentality."[3] A similar use of stereotype can be seen in the interpretations of readers in Solentiname, where commenting on Luke's version of the story (Luke 6:6–11), Alejandro states: "To keep people in sickness and misery is like destroying their lives, because it's a life that's not a life. Besides, they were already thinking about destroying his life. They were criminals" (Cardenal 1976–1982, 2:106).

However, from a textual perspective, interpreters can justify the insertion of malice in the watching of Jesus only anachronistically: by reading back from verse 6 where the Pharisees join the Herodians in conspiring to destroy Jesus.[4] The leap of reasoning that any malice toward Jesus precedes

---

2. For example, Hare 1996, 43; Budesheim 1971, 203; Sabourin 1975, 150; Hultgren 1979, 83; Dewey 1980, 101; Mann 1986, 242; Doughty 1983, 170; Williamson 1983, 74; Hooker 1991, 107; Kuthirakkattel 1990, 230; Hiebert 1994, 84; van Iersel 1998, 160; Marcus 2000, 24.

3. Van Iersel 1998, 161. Similarly, he reads the whole episode to have been a "set-up," with the role of the man with the withered hand to have been no more than a ruse to trap Jesus (160).

4. Indeed, Anderson has argued that 3:6 is an insertion either by the evangelist or

his actions in 3:3–5 cannot be supported by the text, which only suggests that the concern of those watching Jesus was a legal or technical one, not one that was necessarily attached to a motivation to do Jesus harm.[5] Readings that argue for malice between the Pharisees and Jesus in the relational dynamics of 3:1–6 demonstrate less a textually justified interpretation of identity and agency and more the operation of stereotypes.

If the operational stereotype for "the Pharisees" is one centered on malevolence, often the interpretation of Jesus' identity in this text focuses on his supposed benevolence. Jesus' designation as Son of Man (Doughty 1983, 178) and Messiah (Hultgren 1979, 152) is almost by definition a superlative and benevolent identity. For instance, Darrell Doughty sees the establishment of the authority of Jesus as the Son of Man—as the one who is "now clearly portrayed as one who stands in the place of God and acts with the authority of God" (1983, 178)—to be the overall purpose of this pericope.

What is often in operation in such readings of Jesus' part in the acts of 3:1–6 is a theological agenda submerged within other stated hermeneutical interests. For instance, Hultgren's form-critical reading focuses on the significance of Jesus' question to the Pharisees in 3:4, arguing that Jesus is persuasive in the pericope most significantly because putting forth an argument and then acting on it in healing the man focuses attention not just on Jesus' status and authority as a healer, but christologically on Jesus

---

via redaction of the text serving to conclude the larger section 2:1–3:5 as an indication that "Jewish hostility has reached its zenith" (1976, 112).

5. Within the milieu of the synagogue and its traditions of disputation, following the logic of many scholars, one would have to argue that each synagogue disputation was motivated by "underlying" and "unspoken" motivations to destroy one's opponent, unless one can point to evidence to support the notion that disputations involving Jesus were somehow different. Richard Horsley claims that the synagogue was central to the whole life of a village. Its religious identity was inseparable from its sociopolitical function. He argues for a much wider role for the Pharisees—whom he says were unlikely to have been in Galilee during Jesus' lifetime as Jerusalem no longer held direct political jurisdiction over the area. Their concerns were beyond a desire to see Torah narrowly defined and defended as such; they were concerned with life-and-death issues such as the provision of adequate food (interpreted by Horsley as the issue behind 2:23–28) and the disintegration of marriage and the family (10:2–9). Hence disputation was not only likely to have been common in and around synagogues, but would have been vital for the political and religious well-being of the community. See Horsley 2001, 162–66.

4. IDENTITY, LABELS, AND RESISTANCE

as "Messiah" (1979, 152). Mann's reading of 3:1–6 is another example of a theologically driven reading under the hermeneutical category of form criticism. He states "that the dawning of the Reign of God carried with it implications of a new creation—and what more appropriate day to herald the new act of God than the Sabbath" (1986, 242).

The consequence of such stereotypical readings of identity markers is that the dominant concern of much scholarship on the relational dynamics of 3:1–6 is focused on the disputation the pericope narrates between Jesus and the Pharisees. What is placed into submission by this is the other piece of relating the story describes: between Jesus and the man with a withered hand. In interpretations that do focus on the man with a withered hand, a key assumption is that when Jesus encounters the silent compliance of the man this reflects the reality of the identities of both characters: Jesus as active agent and the man as passive recipient. The man with the withered hand therefore falls victim to another stereotypical frame common in biblical narration, as Elly Elshout notes: the disabled are understood as little more than "marvellous plot-devices that show off the power of God or the Anointed One," part of the "group of God's special interests" (1999, 439). Many scholars read the man as the no-man of the pericope: a character who "requests no cure and exhibits no faith" (Sabourin 1975, 151), and the one whom Jesus intends to use "to give a public demonstration of His attitude toward the perverted Sabbath rules of the scribes and Pharisees" (Hiebert 1994, 84). He is at best, then, a man who exhibits no active agency in his healing and at worst, asserts Robert Guelich, merely a dramatic tool playing a supporting role in somebody else's act (1989, 133), a cipher for Jesus to contest his point with his opponents.[6]

What might be seen to be in operation in these readings of Jesus and the man with the withered hand in 3:1–6 is "normate hermeneutics," which some think dominates modern biblical thought (Wynn 2007, 92). The idea of a *normate*, a term coined by Rosemarie Garland Thomson, is the notion that there exists a socially constructed ideal image of personhood "through which people can represent themselves as definitive human beings" (1997, 8). With reference to the "disability" of the man in 3:1–6, some argue that interpretations of this pericope adhere to the normate ideal person embodied in Jesus; the unnamed man's identity and

---

6. Indeed, J. D. M. Derrett argues that Jesus uses the man as an example in an "obviously high-grade legal debate" and pointed to him as "an example of the state of Israel" (1985a, 79).

agency, by contrast, are imposed by disability's perceived deviation from that normate ideal.[7]

This sample of scholarship suggests a pattern in interpretations of this text across a range of hermeneutical interests that overly utilizes stereotype and underemphasizes a closer reading of the actual relational dynamics within the story. In contrast, what the interpretations of the group readers—with their alternative emphases and perceptions of relational dynamics in this pericope—might do to problematize or extend the scholarship described above will be explored in the next section.

4.1.3. Power, Voice, and the Signification of Difference—Group Readers' Perspectives

The most immediate feature that can be noticed in the reading groups' interpretations is that readers also used stereotypes in their interpretations of identity in this pericope. Significantly, their perception of the Pharisees and Jesus was markedly similar to that of trained scholars. For instance, while there was a wider range of interpretations offered of the Pharisees—as potentially "ill,"[8] feeling "foolish,"[9] "stuck" without an answer to offer back to Jesus,[10] hard-hearted,[11] "angry,"[12] "jealous" of Jesus and wanting his power,[13] and even languishing without an answer from the God they

---

7. See Wynn 2007, 92, for a similar argument about biblical criticism in general.

8. "They thought they were better. Personally, I think they looked down on Jesus. You wonder whether they are ill. There are a lot of people like that, unfortunately" (E from Reading Group Two, March 21, 2006).

9. "Maybe they were silent because they realized that what they were doing was just as bad as harm—by this set up, they felt foolish. When he asked them a question, he just saw through them" (C from Reading Group Four, April 4, 2006).

10. "Nothing in the rules spelled out an answer. In the moment they were stuck" (B from Reading Group Three, April 3, 2006).

11. "Jesus brings radical love to a people whose hardness of heart is against him, telling people to love people who hate you. I am sure there were people who demonstrated what love really is, and mercy. … I don't have mercy on myself more than anybody else. Even people who don't like me probably would be more merciful to me" (C from Reading Group Three, April 3, 2006).

12. "They were very angry, always getting angry with Jesus" (A from Reading Group One, March 21, 2006).

13. C: "They were jealous of him." A: "He had power, they wanted that power" (from Reading Group Two, March 21, 2006).

4. IDENTITY, LABELS, AND RESISTANCE 95

had turned to[14]—the interpretations offered largely reflected the trend found in the above sample of academic scholarship toward a malevolent depiction of the Pharisees in the story. Furthermore, none of the interpretations really marked out this group as having identities that were significantly hegemonic; rather they were understood in general as being in some way inferior to and less praiseworthy than Jesus. For instance, answering a question about why "they" remained silent in response to Jesus' question in 3:4 ("Is it lawful to do good or to do harm on the sabbath, to save life or to kill?"), one reader said: "Because Jesus is Jesus and Jesus is superior."[15] Similarly, perceptions of Jesus' character in the reading groups, while varied—interpreted by group readers as a character set apart by his divine power,[16] as a "good guy,"[17] wanting to help people,[18] offering "radical love,"[19] and as one having authority,[20] yet also as one short on patience,[21] and rejected by the crowds[22]—were largely interpreted as being generally positive and superior to the other characters.

By contrast, the interpretations of the man with the withered hand were much more pronounced and divergent from those of the academic community; they focused on the unworthiness and diminished agency of the man. For instance:

---

14. "Sometimes the Pharisees turned to God and didn't get a response" (D from Reading Group Two, March 21, 2006).

15. D from Reading Group One, March 21, 2006.

16. "Because he was the Son of God. He already knew the facts about it" (A from Reading Group One, March 21, 2006).

17. "Jesus was a good guy" (A from Reading Group Two, March 21, 2006).

18. "He wanted to help them but they didn't allow it" (E from Reading Group Two, March 21, 2006).

19. "Jesus brings radical love to a people whose hardness of heart is against him, telling people to love people who hate you" (C from Reading Group Three, April 3, 2006).

20. "These people were seeking to accuse the Father himself. That was the true fight—it was a fight to accuse the Father. The authority that Jesus had was so unbelievable, he could feel God's grace as well as the pain" (D from Reading Group Four, April 4, 2006).

21. B: "He ran out of patience." C: "Oh sure, why not? He was only human. Once in a while we can see his human side" (from Reading Group One, March 21, 2006).

22. "The crowd rejects him the same reason they reject Jesus. They don't want to identify with Jesus" (C from Reading Group Four, April 4, 2006).

D: He knew he was going to be used of Jesus. He did so understanding that he would be the one.
B: Just a spectacle. He didn't understand, he was just grieved.
C: Maybe he felt Jesus had such authority, he felt like a child, he just obeyed him.
B: Unworthy, right.
A: Unworthy.
D: It was a fight against good and evil.[23]

The fundamental point of note about these interpretations of the man was that more than the other characters in the text, a consistent interpretive pattern emerged across the reading groups where the identity of the "man with the withered hand" was explicitly and often spontaneously linked to multiple perceptions of the lived experience of poor mental health by many group readers. For instance, one reader drew out the theme of the unworthiness of the man in relation to a personal experience of poor mental health (in response to the question of how it feels to be the man with the withered hand):

> "I desire mercy, not sacrifice." Makes me think of my own life and how God does want to heal me even if I don't deserve it. Maybe even makes me think I should pray to God. I forget about God and that he wants me to have healing. ... I struggle with God's prestige, so my mind doesn't work, but is it spiritual blindness or physical blindness?... It is said in the Bible, Jesus said go and sin no more. That part always scares me. Somehow sin is attached to affliction. I struggle with that; sin leads to punishment. There are different schools of thought that mental illness is possession or spiritual warfare.[24]

Some readers emphasized how the man was marked out by difference. While it was the case that "everybody else in the place had a good hand,"[25] the man whose hand was not "good" stood out:

B: Something different always stands out in the crowd.
A: That's true.
E: He was very different.

---

23. From Reading Group Four, April 4, 2006.
24. C from Reading Group Three, April 3, 2006.
25. C from Reading Group One, March 21, 2006.

4. IDENTITY, LABELS, AND RESISTANCE

B: Yes.[26]

Indeed, echoing Sander Gilman's argument for the role of fear in the representation and perception of persons with poor mental health (1988, 243), being marked out for difference was read in the text to lead to, and perhaps also to flow out of, a certain predeterminedness generated from various prejudices that left the character segregated.

> B: Yes, I feel that when you are different you stand out. Everybody watches him and is seeing what you are going to do about him. …
> A: Yeah. It's called prejudice. They don't understand, they hate them automatically. They make up stories. Our Lord never had prejudice. He tried to help as many people as possible.
> B: They were probably afraid that sometimes they might find it, might call it an illness in the hand. People are afraid of the mentally ill.
> D: You think so?
> B: Yeah.
> D: Some people, not all.
> Facilitator: Why?
> B: They don't know how to behave toward them.
> E: They think we're crazy. We're not sick. This is not our home, we don't live here.[27]

Other readers emphasized the role of stigma: "Some of the crowd would call him names, making fun of it, because that's the way things are in the world."[28] Similarly, when asked where the man's friends are in this passage, another group responded:

> C: None. He was handicapped.
> B: Sometimes when people are handicapped, people shun them, like the mentally ill, some people shun you. They think that you're crazy.
> C: Some people don't understand.
> A: Some do.
> E: They shouldn't do that. Wouldn't wish it on anyone.
> B: They call you names—loony, crazy.[29]

---

26. From Reading Group One, March 21, 2006.
27. From Reading Group One, March 21, 2006.
28. B from Reading Group One, March 21, 2006.
29. From Reading Group Two, March 21, 2006.

The impact of identities built upon stigma and stereotype was read by some group members to result in the silencing of those set apart for difference: "Maybe he's been praying for a cure. Nobody really hears him. But Jesus hears him and Jesus repairs his hand."[30] Taken together, group readers' interpretations present a radically diminished view of the identity of the man as "different,"[31] "hidden,"[32] "cursed,"[33] "alienated,"[34] "an experiment,"[35] "rejected,"[36] and even "guilty."[37] These render the "man with a withered hand" in the interpretations of group readers as profoundly marked out for difference. The significance of this emphasis offered by group readers is seen in the imagined consequences such a diminished view of identity might have for the perceived potential for agency the man has in comparison to other characters.

For instance, group readers did not take the identity of the Pharisees as significantly compromising their potential for agency in the text. Indeed, they continued to be characterized as people "wanting to argue."[38] Even when the agency of the Pharisees was seen to be diminished in their being silenced by Jesus—"temporarily defeated,"[39] "couldn't

---

30. D from Reading Group One, March 21, 2006.

31. "Yes, I feel that when you are different you stand out. Everybody watches him and is seeing what you are going to do about him" (B from Reading Group One, March 21, 2006).

32. "He hid out. He wasn't accepted, he was different" (B from Reading Group Two, March 21, 2006).

33. "Maybe he had a family but when he got disabled, they said, 'You got yourself cursed, get out of here'" (C from Reading Group Three, April 3, 2006).

34. "When Jesus was going about teaching and preaching, these people were so obsessed with the law. When you were struck with leprosy at that time there was no cure. They were alienated from normal people" (B from Reading Group Four, April 4, 2006).

35. "He became a project—he was used, like an experiment" (B from Reading Group Four, April 4, 2006).

36. "The crowd rejects him [for] the same reason they reject Jesus. They don't want to identify with Jesus" (C from Reading Group Four, April 4, 2006).

37. "I think he was probably ambivalent. He wanted to be healed but he felt guilty. We know how that is. Guilty that he didn't go to Jesus of his own will" (C from Reading Group Four, April 4, 2006).

38. "Maybe they thought he was a fake. They wanted to argue with him" (B from Reading Group One, March 21, 2006).

39. "The Pharisees were temporarily defeated. That's why they are so quiet" (D from Reading Group One, March 21, 2006).

4. IDENTITY, LABELS, AND RESISTANCE 99

give a good answer,"[40] "jealously wanting Jesus' power"[41]—this could be less a product of their identity and more, as I will argue below, a consequence of their own choosing. In terms of Jesus, group readers largely interpreted his identity only to be further augmented by his agency in the pericope. For instance, Jesus was interpreted as one who is in control of the situation,[42] the "center of attention,"[43] already knowing what the man needed,[44] having an effect on people as the "Son of God,"[45] with the "efficient" ministry of a sovereign.[46]

In terms of how identity impacted agency for the man with the withered hand, the interpretations of group readers were split. Some argued that the man's profoundly diminished identity rendered his potential for agency severely attenuated. For instance, some stated that the man was left feeling "nervous" and "in the spotlight,"[47] hiding and "cowering in a corner,"[48] "afraid,"[49] "forced to go" to the synagogue that day,[50] "used of

---

40. C: "Couldn't give him a good answer." D: "If they answer one way, there can be no answer. They would look bad either way" (from Reading Group One, March 21, 2006).

41. C: "They were jealous of him." A: "He had power, they wanted that power" (from Reading Group Two, March 21, 2006).

42. "It sounds like to me that Jesus is in command of the whole situation. He always knows how to defeat plans with a good saying" (A from Reading Group One, March 21, 2006).

43. "Jesus is the center of attention. Helping this man he got more followers" (A from Reading Group One, March 21, 2006).

44. "Reminds me of the woman at the well. She was confronted with what Jesus already knew about her" (C from Reading Group Three, April 3, 2006).

45. "Well, if he was Son of God it has an effect on people. Did he have doubts and then he believed? Jesus has an effect on him" (C from Reading Group Three, April 3, 2006).

46. "In his sovereignty everything is efficient. It doesn't become a matter of what is most important. This one act will heal and demonstrate how wicked they are, right?" (D from Reading Group Four, April 4, 2006).

47. "He might be nervous or afraid, in the spotlight. Before he was not in the spotlight, now everybody can see him" (D from Reading Group One, March 21, 2006).

48. "He's hiding, cowering in the corner. They wouldn't have wanted him to get help just because it was that day" (D from Reading Group Two, March 21, 2006).

49. "Could be afraid to for societal reasons. The fact that they wanted to destroy the man who healed him—I can see he would be afraid they were going to destroy him too, he would be petrified" (B from Reading Group Two, March 21, 2006).

50. "Forced to go there" (A from Reading Group Four, April 4, 2006).

God,"[51] feeling "guilty that he didn't go to Jesus of his own will,"[52] and left there a "spectacle," "grieved," "unworthy."[53] Thus these readers suggested that beyond even the view some scholars offered of the man as one who "requests no cure and exhibits no faith" (Sabourin 1975, 151), this is a man who is profoundly stigmatized such that his mark of difference—withered—renders his agency as decided in advance to be at a dead end. Via such interpretations of agency, this is a man for whom, in Benita Parry's terms, "no alternative texts are supposed to have been written" (1995, 43). He is the subaltern who not only does not, but cannot, speak.

Other group readers, though, saw that despite his diminished identity, the man with the withered hand did act as an agent of change and healing in the pericope, an interpretation that is largely absent from the scholarship reviewed earlier. For instance, some maintain that the man had been praying for help "for a long time,"[54] that he played a big part in his healing,[55] that he went to the synagogue that day in order "to understand how he feels," "to try to cope,"[56] that he wanted to be cured so that "he wouldn't be victimized anymore,"[57] that he "tried to hold on to hope and he got better,"[58] that "he wanted to be whole again,"[59] and that "he showed he believed."[60]

---

51. Facilitator: "What is the 'man with the withered hand' coming forward for?" … D: "Because this being is used of God, he probably wanted to be healed of his deformity. He couldn't even offer things to God because of his deformity" (from Reading Group Four, April 4, 2006).

52. "I think he was probably ambivalent. He wanted to be healed but he felt guilty. We know how that is. Guilty that he didn't go to Jesus of his own will" (C from Reading Group Four, April 4, 2006).

53. D: "He knew he was going to be used of Jesus. He did so understanding that he would be the one." B: "Just a spectacle. He didn't understand, he was just grieved." C: "Maybe he felt Jesus had such authority, he felt like a child, he just obeyed him." B: "Unworthy, right." A: "Unworthy" (from Reading Group Four, April 4, 2006).

54. "He was praying for it for a long time" (D from Reading Group One, March 21, 2006).

55. "He played a big part. He had to believe" (C from Reading Group One, March 21, 2006).

56. "Maybe he wants to understand how he feels. He's going to the synagogue to help him understand, to try to cope" (E from Reading Group Two, March 21, 2006).

57. "He wanted to be cured, so he wouldn't be victimized anymore. He believed Jesus could cure him" (B from Reading Group Two, March 21, 2006).

58. "He accepted what had happened to him and he did not try to deny them because he went and accepted them. He tried to hold on to hope and he got better" (E from Reading Group Two, March 21, 2006).

4. IDENTITY, LABELS, AND RESISTANCE

It is this twin emphasis of diminished identity yet active agency that I examine in an expansion of the frame of this text in the section that follows. To explore such a possibility is to take up the invitation such group readers' interpretations suggest: to probe the thin spaces of often submerged interest in the text. To read the man with the withered hand as an active agent in the text, particularly given the strong emphasis on his diminished and debilitated identity offered by group readers, might be seen to undermine such an important reemphasis on diminished identity for this pericope, particularly given the multiple associations made by group readers between the man's relational predicament and those who experience poor mental health.

Indeed, given the critique I made in chapter 3 of the role of the biblical scholar as the sole arbitrator of interpretive difference, to take up one emphasis (that the man's identity did not preclude his potential for agency) over another (that, to a large extent, it did) might look like I am seeking to sublate the difference in between the different group readers' interpretations. However, the crucial delineation I wish to draw here is that in seeking to probe one of the emphases above, rather than another, I wish simply to explore one possible interpretive response to this text; I am not stating that this is how the text must be read. Furthermore, in pushing at the points of tension between readings of this text, I explore how the argument—that diminished identity might lead to the conclusion that possibilities for agency are precluded—might rely on a view of postcolonial agency limited to the confines of hegemonic power structures, and that the postcolonial praxis of mutuality might suggest an expansion of that limited framing of agency.

4.1.4. "Come Forward": Invitations to the Middle and the Man with the Withered/Divine Hand

The reframing I offer of this pericope is essentially one that seeks to reimagine power. On one hand, one can argue that "the man with the withered hand" has been imagined as one who is subject to others' power in the text: to the power of Jesus, who commands him to come forward, stretch

---

59. "The man's healing. Because he wanted to be whole again" (D from Reading Group Two, March 21, 2006).

60. "He played a very important part. He showed he believed. As tiny as a mustard seed, just a small amount" (E from Reading Group Two, March 21, 2006).

out his hand, and then performs a healing on him (3:3, 5); and to the power of the Pharisees, who many have assumed to have relegated this man to a place of exclusion in the synagogue and perhaps in the wider community (Derrett 1984, 178). With this, one can assert that this man is the product of these powers of assumption that render his identity as "different," hidden, "cursed," "alienated," "an experiment," rejected, and even "guilty."[61]

An alternative view of the man is that he is more than merely the object of others' power, and that he exercises power for himself. It is this second strand of group readers' interpretations, which contend that in spite of his profoundly diminished identity the man does exercise agency, that push at the limits of how this pericope has typically been framed.

Fundamentally, the shift that I am proposing is one that biblical scholars have argued for more widely with regard to "disability," urging a shift in the perception of disability "from pathology to identity," wherein physical difference is not something to be compensated for but seen as a legitimate part of relational power.[62] Thus, along with the group readers who suggested that in spite of the man's diminished identity he was able to exercise agency in the story, I wish to extend the frame of this possibility, in exploring how such agency might operate using mutuality as a postcolonial praxis.

The praxis of mutuality can be discerned in this pericope in the way agency is invited in the relational encounter narrated. In this regard, Jesus can be seen to offer a twofold invitation in 3:1–6. First, viewed through the

---

61. Different: "Yes, I feel that when you are different you stand out. Everybody watches him and is seeing what you are going to do about him" (B from Reading Group One, March 21, 2006); hidden: "He hid out. He wasn't accepted, he was different" (B from Reading Group Two, March 21, 2006); cursed: "Maybe he had a family but when he got disabled, they said, 'You got yourself cursed, get out of here'" (C from Reading Group Three, April 3, 2006); alienated: "When Jesus was going about teaching and preaching these people were so obsessed with the law. When you were struck with leprosy at that time there was no cure. They were alienated from normal people" (B from Reading Group Four, April 4, 2006); an experiment: "He became a project—he was used, like an experiment" (B from Reading Group Four, April 4, 2006); rejected: "The crowd rejects him the same reason they reject Jesus. They don't want to identify with Jesus" (C from Reading Group Four, April 4, 2006); guilty: "I think he was probably ambivalent. He wanted to be healed but he felt guilty. We know how that is. Guilty that he didn't go to Jesus of his own will" (C from Reading Group Four, April 4, 2006).

62. See Wynn 2007, 92, who cites Thomson's work on the normate principle (see Thomson 1997, 24).

4. IDENTITY, LABELS, AND RESISTANCE

lens of the praxis of mutuality, Jesus offers the invitation to those who were watching him to share a space of dialogue, even if that dialogue takes on a disputational form.[63] To see Jesus' question in 3:4 ("Is it lawful to do good or do harm on the sabbath?") as an invitation to share dialogue is not a common view. Some interpret Jesus' question to those who were watching him as an act that reduces those being asked to silence.[64] However, from the text alone it is hard to see how the Pharisees as composite characters in Mark would be so easily reduced to silent compliance in this exchange. Indeed, according to the Gospel as a whole, "the Pharisees" are not a group that are often shy to offer an opinion (e.g., 2:15–17, 18–20, 23–27). Moreover, the indication at the end of the pericope (3:6) in the "plot" of the Pharisees with the Herodians is that the Pharisees were far from feeling marginalized by Jesus. Rather, if the text is to be taken at face value, they were choosing to respond to Jesus' invitation to dialogue and to his actions following it in a definitive way: "plotting to destroy him" (3:6). Whichever way the silence is interpreted, such arguments suggest it was not out of an inability to answer Jesus' clever rhetoric that those who were watching him did not reply. The Pharisees made a choice not to take up the invitation to the praxis of mutuality in dialogue.

The second invitation to a praxis of mutuality Jesus offers is to the man. Apart from the more conventional interpretations of Jesus' "sovereign" status[65] as the "Son of God"[66] in relation to this man in the pericope, whereby Jesus' "invitation" is read as a command, certain group readers focused on the quality of the encounter between Jesus and the man as invitational:

---

63. For instance, José Cárdenas Pallares argues that Jesus invites "his adversaries" to question themselves and answer whether God is on the side of oppression and tyranny or that of succor and life (1986, 24).

64. For instance, John Painter argues that Jesus' question neutralizes any objection that might be raised (1997, 63); Hugh Anderson argues that the Pharisees' choice to remain silent is an attempt to indicate their disagreement to any principle that would undermine the sovereignty of the law (1976, 114); and John Heil assumes that the Pharisees remain silent either because Jesus' question is to be read as a rhetorical one or because of the "stubbornness" of those who were watching Jesus (1992, 75).

65. "In his sovereignty everything is efficient. It doesn't become a matter of what is most important. This one act will heal and demonstrate how wicked they are, right?" (D from Reading Group Four, April 4, 2006).

66. "He saw the Son of God and knew he could help him" (A from Reading Group One, March 21, 2006).

> I can see how he was trying to help this man. Not just physically if we consider he was outcast, shunned. He encountered him, calling him publicly. Basically through the people, Pharisees, and the crowd he's healing him right in front of them and defends that action. In fact that may not be the most important thing he's doing. The most important thing might be the way he is doing it. Healing is the operative thing. If he was using the guy to make a point, then I think that would be going in the direction of the people he is saying this to, and I think one of the huge points is that he is completely different in important ways. There's no way he's embodying objectifying. To the Pharisees their relation to the law was more important than whether this guy is suffering. The most obvious thing in this passage: Jesus feels different.⁶⁷

I would argue along with this reader that the difference Jesus "feels" is that he acts in this story as one who seeks out the agency of both the Pharisees and the man. That is, Jesus seeks to cultivate the praxis of mutuality and exercises it himself as a resistive and transformative praxis: in dialogue with those who were watching him, and in action with the man. What I am arguing for here, then, is that the praxis of mutuality is used by Jesus as a way of reimaging discursive power. In response to Jesus, the Pharisees choose to deviate the potential for a praxis of mutuality in that moment of the encounter to a discussion "outside" the presence of Jesus and his invitation. Also in response to Jesus, the man chooses to take up that invitation to a praxis of mutuality within which identity might be reimagined. Within postcolonial criticism, such acts of reimagining thus challenge the notion of identity as fixed, re-presenting identity as something that "evolves through a continuing process of interrelation, identification, and differentiation" (Keller et al. 2004, 11–12). That is, the man himself exercises a praxis of mutuality and thus acts to forge a new wholeness not by negating difference but by choosing to act within the very reality of the conflict that difference presents.⁶⁸ What I am suggesting here is that, in

---

67. B from Reading Group Three, April 3, 2006.
68. See Elshout 1999, 432, who holds that the disabled body represents the reality of differences and conflicts. Consequently, new relationships and new wholeness can be forged only in difference and conflict. Indeed, as Elshout contends in relation to the role of the "dis-abled" body and transcendence, "overcoming barriers and locating freedom in physical restrictions constitute my idea of transcendence. In other words, it is the body which provides the location and possibility for transcendence" (451).

4. IDENTITY, LABELS, AND RESISTANCE

Carter Heyward's terms, the man and Jesus choose to exercise δύναμις, a power underneath the authoritative order of external power.[69]

Yet it is the specifically strategic nature of this exercise of δύναμις that I wish to emphasize here. For the praxis of mutuality, seen in the invitational agency of Jesus and in the man's response, operates in tandem with another postcolonial praxis: hybridity. Specifically, the man's agency of choosing to respond to Jesus' praxis of mutuality reimagines a symbol previously interpreted as a mark of difference in the text—the withered hand—as a symbol of divine activity. In responding to the invitation of Jesus to "Come forward" (3:3), the man produces a fuller and hybrid knowledge of his identity symbolized in the man's stretching out of his hand in 3:5.

That the outstretched hand of the man in 3:1-6 might be viewed as a praxis of hybridity can be seen by placing the symbolism of such an action within Judaic tradition. For instance, J. Duncan M. Derrett thinks that the symbolic resonance of such an action cannot be missed: the man, in stretching out his hand, produces/performs "divine knowledge."[70] Similarly, Kurt Queller suggests that 3:1-6 contains echoes of Deuteronomy that show the stretching forth of the man's hand as a faithful response to "a prophetic Deuteronomic understanding of the Sabbath as commemorating God's liberation of the people from slavery" (2010, 757). Indeed, the textual allusions of stretching out one's hand are abundant (e.g., Exod 6:6; 14:21, 27; Deut 4:34; 5:15; 1 Kgs 8:42; 2 Kgs 17:36; 2 Chr 6:32; Isa 50:2; Ezek 20:33-34).

While Derrett goes on to interpret the act as potentially having political overtones,[71] I would like to focus on the relational overtones of the encounter. That is, this encounter takes place in a space wherein the dynamism of the encounter is contained not in the issuing forth of "divine power" from one character to another, but is expressed in the praxis of mutuality between characters who actively choose to exercise agency.

---

69. Heyward 1982, 44. Furthermore, the role that Jesus plays in encounters such as this "confronts the traditional beliefs about disability" that associate "disability" with sin and punishment from God, and establish a new relationship based on forgiveness and healing. See Hentrich 2007, 86.

70. Derrett 1984, 183. A similar point is argued by Smith 1994.

71. He maintains that the reaction of the Pharisees and Herodians in 3:6 might not have focused only on Jesus but on the now divinely strengthened hand of the "mighty army" Jesus was equipping (1984, 183).

Thus, through the lens of the postcolonial praxis of mutuality, the colonial space of this pericope may be seen as not only fertile for the resistance of stigmatizing, stereotyping, and the negation of agency but also a space for a strategic transformation of hegemonic relational dynamics via the renegotiation of identity as hybrid.[72] In taking up Jesus' invitation to stretch forth his hand, the man imbues the encounter with hybridity: he is at one and the same time the man with the withered and the man with the divine hand. He symbolizes both stigma and a debilitation of relational power and the divine inbreaking of transformative and saving/healing power in the midst of the relational encounter with Jesus. At Jesus' invitational praxis of mutuality, the man stretches forth his withered/divine hand and tears at the fabric of binaristic patterns of power.

In Homi Bhabha's terms, the man with the withered/divine hand repeats the act of divine stretching forth, yet his ambiguous presence means that this repetition is not quite the same as the biblical imagination normatively conceives of it (1994, 5). One might even argue that it is in this "hybrid moment of political change" (28) made possible by Jesus' invitational praxis of mutuality that the hybridity of the man with the withered/divine hand offers him the room to maneuver in the space between Jesus and the Pharisees (if it can be assumed from the text that the "they" who were watching him were the Pharisees named in v. 6), and so to resist not only the debilitation of his physical condition but also the marginalizing of his societal location.

One of the readers comments in response to a question about what "they" care about concerning the man, "I think it's psychologically normal for people at times to do things outrageous or provocative."[73] It might be that this biblical instance of reimagining difference not as dis-abled but as divinely abled models hybridity as a form of resistance and transformation, which might offer ways for those who have been subjugated by the imposition of identity to estrange the basis of that hegemonic power. This interpretation of the actions of the man with a withered/divine hand, then, stands in tension with the earlier readings that submerged the significance of the sharing of space between Jesus and the man, and relegated the role of the "no-man" of the encounter to little more than, in Tat-siong Benny

---

72. Indeed, more broadly, Keller et al. maintain that postcolonial criticism rightly recognizes that hybridity contains "great potential for resistance," turning hybridity to "transformative use" (2004, 13–14).

73. B from Reading Group Three, April 3, 2006.

Liew's terms, a "sidekick" or "gopher" (2006, 212). Indeed, this reading also stands in tension with theological interpretations of the significance of an outstretched and withered hand that do not designate such an act as being symbolic of the divine. Yet the theological postcolonial lens is one that is open to boundary crossing in the interpretation of biblical texts, both in terms of culture and theology, a possibility that is open not only to Jesus[74] but to other characters too.

In this regard, there is an invitational element to the praxis of mutuality in the man's action too. For, in his choosing to enter into the tenuous middle space of the synagogue, the man models the risky living of exercising a praxis of mutuality in the face of excluding and imposing power. There is a sense in which his action serves as an invitation to others present, and perhaps by extension to the reader, to take up the resistive praxis of hybridizing narrow relational "spaces" by reworking symbols of assured theological or ideological value and resonance. Such a hybridizing praxis presents the man's "disabled" identity in this pericope not primarily as a sign of a loss of status, but as the means through which he reimagines power in relational dynamics. For, if not withered, his hand is not imbued with the hybridity that makes it such a subversive symbol of resistance. Indeed, his status might be reconfigured as augmented, not diminished, by his hybrid praxis.[75]

However, before the potential of hybrid identity and "disabled" agency is celebrated via the invitational praxis of mutuality, two caveats need exploring. The first is the simple textual fact of the matter that "disability" is not retained in 3:1–6; to the contrary, it is transformed in an act of healing (3:5). The principle that disability is something to be overcome, even metaphorically, by a divine restorative power is dominant in biblical texts.[76] Indeed, such healing power is read to indicate God's salvific action toward his people.[77] And so, with particular reference to Jesus' healing acts in general and in 3:1–6 in particular, one can argue that Jesus treats the disabled

---

74. Postcolonial interpretations of Jesus as a boundary crosser are numerous. See, e.g., Nausner 2004; Joh 2004.

75. See Wynn 2007, 101, who thinks that disability might be conceived of not as a loss of status but as a mark of it.

76. See, e.g., Isa 6:10; Jer 31:8; Zeph 3:19.

77. See Melcher 2007, 123, who emphasizes the problematic nature of this sort of interpretation when considering biblical texts as sources of liberative rhetoric in relation to disability, resulting in a devaluing of persons with disabilities.

body as something to be healed so that a barrier to full participation in society might be overcome.[78] Such a critique is significant for my reading of 3:1–6, as implicit in my interpretation of this text is an assumption that the "withered hand" is something to be overcome. That such an assumption might be problematic for those readers who experience chronically poor mental health is clear.

The second potential caveat is whether hybridity exercised via the invitational praxis of mutuality—in this case openly transgressive of hegemonic relational dynamics—is effective as a form of reimagining identity. Some of the readers commented on this symbolic and transformative act:

> D: He may be a little afraid of the Herodians.
> A: They might cut off his head.[79]

The applied efficacy of these postcolonial praxes remains an open question, for it is not to a safe or liberated place that this story makes its end, but one fraught with danger and foreboding (3:6). What is clear, though, from rereading this pericope, is that when stereotype is allowed to predominate in the interpretation of this text, the full extent of the agency exercised in 3:1–6 is missed. Furthermore, the emphasis group readers offered this rereading of a man who is profoundly diminished and reduced accentuated the significance of the man's choice to accept what I have maintained to be Jesus' invitational praxis of mutuality to exercise agency, thus significantly altering the view of the "man with a withered hand" as an agent in this story. Not only is the interpretation of this man as a passive character in the text challenged by this rereading, so also is the interpretation of what is transforming. That is, I contend that transformation occurs in this pericope both because of Jesus' exercise of an invitational praxis of mutuality and because of the healing that came forth following the man's choice to respond positively to that invitation.

I have argued that the praxis of mutuality is more than an interesting motif in the interpretation of this text—it is central to the text's narrative development. The praxis of mutuality opens the way in this pericope for

---

78. "Not only does the New Testament cultivate social contexts that expect the eradication of disability as a resolution to human-made exclusion, it does so by depicting disabled people as the agents of their own curative ambitions" (Mitchell and Snyder 2007, 179).

79. From Reading Group Two, March 21, 2006.

4. IDENTITY, LABELS, AND RESISTANCE

the exercising of agencies of resistive survival and transformation. In the second of the pair of pericopae we consider in this chapter, by contrast, the absence of the full form of the praxis of mutuality opens up quite different possibilities, as the shadow of the cross is cast from Golgotha all the way to Capernaum.

4.2. Mark 3:19b–35

19b Then he [Jesus] went home; 20 and the crowd came together again, so they could not even eat. 21 When his family heard it, they went out to restrain him, for people were saying, "He has gone out of his mind." 22 And the scribes who came down from Jerusalem said, "He has Beelzebul, and by the ruler of the demons he casts out demons." 23 And he called them to him, and spoke to them in parables, "How can Satan cast out Satan? 24 If a kingdom is divided against itself, that kingdom cannot stand. 25 And if a house is divided against itself, that house will not be able to stand. 26 And if Satan has risen up against himself and is divided, he cannot stand, but his end has come. 27 No one can enter a strong man's house and plunder his property without first tying up the strong man; then indeed the house can be plundered.

28 "Truly I tell you, people will be forgiven for their sins and whatever blasphemies they utter; 29 but whoever blasphemes against the Holy Spirit can never have forgiveness, but is guilty of an eternal sin"—30 for they had said, "He has an unclean spirit."

31 Then his mother and his brothers came; and standing outside, they sent to him and called him. 32 A crowd was sitting around him; and they said to him, "Your mother and your brothers and sisters are outside, asking for you." 33 And he replied, "Who are my mother and my brothers?" 34 And looking at those who sat around him, he said, "Here are my mother and my brothers! 35 Whoever does the will of God is my brother and sister and mother."

4.2.1. Introduction: Labels, Binarism, and Ambiguity

In the interpretation of 3:19b–35 I ask how relational dynamics are negotiated in the unfolding of this narrative. Central to this question is the assertion that in 3:19b–35 Jesus is faced with a radical challenge not only to his authority but to his very person, by labels that seek to point to an inner, spiritual/theological, and psychological depravity. My interest is in Jesus' response to these labels, and whether the binarism that he employs is an attempt to offer a resistance of clarity or one of ambiguity. While both possibilities are explored by group readers, it is their emphasis on ambiguity that prompts my interpretation of Jesus' resistance in this encounter as one that employs ambiguity as a postcolonial strategy. Furthermore, I explore how the relative absence of a praxis of mutuality in its full form ultimately shapes the encounter as it is narrated.

4.2.2. Jesus, Labels, and Binaristic Resistance—Scholars' Perspectives

In assessing Jesus' response to the questioning of his identity narrated in 3:19b–35, scholars who have an interest in the relational dynamics of the text tend to argue that Jesus resists the acts of labeling he is subjected to by utilizing a similarly binaristic type of argument, turning it to his own advantage. Furthermore, many assert that Jesus not only uses binarisms in contending with his accusers, but he does so with clarity of expression. For instance, Sharyn Dowd argues that, unlike later passages in the Gospel, here in this pericope the contrast between insiders and outsiders is clear-cut.[80] That is, while in the first pericope examined in this chapter (3:1–6) Jesus' invitational praxis of mutuality with those around him sought to open up a space between the persons involved, on the face of it Jesus' response to his own experience of "othering" in this second pericope (3:19b–35) does the very opposite. He appears to allow no shared space within the relational dynamics between himself and those who accuse him. Instead he creates a binary distinction between insiders and outsiders; between himself and those who accuse him of being "out of his mind" (3:21); and between himself and those who accuse him of "having Beelzebul" (3:22), to whom Jesus offers a series of parables about devils, kingdoms, and houses (3:23–25) couched in a binaristic form, the implication being that he stands on one side and cannot therefore stand on the other.

The argument that Jesus negotiates the relational dynamics he is faced with in this pericope with binaristic clarity has focused on what a number of biblical scholars have interpreted to be at the heart of the

---

80. Dowd 2000, 37. For interpretations that see Jesus' argumentation in 3:19b–35 similarly based on clear binaristic distinctions see Heil 1992, 88; Hare 1996, 50; Broadhead 2001, 42; Bowman 1965, 131; Guelich 1989, 175–76; Painter 1997, 72. Moreover, Liew argues that Jesus' use of binarism in 3:19b–35 duplicates an insider-outsider model that spells violent destruction for those "outside," and serves the purpose of assisting in establishing Jesus' absolute authority upon the colonial landscape of the Gospel (1999, 103).

entire passage: the charge that Jesus "has Beelzebul" (3:22).[81] The postulation of the central importance of 3:22 is often based on the supposed predominance of a theological dualism between "powers of good and evil" contemporary in the story's historical location. That is, Jesus' binaristic response to the charges before him typifies a dominant discourse of first-century Palestine.[82]

While arguing that Jesus responded to the acts of labeling he faced utilizing a clear binaristic strategy of resistance, scholars often wish to retain the critical distance Jesus creates in relation to others in this text, at the same time maintaining that he does not lack compassion for them. Take, for instance, the first act of labeling, that Jesus is "out of his mind" (3:21). This troubles scholars who presume that Jesus' family are responsible for saying this, when they wish also to argue that a good relationship is maintained in this pericope between Jesus and his family. For example, Joel Marcus sees the presence of an antagonism between Jesus and his family as necessary, wherein "somehow such strange antagonisms must serve God's purpose."[83] In this vein, some scholars want to abdicate the family's role in the act of labeling altogether. John Painter believes that the textual context of the appointment of the Twelve by Jesus to do his work in 3:13–19 is evidence enough that the intended referent in the phrase in 3:21 is Jesus' disciples, not his family.[84] Others interpret the role of the family in positive terms even if they demonstrate a "lack of sympathy" (Hiebert 1994, 97). Of course, most scholars who take such a position assert the opposite lack of personal regard for Jesus on behalf of the scribes, described by D. Edmond Hiebert as "deliberately malicious" (99).

Alternatively, those who wish to accentuate the critical distance between Jesus and his family contend that Jesus' family should be impli-

---

81. See, e.g., Hiebert 1994, 97–102; Best 1990, 12–15; Mann 1986, 254; MacLaurin 1978, 157–59; Hiers 1974.

82. Indeed, Mann (1986, 254) has argued that Zoroastrianism was a contemporary influence on Jewish thinking through both the earlier Persian period and later Hellenistic one. For instance, Essene theology, one of a dualism between "good" and "evil," may have depended on Zoroastrianism in some form.

83. Marcus 2000, 280. See also Hiebert's argument that the attempt by the family of Jesus to restrain him represented nothing more sinister than a misplaced, well-meaning desire to protect (1994, 97).

84. Painter 1997, 70. This argument is refuted by those who privilege the "Markan sandwich" form, of which 3:19b–34 (with 3:19b–21 and 3:31–34 around 3:22–30) is taken to be an example (see, e.g., Guelich 1989, 172).

cated in the accusation made against him, and Jesus' resistance should be read within a wider framework that challenges the ancient notion of traditional family ties with an alternative "strategy for good living" centered on the "kingdom of God" (Ahearne-Kroll 2001). This alternative strategy, according to Stephen Ahearne-Kroll, demands that when those ties interfere with the "way of the kingdom," then doing the will of God must come first, even if it means severing family relations (19). Thus Jesus redefines family by its relation to God as its creator and binding force (22), with conventional family relations no longer completely conditioning one's life choices.[85]

Other scholars' interpretations imply that a clearly defined binarism must lie at the heart of Jesus' responses to undergird his telling of parables. For instance, interpreters of the enigmatic parable of the Strong Man suggest that it means that Jesus has already "bound" or defeated Satan,[86] perhaps in the temptation in the wilderness (1:12–13). Contrary to this assertion is the position that the parable of the Strong Man refers not to Satan but to demons.[87] This sort of argument wishes to further the analysis of Jesus being in the process of "binding the strong man" by associating it with a theology of Jesus as eschatological agent (see Hiers 1974, 43; Marcus 2000, 270–87). Therefore, rather than seeing Jesus' exorcisms as signs of the "kingdom of God" about to break in, these interpreters view them as signs of the present action of that kingdom through Jesus. Whichever interpretation one favors, the implication is clear: Jesus cannot be on the side of those he is binding.

Alternatively, Jesus' seemingly binaristic use of parables to resist the labeling of the scribes has been thought to have political resonances. For instance, Ched Myers (1988) argues that Jesus has to be the "strong man," whose role is less to bind the cosmic powers of evil and more related to the socioeconomic powers under whose bondage the people languished.[88]

---

85. A similar argument about the need to break conventional family ties for the sake of the cause being struggled for is emphasized by readers in Cardenal's *Gospel in Solentiname*. For instance, Laureano argues, "Jesus has a very revolutionary attitude here I believe, because every revolutionary has to break loose from his family" (Cardenal 1976–1982, 2:160).

86. Herman Waetjen has linked the overpowering of Satan in this parable to the work Jesus is now doing in the liberation of "the possessed and dispossessed" (1989, 99).

87. According to Richard Hiers, the binding of demons is attested to in other scriptural literature, e.g., Tob 8:3; Jub 10:7ff. (1974, 43).

88. Myers's reading of the prevalence of oppression at the hands of Roman rule

4. IDENTITY, LABELS, AND RESISTANCE

Richard Horsley agrees with Myers that the notion of "plundering a strong man's house" resonated politically in first-century Galilee, citing accounts in Josephus where both Judas in Sepphoris and Simon in Jericho broke into, and in Simon's case burned down, royal palaces and then plundered "the things that had been seized there" (Horsley 2001, 139, 273–74 n. 30, citing *Ant.* 17.271, 274).

From a slightly different angle, Douglas Oakman argues that the entire set of parables and indeed the whole pericope should be read more allegorically than has previously been done, with the unifying focus found in the word *basileia* (reign) (1988, 114). For Oakman, the conflict with Beelzebul underscores not spiritual/cosmic concerns but economic and political ones. He further asserts that the parables of strong men, houses, and kingdoms in 3:19b–35 were crafted with the reign of Herod Antipas in sight, and operates as a hidden transcript of resistance (see Scott 1990) against such political and economic realities due to the dire consequences that could follow candid speech (Oakman 1988, 112). Thus the conflict between Jesus and the scribes concerning Beelzebul underscores the political and economic dimensions of underprivilege, malnutrition, endemic violence, and the destruction of rural families (115).

Despite the diversity, all of these interpretations of Jesus' responses to the labels he is given in this pericope, sampled above, share a common feature: the responses Jesus makes are intended to communicate a clear polar opposition between himself and his detractors. Yet it is this very issue of clarity that is questioned in relation to the nature of Jesus' resistive rhetoric in 3:19b–35 when the insights of group readers are brought into the hermeneutical circle of this text's interpretation. What group readers offer the interpretation of this pericope are the particular vantage points from personal experiences of being labeled, and insights via this experience into both the impact of labeling on Jesus and the agency he exercises resisting the same.

---

and their Jewish client rulers is supported by other readers, e.g., Horsley: "The Gospel of Mark ... [is] about people subjected by an ancient empire," wherein the effects of imperial exploitation led to a breakdown the traditional socioeconomic infrastructure. Exorbitant taxes and tributes led to a rising indebtedness and loss of the land for a people whose subsistence relied upon it. Horsley goes on to propose that the reign of Herod Antipas intensified this economic exploitation (2001, 30, 35; 1993, 401).

4.2.3. External and Internal Struggles—Group Readers' Perspectives

In a story punctuated by labeling and resistance, one of the most prominent features group readers reflected on in their interpretations of this pericope was the struggle for power. On one hand, the scribes from Jerusalem were read as wanting to "maintain power."[89] On the other hand, the power the scribes represented, and its influence over the people, were perceived to have been somehow threatened by Jesus' own power, such that one reader interpreted the scribes' accusations against Jesus as an indication that they wanted "the criticism to go away."[90] In their interpretations of this text, group readers saw power in a Foucauldian sense as a complex web of power struggles present both between characters and as conflicts within them. For instance, interpretations of Jesus were offered that portrayed him as a character who, in a sense, inhabits internally the power struggle that he faces externally. That is, among certain group readers, Jesus' identity is considered to be ambiguous;[91] his home is not only a place of rest but is also a place of entrapment;[92] and he is identified as a person whom others often fail to understand.[93] Group readers strongly associated this sense of Jesus' internal and external struggle with their own experiences of poor mental health. For instance, with regard to the labeling of Jesus as being in league with Beelzebul and Jesus' parabolic response to that charge, some readers interpreted this to correspond to the notion of a divided self, expressed as an "inner conflict."[94] One of the same read-

---

89. "They might have been concerned that they were losing popularity. They wanted to maintain power" (B from Reading Group Three, April 10, 2006).

90. "I think they might want the criticism to go away" (A from Reading Group Three, April 10, 2006).

91. "What was Jesus? Couldn't have been human. What was he? A superhuman? Batman or Hercules?" (C from Reading Group One, April 4, 2006).

92. "He's home but the crowd are eager to seize him. He's tired, couldn't get any rest" (B from Reading Group One, April 4, 2006).

93. "They didn't understand what he was trying to do. They wouldn't believe what he had done. He keeps doing these strange things, they couldn't understand him so they told him that he was out of his mind" (A from Reading Group One, April 4, 2006).

94. B: "I think it's something about yourself. A soul divided into pieces cannot function properly. It's hard to believe it's a real house." D: "A soul divided against itself, given over to sin and personal pressures. Before you know it, it is all messed up." C: "Every day I'm called that. They said it was an inner conflict" (from Reading Group One, April 4, 2006).

4. IDENTITY, LABELS, AND RESISTANCE

ers, later in the session, went on to expand on the quality of that conflict: "Sometimes I suffer so much I don't see reality."[95]

The striking commentary that these group readers offered of Jesus' sense of self in this pericope, then, is of a man in profound distress as a result of the labeling that he is subjected to. The emphasis here is not so much on a postulation that Jesus as a character is something of a divided self; rather it is an emphasis on the divisive and hegemonic impact of labeling, of power exercised upon Jesus. While there were divergent views of which label might have been worse for Jesus to have received—for some being labeled as "having Beelzebul" was worse,[96] for others being labeled as "out of his mind" was the more damaging identifier[97]—the impact of acts of labeling and their associations with mental health for group readers was strong in their interpretations. Group readers spoke of the experience of being labeled by others as one that encouraged them to act "as if we are a separate category of people."[98]

For group readers, labeling was seen as a threat not only to a person's ability to express identity for oneself but also to the sense of integrity a

---

95. "Sometimes people suffer for real. Sometimes I suffer so much I don't see reality and I don't realize what people are doing. When I finally get through I find that people are just living. It's all a racket. You've got to even pay to die. It's not worth it. If you really think about being in the world today you go nuts. You go off the deep end. When a person has faith, these people don't think about these things. It is the small things that put you over. You can't think over and over about the same thing" (C from Reading Group One, April 4, 2006).

96. B: "They were saying he is of Satan, that is more damaging because Satan is Satan, he wants to destroy everything he's teaching." A: "Satan existed in those days." B: "The devil is the antithesis of what he is trying to teach. 'Out of his mind' is a physical model. Satan, that's spiritual, not physical" (from Reading Group Four, April 11, 2006).

97. "It's worse being called crazy. It's unfair" (C from Reading Group One, April 4, 2006).

98. C: "We have to live and act like we are a separate category of people." D: "Oh no we shouldn't." C: "It's just the way of life, that's all" (from Reading Group One, April 4, 2006). That said, it should be noted that for two readers the impact of labels was perceived more positively: B: "I guess for me it's not as much about the label than how well I'm doing. Am I safe? Am I in touch with reality? Are my moods stable or not? I don't know that people respect me or consider me mentally ill." A: "I have no problem with labels." B: "Labels can be useful, giving people an idea of what history might be there, what symptoms to look for with family and friends. Really getting a sense of the problems I've been facing" (from Reading Group Three, April 10, 2006).

person has within. For instance, one reader emphasized how labels can lead to an estrangement from the self,[99] and another reader stated how it becomes hard not to believe the things people say and then "lose yourself for a while."[100] The impact of such threats that labeling presents, both externally and internally, was interpreted by some group readers to lead to "surrender"[101] and to resolving to "shut up."[102] From this perspective, then, in making an association between their own experiences and the imagined experience of Jesus in this pericope, power as it operates in 3:19b–35 seems to render Jesus' identity as other in a coercive and objectifying way: Jesus is designated as spiritually and psychologically other.

However, being objectified by acts of labeling was not all that group readers emphasized. The other feature of power that group readers highlighted was the necessity of having something to say back to those who label.[103] Fundamentally, certain group readers thought that people facing labels need to defend themselves somehow,[104] even though it is "never easy to defend yourself."[105] It is against this backdrop of the profoundly debilitating effect of labels on a person's sense of identity and agency and the

---

99. C: "People like to label, it's convenient." A: "And especially when a person is troubling you but you don't want to argue with them. It's easy to say, 'He is an idiot.' Then deep down I need to be in conflict with myself about those things he is saying" (from Reading Group Three, April 10, 2006).

100. "You have to defend yourself somehow. Have to say something. They will walk all over you and you believe all these stupid things about yourself and you lose yourself for a while. It's very difficult for you" (B from Reading Group One, April 4, 2006).

101. "It's tough, words are worse than the sword emotionally. I faced a family member head on, straight to the matter, who said I was crazy, 'You've been smoking too much crack.' I had to surrender right there. But for Jesus it was different; he knew exactly what was going on" (C from Reading Group Four, April 11, 2006).

102. "Even so-called regular people, if you say the truth, people let you have it. Even regular people have to shut up. Jesus had to keep his mouth shut sometimes. That's the way of society" (A from Reading Group One, April 4, 2006).

103. "It depends on the person. He does a good job of thinking of something to say" (B from Reading Group Three, April 10, 2006).

104. "You have to defend yourself somehow. Have to say something. They will walk all over you and you believe all these stupid things about yourself and you lose yourself for a while. It's very difficult for you" (B from Reading Group One, April 4, 2006).

105. "It's never easy to defend yourself against the Pharisees and the scribes. Always trying to trap you" (A from Reading Group One, April 4, 2006).

4. IDENTITY, LABELS, AND RESISTANCE   117

utter necessity of saying something back that Jesus' acts of resistance in this pericope should be read.

What group readers' interpretations offer to our understanding of this pericope, then, is a sketch of the human quality of the encounters narrated. Furthermore, the person of Jesus who emerges from these interpretations is not simply the monochrome master of rhetoric and parable who remains altogether unfazed by the labeling he faces. Rather, he is presented as a figure who is imagined to face external and internal conflicts and ambiguities. It is this thicker description of Jesus' character and identity that offers a fuller perspective from which to view his resistance.

Where group readers offer the depth of insight into this particular option for reading this pericope is in their descriptions of the lived experiences of poor mental health that they associated with the struggles of Jesus as narrated in 3:19b–35. For instance, one reader recounted the experience of a friend who, when faced with the exclusionary act of another person, responded in a way that reflects the agonistic tension that people who experience poor mental health can often face when attempting to assert their resistance to pejorative remarks:

> There's a woman I know with bipolar. She has a guy friend who tells her that she is a manic depressive. She left, sat in the car, and cried. Then she went back and said, "Go to hell." Then she left, she didn't want to give him more fuel. I think she wanted to represent herself and all people with bipolar in a positive light. If she had stayed to argue she might have got angry in the heat of the moment and wouldn't have helped this guy to see mental illness in a positive light.[106]

This episode reflects the tension of the relational dynamics that persons who experience poor mental health can often face between the desire to defend oneself and the contrary presence of "self-defeating thoughts";[107] and, similarly, the tension between the pejorative representations of the identity of mental health others present (such as the man in the episode

---

106. B from from Reading Group Three, April 10, 2006.
107. "I'm a firm believer that Jesus will not give up on me. I've seen work in my life I really believe is of God. Only be taught as a child. When you are subject, then there is freedom to rationalize it and continue to do something wrong. I knew that I was enslaved to my disease. When I used to get high I was a devil. The walking dead. Trying to use self-defeating thoughts to be my excuses" (B from Reading Group Four, April 11, 2006).

narrated above) and the difficulty of responding to such labeling without being reduced by the other person to the "sound of their illness."[108] With this contextual reality in mind, being labeled as one who is out of his mind and as having Beelzebul/Satan may have a more debilitating effect on Jesus' ability to exercise resistance than has hitherto been acknowledged.

What then of Jesus' resistance? As noted earlier, some scholars emphasize or imply the binaristic nature of Jesus' response to the labeling he faces in this pericope. A similar view was offered by some group readers, such as one who highlighted how Jesus manages to flip the power relations in the story,[109] thus assuming the teaching authority previously held by the scribes. Yet as well as these emphases, group readers offered insights on the inherent ambiguity in the relational dynamics of the passage. Jesus' home is an ambiguous symbol of security yet entrapment;[110] his identity is an ambiguous expression of teaching with authority[111] while having that authority undermined by both scribes from Jerusalem and his own family, by whom he is partly identified in the Gospel (6:3); and his ministry remains ambiguous to those who fail to understand him.[112]

---

108. "Madness, which for so long had been overt and unrestricted, which had for so long been present on the horizon, disappeared. It entered a phase of silence from which it was not to emerge for a long time; it was deprived of its language; and although one continued to speak of it, it became impossible for it to speak of itself" (Foucault 1976, 68).

109. "Well, I mean it is no longer the religious authorities who are deciding. He has flipped the power relation and he is teaching to students" (A from Reading Group Three, April 10, 2006).

110. "He's home but the crowd are eager to seize him. He's tired, couldn't get any rest" (B from Reading Group One, April 4, 2006).

111. "Anybody could be not trusted. God could make a spectacle. He [Jesus] could be drunk on beer or wine and go crazy that way too" (C from Reading Group One, April 4, 2006). "Yeah, depending on what it means. I feel like it's a strong psychological temptation to be megalomaniac, where you consider yourself to be really great. I imagine Jesus to be a really good teacher. It's plausible that hearing the crowd this could go to his head. He could convince himself that he could do more than he really could, more than just an ordinary man" (A from Reading Group Three, April 10, 2006).

112. "They didn't understand what he was trying to do. They wouldn't believe what he had done. He keeps doing these strange things, they couldn't understand him so they told him that he was out of his mind" (A from Reading Group One, April 4, 2006).

Prompted by these emphases of group readers, one might think that Jesus' resistive responses in 3:19b–35 reflect this strain of ambiguity. Rather than employing a binaristic strategy of clarity in answering the labels that question his spiritual and psychological integrity, Jesus, in exercising resistance, might utilize a binaristic strategy of ambiguity. It is this very possibility that I explore in the next section.

4.2.4. Rearticulating Identity in Ambiguity: A Viable Strategy?

At first it may seem that the possibility that Jesus' rhetorical resistance in 3:19b–35 intentionally employs a strategy of ambiguity is to push a little too far out both from what group readers' interpretations have suggested and also from the text itself. It is, after all, a thin slice of the interpretations offered by the group readers that I have decided to take as a lead in considering ambiguity as a praxis of resistance in this encounter. Yet for two reasons I do not believe that to push at the received boundaries of how this text has been understood in its interpretation by other scholars is a move too far.

First, if the assumption that Jesus in his argumentation in this pericope is by default coherent and even masterful[113] is suspended momentarily, then it is possible to view this encounter as between a man under considerable and immediate public scrutiny and his detractors. This is where the significance of some of the diversity of interpretations offered by group readers comes in. Jesus' responses viewed in light of group readers' emphases on the debilitating impact of labeling offer an alternative to the assumption that Jesus must have been altogether composed in this pericope in order to have reasserted his identity. Second, if the text is considered again not with the expectation that the terms of Jesus' argumentation are necessarily clear, but open to the possibility that a lack of clarity is also a possible finding, then the examination of ambiguity as a strategy of engagement by Jesus is more possible.

To establish that Jesus achieved a clear delineation in his use of binarisms in his resistance to the labeling he faced, two points would need to be clarified. First, to whom is Jesus referring in his argumentation for the delineation of insiders and outsiders to be beyond doubt? It is not clear at

---

113. See, e.g., Liew's portrayal of Jesus' superlative rhetorical agency (1999, 103) and the group reader who describes Jesus' agency thus: "He is God; just God" (A from Reading Group One, April 4, 2006).

all from the text alone who Jesus means when he talks of his "true family" (3:35), who have assembled in his home (3:33). While it cannot be his mother and brothers, who are standing outside (3:31), could it be his disciples? the neighbors who earlier wanted to restrain him? the scribes whom he has just called to him for a parabolic teaching?

This lack of clarity abounds in the entire pericope. Who cannot even eat because of the crowd (3:20)? Jesus and his disciples? Jesus and his family? Jesus and the scribes? Who thinks that Jesus has gone out of his mind (3:21)?[114] Is it his family?[115] Is it the crowd or the mob (Hamerton-Kelly 1994, 82)? Could it be the disciples? Or the scribes? Or perhaps just some neighbors who have had enough of all the commotion? And why was this charge being made against Jesus in the first place (see Gundry 1993, 171)? Was it because it reflected the reality of the situation or was it a more politically or theologically motivated attack? Then, after the charge by the scribes that Jesus "has Beelzebul," whom does Jesus call to him? The scribes? Or is it a teaching episode for his disciples?[116]

The second feature necessary for the binaristic strategy to have been used effectively is that the terms of reference would need to be clear. With regard to the second accusation, for instance—"He has Beelzebul" (3:22)—the search for clarity in Jesus' response to this charge has inspired a wide range of interpretive maneuvers. One approach has been to focus on Jesus' response in 3:28–30, wherein he rebuffs the charge of having an unclean spirit, the charge of being in league with Beelzebul (which in the narrative Jesus conflates with Satan).[117] Some contend that Jesus resists

---

114. In addressing this quandary some scholars choose to spread their bets: "'Those with Jesus' likely refers to family or friends or followers. Believing Jesus to be beside himself, they come to take him away (3:20)" (Broadhead 2001, 42).

115. See, e.g., V. Taylor 1966, 235–36; Johnson 1960, 80; Waetjen 1989, 98; Dowd 2000, 34; Gundry 1993, 171; Crossan 1999, 55; Lambrecht 1999, 94.

116. Indeed, Aichele argues that Jesus summons the scribes as though they were his disciples (1999, 41).

117. Few would argue that "Beelzebul" and "Satan" somehow refer to different subjects or have a rhetorical purpose. Therefore, when considering the resistance to the labeling as "having Beelzebul" Jesus displays in his parabolic response, which includes references to Satan, I will not pursue the argument that Jesus rebuffs their charge by changing the terms of reference from Beelzebul to Satan. As with the majority of scholarship, I will not assign any greater significance to this change other than that the two names were considered to be coterminous. See, e.g., Hiebert 1994, 97–102; Best 1990, 12–15; Mann 1986, 254; MacLaurin 1978, 157–59; Hiers 1974, 35–47.

4. IDENTITY, LABELS, AND RESISTANCE

the charge with the implication that the scribes had blasphemed against the clean Spirit, the Holy Spirit, with whom by his comment Jesus implies he is associated, or even identifiable.[118] However, is Richard Hiers right in assuming that it is the scribes who are never to be forgiven for blaspheming against the Holy Spirit? Could it also be Jesus' family, or those others who labeled him as being "out of his mind," who have blasphemed? George Aichele argues that it could be both, that each seeks to control Jesus, to define his identity. Perhaps attempting to control Jesus is what counts as blasphemy (1999, 44)?

Indeed, the very diversity of interpretations of the various terms and turns of Jesus' acts of resistance to labeling in 3:19b–35 demonstrates that the search for clarity in Jesus' resistive rhetoric in this pericope remains elusive. Given this, I take up the emphases of some of the group readers who point to the ambiguity in this pericope, and suggest that Jesus' strategy for resistance in 3:19b–35 is less an attempt to make things clear and more an attempt to make things opaque, and that Jesus employs a strategy of ambiguity in making his defense against those who question his identity.[119] In positing this, I am seeking to explore the tension between group readers' interpretations that suggests both this pattern of ambiguity in the pericope and the conviction that Jesus' resistance is effective such that it "flipped the power relation" (see n. 109) in the relational dynamics he encounters. What I am seeking to do here, then, is to practice a technique common to postcolonial biblical criticism of probing the points of tension between competing readings of texts without seeking to sublate the difference that this tension provides.

If ambiguity is the praxis that Jesus employs in this pericope, then how might it be understood? Within the relational dynamics of this peri-

---

118. See Hiers 1974, 43. Anderson (1976, 123) argues that a contrast is now drawn between the "lavishness of God's grace" and the "the incredible hardness of those who by their wilful spurning of that grace shut themselves off from its blessing."

119. Although not arguing that Jesus necessarily intends to use a strategy of ambiguity in this pericope, John Keenan does assert that both the attempts of his family to restrain him and of the scribes to exclude him from their tradition by placing him beyond it in the "false otherness of the demoniac" can be interpreted as attempts to "bind and negate the middle path and its practice of abiding in a tensive and healthy differentiation of two truths" (1995, 111). Similarly, my own postulation that Jesus' responses to labeling in 3:19b–35 might be read to utilize a strategy of ambiguity is not unlike Robert Fowler's suggestion that there is a strategy of indirection in Mark, shaped by the evangelist himself (1989, 15–34).

cope, ambiguity is akin to Bhabha's notion of ambivalence that operates as a strategy that fluctuates between complicity in and resistance to colonial discourse.[120] Thus Jesus might be seen to employ ambiguity as a postcolonial praxis in this pericope in an attempt to create what has been termed an "interstitial space of doubt" between himself and the accusations laid before him.[121] Furthermore, from the perspective of the postcolonial praxes that I described in chapter 2, this strategy of ambiguity as used by Jesus in this pericope is not a strategy of hidden resistance. To the contrary, it is clear from 3:19b–35 that this is a strategy of open defiance before one's detractors. And, as Scott suggests in his work on the hidden transcripts of resistance, open defiance is a risky strategy to employ in the face of hegemonic power.[122]

Putting these two pieces, doubt and open defiance, together, one might argue that Jesus inserts doubt within the framework of hegemonic power while still maintaining the appearance of complicity with that power by utilizing the strategy of ambiguity within the binaristic terms of reference his accusers use to label him. Why, though, couch his rhetorical resistance in terms that both comply with the binarism he is presented, and yet do so ambiguously? It is here that mutuality is informative, particularly when taking into account the group readers' emphases on the profound struggle Jesus may well have experienced in the face of labeling that questioned his identity and integrity.

The key emphasis that group readers offered of this pericope, in terms of the impact of the acts of labeling Jesus faced, centered on the theme of power. Drawing on their own experiences of the debilitating impact that

---

120. See Ashcroft et al. 2000, 12. That ambiguity might be a postcolonial praxis of resistance is a possibility that has been explored by other postcolonial thinkers. For instance, Paul Gready has examined the role of ambiguity among other resistive strategies in the context of South African resistive praxes in the era of apartheid (2003, 275). See also Jefferess 2008, 57–94. Likewise, within postcolonial biblical criticism, Liew (2002) has explored the role of ambiguity in John's Gospel in terms of the evangelist's construction of community in the Gospel via a motif of misunderstanding and miscomprehension.

121. See Logan 2008. In literary theory, this has been understood as the doubt created for the reader by ambiguity between what is fact and what is fiction.

122. The specific proposition that Scott wishes to put forward is that subordinate groups have "learned to clothe their resistance and defiance in ritualisms of subordination that serve both to disguise their purposes and to provide them with a ready route of retreat that may soften the consequences of a possible failure" (1990, 96).

labeling can have on individuals, readers offered what I termed a "thicker" description of Jesus' character as facing both external and internal struggles for survival in the heat of that relational encounter. That is, if the interpretive insights of group readers who see the reception of acts of labeling as debilitating to the point of leading to "surrender" (see n. 101), to feeling like a "separate category of people" (see n. 98), and to "losing yourself for a while" (see n. 100), are to be taken seriously, then it is reasonable to conclude that the struggle that Jesus faces in this pericope is the struggle between the need to defend himself and the fact that it is "never easy" (see n. 105) to do so when the mutual relating is seemingly so profoundly lacking.

From this vantage point that group readers offer, I argue that Jesus employs a strategy of ambiguity in this pericope in response to a level of scrutiny so intense that it appears to have leached the encounter of any hope of a mutual exchange. It is my contention here that Jesus may well have perceived that there was no space within the relational dynamics he faced for him to renegotiate anything more aspirational for his societal location in that community other than a rhetoric of survival. It may seem, then, that mutuality serves as a heuristic for this pericope not for praxis that is present but for that which is absent. The question that remains is whether Jesus' response to this lack of the praxis of mutuality can be only be understood as similarly lacking mutuality.

On one hand, Jesus' action of calling the people to himself in 3:23 looks like a clear instance of a praxis of mutuality. The parabolic teaching that he offers to those he gathers around him is an agency that seeks to renegotiate the terms of the relational dynamics he finds himself in. As I laid out in chapter 2, mutuality is a praxis of resisting hegemonic relational dynamics via the renegotiation, in this case, of perceptions of identity. Thus Jesus' actions here might be seen to exercise a praxis of mutuality via terms of engagement that are ambiguous as the reassertion of an individual's rights to self-identification and properly represented agency. Jesus' use of ambiguity as a postcolonial praxis of resistance is a praxis of mutuality as much as it stakes for him a "place at the table." In this praxis of mutuality, he reasserts that he should be viewed as a legitimate participant in the relational dynamics of that community, and his agency embodies the refusal to be written out of the same. His reassertion, then, is the postcolonial reimagining of a relational space of encountering that has, through the imposition of labels, taken on a heavily hegemonic form.

That said, what is limiting in Jesus' praxis of mutuality here is that in tandem as it is with a praxis of ambiguity, it is unable to be truly effective as a praxis of transformation. Thus what is revealed in this particular pericope is the truly compound nature of mutuality as a postcolonial praxis. Used as a praxis of resistance alone, it acts in this case as a reminder that each person should be related to as a full partner in the space of relational encounters; yet without the transformational (or what I termed in chapter 2 to be the aspirational) components of this praxis, it fails to fully realize the mutual sharing of that space. It is, then, the lack of the praxis of mutuality in its full form—as both resistive and transformative—exercised in the postcolonial praxis of ambiguity in this pericope that ultimately determines the narratival outcomes of this particular reassertion of Jesus' identity. Indeed, without the aspiration for a transformation of hegemonic relational dynamics that the praxis of mutuality embodies, the effectiveness of this praxis as a form of postcolonial agency is limited.

This limit to effectiveness can be seen by reading on in the Gospel. With Jesus' resistance to the first act of labeling in mind—that he is "out of his mind" (3:21)—the resultant effect is that Jesus' "old family" is left out of the house, outside the inner circle. Even with the ambiguity that surrounds the identity of the new family of followers—neighbors? the crowd? the scribes?—the impact of this resistance is difficult to see in a positive light. As one set of readers put it:

> C: It's sad for him, there's a wall between them [Jesus and his biological family].
> A: I don't know, it's sort of like his followers were his family, that could be part of this radical love thing—love as if they were your family.
> B: I don't know, it sort of seems he usually forgives them. What you've done proves you're not on my side, so get this, this is my real family.
> A: It's hard.[123]

Indeed, placing the pericope into its fuller Markan context, the relationship between Jesus and his biological family only continues to take negative turns. In 6:1–6 Jesus is rejected by those in his hometown and so is distanced from even more levels of his family (see Ahearne-Kroll 2001, 15). While the townspeople think that they know Jesus because they can situate him within their notions of family structures as "the carpenter, son of Mary and brother of James and Joses and Judas and Simon" (6:3), the next sentence is telling: "And they took offense at him" (6:3b). Following

---

123. From Reading Group Three, April 10, 2006.

the rejection of Jesus in the hometown of his family, Jesus immediately commissions his disciples to "shake off the dust" of any house or place that refuses to hear them "as a testimony against them" (6:11). In 10:29–30 Jesus' response to Peter's contention, that the disciples had left everything to follow him, rather enigmatically lists brothers and sisters, mothers and children, along with persecutions, in contrast to what they had left. The next significant mention of family by Jesus relegates them to an even more serious level of estrangement where, instead of family relations being a source of minor conflict, they now become a source of violence, persecution, and death: "Brother will betray brother to death, and father his child, and children will rise against parents and have them put to death" (13:12; see Ahearne-Kroll 2001, 18).

Rejection takes place on both sides. Jesus' rhetoric about the conventional family continues to paint that cultural norm as a source of deepening constriction and woe. He states categorically how he is without honor among his own kin and in his own house (6:4). Jesus' view of his townspeople, and presumably also the members of his own family who lived there, is dismal as he leaves there for the final time: "he was amazed at their unbelief" (6:6). Likewise, the family's view of Jesus in Mark, no longer mediated by the family members directly, who are left outside (3:31), is mediated by the extended cultural family of his hometown. Their view of Jesus, as has already been alluded to ("they took offense at him," 6:3b), is equally dim. Here the strategy of ambiguity is much less prominent. Jesus names his "kin" as those who fail to show him honor (6:4).

The strategy of using ambiguity as a form of resistance in the face of a potentially hegemonic relational encounter can hardly be lauded as an unqualified success. Furthermore, the "new family" does not exactly provide Jesus the comfort and support that one might hope for a family to offer. By the end of the narrative, this new "eschatological family" (Brown et al. 1978, 286) deserts him (14:50), one member betrays him (14:44), another denies he ever knew him (14:71), and only some of the women of his "new family" are with him to the very end at the foot of the cross (15:40–41).

A similarly bleak outlook can be traced with regard to Jesus' response to the second accusation—"He has Beelzebul" (3:22)—made by the scribes. Jesus' parabolic and ultimately enigmatic response to this act of labeling leads to an almost consistently negative series of encounters. The next reference to scribes after 3:19b–35 is in 10:33, and it begins a theme that foreshadows Jesus' death, which, according to the text, is at the hands of (among others) the scribes, "who will condemn him to death." Similarly in 11:18 it is the Jerusalem scribes and the chief priests who "kept looking for a way to kill him" (11:18). It is scribes along with elders and chief priests in the temple who question Jesus' authority (11:27–28). Jesus then tells the parable of the Wicked Tenants, who put the beloved son of the vineyard owner to death (12:8)—a parable the scribes, elders, and chief priests then realize is directed against them (12:12). In 12:38 Jesus warns the crowd to beware of the scribes, who "devour widow's houses" (12:40). The inevitable dramatic momentum toward Jesus' death is again emphasized in 14:1 with the scribes and chief priests "looking for a way to arrest Jesus by stealth and kill him." Indeed, at the end it is from the scribes, chief priests, and elders that a crowd with swords and clubs comes to arrest Jesus (14:43); and it is the same combination who assemble to try him (14:53) and hold a council the next morning (15:1). And the scribes and chief priests mock him on the cross (15:32). The only positive note between Jesus and the scribes following 3:19b–35 is in the encounter where the scribe who calls Jesus "Teacher" is told by Jesus that he is "not far from the kingdom of God" (12:24–34).[124]

Of course, this textual trajectory of Jesus' praxes of ambiguity and partial mutuality is a presentation of what has to look like a failed strategy. To present Jesus in a way that suggests that his agency might be somehow limited in his encounters with others runs counter to the "normate hermeneutics" (Wynn 2007, 92) often associated with this passage that Jesus is normatively a character who is almost by definition taken to be a superlative agent in every instance. Yet, as I explored in chapter 3, the form of dialogical postcolonial biblical criticism that I seek to employ in this work is one that wishes to have room for any questions to be asked and any answers to be argued with regard to biblical texts. Fundamentally, this interpretation of this particular pericope is not presented as the definitive way that this story might be understood; rather, it is presented as one way

---

124. True to this work's stated reader-response criticism approach to the Gospel of Mark that views the text fundamentally as story, this paragraph relates the textual pattern of Jesus' deteriorating interactions with scribes. That said, I offer this series of encounters between Jesus and these religious leaders keeping in mind the history of the interpretation of these texts that has at various times been anti-Judaic. Given that this work is not primarily interested in the context "behind the text" of Mark as much as it is in the text itself, I present this as a textual trajectory not intending it to imply the complicity of religious leaders in Jesus' execution as those events may have occurred in history.

that sees the text through the emphases of readers who offer insights into the lived experience of some of the relational dynamics the text narrates. It is my contention that the sometimes transgressive expansions that these readers' emphases offer biblical interpretation are worth noting, not only for the ways in which they expand understandings of textual concerns, but for the important ways in which they draw multiple associations from text to context and vice versa.

4.3. Conclusion

What, then, are we to conclude about the struggles for identity that these two pericopae narrate? On one hand, the fractured picture of relating that 3:19b–35 narrates and foreshadows is far from the "celebration" of the reimagining of the identity of the man with the withered/divine hand in the first pericope (3:1–6), whose hybrid identity and agency were transformative and made in response to the transformational invitation to a praxis of mutuality. Indeed, for the man with the withered/divine hand, stepping into the middle of the relational "space" of that encounter is a "hybrid moment of political change" (Bhabha 1994, 28) that offers him the room to maneuver in that space between Jesus and the Pharisees. By contrast, Jesus' own maneuvering is a moment of political change that does not seem to point to the restoration and transformation of relating but rather to relational encounters with family and scribes wherein the praxis of mutuality is increasingly diminished. On the other hand, bearing in mind Bhabha's stated wariness of placing agencies of survival within the "uplifting, tall stories" of progress (Bhabha and Comaroff 2002, 31), the celebration of hybrid over ambiguous assertions of identity in a comparison of these two stories should be tempered by the foreboding ending to 3:1–6 that speaks of the destruction of those who would challenge discursive patterns of power.

A further conclusion that one might draw from our reading of 3:1–6 and 3:19b–35 is that the relational dynamics in such encounters are complex. A recognition of such a complexity naturally resists the temptation in interpretations of Mark to conceive of characters (such as Jesus and the man with the withered hand) or composite characters (such as the Pharisees, the scribes, and Jesus' family) stereotypically, in ways that run the risk of oversimplifying their praxes. For, in these pericopae, while it might be tempting to perceive binaristic delineations of oppressor-oppressed, a colonial landscape wherein expressions of identity are had in the complex and fluid postcolonial praxes of mutuality, hybridity, and ambiguity is more evident.

Looking at the praxis of mutuality in 3:1–6 and 3:19b–35 more closely, on a broad level we saw mutuality not only to be at the heart of 3:1–6 and only partially present in 3:19b–35, but in the former it was interpreted to be what enabled a resistive transformation to take place through Jesus' invitation to exercise agency. More subtly, though, what group readers brought out in their varied readings of these pericopae was something of the texture of relational dynamics. Interpretations of 3:1–6, for instance, highlighted the profound deficit of the praxis of mutuality as something that was true of the imagined life of the man with the withered hand, seen not only as central to an understanding of the audacity of his hybrid agency of self-identification as withered/divine, but also as a deficit that might not dissipate when the miraculous participation of Jesus in the man's life ended. Focusing on the praxis of mutuality, then, does not reveal a "tall story" of postcolonial celebration, but rather paints a picture of transient survival: a hybrid word returned to hegemonic discourses of "witheredness," yet at the same time a word that runs the risk of the ultimate denial of any praxes of mutuality—death (3:6).

Similarly, I argued that the relational struggles in Jesus' hometown narrated in 3:19b–35 are ones where the relative absence of mutuality as a postcolonial praxis do not reduce the quality of that relating to simple binarisms. Indeed, as certain group readers highlighted, tracing the contours of the relative lack of the praxis of mutuality in 3:19b–35 reveals the complexity of the struggles necessitated by its absence: struggles with both external and internal conflicts. The Jesus interpreted to inhabit such struggles in this pericope is one who reveals the complexities and contradictions of colonially situated praxes of identification.

In the next chapter, this theme of the complexity of struggles to assert identity and to exercise agency in hegemonic relational dynamics is continued. I explore some of the further dimensions of the praxis of mutuality with regard to the agonisms necessitated by the construction of difference along lines of gender and ethnicity.

5
NEGOTIATING MARGINAL AGENCY:
MARK 5:21–43 AND 7:24–30

The interpretations of the first pair of encounters in chapter 4 forefronted the role of power in the renegotiation of relational dynamics. There power was manifest in religious authority, physical deformation, and the significance of labels as marks of identity. This second pair of encounters (5:21–43; 7:24–30) also forefronts power differentials: bleeding as a sign of physical difference, and sickness and demon possession as marks of narratival exclusion. These two pericopae also forefront particular power differentials with regard to gender and ethnicity. In this chapter I consider each of these differentials, asking how they impact the praxis of mutuality in ways that reflect the heterogeneity and the gradated nature of exclusion. Furthermore, I consider how agency might be practiced within such gradations and how the struggle for relating does not always assume an altogether respectful dialogical exchange. That is, while the agency of the doubly othered female might be celebrated in these biblical texts, the space between does not emerge as one that offers a panacea to the social ills of relating between both sexes and ethnicities. Rather, the marginal agency of females, taking place in a space of conflict and struggle, responds to hegemonic discourse utilizing postcolonial praxes that are supplementary to and mimetic of gradations of power.

5.1. MARK 5:21–43

21 When Jesus had crossed again in the boat to the other side, a great crowd gathered around him; and he was by the sea. 22 Then one of the leaders of the synagogue named Jairus came and, when he saw him, fell at his feet 23 and begged him repeatedly, "My little daughter is at the point of death. Come and lay your hands on her, so that she may be made well, and live." 24 So he went with him.

And a large crowd followed him and pressed in on him. 25 Now there was a woman who had been suffering from hemorrhages for twelve years. 26 She had endured much under many physicians, and had spent all that she had; and she was no better, but rather grew worse. 27 She had heard about Jesus, and came up behind him in the crowd and touched his cloak, 28 for she said, "If I but touch his clothes, I will be made well." 29 Immediately her hemorrhage stopped; and she felt in her body that she was healed of her disease. 30 Immediately aware that power had gone forth from him, Jesus turned about in the crowd and said, "Who touched my clothes?" 31 And his disciples said to him, "You see the crowd pressing in on you; how can you say, 'Who touched me?'" 32 He looked all around to see who had done it. 33 But the woman, knowing what had happened to her, came in fear and trembling, fell down before him, and told him the whole truth. 34 He said to her, "Daughter, your faith has made you well; go in peace, and be healed of your disease."

35 While he was still speaking, some people came from the leader's house to say, "Your daughter is dead. Why trouble the teacher further?" 36 But overhearing what they said, Jesus said to the leader of the synagogue, "Do not fear, only believe." 37 He allowed no one to follow him except Peter, James, and John, the brother of James. 38 When they came to the house of the leader of the synagogue, he saw a commotion, people weeping and wailing loudly. 39 When he had entered, he said to them, "Why do you make a commotion and weep? The child is not dead but sleeping." 40 And they laughed at him. Then he put them all outside, and took the child's father and mother and those who were with him, and went in where the child was. 41 He took her by the hand and said to her, "Talitha cum," which means, "Little girl, get up!" 42 And immediately the girl got up and began to walk about (she was twelve years of age). At this they were overcome with amazement. 43 He strictly ordered them that no one should know this, and told them to give her something to eat.

5.1.1. Introduction: Agency and Power

Mark 5:21–43 is often interpreted as a teaching about the significance of faith in an encounter with Jesus. As an example of a Markan sandwich or intercalation,[1] the pericope is often read such that the roles of Jairus and the woman with hemorrhages are understood to exemplify the centrality of faith for a life of discipleship. Other scholars argue against the grain of this interpretive trend. Particularly, feminist rereadings of 5:21–43 empha-

---

1. The fitting of one story into another is one of the most characteristic compositional features of Mark (3:20–35; 5:21–43; 6:7–32; 11:12–26; 14:1–11, 10–25, 54–72). See Marshall 1989, 91.

size how the female, both within the text and in the interpretation of the text, is diminished, with attention given to the significance of bleeding, corpses, and cleanliness.² I argue below for the significance of social and economic power in this pericope in as far as it relates to the bargaining capabilities of the different characters in the story. In this regard I will focus specifically on the contrasts within the relational dynamics between Jairus, one of the leaders of the synagogue (5:22), and a woman who has spent all that she has (5:26).

My central interest is to see how relational dynamics are negotiated by the different characters in the pericope, paying attention to the varying gradations of power the pericope narrates. Specifically, via the interpretations offered by group readers who emphasized the power differentials between males and females in the text, both in terms of internal struggles and external actions, I contend that the agency exercised in this pericope demonstrates the supplemental nature of resistive and transformative praxes necessitated by the gradation of power. This pericope paints a picture of relational dynamics being struggled over in which the possibility of the praxis of mutuality is already lesser for some characters than for others: relational "space" may be shared in this pericope, but it is not done so on a level playing field.

5.1.2. Beyond Modeling Faith: Gender and Power—Scholars' Perspectives

In the interpretation of 5:21–43, a number of scholars give the theme of faith center stage. Many maintain that faith is the hermeneutical key to unlocking the door to the meaning of the pericope, and even of the Gospel as a whole (e.g., Marshall 1989, 90–109), with some even indicating their preference in the title of their work (e.g., Beavis 1988, 3). Whether made explicit or implicit, the agency of the so-called minor characters in the text is most often defined and measured in terms of their faith in Jesus.³

Some maintain that faith in the Gospel as a whole operates as the conduit for all of the miracles in Mark.⁴ In this particular pericope, some

---

2. Haber 2003; Selvidge 1990, 47–70, 83–91; Swidler 1971; Barta 1991; D'Angelo 1999, 83–85.
3. Marshall 1989, 93, 95, 100, 108; Beavis 1988, 3, 6; Gundry 1993, 272; Juel 1999, 115; van Iersel 1998, 204; Tolbert 1989, 169–71; Cotter 2001, 76; Williamson 1983, 110.
4. "Faith, then, is the prerequisite of healing for the Gospel of Mark, not its result.

scholars emphasize that faith operates in dramatic tension with fear.[5] That is, faith is demanded of each of the characters involved in the story even in the face of considerable fear for their own and for others' lives.[6] This theme of faith and fear is associated with the character of Jesus in such a way that subordinates other characters' agencies to the authority and power of Jesus. Leopold Sabourin states that others need have no fear of storms or death but only need faith in Jesus (1975, 151). In other words, the supreme agency of Jesus removes the need for other actors in the text to exercise judgments eliciting fear. The only response left for those who encounter Jesus is that of faith, such that in 5:21–43 minor characters are read as submitting to Jesus' shaping of the narrative, none more profoundly submissive than the dying/sleeping girl. They have stood as ciphers for the characters whom Jesus condescends to help (as in the case of Jairus) or to touch (as in the case of the girl) or to be touched by (in the case of the woman with hemorrhages).

However, the exercise of faith demonstrated by characters in this pericope does not necessarily take place on a level playing field. One of the most prominent contrasts in this regard is between and within genders.[7] Mark 5:21–43 is a story about two men—Jesus and Jairus—both of whom might be read to possess a certain amount of power within the narrative. On one hand, there is Jairus, a man of religious authority and, one might presume, power within his community; on the other hand, there is Jesus, a man whose authority and power is at such a level that Jairus is willing to fall at his feet (5:22) and beg him repeatedly to save his daughter's life (5:23). Similarly, for the females in 5:21–43 there are also significant contrasts. One female is twelve years old (5:42); the other has suffered with hemorrhages for over twelve years (5:25). Jesus goes to one (5:24), while

---

… The miracles in Mark are not intended as signs to induce belief; they are, instead, the visible, tangible fruits of faith" (Tolbert 1989, 159).

5. Keenan 1995, 145. See also Beck, who argues that faith as confidence in God replaces confidence in the usual "realistic" answer to fear, namely courageous strength (1996, 79).

6. Shalini Mulackal (2010) draws the comparison between faith and the fearfulness in Mark 5:21–34 and of Dalit women in India, where both sets of women are affirmed by Jesus though despised by society.

7. Rodney Bomford argues that the contrasts in this regard contained in this pericopae offer a "symmetric logic" such that the author of Mark's Gospel can be seen to utilize a "calculated rhetoric" that enables the union of seeming opposites (2010, 46).

the other has to go to him (5:28). One is represented by someone presumably well known in the area (5:22); the other is represented by no one. One is silent; the other tells "the whole truth" (5:33). One arouses the manic interest of the crowd (5:38); the other interrupts it (5:37).

However, the importance of gender in this story is significant beyond these literary contrasts. This is true not only of the text itself but also of the interpretation of the text. Mark 5:21–43 is often read as reflecting on the question of religious power and specifically the question of purity. Typically, these themes are emphasized in ways that contrast the agency of males and females in the text. It is a widespread assumption that both of the females in question, in different ways, should be considered unclean. For Jairus's daughter, such a state of uncleanness is physically manifest in her dying state (5:42). A dead body would have been considered unclean, asserts Susan Haber, citing Num 19:11–21, wherein anyone who touches a corpse or enters a dwelling in which there is a dead body is rendered impure for seven days, during which their impurity may be transmitted to others.[8]

Ironically, as far as the girl's dramatic role in the narrative is concerned, her sickness and impurity in death do not limit her agency. Rather, her nonrole does—her condition renders her powerless of judgment and agency in the text. Both of those roles go to her father, Jairus. When her death renders her utterly obsolete, it is her father's faith that must make her well. This sort of nonrole is not, though, the case for the woman with hemorrhages, whose designation as unclean interpreters emphasize to have drastic consequences for her potential as an active agent in the narrative. Her bleeding in and of itself is taken for a hegemonic mark of exclusion. Some argue this on grounds that her bleeding makes her ceremonially unclean (Marshall 1989, 104; Kinukawa 1994, 35) and so ineligible for public worship (Dowd 2000, 56; Kinukawa 1994, 35). Those scholars who interpret the bleeding to be vaginal in nature interpret its significance in multiple ways, from mysterious to polluting (Dowd 2000, 57).

The significance of this designation of impurity for the woman's role as a potentially active agent in the community is interpreted in a number of different ways. For instance, the ritual uncleanness of the woman is often

---

8. See Haber 2003, 187, citing attestation that these purity laws were "widely observed in the Second Temple period" in Philo (*Spec.* 3.205–209), Josephus (*Ant.* 4.81), the Dead Sea Scrolls (11Q19 49.16–17; 50.10–14; 1QM 14.2–3), and rabbinic texts (t. Parah 3.14; 10.2; 5.6; 7.4).

extended as a factor that excludes her socially (van Iersel 1998, 205; Kinukawa 1994, 40). Such an exclusion relies heavily on the sociocultural role of gender as well as the physical fact of bleeding. On one level the woman is considered to be other to Jesus and Jairus, simply because her body is female, not male. In addition, there is a combination of ritual uncleanness and social obscurity that contrasts sharply with the figure of Jairus, who has both an elevated social position and leadership in the synagogue: Jairus, as a socioreligious officeholder, is contrasted to the nameless, "office-less" woman, according to Donald Juel (1999, 115). In addition to being other, the woman is interpreted as having no class or authority and as one, unlike Jairus, who is not entitled to speak (Kinukawa 1994, 34).

Some assert that the woman's bleeding leads not only to social exclusion but to theological exclusion as well. For instance, Hisako Kinukawa (1994, 35–36) contends from an intertextual viewpoint (Lev 12, 15, and 20) that menstrual bleeding was considered sinful, and resulted in seclusion and in "the ultimate humiliation" of the sin offering required after both menstruation and childbirth (Lev 15:29–30; 12:6–8).[9] J. Duncan M. Derrett takes the debate a step further, arguing for a deeper significance for blood in the text, both for the woman with hemorrhages and for the girl. He maintains that within a Hebrew Bible framework the blood of

---

9. However, it is not clear that these widespread interpretations of the nature of the impurity and consequent sociocultural and even theological exclusion of the woman with hemorrhages can be supported by the text and its presumed context. First, some have argued that both men and women found themselves in situations of being impure, and so it was not women in particular who were stigmatized (see Horsley 2001, 208). Second, according to Haber there is no suggestion in 5:21–43 that the contact Jesus has with the woman with hemorrhages led to his "contamination." She has pointed out that there are two potential sources for the Second Temple period's understandings of purity. Arguing that the woman in Mark 5:24–34 is an example of a זבה (a female with an abnormal genital discharge) as opposed to a woman with normal menstrual bleeding, Haber cites two possible sources for how such a ritually impure person might be dealt with. One is Lev 15:11, which states that via the rinsing of hands a זבה could make herself no longer contagious by touch. With such room to maneuver, a זבה might reasonably be assumed to have been able to lead a relatively normal life over the course of the condition. Indeed, as Haber notes, the scribes and Pharisees of Mark, usually guardians of the purity codes, are nowhere to be seen in this scene, and so this omission places the pericope in sharp relief to other such pericopae concerned with purity (2:13–22; 7:1–23). However, such leniency is contrary to the alternative source in Num 5:1–4, which outlines the complete exclusion of such a person from the Israelite camp. See Haber 2003, 189.

these females is an allusion to the blood of Israel in Ezek 16:9. The significance of these females' blood, then, is not for their own status as subjects of agency in the text, but as ciphers of Jesus' supremacy over the temple, for which, Derrett asserts (1985a, 106), Jesus is the "total substitute" by means of expiation (Rom 3:25). Derrett's reading, which heavily relies on the assumption that Mark's theological interpretation of the significance of Jesus is to be found in his use of allusions to the Hebrew Scriptures, takes the utility of the females as ciphers in the text to another level. He asserts that they stand not as characters with potential for agency in the text, but as two characters forming a composite, each sharing central characteristics as a "daughter of Jerusalem." Their faith and salvation is taken as paradigmatic for salvation to come to Israel through Jesus (107).[10]

Such acts of interpretation in the reading of females in the pericope not only reduce their potential for agency via the designation of impurity; they also relegate the role of females to that of theological conduits for Jesus' identity and mission. In this vein it is interesting that some interpretations assign the significance of the consequences of the woman's uncleanness not as much to her but to Jesus. For instance, Sharyn Dowd interprets the significance of the woman's uncleanness, and indeed the uncleanness of the girl, once dead, as evidence that Jesus crosses boundaries: the boundaries of Jew-Gentile in 5:1–20, and the boundaries of clean-unclean in 5:21–43 (2000, 56). Vernon Robbins goes as far as to say that Jesus "controls the feelings and thoughts of the woman," controlling and interpreting her knowledge, feelings, and action (1994, 196).

Similar concentrations on the role of Jesus, and the subsequent relegation of the role of females, can be found in the work of scholars who suggest that the significance of the pericope is not in the acts of healing themselves but in the proclamation they point to. For instance, Morna Hooker argues that in the narrative Jesus does not want the woman with hemorrhages to go away thinking him to be a "magician-healer," nor does he want the family of the girl to "babble about his ability to raise the dead." Instead, Hooker claims that Jesus wants the focus to be on the "proclamation of God's Kingdom" (1991, 151). In relation to Jairus's daughter,

---

10. Similarly, Ched Myers et al. argue that within the "family" of Israel, these "daughters" represent the privileged and the impoverished, respectively, and because of such inequality the body politic of the synagogue is on the "verge of death" (1996, 66). For Herman Waetjen (1989, 122), Jesus is the "New Human Being" who saves the woman with hemorrhages (as representative of "tradition-bound mother Judaism").

Mary Ann Beavis (2010, 59–61) sees the theological significance of Jesus' action as establishing his "God-given power to bring life out of death," thus reworking the story of Jephthah (Judg 11:34–40), who sacrifices his daughter. Thus the significance of the agency of the females in the pericope is not only subordinated in these interpretations of the text to the presumed necessity of Jesus' agency to be dominant in the encounter of healing; the very episodes themselves are subordinated to an assumed wider theological significance.

It is clear, then, from assessing the various interpretations of female agency in this text, that the issues of ritual purity and even guilt have led to a radically diminished view of that agency. Given this, I would like to consider again the relational dynamics narrated in 5:21–43 and explore how group readers' emphases in interpreting this text highlight the negotiation of healing in light of other markers of agency beyond purity.

5.1.3. Gendered Alterity: Agency on an Unlevel Playing Field—Group Readers' Perspectives

Much like scholars who attempt to frame the Markan intercalation narrated in 5:21–43 around responses made to Jesus, group readers to a large extent read this pericope as a story about faith.[11] Also, scholars differentiate between the agency of the characters in this story along gender lines, as do group readers. However, while much scholarship focuses on issues of ritual purity and religious-cultural exclusion, that is, on external features that characterize females as distinct from males and impose a postulated

---

11. C: "He's a believer. He doesn't say, 'Do something,' he says, 'Lay on your hands.' He believes Jesus can do it." ... D: "I see her just going forward. Her faith overcoming everything. Jesus already knows. Her faith is beyond that obstacle, somehow she is going to get there and she does. She's not thinking, 'Am I able?'" B: "She's on a mission" (from Reading Group Four, April 25, 2006). "He knew that she was somebody's daughter. By her faith she became Jesus', God's daughter" (D from Reading Group One, April 18, 2006). D: "I don't know, she was a little bit overwhelmed with everything. Jesus felt her faith, he felt everything about her. Her faith was too much for her to think she was doing something wrong. She knew that he was the Messiah." A: "She knew it was God." D: "Yeah, exactly. Her faith told her what this person is going to say. Not wrong, not in fear because she knows she is touching God." ... B: "Jesus said, 'Your faith has made you well.'" C: "She doesn't know it's her faith that's healed her. She has faith but at the moment she is not thinking about anything: 'I've just gotta touch him'" (from Reading Group Four, April 25, 2006).

external religious-cultural paradigm on the story, a significant pattern that emerged from group readers' interpretations was that gendered agency was delineated via a contrast between external and internal parameters.

One way this difference can be illustrated is by comparing group readers' interpretations of Jairus and the interpretations of the woman with hemorrhages. One of the most consistent features of the reading groups' interpretations was an accentuation of the overwhelming presence of emotional distress in the woman's life as it intersects with the story narrated in 5:21–43. While one reader saw little difference between Jairus and the woman in this regard,[12] many others perceived the woman to be distinguished by fear and doubt. For instance, one exchange between group readers incorporated feelings of doubt, attraction, being impressed, and fear as they imagined how the woman felt as she came before Jesus in 5:33–34.[13] Other readers associated the woman's struggle with physicians' care, with their own desires to "get help":

> Facilitator: Do you know how she feels to have endured much at the hands of doctors?
> B: Like the blind leading the blind. Dark doctors don't see the light.
> D: Scary, frustrating. It hurts, it's hateful.
> B: For every antagonism, there is an equal antagonism.
> C: I'd be afraid of not getting the help I needed, of not getting better again.
> A: A little hopeful that I'd heal.
> E: She gave up.[14]

Similarly, another reader associated the experience "of not getting the help you need" with anger, sorrow, and despair.[15] Beyond associations around the theme of needing to get help from others, some group read-

---

12. "She was helpless and hopeless at this point, and sure I would be hoping for something to happen so she could stop bleeding. She was desperate for a cure, like Jairus" (D from Reading Group One, April 18, 2006).

13. C: "Maybe she thought it wasn't Jesus. She had to tell him the whole truth who did that. Maybe she had doubts. Looks like she had doubts." B: "Don't forget our Lord had a magnificent presence. People were attracted to him and his charisma." A: "I think that the woman is so impressed by him and so afraid and now healed she feels a lot different—standing in the presence of the God who healed her" (from Reading Group One, April 18, 2006).

14. From Reading Group One, April 18, 2006.

15. "You get angry, pissed off, disgusted, every time you try you end up with a

ers perceived the woman's struggle in increasingly desperate terms. One reader saw her as one struggling with herself, even imagining her to crawl on the ground to touch Jesus.[16] Similarly, another reader emphasized her desperation in having tried "everything she could" and still not being able to "keep her stasis."[17]

The pattern that emerges here is a marked deviation from typical views of some scholars, which tend to concentrate on the external religious-cultural frames of reference regarding the state of the woman and on postulated purity codes. By contrast, group readers' interpretations viewed the woman's agency as punctuated by an overwhelming internal emotional state that, to an extent, governs her internal world. She was viewed, then, through this lens as one who has internalized her physical status on a psychological level, thus reducing her agency to the acts of a desperate woman who has no other options left but to silently stretch out to touch Jesus.

Some group readers' interpretations moved beyond this emphasis on the woman's internal emotional distress and suggested, if rather idiosyncratically, that she might be in some way responsible for her condition:

> B: She led a disordered life. She became straggly and bitchy.
> C: It's not her fault. I don't think she is to blame.
> B: Imperfection is disease. When does the world begin to die?
> C: No one's perfect.[18]

It is worth noting here that this association of the woman's afflicted state with her own culpability for that state was not read universally across

---

problem. You have no hope anymore. Sorrow and tears and despair" (B from Reading Group One, April 18, 2006).

16. "She knew she had to struggle with herself. Had to crawl on the ground to get to that cloth and when she touched, she knew" (D from Reading Group Four, April 25, 2006). It should be noted that while it is not an unreasonable assumption that the woman may have crawled on the ground to reach Jesus, the text itself may not support such a view in its explicit description of the woman falling before Jesus to tell him the "whole truth" a few verses later (5:33).

17. "Desperate. She knows she's tried everything she could. Maybe not just one, not just local, and at that time there probably weren't more than one doctor in a town. She had sought help from other places. Spent all she had. She had a lot of money to do that but now she has no money left, and there's no recovery for herself and plus, she is getting worse. She couldn't even keep her stasis" (D from Reading Group Four, April 25, 2006).

18. From Reading Group Two, April 18, 2006.

reading groups, but was often made by male readers in particular. For instance, if one compares the interpretations of group reader B in this exchange to the interpretations of A, while the latter (a female reader) seemed to wish in some way to exonerate the woman, the former (a male reader) sought to implicate her. A similar pattern of differential perceptions of the woman can be seen in other reading groups. For instance, an interpretation of the woman that associated her condition with guilt and fear was made by a male reader.[19] Similarly, one male reader took this perception of the woman even further, arguing that she was "a bit of a devil," unable to say that she was "a good woman" or to "show herself as a true person."[20]

This pattern of interpretation is quite different from the interpretations group readers offered of Jairus, who in contrast to the woman was characterized by markers external to his person. For instance, he is portrayed as one who ignored his power[21] and overcame his pride,[22] both facets secured by his externally derived status as a cultural-religious leader. Furthermore, while he was read to have shocked the crowds by begging

---

19. "She felt guilty. Knowing what had happened, she was afraid. Maybe she felt guilty because she stood out there—not good enough for Jesus to come to her. Afraid Jesus thought she was sneaky or something" (C from Reading Group Four, April 25, 2006).

20. "He's powerful and beautiful—his manifestation. She's afraid. She's only a woman and does not have any ability to say she was a good woman, a happy woman. Unable to be working, unable to get rid of the malady which scorned her—a bit of a devil. Unable to show herself as a true person" (B from Reading Group Two, April 18, 2006). The etiology of this gendered differential among group readers is difficult to ascertain. It could be that some female readers offered more sympathetic interpretations of the woman because she is the female other in the story. Indeed, beyond this simple association of gender, there might be a deeper association between the woman's peculiar struggle with male power in the guise of leaders like Jairus and doctors who offered no help to her in the end, and female readers' experiences with the same sort of societal and medical/professional power.

21. "Emotional to start with. He ignored his power. His emotions had gone beyond his position in life. He was just a human being and caring about his daughter" (A from Reading Group Four, April 25, 2006).

22. "Well, along his ministry there were great crowds, many miracles. Jairus was overcoming his pride, he was desperate for his daughter" (B from Reading Group One, April 18, 2006).

Jesus to heal his daughter,[23] Jairus was also interpreted to have impressed the crowd with his public show of obsequiousness.[24]

This differentiation between genders is even more pronounced when one considers the group readers' interpretations of the agency of Jesus. If the woman and Jairus are delineated in terms of her internal state and his external status, then Jesus is more akin to the woman in this regard. The significant difference in interpretations of the two, though, is that while the woman was interpreted to be "afraid" and "unable," Jesus by comparison was seen to be "powerful and beautiful."[25] His agency is interpreted by group readers as intrinsically superlative to that of the other characters around him. For instance, Jesus is presented in the story by multiple group readers as the one who can do what doctors cannot,[26] as the one having command over women and men,[27] and as the master to his students.[28] Furthermore, this intrinsically superlative agency is even taken to extend to his exterior and to his "magical" clothes: "She feels his clothes are magical, representative of him, because at that time if a boy was missing they'd grab his clothes and remember. They think clothes have some living part of him. That is miraculous."[29]

However, this gendered power differential along internal and external lines is not all that is suggested by group readers' interpretations. When asked what part the characters played in their own healing in the story, one group reader stated: "A major role: they heal themselves. It's just the way

---

23. "Shock. The fact that he begged. Mixed feelings I guess" (D from Reading Group One, April 18, 2006).

24. "I think the crowd were amazed, one of the most prominent members. It's very impressive to the crowds" (B from Reading Group One, April 18, 2006).

25. See n. 20 above.

26. "That's right, Jesus can do this, doctors can't" (B from Reading Group One, April 18, 2006).

27. "He is responsible for a lot of people. He has a large following himself. By making her better, Jesus would pass the word along. He did not want to convince this guy, but to show God's love to Jairus and Jairus will show that to his congregation. What better than the leader of the community? Jairus didn't pick Jesus out. Jesus picked out Jairus" (A from Reading Group Four, April 25, 2006).

28. "No. It goes from black to blue, yellow, white. Always travel through what it means. That is why it is always a master and a student. That is what this is" (B from Reading Group Two, April 18, 2006).

29. B from Reading Group Two, April 18, 2006.

it happens, you have to do certain things."[30] Another reader emphasized the importance of "taking care of the situation you are in" and practicing "self-healing."[31] The question arises, what sort of things did group readers imagine the characters in this pericope were doing to take care of their situations and bring about their healing?

As one reader put it, getting healed depends a lot on how you are trying.[32] It is here that the exercise of an agency beyond the seeming constraints of gendered power differentials is suggested. For the woman, her approach to Jesus, as surreptitious as it was, was seen to exercise an agency quite different from male agency in the pericope. As two of the group readers put it: "the fact that she touched his clothes, she gets herself saved";[33] moreover, "the crowd think she's ripped off this situation. She takes something from him. He was going to see someone else."[34]

What, though, does the woman "take" from Jesus? One reader suggested that the woman touches Jesus' divinity and so in some sense takes it from him:

> She knew she had to struggle with herself. Had to crawl on the ground to get to that cloth, and when she touched, she knew.[35]

> I think the crowd thinks she is insignificant. They couldn't feel what Jesus feels. There was something more to that touching. The crowd was indifferent to this woman, still Jesus turns around. ... She touched him in a certain way—in a way that through him she was healed, through his power. ... Like the armor of God. Someone touched his divinity and it went out from him.[36]

---

30. B from Reading Group Two, April 18, 2006.

31. "An important role. Not sure if it is small or large. I hope it would be large. You have to take care of the situation you are in. There was not much knowledge about medication, so there was a lot of self-healing" (D from Reading Group Two, April 18, 2006).

32. 'Yeah, there was a point in my life, two years ago, a situation in my life. I tried everything. My expectations were unrealistic, because I wasn't looking for God. I tried to do it my way, but to no avail. When weakness came, I gave in straightaway. I had played both roles: a father and a very active drug addict. It depends on how you are trying. She tried all those physicians" (C from Reading Group Four, April 25, 2006).

33. C from Reading Group Two, April 18, 2006.

34. B from Reading Group Two, April 18, 2006.

35. D from Reading Group Two, April 18, 2006.

36. D from Reading Group Four, April 25 2006.

I will explore this possibility of the woman taking healing from Jesus more below. It will suffice here to compare this notion of the woman's surreptitious agency to that of Jairus. For Jairus, agency was read to have been exercised in quite a different way. While some readers saw Jairus to be in a desperate state due to the condition of his daughter,[37] he still is seen as one who exercises agency publicly and openly, "amazing" the crowd.[38] Similarly, seen to operate in open and in public, Jairus was interpreted by another reader to be effectively challenging Jesus in a show of power, suggesting that perhaps Jesus heals Jairus "of the fact that it is not good to play double games on whether or not the kind of power you have," going on to point out that while Jesus "doesn't need to play games with anybody," he does want "everything to be foolproof, and the greater the trial, the stupider the man."[39] While offering a rather idiosyncratic interpretation of Jairus's act of negotiating in the pericope, this reader does concur with the general point about Jairus's agency in the text, that his action is open and public.

In the section below, I explore how this emphasis on a gendered differentiation of agency—between external and internal markers of character and agency, and between publicly and privately exercised agency—might have implications for how healing is negotiated in this story. Particularly, I wish to explore how, even with the radically subaltern status the woman with hemorrhages is interpreted by group readers to have, in 5:21–43 she does exercise agency. In doing so, I hope to ask again how agency in this text, which has predominantly been read within a paradigm of purity, power, and exclusion, might be read, despite its liminal nature, as unrelentingly resistive and participatory.

---

37. "He was desperate, fearful because of his daughter" (D from Reading Group Two, April 18, 2006).

38. "I think the crowd were amazed, one of the most prominent members. It's very impressive to the crowds" (B from Reading Group One, April 18, 2006).

39. "I think Christ is an unassuming man. He doesn't need to play games with anybody. He is the all-powerful God. 'I have come here to teach you to love.' He's concerned about the man's little girl. He's concerned about the man's concern. He wants everything to be foolproof, and the greater the trial, the stupider the man" (B from Reading Group Two, April 18, 2006).

5.1.4. From Exclusion to Participation: Subaltern Agent, Liminal Agency

In this final section on 5:21–43 I wish to take up the strands of the emphases present in group readers' interpretations about the differential agencies acted out in the relational dynamics of this story. There was a shared perception across reading groups that the woman with hemorrhages could be characterized as overwhelmed by significant emotions, including doubt and fear,[40] anger, sorrow, and despair.[41] She was seen as a character who "struggled" with herself (see n. 16), doing "everything she could," and still not being able to "keep her stasis" (see n. 17). Contrasts were drawn between this perception of the woman's internal struggle diminishing her status, the externally mediated status of Jairus as one who ignored his power (see n. 21) and overcame his pride (see n. 22) to get healing for his daughter, and Jesus' intrinsic status as "powerful and beautiful" (see n. 20). The strong delineation above argues for a differentiation of power along gendered lines. This differentiation was argued by group readers to impact how agency is exercised within such a stratified relational dynamic. This was seen with regard to the public versus private nature of the negotiation of healing that was interpreted to take place in the pericope.

Looking at the text again, one can clearly see a parallel process at work in the story between the actions of Jairus and those of the woman. The woman comes to Jesus surreptitiously, privatized in a very public scene, by being camouflaged by the pressing crowd (5:24b, 31). She is then brought out into the open by Jesus' demand to know who had touched him (5:30), by her own response in coming forward, and by telling the truth (5:33). Indeed, her falling at Jesus' feet is read by Myers and colleagues (1996, 65) to suggest that she now has attained equal status to Jairus, who himself began his encounter with Jesus by falling at his feet (5:22).[42] Following

---

40. C: "Maybe she thought it wasn't Jesus. She had to tell him the whole truth who did that. Maybe she had doubts. Looks like she had doubts." B: "Don't forget our Lord had a magnificent presence. People were attracted to him and his charisma." A: "I think that the woman is so impressed by him and so afraid, and now healed she feels a lot different—standing in the presence of the God who healed her" (from Reading Group One, April 18, 2006).

41. "You get angry, pissed off, disgusted, every time you try you end up with a problem. You have no hope anymore. Sorrow and tears and despair" (B from Reading Group One, April 18, 2006).

42. Beyond this, Myers et al. contend that Jesus' exhortation to Jairus to believe

this movement from private to public, Jesus then publicly calls the woman "daughter," and he states that her faith brought about healing (5:34).[43]

In contrast, Jairus begins to negotiate the healing of his daughter in public, begging Jesus repeatedly to come and lay hands on her (5:23). As the narrative progresses, public attention to his concerns diminishes. The synagogue leader's public obeisance toward Jesus is followed by his hopes for his daughter's healing being stalled by an unnamed and previously hidden woman. People then come from his house to urge Jairus not to bother Jesus further (5:35). Jairus is led home by Jesus, past the people weeping and wailing loudly at the house (5:38),[44] and into a small, unseen gathering of three disciples of Jesus and Jairus's immediate family and companions. It is here, in private, that Jesus strictly orders those gathered that "no one should know this" (5:43).

What, then, is to be made of this public/private reversal between Jairus and the woman? One way to view this delineation is to explore the disparity of economic power it represents. For instance, Christopher Marshall (1989, 94–95) holds that Jairus's greater wealth relative to the woman might be presumed by the fact that he has a many-roomed house (5:38–40) and has sufficient means to attract a number of mourners to the scene (5:38). By contrast, it is clear from the detailed description of the text that the woman's economic status has been radically undermined by her previous attempts to find healing, spending all that she has, getting no better, and indeed only growing worse (5:26).[45]

From the standpoint of the relational dynamics of the story, this emphasis on two levels of agency—public and private—begs the question of whether conventional views of agency in the text might have obviated the potential for agency for these characters. That is, it is an assumption of the scholarship sampled earlier that the woman is effectively excluded

---

and not to be afraid (5:36) suggests that Jairus should learn about faith from the previously outcast woman (1996, 66).

43. Some think that Jesus' public designation of the woman as "daughter" is intended to free her from fear and reintegrate her into the life of the community. See Williamson 1983, 110.

44. The significance of disallowing the crowd from being with Jesus when he raises the girl is sometimes taken to reflect the "messianic secret" or the crowd's unbelief. See Brooks 1991, 94.

45. Waetjen argues that this level of description of the woman's poor socioeconomic status reveals the narrator's own "lower-class bias" with the "bitter indictment" that she had spent all that she had, "all for nothing" (1989, 120).

from practicing agency in her context, due to her impurity, or her poverty, or as some group readers perceived it, due to an intrinsic and internal lack on her part. Thus her liminal agency, her reaching out to Jesus, is not a display of an agency commonly in operation by the woman, but rather is the last attempt at survival of a desperate person.

However, the second strand that group readers suggested in terms of the agency of the characters in the pericope was that while healing power might have been openly negotiated by Jairus, the woman may have done something more akin to taking power from Jesus. Relating this emphasis to scholars' perspectives on this point reveals diverging views of the agency of the woman. For instance, Marshall argues that if 5:29 ("Immediately her hemorrhage stopped; and she felt in her body that she was healed of her disease") were to be read in isolation, then it could be implied that an autonomous transference of "healing mana" took place, since "power is appropriated by the woman without Jesus consciously imparting it" (1989, 106). However, as soon as this possibility is raised, it is quashed by the imposition of the theological panacea of the "wider context," which according to Marshall (106) shows that power is not automatically released but is "under the governance of God, determined to limit it to the arena of repentant faith (1:15)."

Other scholars decide not to rule out so quickly the possibility of Jesus' not knowing who had "taken power" and instead posit that power is "free-flowing" and "spontaneous" in the scene (Keenan 1995, 147). Candida Moss asserts that the flowing of power from Jesus reveals him as "weak and sickly … unable to control, regulate, or harden his own emissions" (2010, 516). Moreover, some scholars not only argue for a strong role for the woman, but go on to say that, in contrast to her, Jesus is "utterly passive," with the initiative, action, and confirmation all in her hands.[46] For example, according to Richard Horsley, in the end Jesus "simply confirms what she already knows: that it is her own faith that has made her well." It is the woman with hemorrhages whose "'courageous work' is solely responsible for the healing in this episode. … Restorative, healing power becomes operative in this episode by the initiative and aggressive action of one perceived as weak who reveals the divine way of power."[47]

---

46. Horsley 2001, 209. Moss makes a similar point, arguing that it is the "sickly woman who exerts control over the body of the physician savior … able to pull divine power out of the passive, leaking Jesus" (2010, 516).

47. Horsley 2001, 210–11, referring to Brock 1988, 84, 87.

Similarly, feminist rereadings of 5:21–43 hold that the woman's reaching out to Jesus enlivens a relationship that had previously been dormant or bound by the societal double debilitation of sickness and womanhood. Hisako Kinukawa contends that in the reciprocity of the relational encounter between the woman and Jesus they both subvert the myth of contamination and break down the barrier between clean and unclean (1994, 44). Or, as Carter Heyward asserts regarding this pericope, it is because of the woman's confidence in the potential mutuality shared between herself and Jesus that she initiates an acknowledgment of that relation as δύναμις (καὶ εὐθὺς ὁ Ἰησοῦς ἐπιγνοὺς ἐν ἑαυτῷ τὴν ἐξ αὐτοῦ δύναμιν ἐξελθοῦσαν, "Immediately aware that power had gone forth from him," 5:30), as power in relation between persons (1982, 45).

Taking up these scholarly and group reader emphases, one can argue that the woman's decision to approach Jesus, not openly but surreptitiously, needs to be interpreted not only as the reactive urge for survival of a desperate woman but also as an intentional and strategic praxis of agency. The question that remains here is how agency is exercised by the woman as the strategic element of the encounter is considered.

On one hand, the strategically surreptitious approach of the woman might be seen to be agency exercised under the guise of hegemonic structures of power ordered by the rules of formation of gender discourse. With these structures of hegemonic power in mind, the agency of the woman in reaching out to Jesus inhabits a strategic edge in as much as it points to a possible recognition by the woman of the thinness of the relational space within which she knows she has to operate. This thinness can be seen through the lens of the praxis of mutuality. For with gradations of gendered and socioeconomic power an open space for the negotiation of a healing from Jesus is not a viable option for the woman. In this sense, the woman's actions betray the lack of the praxis of mutuality between a woman in her situation—sick, impoverished, and female—and the charismatic rabbi who is soon to pass her by. Unlike Jairus, whose social capital affords him the opportunity to openly negotiate a healing for his daughter, the woman with hemorrhages has no such standing.

I contend, then, that the agency of this woman as narrated in 5:21–43 cannot truly be described as a praxis of mutuality. Contrary to Heyward's interpretation of this pericope, I assert that the woman's actions are not an indication of her confidence in the presence of mutuality as power in relation; rather they are an indication that she is certain that mutuality does not exist between herself and Jesus. Thus the agency of the woman in approaching Jesus is not truly an exercise of agency that seeks to reimagine hegemonic relational dynamics. Her approach of Jesus is, in the end, the best chance for healing that this woman opts for in the knowledge that mutuality in this encounter is apparently a lost cause. Healing occurs for the woman while the relational dynamics between Jesus and her remain unaltered. It is only subsequent to the healing, and Jesus' knowledge of power having left him (5:30), that the relational dynamics between them are addressed.

On one hand, asserting that the woman's agency in 5:21–43 is not an exercise of the praxis of mutuality may seem to contradict the definition of mutuality presented in chapter 2: the agency that seeks to renegotiate diminished views of identity and power thereby staking a claim for the voices of othered persons in hegemonic relational dynamics. However, while the woman does act, her actions do not appear in the text to indicate any intent on her part to enter into such a renegotiation. Indeed, her concern, explicit in 5:28 ("If I but touch his clothes, I will be made well") is only that she be healed.

On the other hand, it may be that this apparent lack of intent to renegotiate is misleading. The group readers emphasized not only the imagined liminal societal location of this woman but also her desperate internal state. From their perspectives, she very well might desire social reintegration. Whether the woman in this story is read to seek this reintegration and thus practice mutuality, or whether her concerns are purely for physical healing, in Jesus' response to her agency in 5:29–34 I would contend that he does exercise a praxis of mutuality in his dialogical engagement with her. How far, then, might Jesus' praxis of mutuality extend? While I have argued that the woman may be seen initially not to seek to renegotiate the relational dynamic she shares with Jesus, once her hiddenness is exposed, she does choose to tell him "the whole truth" (5:33). In return, Jesus calls her "daughter" (5:34). Does this then speak of a transformation of the relational dynamics between male and female through this encounter?

There may be reason to pause at this interpreted picture of reciprocity and note that the woman who tells the whole truth to Jesus does so in "fear and trembling" (5:33). Indeed, Tat-siong Benny Liew maintains that the significance of being named "daughter" is less of a celebratory moment for the woman than it seems. He asserts that in naming her thus, Jesus incorporates her into his family and "establishes himself as her spokesman, provider, and protector in a way that Jairus is to his daughter" (1999,

139). Furthermore, Liew interprets Jesus' command for her to "go in peace" (5:34) as corroboration that she is "placed under the direction of a man" (139). The praxis of mutuality in this encounter is thus tempered by the gradations of colonial power within which it operates. Indeed, there is no initial welcome into Jesus' space for the woman, no invitation as such, and following her breaking in and her attempt to "seize the rules" of the gendered discourse that had seen her suffer much at the hands of men who had taken all that she had (5:26), she too is seized with fear and trembling as her liminal agency is uncovered.

What then are we to conclude regarding this pericope and the gradations of gendered power it narrates? The question calls to mind the apprehension of Homi Bhabha over "uplifting" and "tall stories" of progress (Bhabha and Comaroff 2002, 31). That is, there is a danger in seeing the encounter between Jesus and the woman healed of her bleeding narrated in 5:34 as one such "tall story." If there is any transformation of relational dynamics in this pericope, it may occur only corresponding to hegemonic power in what Bhabha calls a "supplemental position" (Bhabha 1995, 82). The relational dynamics of 5:21–43 might thus be viewed as operating in a site not of utopian relating but of struggle that bears the marks of "fear and trembling" (5:33).

That said, Bhabha's description of the "supplemental position" as possessing "often the most significant elements in a process of subversion and transformation" (1995, 82) gives pause for thought. While the end of the exchange between the woman and Jesus in 5:21–43 looks sparse in its possibilities for the transformation of relational dynamics, I conclude that these possibilities should not be overlooked. Indeed, with this work's dialogical reading of the text with persons with poor mental health in mind, and with a particular focus on female readers who may have experienced the assumption of an inability to be fully active agents in relational encounters in their particular experiences of poor mental health, this opening of possibilities, even if supplemental, is significant. Indeed, as the readers of one of the groups emphasized, the personal experience of societal reactions to poor mental health is in the end not something that can be had from the outside:

> C: You have to know. You have to have some idea of what is going on to tell somebody else.
> A: Better than reading it in a book.
> C: To actually explain it, not unless it is happening to them.

5. NEGOTIATING MARGINAL AGENCY

D: Sometimes I wonder if anyone really knows anything anymore.[48]

So too might it be regarding the significance of the supplemental change in the lived experience of hegemonic relational dynamics. Slight alterations might be more significant than they first appear. With this in mind, the second pericope of this pair narrates the role of marginal agency beyond the intimacy of touch and within the invective world of rhetoric. In it, I explore how agency might be exercised in a relational dynamic where the deficit of a praxis of mutuality is not merely assumed—it is declared.

5.2. Mark 7:24–30

24 From there Jesus set out and went away to the region of Tyre. He entered a house and did not want anyone to know he was there. Yet he could not escape notice, 25 but a woman whose daughter had an unclean spirit immediately heard about him, and she came and bowed at his feet. 26 Now the woman was a Gentile, of Syrophoenician origin. She begged him to cast the demon out of her daughter. 27 He said to her, "Let the children be fed first, for it is not fair to take the children's food and throw it to the dogs." 28 But she answered him, "Sir, even the dogs under the table eat the children's crumbs." 29 Then he said to her, "For saying that, you may go—the demon has left your daughter." 30 So she went home, found the child lying on the bed, and the demon gone.

5.2.1. Introduction: Agency and Rhetoric

The encounter of Jesus with a Syrophoenician woman in 7:24–30 looks like an exchange in a relational space thin on the praxis of mutuality. Difference is foregrounded in this pericope as the Jewish man and the Gentile woman strike up an unlikely conversation. Between comments about food and dogs this conversation has all the hallmarks of a colonized relational milieu with the "us, not them" paradigm of hegemonic parlance at the forefront, this time with Jesus in the stead of the colonizer. This emphasis on difference is a consistent feature of group readers' interpretations of this text that focus on the significance of power, faith, ethnicity, and the profound struggle with the self and as well as with

---

48. From Reading Group Two, April 18, 2006.

others that this sort of encounter can lead to. Building on these insights, I argue that the strategic element of postcolonial resistance evident in the text is seen in the woman's mimetic repetition of Jesus' authoritative voice in her rearticulation of the discursive rules of bread and miracles. Yet the extent to which this subversive act of mimicry relates to the praxis of mutuality in this pericope remains unclear. In the end, Jesus is still a character who is difficult to place, split between his appearance as healer and his troubling rhetoric.

5.2.2. Unblotting Jesus' Copybook: Saving Jesus from Throwing Food and Insults—Scholars' Perspectives

Mark 7:24–30 is a brief yet deeply problematic pericope in Markan scholarship. Apart from the fact that during the course of a private conversation with a Gentile woman he appears to change his mind about whether he should or should not heal a "demon-possessed" girl, Jesus appears to throw insults in the process. On one hand, this should not be surprising given that the Jesus we meet in Mark is not always a man on his best behavior. In 5:13 he causes a zoological disaster outside Decapolis; in 11:14 he continues the agricultural theme by cursing the fig tree outside Bethany, which later withers away (11:21). Later that day (11:15) he causes a ruckus in the temple, turning over tables and preventing people from carrying anything inside. During his ministry he calls the Pharisees and scribes from Jerusalem "hypocrites" (7:6), and he calls one of his disciples "Satan" (8:33). Added to this litany are his comments to the Syrophoenician woman seeking healing for her daughter in 7:27: "it is not fair to take the children's food and throw it to the dogs."

The scholars I sampled tend to frame the brief events of 7:24–30 within various mitigating circumstances, with the resultant effect that the relational conflict that specifically 7:27 narrates is in some way or another palliated. Such analyses seek to attenuate the struggle for power the pericope narrates by the imposition of various paradigms that for the most part serve as apologies for Jesus' rhetoric. Some interpretations of 7:24–30 strongly condemn Jesus' rhetorical actions in the text, ranging from accusations that Jesus is "insulting to the extreme" (Ringe 2001, 89), to views that his behavior is "morally offensive" (Theissen 1991, 61) and "abhorrent" (Gnanadason 2001, 163). In light of these, it might be that scholars feel all the more inclined to offer extenuating explanations for Jesus in this story.

The several attempts to exonerate Jesus with regard to this pericope are carried out on a number of levels; one is on the level of theology. Some argue that Jesus' use of the word *dog* is intended to be a test of the woman's faith (Brooks 1991, 120). Others justify the harshness of the term in 7:27 as a rebuke of the woman whose request constitutes an attempt "merely" to take advantage of Jesus as a miracle worker (Hooker 1991, 182). The woman's perceived fault here is that she fails to realize that this singular act of healing is part of something greater: the breaking in of the kingdom of God. The argument follows for Hooker that the woman's reply does not represent her resistance to Jesus' act of labeling, but rather her acceptance that "salvation belongs to Israel" and thus shows her faith in something far greater than Jesus' miraculous power to heal (ibid.). Also arguing that the pericope is fundamentally one that communicates a theological lesson, Rebekah Liu (2010) suggests that viewed through the lens of the motif of the messianic banquet, the rhetoric Jesus employs indicates to the Syrophoenician woman that she may also be a partaker in Jesus' messianic blessing.

Other analyses proceed from a postulated socioeconomic perspective. Gerd Theissen believes that Jesus' response must be seen within the context of the enmity that existed between Jews and non-Jews, particularly at the largely agricultural border of Tyre and Galilee. Based on the Roman control of the supply of food and the enormous demand for grain grown in that border area, Theissen argues that the local populations had scarce food supplies. In particular the local Jewish populations of the Hellenistic cities such as Tyre, being a minority group, suffered greatly. He contends that the woman in 7:24–30 is not from a socioeconomic location that is impoverished (contrary to Horsley's depiction of the woman as representative of "all who are threatened with similar circumstances"[49] of poverty and abandonment) but from a more advantaged background. Poling Sun makes a similar case, arguing that the woman comes to Jesus as "Syrophoenician power, a dominant and oppressing group," and so "naming the dog does not refer to the woman as such but the power and domination she embodies" (2010, 389).

Others assert that Jesus' response is mediated by cultural factors beyond the economic realities of the day. Some purport that Jesus is a

---

49. Horsley 2001, 213. See also LaVerne Gill, who argues that the woman is "of mixed race, coming from a conquered people, a second-class citizen in a country that once belonged to her people" (2000, 99).

"victim" of his historical context, which subsequently shapes his response to his ethnic foe (Gill 2000, 101). Alternatively, the significance of ethnicity arises in terms of a supposed honor and shame framework. Myers and colleagues, for example, argue that it would have been inconceivable for an unknown, unrelated woman to approach a man in the privacy of his residence, particularly a Gentile woman soliciting a Jewish man.[50] Hence Jesus' words are seen as a justified response to the indignant situation that the woman's approach precipitated.

At an intertextual and cultural level, the exchange about dogs and food is often taken as an allusion to the pericope immediately preceding, 7:1–24, wherein Jesus has declared all foods clean (7:19). On a general level, Jesus in 7:24–30 could be declaring all persons clean, according to Lamar Williamson (1983, 137; cf. Brooks 1991, 120). Conversely, Robert Beck maintains that because food laws prohibit Jews from eating unclean food intended for dogs (e.g., Exod 22:31), Jesus' statement in 7:27 articulates the opposite principle, that no dogs should eat clean food that is fit for humans (1996, 81). It would follow that the problem in this pericope is not with unclean foods but with unclean eaters of food—Gentiles.

On a missiological level, one approach shifts the focus to the first-century evangelist and his concern for the mission to the Gentiles.[51] The contention here is that the evangelist wishes to address a contemporary need in his own community to resist a division between Jewish followers of the Jesus movement and Gentile followers (Dowd 2000, 76). Also referring to the supposed context of the production of the text, Mary Ann Tolbert argues that the use of the metaphor "dog" is an intentional reference to Cynic philosophers, who were distinguished not for their philosophy but for their "impudent and argumentative style" (1989, 183). Indeed, Diogenes of Sirope, the fourth-century B.C.E. Cynic founder, was called "the dog" for his rudeness and impudence (ibid.). However, not only is Tolbert's argument tenuous—it would be the only reference to Cynic philosophy in the Gospel and so a rather odd anomaly—it also does nothing to alter the fact that Jesus' reference for the woman who is at his feet is to a group whose reputation is tarnished as rude and impudent.

It seems, then, that there are as many mitigating paradigms used to exonerate Jesus as there are scholars to propose them. While these inter-

---

50. See Myers et al. 1996, 82, who argue that this affront explains Jesus' initial rebuff of the woman.

51. See, e.g., van Iersel 1998, 250; Painter 1997, 116; Williamson 1983, 138.

pretations that attempt to explain Jesus' behavior—whether from a linguistic, theological, or contextual perspective—do offer some valuable insights, they can do nothing to alter the textual presence of 7:27. Indeed, it is interesting that both the theological and contextual approaches attempt to offer justifications for behavior that is taken in some way to be a blemish on Jesus' character. That is, whether attributed to the evangelist's later concerns or to Jesus himself, 7:27 still undercuts the image of Jesus' benevolence.[52]

With this tendency to palliate the conflict between Jesus and the Syrophoenician woman in 7:24–30, when scholars offer interpretations of the character of Jesus, for the most part they do not address analyses of the relational dynamics of this conflict. Interpretations tend to move straight to the *why* of the encounter, leaving the questions concerning *what* actually takes place unexplored. If we consider interpretations that directly focus on the role of the woman, this trend is somewhat reversed. Many of these attempt to champion the rhetorical agency of the woman, such that the *what* of the encounter is taken to be central to an appreciation of the pericope.

For instance, Dowd argues that the woman does not so much win the argument in 7:24–30; rather she solves a riddle by changing the terms of the discussion (2000, 76). By changing the cultural context (while Jews did not keep house dogs, Greeks and Romans did) from Jewish to Greek (77), the Syrophoenician woman solves the problem of priority by replacing an image of scarcity (Jews do not have enough food for themselves, let alone for scavenger dogs) to one of abundance (Greeks have enough food to share it with their pets). Similarly, R. C. Spargo argues that the textual location of 7:24–30, between two feeding narratives (6:34–44 and 8:1–10), suggests "an economy which is of the woman's making" (1999, 323): that she is able to translate leftovers into a symbol of having plenty to share. Thus her response to Jesus (7:28) can be seen as a corrective of Jesus' misunderstanding of his own miracle working (ibid.).

Other interpretations of the exchange between Jesus and the Syrophoenician woman that focus on the rhetoric employed between them have made the case for the importance of the type of rhetoric being employed. Lawrence Hart maintains that Jesus can be seen in this peri-

---

52. Indeed, some maintain that in no other place is Jesus found to treat any other character in such a harsh manner; see Donahue and Harrington 2002, 233.

cope and more broadly in Mark's Gospel as a sage who presents the woman with a paradox in the form of a proverb or *mashal* that she must resolve. Consequently, Jesus' words might be characterized less as pejorative and more as playful (2010, 23–24). Similarly, Kelly Iverson contends that Jesus' response to the woman is not a rejection but a test, an instance of "peirastic irony"—a verbal challenge intended to test the other's response (2007, 52). Beyond rhetoric alone, and viewing the text from the perspective of the Indian subaltern, David Joy argues that the Syrophoenician woman is a "true representative of postcolonial native women" due to her courage in breaking boundaries of gender and colonial power, challenging Jesus to treat her situation with care (2008, 160–61).[53]

While these interpretive lenses shift the focus of biblical scholarship to the internal power dynamics of the story rather than elide such concerns, they still tend toward a movement to resolve the conflict being narrated and the struggle for and the ambiguity of power in this story. For instance, Joy makes the strong claim that from within a colonial context of the subjugation of ethnically and gendered otherness, "the dialogue between Jesus and the Syrophoenician woman breaks the boundary of gender, breaks the boundary of race and ethnicity, also breaks the boundary of religionism, and finally it redefines those boundaries" (2008, 165). Yet, as Musa Dube highlights in her rereading of the Matthean counterpart (Matt 15:21–28) to Mark 7:24–30, depending on the perspectives individuals have concerning the power relationships narrated in the pericope, the Syrophoenician/Canaanite woman can be read to be either a heroine paradigm for feminists who transgress intellectual and religious boundaries (Schüssler Fiorenza 1993, 12, 97) or a victim of patriarchal and imperial ideology (Dube 2000, 170).

As a segue from this section that has focused on a sample of scholarly approaches to the text to group readers' interpretations, it is interesting that Dube's own work with reading groups from an African context found that readers tended to emphasize the ways in which conflict and struggles for power gave way to the centrality of interdependence in acts of healing. This interpretive trend was guided by the readers' contextual concept of

---

53. Jennifer Glancy (2010) makes the case that an analysis of the operation of power in the encounter between Jesus and the woman must take into account all the dimensions of identity at play such as gender, ethnicity and corporeality, arguing that the woman's posture before Jesus at his feet is as significant to the analysis of power as other factors.

Semoya, a mode of reading that resists discrimination and articulates a reading of healing of race and gender relations as well as of individuals, classes, and nations, by underlining the interconnections of things and people rather than the disconnections (Dube 2000, 192). While this stress on interdependence directly considers the relational dynamics of the text, my own interest is to stay with the tensions of the story and ask group readers to consider how they read the power struggles narrated in 7:24–30, in the hope that the tendency to sublate the agonistic tensions of the story will be resisted to some extent.

5.2.3. Power, Difference, and the Fracture of Mutuality— Group Readers' Perspectives

As demonstrated above, in reading 7:24–30 scholars tend to palliate the tensions inherent in the pericope—by placing an imagined exonerating paradigm for Jesus' behavior or an imagined heroism of the woman— onto the text. Such a tendency leaches this story of the agonisms of its relational dynamics. No such tendency was found among group readers' interpretations. For example, when asked to reflect on how the exchange with Jesus might have made the Syrophoenician woman feel, readers variously responded in a negative light. One reader stated self-reflectively that it would make her feel "humiliated,"[54] while another reader postulated that the woman must have internalized the rhetoric she was receiving and be left feeling "like a dog" and thinking "of herself as a child."[55] Yet, despite these imagined hegemonic effects of the actions described in 7:24–30, the woman is also interpreted by some group readers as one whose faith makes the demons leave,[56] and, according to another reader, as one who was stronger than Jesus.[57]

---

54. Facilitator: "How would you feel if you were called a 'dog'?" A: "I would feel humiliated" (from Reading Group One, April 25, 2006).

55. Facilitator: "How do you think the woman feels now? Like a woman, a child, a dog?" A: "I think she thinks of herself as a child now, 'cause I think after this she changed her life around." C: "She felt like a dog, because of what happens to her. She's been treated like a dog" (from Reading Group One, April 25, 2006).

56. Facilitator: "What do you think has made the demon to leave her daughter?" B: "I think the mother's faith" (from Reading Group One, April 25, 2006).

57. "Because I think she's stronger than him, because she comes from another area and the area she comes from is probably very powerful" (C from Reading Group One, April 25, 2006).

The question that arises from the tension perceived to be at the heart of this pericope is, Who in the end is in control of the conversation? On one hand, group readers thought that Jesus has the advantage: he is sought out by the woman, he then sets the terms of the conversation, and it is he who decides that the woman can go,[58] declaring that the demon has left the woman's daughter (7:29). Similar conclusions were reached by other group readers, with Jesus, as "Messiah"[59] and "Lord,"[60] associated by one reader with experiences of encountering mental health professionals: "I remember a psychiatrist when starting would always have his head above mine. I've never felt that kind of thing with people I am working with now. Although I do remember trying to get into a certain living situation and my caseworker was holding the reins."[61] The notion that Jesus might have been "holding the reins" of this encounter with the Syrophoenician woman was supported by other readers who emphasized the woman's situation, in contrast to Jesus' status. She "begs"[62] and requires "mercy."[63] Her position, at Jesus' feet, signified to other readers that she had placed herself in a position of trust in someone she does not know,[64] and this could be seen as the risky action of a "desperate" woman.[65]

In contrast, some group readers felt that it is the woman who, in her response, has the upper hand. For, while she is the recipient of the enigmatic riddle concerning dogs and bread, she is also the one who reimag-

---

58. "I think Jesus is trying to exhibit control by saying, 'You may go now'" (A from Reading Group Two, April 25, 2006).

59. "She has faith that he is the Messiah" (D from Reading Group One, April 25, 2006).

60. "She saw the Lord, she was astonished" (B from Reading Group One, April 25, 2006).

61. A from Reading Group Three, April 24, 2006.

62. "She had humility. I beg to people sometimes, well yeah, if I'm asking for forgiveness or I don't want to be punished. Like with the staff at the home—be merciful, have mercy" (C from Reading Group One, April 25, 2006).

63. "For her forgiveness, she needs to be forgiven" (A from Reading Group One, April 25, 2006).

64. A: "Could be, opening up to someone you don't really know." B: "Where he comes from it is." A: "It shows trust. I myself wouldn't trust in doing it like that" (from Reading Group Two, April 25, 2006).

65. "Well, it seems to me that she's kind of desperate. Her daughter has a demon or whatever. She doesn't quite know what to do about it. She's probably tried numerous things without getting anything out of it. So she's looking to somebody to help the situation she has" (A from Reading Group Two, April 25, 2006).

ines the terms of the debate (7:28), and in the end gets what she desires.[66] Perhaps she has the advantage because as a recipient of Jesus' rhetoric she now holds his reputation in her hands. Jesus offered the woman what could easily have been interpreted as an insult in a place where his fame had spread (3:8); the choice is hers as to how she might respond. As one of the group readers commented, Jesus' agency in the encounter "depended on her saying the right thing."[67]

The question of power in 7:24–30, then, is fraught with ambiguity. Indeed, reflecting on the psychological tension inherent in the exchange between Jesus and the woman, not only is the question of who has control of the exchange not clear, one reader suggested that the encounter is itself set on edge between control and the loss of control:

> Facilitator: How do you think Jesus felt about her doing that [bowing at Jesus' feet]?
> A: Merciful.
> C: He probably said, "You don't have to keep crying all the time," otherwise she might go into a frenzy and go mentally ill.
> A: She could have been in danger of losing her mind.
> C: Sure they had mental illness, even in those days.[68]

Another feature that group readers emphasized was the dynamics of difference in the story. Specifically, readers stressed the difference Jesus sees between himself and the sociocultural group represented by the Syrophoenician woman. For instance, one reader suggested that "dogs" referred to the scarcity of faith as well as of food among those whom Jesus is addressing.[69] Another reader suggested that "dog" referred to a lack of equality between Jesus and the others the woman represented, with the implication

---

66. "Does the Syrophoenician woman expect too little? Should she also have a place at the table? I don't know. Her kid gets cured. It seems that this is all she is asking for in the first place" (A from Reading Group Three, April 24, 2006).

67. "Who is in control of this situation? Definitely I think Jesus. It seems almost like he's saying aphorisms, it's like he's throwing something at her, something small and profound for her to think about. I guess Jesus … but it depended on her saying the right thing" (A from Reading Group Three, April 24, 2006).

68. From Reading Group One, April 25, 2006.

69. Facilitator: "And the dogs?" A: "People who don't have any food." D: "Or the people who don't believe" (from Reading Group One, April 25, 2006).

being that these others were "people beneath him."[70] For another reader, the difference was just a matter of ethnicity: "Well, the dogs are the people whom Jesus doesn't recognize as part of his people."[71] In multiple ways the difference of the other is not recognized and embraced in this encounter. Instead of offering words of healing, as one group reader stated, Jesus is found to be "throwing an aphorism" at a woman in need.[72] In return, another group reader does not see Jesus here necessarily gaining a follower but perhaps ending up "with a fight" on his hands.[73]

While some scholars celebrate the Syrophoenician woman as a biblical heroine of female rhetorical agency (Schüssler Fiorenza 1993, 12, 97), for some group readers the impact of the fractured relational dynamic narrated in this story was associated with experiences of othering in relation to mental health. One reader stated simply that in the face of such an encounter you can end up "hating yourself."[74] Other readers suggested that there might be a danger of "losing your mind" and going "into a frenzy."[75] Such reflections were put into sharp contextual relief by one reader who found the begging woman in 7:24–30, who would be called "dog" by the one from whom she is begging, to be a reminder of his own experience of begging from others: "She had humility. I beg to people sometimes, well

---

70. "Doesn't sound too good, no, when he calls them dogs. Those are people beneath him, he doesn't recognize them as equal" (C from Reading Group One, April 25, 2006).

71. B from Reading Group One, April 25, 2006.

72. "It's enigmatic. It's metaphorical. She's asking him for something, he is throwing an aphorism at her. It doesn't really make sense to me. It's definitely open to interpretation, that he is calling her a dog. It's disturbing. It's not a compassionate, loving thing to do" (A from Reading Group Three, April 24, 2006).

73. Facilitator: "Does the way the woman answers back work as a way of resisting the label Jesus offers?" B: "You might end up with a fight on your hands." A: "If you wanted a fight, I presume it would be fine to do that." B: "Could be verbal or physical." A: "It could happen" (from Reading Group Two, April 25, 2006).

74. "I think some people have this mental constitution to react in that way but to the extent that mental health problems can overlap with problems with hating yourself, feeling depressed, and getting really high and manic—yeah, this part just feels like a story, it doesn't feel like something that could really have happened" (A from Reading Group Three, April 24, 2006).

75. C: "He probably said, 'You don't have to keep crying all the time,' otherwise she might go into a frenzy and go mentally ill." A: "She could have been in danger of losing her mind" (from Reading Group One, April 25, 2006).

yeah, if I'm asking for forgiveness or I don't want to be punished. Like with the staff at the home—be merciful, have mercy."[76]

Such emphases, then—of an ambiguous struggle for power, the significance of difference, and fractured relating resonating with the dissonances of living with poor mental health in today's North Atlantic societies—are distinct from scholarly perspectives sampled earlier that elect to palliate the conflict inscribed in the encounter. Building on the expansive interpretive work of these group readers, I will now turn to the pericope again and ask how the forefronting of these emphases might inform readings of the text in ways that honor both the potential that in this story the Syrophoenician woman is left "hating herself," and a contrary possibility that she might have ended up feeling transformed and empowered by the exchange.

5.2.4. Mutual Transformation? The Cost of Negotiation

Above all, what the emphases of the group readers point to in the relational dynamics of 7:24–30 is the predominance of difference. First, there is no clarity as to who might have had control of the pericope in the end. The network of power in this pericope is diffuse and unclear. Second, faith, ethnicity, and some measure of equality were all seen to create tensions between Jesus and the Syrophoenician woman such that group readers did not see these various marks of difference resolved. Third, and similar to the second point, the picture of relating that group readers painted of the encounter narrated in 7:24–30 is one where the fractures of difference are not somehow healed by the end of the exchange; rather they remain as an agonistic presence that is not in the end overcome.

What, then, do these various emphases point to in terms of the praxis of mutuality in this pericope? As I defined it in chapter 2, mutuality in its full form is a praxis wherein both the self and the other are recognized as mutual partners in a relational encounter, and where there is the establishment of forms of relating where each has room for the difference of the other. With this definition in mind, it is hard to see through the lens of group readers' interpretations how mutuality is practiced in its full form in this pericope. What is seen is more a partial resistive strand of the praxis of mutuality wherein the Syrophoenician woman seeks to reassert her

---

76. C from Reading Group One, April 25, 2006.

agency and her rights to healing power in her renegotiation of the terms of the hegemonic relational dynamics Jesus puts forth to her.

Beyond this, though, and contrary to the limit of mutuality that I think is prevalent in group readers' interpretations, some scholars suggest by their interpretations of this pericope that mutuality as a praxis of resistance and aspirational transformation is present in its full form in this encounter. Arguing such a case for transformation, Kinukawa postulates that the woman knowingly neglects social custom and bows down to Jesus, which is an expression not of honor and respect to him, but of disgrace, all in an attempt to bring healing to her daughter.[77] Via the woman's crossing of her cultural border, she frees Jesus "to be fully himself … the boundary-breaker" (Kinukawa 1994, 60). By this interpretation, it is Jesus who is encouraged to step across the boundary, to the woman's side. Kinukawa asserts that the woman enables Jesus to see the situation in a different way via a mutual transformation (61).[78]

Similarly, in another article, Kinukawa contends that what is predominant in this pericope is not a segregation of the Syrophoenician woman from Jesus, but an interdependence between them. Arguing that the woman identifies not with the referents of "the dogs" in 7:27 but more with Jesus and the economic struggles of his own people, Kinukawa posits that what the woman negotiates in this story is not one side of a relational dynamic of difference, but the solidarity that Jesus and she share. That is, she leads the dialogue toward an interdependent relationship among Jesus, the children of Israel, herself, and her daughter (2004, 372).

Through a Bhabhian lens, Jim Perkinson's work (1996) also can be seen to suggest that mutuality is practiced as a form of both resistance and transformation. Perkinson contends that Matthew's treatment of Mark's encounter between Jesus and the Syrophoenician woman represents an iteration of the word of Jesus. That is, he argues that Jesus' words to the

---

77. She maintains that women of that time were not expected to come out of their homes, much less make a plea in a public setting. Her invasive solicitation would make a man "lose his face in a culture of honor/shame" (Kinukawa 1994, 54).

78. A similar cultural argument is proposed by Gill, reading from an African woman's perspective with a particular eye on Matthew's account of the story. Her reading emphasizes the perseverance of the woman even in the height of her humiliation before Jesus. She is likened to, then, black women in Africa whom Gill argues have persevered in spite of degrading circumstances, "retaining the core virtues that black women have had to internalize in order to survive in a country that humiliated them and considered their people dogs" (2000, 102).

woman—who in Matthew's Gospel is presented as a Canaanite—are interrupted by the woman and repeated back to Jesus, thus negotiating difference with the discourse's own terms. Again utilizing Bhabha, Perkinson describes this dialogical exchange as the presence of a time lag in that the past catches up to the present with the Canaanite (Syrophoenician) difference included in the repetition of the authorial voice of Jesus, thus shifting the boundaries of the discourse. What Perkinson suggests is in operation here is the praxis of mimicry, such that the terms of hegemonic discourse are rearticulated in an act of dialogue. This is not, though, just a renegotiation of difference on ethnic grounds, or on grounds of who is permitted to receive healing from the hand of Jesus; this is also the inscription of a theological transgression. In this mimetic return of Jesus' seeming disavowal of the Canaanite (Syrophoenician) woman, Perkinson asserts that a hybrid space opens up between Jesus and the woman (80). He argues that for a brief moment, as she returns Jesus' words to him, she speaks not only to Jesus but also in his place: "She briefly occupies the space (even the subject-position) of 'Christ' in her speaking to and against Jesus, speaking briefly 'in his place' without entirely giving up her own" (81).[79]

Is this, then, a happy resolution to the problem of "dogs" and "bread" in 7:24–30? Following along the grain of Perkinson's thesis, one could say that not only is this the resolution in the encounter that the mother of the sick girl desires—her daughter's healing—but the relational encounter also displaces the power imbalance presented by the knowing lord and the bowing servant. In a similar vein some contend that Jesus' ministry is enlarged by the woman's ministry to Jesus (Kwok 1995, 80), and that "it is the evangeliser who is being evangelised now" (Sugirtharjah 1986, 14). Joan Mitchell asserts that the happy resolution might be that the woman offers a model of emancipatory dialogue. That is, 7:24–30's rhetoric "demonstrates how personal speech can create tension with oppressive social assumptions and redescribe reality" (2001, 110). Mitchell goes on to claim that this particular pericope offers dialogue as a potential space where people can "entertain one another's truth claims, deconstruct oppressive social reality, and construct inclusive Christian community" (113).

Difference is thus present in this pericope not only between the characters in the text but also clearly between scholarly interpretations such as

---

79. Gill argues even more strongly, stating that the healing that the woman persuades Jesus to perform authenticates Jesus' divine status (2000, 104).

the ones described above and the emphases of group readers. The question remains, then, whether the praxis of mimicry that Perkinson thinks was exercised by the Syrophoenician woman operates as an enabler of a mutual relating or whether the group readers' reluctance to see mutuality in this encounter subverts such confidence. That is, is it reasonable to suggest, with Perkinson's reading of the woman's use of mimicry, that this is a form of postcolonial praxis that not only expects a more spacious set of relational dynamics to be created, but also offers to Jesus an invitation to the same? Moreover, can Jesus' word offered in return to the Syrophoenician woman in 7:29— "For saying that, you may go"—be reasonably seen as a reciprocation of such a postulated invitation to mutuality?

It is my contention that in the end such definitive conclusions about the mutual nature of the exchange between Jesus and the Syrophoenician woman between verses 28 and 29 remain elusive. It is not clear at all that Jesus practices mutuality in his encounter with the Syrophoenician woman in 7:24–30, and so one cannot conclude that the postcolonial praxis of mimicry that Perkinson reads to be present in the relational dynamics of this text actually enables anything more than healing for the woman's daughter. That is, it is reasonable to conclude that the agencies in this pericope are exercised without any certainty as to the status of mutuality in the encounter. The presence of mutuality remains a question that hangs over interpretations of the text.

I contend that such irresolution is created by the ambivalence of Jesus' presence in the text. Jesus in this pericope remains a character who is difficult to place. Every designation of Jesus in 7:24–30 is undercut by a contrary designation that in the end subverts the attempt to come to definitive conclusions about his agency and the agency of the woman in return that he inspires. Jesus' presence in the text and the humiliation he perpetrates still, in Mitchell's words, bring the reader "up short" (2001, 97). As Mitchell argues, there is a disturbing ambivalence here that tears the reader between a celebration of the woman's agency and "lament or even rage" at the treatment she receives (99). Similarly for the varied interpretations of group readers, the presence of Jesus remains ambivalent. He is for some readers the "Messiah"[80] and "Lord,"[81] yet for others he is the one who

---

80. "She has faith that he is the Messiah" (D from Reading Group One, April 25, 2006).

81. "She saw the Lord, she was astonished" (B from Reading Group One, April 25, 2006).

leaves the woman feeling "beneath him" (see n. 70). "humiliated" (see n. 54), "like a dog," and left thinking of "herself as a child" (see n. 55).

With the troubling presence of Jesus in this text—split between an appearance as both one who heals and one who "humiliates"—this state of irresolution in the interpretation of this text is consonant with Laura Donaldson's suggestion that a third ambivalent character in this story might leave the tension between Jesus and the Syrophoenician woman unresolved. This character takes the form of a seemingly absent body: that of the Syrophoenician girl. While for some of the group readers she is "auctioned, a bargained thing,"[82] for Donaldson she is a spectral presence in the text (2005, 101), calling forth a silent witness to both her absence and her presence in the text. For while she remains silent and nameless, what the text is also very clear about is that she is restored to health (7:30). The very ambiguity of her presence, as Donaldson suggests, haunts the text and the conclusions that might be brought to bear upon it, for she is at the same time both written out yet indelibly written into the text, and into the encounter between Jesus and her mother who appeals to him for healing. Indeed, to view the girl in 7:24–30 as a spectral presence in the text is to move beyond the role of persons with disabilities as "the body silent," "not allowed to speak," and designated as "not able to speak up," thus leading to "representative others" assuming the need "to step in—like ventriloquists—as 'voices of the voiceless'" (Betcher 2004, 97). Rather, as a spectral presence, the girl, though silent in the pericope, continues to undo speaking done for her that might rest at easy resolutions.

Thus, when no longer seen as a discreet encounter between Jesus and his ethnic other, but one between a healer, a mother, and an absent-yet-present sick girl, the ambivalence that might be felt concerning Jesus' rhetoric in this pericope is only accentuated, especially when the insights of the group readers are brought to the fore as ones who have known what it is to beg for mercy (see n. 62) from those who seemingly "hold the reins" (see n. 61) of power and wellness.

So, while Leticia Guardiola-Sáenz's comment on this pericope—that it is only at the level of the table (as equals) and not under the table (as inferiors) "that a constructive dialogue and a fair reconstitution of the world can be achieved" (1997, 69)—is true in as much as that is what might constitute "fairness," it is not where the dialogue of this text takes place. The

---

82. A from Reading Group One, April 25, 2006.

relational space of 7:24–30 is not "fair." It is not a space of equality wherein "constructive dialogue" takes place; it is a space where agency both transforms and at the same time tears at the fabric of relational dynamics.[83]

5.3. Conclusion

Drawing these two pericopae together that narrate the struggles of females in Mark's Gospel, one can conclude a fundamental feature about the kind of postcolonial reading that I have offered of the texts: the agonisms inscribed in those relational encounters cannot easily be sublated. The relational encounter with Jesus is not a panacea for hegemonic power wherein power relations are neutralized via some sort of theological conjuring trick. Rather, it is an encounter within which the praxis of resistive and transformative mutuality is played out in the midst of that power.

Given this, what might be made of the forms of female agency that I have highlighted in these two stories? On one hand, the forms of agency exercised by females in these pericopae can be seen to achieve what they desired: healing. At the same time, both forms of agency achieved their ends only at a cost. For the woman with hemorrhages the cost entailed being made public; for the Syrophoenician woman the cost entailed a potentially humiliating dialogue. One significant difference in how group readers viewed the two women was in their perception of the characters' subject locations. While the Syrophoenician woman was viewed as suffering humiliation at the hands of Jesus, to the point that she might have ended up "hating" herself (see n. 74), she was not interpreted to have begun the encounter at a significant loss in terms of her potential as an agent in the negotiation of relational dynamics other than facing the power gradations of gender. Indeed, while scholars emphasize the significance of the ethnic and possible economic subject locations of the Syrophoenician woman, the group readers offered little implication that these differentials rendered her fundamentally debilitated in terms of her internal state.[84]

---

83. Indeed, Liew argues strongly that 7:24–30 "betrays an alliance between racism, or ethnocentrism and sexism" (1999, 135–36). He goes on to argue that this is true of Jesus' interactions with women throughout the Gospel, such that Jesus' so-called redefinition of the family in 3:19b–35 does not free women from "obligations of home and family" (139).

84. Although there was some reference to the torment she might have endured over the suffering of her child (e.g., "Well, it seems to me that she's kind of desperate.

5. NEGOTIATING MARGINAL AGENCY   165

This was not the case for interpretations of the woman with hemorrhages in 5:21–43, whose very person was perceived to be characterized in her "desperate" attempt to reach out to Jesus. Indeed, while it was the case that the Syrophoenician woman was seen to display desperation for her daughter in her begging Jesus, bowing at his feet (7:25), the woman of 5:21–43 is seen as desperate *for herself*, and this attracted more attention from readers, leading to much more pointed portrayals of her diminished selfhood. So, whereas the Syrophoenician woman was seen to leave her encounter with Jesus feeling "humiliated" (see n. 54), feeling like a "dog" or a "child" (see n. 55), this paled in comparison to the woman with hemorrhages in 5:21–43, who was seen as one who "led a disordered life," and who "became straggly and bitchy," as "a bit of a devil,"[85] "unable to say that she was a good person" or to "show herself as a true person" (see n. 20), and even as one who was overtaken by fear and guilt for her condition (see n. 19) and was left "struggling with herself" (see n. 16)—all in some sense exposed publicly to the crowd.

Is this, then, a fundamental difference in the strategies of agency exercised in the two pericopae? Is it the case that while both the liminal supplemental agency in 5:21–43 and the rhetorical agency that took place behind the doors of a home in 7:24–30 operate necessarily within the hegemonic discourses of gendered alterity, that it is the internal malaise of the woman with hemorrhages that sets her agency apart? If this is so, then one can argue that what sets these two acts of agency apart is the perception of wellness. As was the case with the man with the withered hand in 3:1–6, when the wellness of the individual in question is in doubt, there seems to be in the interpretations of group readers a much greater obstacle to overcome in terms of agency.

Taking this observation a step further, I maintain that, in relation to mental health and wellness, we might conclude from the collective interpretations of these pericopae that the presence of the praxis of mutuality is put into question by perceived unhealthiness. It is more difficult for characters perceived as lacking wellness to overcome a deficit in mutuality than for the well to do the same. What group readers might be recognizing

---

Her daughter has a demon or whatever. She doesn't quite know what to do about it. She's probably tried numerous things without getting anything out of it. So she's looking to somebody to help the situation she has" (A from Reading Group Two, April 25, 2006).

85. B from Reading Group Two, April 18, 2006.

in these characters is a sense of estrangement that accompanies seasons of poor mental health, and in that estrangement the status of the self in relation to others becomes questionable. How this observation might relate to the lived experience of persons with poor mental health in contemporary societies I will address in the final chapter of the book. However, before moving on to that, I will explore the last of the three pairs of pericopae, one of which narrates the story of the man among the tombs (5:1–20), and the other Jesus before Pilate (15:1–5).

6
Dialogue and Mutuality: Mark 5:1–20 and 15:1–5

The final pair of readings considers the encounters of Jesus with two men: the first is the demon-possessed man found outside the city in the country of the Gerasenes (5:1–20); the second man symbolizes the imperium of Rome in the city of Jerusalem—Pontius Pilate (15:1–5). With these two texts I consider dialogue and how in 5:1–20 it enables one man to proclaim what has been done for him, while in 15:1–5 the relational encounter inhibits further possibilities for dialogue and relational exchange. Both the content and form of dialogue will be considered in this pair, as well as the potential of the praxis of mutuality as an enabler of dialogical praxes of resistance and transformation.

6.1. Mark 5:1–20

1 They came to the other side of the sea, to the country of the Gerasenes. 2 And when he [Jesus] had stepped out of the boat, immediately a man out of the tombs with an unclean spirit met him. 3 He lived among the tombs; and no one could restrain him any more, even with a chain; 4 for he had often been restrained with shackles and chains, but the chains he wrenched apart and the shackles he broke in pieces; and no one had the strength to subdue him. 5 Night and day among the tombs and on the mountains he was always howling and bruising himself with stones. 6 When he saw Jesus from a distance, he ran and bowed down before him; 7 and he shouted at the top of his voice, "What have you to do with me, Jesus, Son of the Most High God? I adjure you by God, do not torment me." 8 For he had said to him, "Come out of the man, you unclean spirit!" 9 Then Jesus asked him, "What is your name?" He replied, "My name is Legion; for we are many." 10 He begged him earnestly not to send them out of the country. 11 Now there on the hillside a great herd of swine was feeding; 12 and the unclean spirits begged him, "Send us into the swine; let us enter them." 13 So he gave them permission. And the unclean spirits came out and entered the swine; and the herd, numbering about two

thousand, rushed down the steep bank into the sea, and were drowned in the sea.

14 The swineherds ran off and told it in the city and in the country. The people came to see what it was that had happened. 15 They came to Jesus and saw the demoniac sitting there, clothed and in his right mind, the very man who had had the legion; and they were afraid. 16 Those who had seen what had happened to the demoniac and to the swine reported it. 17 Then they began to beg Jesus to leave their neighborhood. 18 As he was getting into the boat, the man who had been possessed by demons begged him that he might be with him. 19 But Jesus refused, and said to him, "Go home to your friends, and tell them how much the Lord has done for you, and what mercy he has shown you." 20 And he went away and began to proclaim in the Decapolis how much Jesus had done for him; and everyone was amazed.

6.1.1. Introduction: Radical Alterity and the Possibility of Dialogue

The Markan narration of the story of Jesus' encounter with the man who lived among the tombs is a text rich with interpretive possibilities. It has been explored as a story narrating the expansion of Jesus' ministry among the Gentiles, as a cosmic struggle with the powers of evil, as a critique of Roman hegemonic power under the guise of a story about demon possession, and as a prime case for Jesus' superlative status as an exorcist. Such interpretive work typically pays little attention to the existential condition of the man among the tombs around whom the story revolves. Building on the insights of group readers, I explore how an appreciation of the man's condition extends the frame of this interpretive work to include a view of the man as a survivor of dead ends. Thus 5:1–20 as a survivor's recovery story is able to emphasize more centrally the emancipatory potential of dialogue as a postcolonial praxis of mutuality and strategy of relational transformation.

6.1.2. Deciphering the Man among the Tombs—Scholars' Perspectives

The man possessed in 5:1–20 is a character whose identity in any sort of complex form is submerged in much interpretation of the story. Even though the opening verses of the pericope (vv. 3–5) offer a rare detailed description of the lived experience that the man endures, the scholars I sampled tend to move past this textual feature.[1] That is, while Bas van

---

1. The other pericope studied that has a similarly detailed description of a minor character's circumstances is 5:21–43 in its description of the woman with hemor-

Iersel is right to state that "words are inadequate" to express the man's suffering (1998, 198), most scholars do not make any real attempt to explore the quality of the man's existence.[2] Those who do tend to pay at least some attention to his existential condition usually limit such descriptions to simple phrases. For instance, for Richard Deibert, the man is "a mere shell … inhabited by evil" (1999, 50), while for Lamar Williamson he is "a tormented personality" (1983, 108). Similarly, Hugh Anderson points out how the textual emphasis in 5:3–5 on the setting of the man's life among the tombs "vividly describes the utter lostness of the man" (1976, 148).

Much of the reason for this scant attention to the man's existential condition is that he is often taken as a symbol. He is the "Gerasene demoniac"[3] whose significance in the pericope is read variously: for some he is a supporting actor in Jesus' eschatological victory over the chaos of the "demonic sea" and then the "demonic man,"[4] for others he serves the text's notion of Jesus' evangelistic purpose for the Gentiles.[5] Alternatively, the man is read to serve the text's purpose in making a christological point about Jesus' greatness (Gundry 1993, 255). Indeed, in light of this tendency in scholarship to categorize the man in 5:1–20, there is some irony to Chris Benjamin's assertion that the man among the tombs fears that he will forever be known by his past, known only as "Legion" (2006, 134),[6] and also to John Painter's point that the man's own identity in the story has

---

rhages. Jeremy Schipper argues, though, particularly in relation to disability, that such detail is something of an anomaly in biblical texts with narratives found largely to pass over the lived experience of disability "in favor of the metaphorization of disability as a tool for social commentary" (2007, 113).

2. For example, Sharyn Dowd briefly describes the man as a "tormented specimen of humanity" and then goes on to describe Jesus' transformation of the man as a demonstration of "his Creator's" power (2000, 55).

3. See, e.g., Gundry 1993, 256–57. Gundry actually refers to the man as the "Gergasene demoniac" (248) so as to make sense of both geographical and extracanonical referents. See also Kinukawa 2004, 367; Derrett 1985a, 98; Camery-Hoggart 1992, 135; Hamerton-Kelly 1994, 93.

4. Dowd 2000, 52–53; Camery-Hoggart 1992, 135.

5. Van Iersel 1998, 201. Furthermore, Kelly Iverson argues that "the healing of the Gerasene demoniac represents the revelation of God's kingdom in Gentile territory" (2007, 39).

6. James Brooks also contends that while at times the man seems to speak and at other times the demons do, "inasmuch as he was possessed, no distinction should be made." The man is thus, according to Brooks's reading, reduced only to the sound of his possession/illness (1991, 90).

become destroyed or obscured, "leaving only the fragmented voice of the demons" (1997, 90).

Similarly, in terms of the circumstances in which the story finds the man, some scholars are less concerned with the experience of such living conditions and more interested in intertextual and intratextual associations. For instance, Rikki Watts argues for two intertextual allusions in 5:1–20: one to Isa 65:4, in relation to the presence of tombs and swine (1997, 157),[7] and another to Exod 14:26–28, the drowning of the swine in the sea echoing Israel's deliverance from bondage in the drowning of Pharaoh's armies (159).[8] Others similarly overstep the human level of the story in highlighting the significance of intratextual links between Mark 5:1–20 and the preceding pericope, 4:35–41, with the movement in 4:35–41 from storm (4:37) to calm (4:39) paralleled in 5:1–20 with the movement from possession and terror (5:3–5) to peace in the man's right mind (5:15) (Camery-Hoggatt 1992, 135). Intratextual links also are forefronted with regard to a previous Markan instance of Jesus healing a man with unclean spirits in 1:21–28. Here Edwin Broadhead highlights various parallels: both of the men are described as violent and cry out to Jesus (1:24; 5:7); both recognize Jesus and seek to name him (1:24; 5:7); and both fear torment at the hands of Jesus (1:24; 5:7). These parallels lead Broadhead to suggest that 5:1–20 should be read not only as a variation on a traditional story form, but also as a second reading of the exorcism in 1:21–28. That is, as Broadhead presents it, 5:1–20 serves to demonstrate Jesus' power in a setting much more foreboding than Capernaum. Here, he asserts, the scene is saturated with uncleanliness and the exorcism becomes an event of regional significance. Hence Jesus' status is elevated even more by this second reading of the earlier pericope (2001, 50). The man's significance, on the other hand, is left unaddressed.

---

7. Watts argues that the combination of tombs and swine points to the Isaiah text, particularly given the presence of demons in the LXX version (1997, 157).

8. Indeed, Watts maintains that the total loss of the Egyptian army (Exod 14:28) parallels the unclean Romans, personified in the two thousand pigs, being totally lost. Furthermore, Derrett argues for parallels between the Markan narrative and haggadic accounts with both cases of drowning inspired by demons (1979, 7). That there might be a connection between foreign rule and the rule of demons is plausible according to Theissen (1978, 102). He emphasizes that the Roman standard was suspected as an idol (1QpHab 6.3ff.) and that idols were considered demons (Deut 33:17; Ps 95:5; 1 En. 19:1; 99:7; Jub. 1:11; 1 Cor. 10:20).

Postcolonial and other sociopolitical interpretations of the pericope foreground the struggle of the man among the tombs as set within a colonial landscape, yet focus on this in that it speaks allegorically to the struggle of an entire people. For instance, Richard Horsley argues that the pericope serves as a counter-Rome Markan metanarrative and thus emphasizes the colonial structures of power that dominated communal life.[9] Similarly, Ched Myers and colleagues assert that the story offers a symbolic portrait of how Roman imperialism was destroying the hearts and minds of a colonized people (1996, 59). Given this, a common tendency of such interpretations is to focus on the pericope's military imagery. The primary term of interest is the name of the unclean spirit, Legion (5:9), which Myers asserts connotes a division of Roman soldiers.[10] Many scholars see the use of this imperial reference as an attempt to connect "demon possession and colonial oppression."[11] In a similar vein, J. Duncan M. Derrett argues that Jesus' command for the demons to leave the man (5:8) contains military overtones.[12]

With this symbolism in mind, one can argue that 5:1–20 might be understood in a way that is subversive to colonial rule: the violence done to the local Galileans is to be done to the Roman legions in return. Moreover, Stephen Moore contends that the pericope can be read to

---

9. Horsley is clear about the political context for Mark as a whole: "The Gospel of Mark ... is about people subjected by an ancient empire" (2001, 30). He describes the systems of imperial exploitation as breaking down traditional socioeconomic infrastructures with exorbitant taxes and tributes, leading to a rising indebtedness, and a loss of land for a people whose subsistence relied upon it (1993, 401).

10. Myers argues that the term had only one meaning in Mark's social world: a division of Roman soldiers, perhaps referring to the presence of the Tenth Roman Legion garrisoned in Palestine (1988, 191).

11. See Crossan 1994, 89; and Moore 2006a, 194. Beyond this simple allusion, Douglas Geyer argues that there might reasonably be two associations with legions that were common during the imagined historical location of the story. One is the image of a legion of soldiers as "a tenacious corporate entity that seeks to resist confronting powers" and to maintain itself as a unit while doing so. Fundamentally, the argument is that the legion was seen as a unit that worked together powerfully. The second association is that legions hated to be defeated, and any loss was typically followed by massive retaliation whenever the opportunity presented itself (2002, 137).

12. Derrett contends that Jesus' command in 5:8 for the demons to leave the man may mimic the issue of a military command. Also, he asserts that the number of pigs is not accidental, with a thousand being a military unit in ancient Hebrew idiom (1979, 6).

suggest that it is not just "the invaders who must be swept away, but the comprador class who have made the invaders' continuing control of the land and its people possible," linking the exorcism of the man among the tombs to the "exorcism" of the temple in Jerusalem.[13] From a similar postcolonial stance, Joshua Garroway argues that the colonial ideology of invasion is mimicked by the man in this story through his entry into the pigs, yet at the same time "subversively altered" by resulting not in the annihilation of others but in the "peaceful invasion" of the kingdom of God (2009, 60).

However, when it comes to the relational dynamics of the text, the above postcolonial readings of 5:1–20 tend to constrict a narrative of individual struggle and transformation to a metanarrative of communal struggle. These sorts of postcolonial readings are in danger of being too selective, predominantly asking only those questions of texts that point to subtextual critiques of empire. Thus, as with the interpretations assessed earlier in this chapter, the personal quality of the man's struggle is somewhat elided in favor of other textual and ideological concerns that end up leaving little consideration of the agency of the possessed man himself.

With this critique in mind, I explore another strand of postcolonial interpretations that address the role of individual agency. For example, Paul Hollenbach pays attention to the interpersonal level of the encounter, attempting to emphasize both the significance of the sociopolitical and the personal context of the pericope. He offers two interpretations of "possession" in 5:1–20. First, possession is interpreted as a form of defense or retreat in the face of colonial oppression, what Hollenbach calls "salvation by possession" (1981, 577). That is, "mental disorder" becomes an escape from, as well as a symptom of, hegemonic relational dynamics (575).[14] Hollenbach's second interpretation is the reading of

---

13. Moore 2006, 195–96. The argument that justifies such readings is that below the surface, "hidden transcripts" of resistance can be discerned in the text via an assumption of the knowledge of events recent to the postulated production of the pericope. For instance, Myers (1988, 191) suggests that there might be an allusion in the drowning of the legion of swine in the nearby sea to the account in Josephus (*Ant.* 14.450) to "seditious Galileans" who drowned Herodian nobles in a lake during one of the uprisings, and is "*surely*" to the "Roman retaliation during Vespasian's reconquest of northern Palestine during the late years of the Jewish Revolt" (*War* 4.486–490).

14. However, is such a defense sustainable? Frantz Fanon, whom Hollenbach's interpretation of this pericope draws upon, argues that "ego-withdrawal as a success-

"possession as protest," what he terms an "oblique aggressive strategy where the powerless deal with their powerful oppressors ... in a way that does not threaten the social position of the latter" (577). What he means by this is that the demoniac is able to "give the Romans the devil" by identifying their legions with demons. He is only able to do this obliquely—as a hidden resistance—through "madness."

Hollenbach thus leaves Jesus' exorcism of the "Gerasene demoniac" to be interpreted in two ways. With his first possession-as-salvation interpretation in mind, one might see Jesus' action as one that liberates the man—and perhaps by extrapolation, colonized people more widely—from a delusional and ineffective means of escape. However, his second possession-as-resistance reading might lead to a different interpretation of the liberative quality of Jesus' action. For instance, R. S. Sugirtharajah suggests rather than seeing Jesus' action as restorative and liberative, one could see it as removing "one of the potential tools in the hands of subjugated people." Thus Jesus is not the liberator but is colluding with colonial domination by unmasking an act of hidden resistance. This is not a claim that Jesus in Mark is a coconspirator with the Roman authorities against the colonized people of Palestine; rather, Sugirtharajah's point here is that "Jesus simply treated the symptom without confronting the system which produces such behaviour" (2002, 94).

Hollenbach's twin readings of 5:1–20 remain intentionally ambiguous. However, as far as the Gerasene demoniac is concerned, Jesus' actions—whether viewed as an emancipation from an ineffective form of escape or a denial of the man's form of resistance—seek to remove the condition that typifies him: his "demonic" state. On one hand, as a textual feature this is not objectionable: the man is recorded as "living among tombs, ... restrained with shackles and chains, ... always howling and bruising himself with stones" (vv. 3–5). On the other hand, as a pointer to the lived experience of persons with poor mental health, Jesus' actions might be viewed not to speak to this condition or to engage with the person living with it, but only to subdue it.

In contrast, I wish to explore a reading that sees Jesus engage, not subdue, the man among the tombs in this pericope. Indeed, considering the interpretations of group readers in the section below, a complex

---

ful defence mechanism is impossible for the Negro. He requires a white approval" (1967, 51).

exegesis of both the man's human condition and his encounter with Jesus is possible if the reading explores more deeply the question of identity.

6.1.3. "It's So Painful, This Story": "Thick" Hermeneutics? Group Readers' Perspectives[15]

Unlike biblical scholars, who either overstep the human quality of the opening verses of this pericope (vv. 3–5) or consider that the character's designation as "demoniac" makes his residence among the tombs "a suitable spot" (Hooker 1991, 142), the group readers emphasized, with Robert Gundry, that the context of the man's life reflects the power of death (1993, 249), and with Hisako Kinukawa, the total isolation of the man's existence (2004, 368). Indeed, readers' descriptions of the man's condition were overwhelming in their emphasis on negation and despair. Across the reading groups the man was described as "troubled,"[16] punished,[17] "a loser" whom nobody liked,[18] as one who "belongs with the dying,"[19] "worthless" and "desolate,"[20] "in bondage, trapped in his suffering," "helpless" and "howling,"[21] one who was "polluting," one who might "have caused others to go insane," and someone they did not want their children to be around.[22]

---

15. B from Reading Group Three, April 17, 2006.

16. "Troubled. Seeking a miracle in life from the Lord. He's going through hard times and needs a good miracle. He really needs something good to happen to him" (B from Reading Group One, April 11, 2006).

17. "It's a kind of punishment. Maybe they thought they were protecting him" (D from Reading Group One, April 11, 2006).

18. "He might have seemed a loser, might not have liked him. No one wanted to have anything to do with him" (C from Reading Group One, April 11, 2006).

19. "Close to the spirit world. He's probably unconscious of that being a taboo. He feels he belongs. That means that he belongs with the dying" (B from Reading Group Three, April 17, 2006).

20. B: "Suffering. He seems like he's worthless. I relate—when I'm tormented by my thoughts I have a tendency to say, 'What do you want from me, God? Why are you doing this?'" A: "It's like there is a piece of him that is aware. He's so broken, so ill, that he lives in this desolate existence. Mental illness can be like that. There is a lot of anguish in mental illness" (from Reading Group Three, April 17, 2006).

21. B: "In bondage, trapped in his suffering. No one can help him. He can't help himself." A: "Helpless, he's howling" (from Reading Group Three, April 17, 2006).

22. "They might have had the assumption that someone with insanity would be polluting for them to be among the rest of society. They might have thought it would

6. DIALOGUE AND MUTUALITY 175

In other words, as one group reader put it: "There is war inside of him battling it out. He gets left in the corner with all the voices."[23]

What is striking about this strong and relatively consistent set of interpretations that emphasized the profound level of alterity of this man is that group readers did not interpret his agency with the same consistently dim view. Indeed, for group readers, the man among the tombs was an ambiguous figure in this regard: "We don't know who's speaking, the man or the demons."[24] He is both a man inhabited by a legion of demons and also a man who "needs" "a life ... like everyone else ... maybe he needed somebody just to listen to him and just to care."[25] Likewise, while one reader saw the man as someone who wanted to be "taken care of,"[26] another reader saw him as a bold representative of the needs of others, of the "lot who were left out because they were a little different."[27]

Along with this pattern of contrasting reads, the group readers more consistently interpreted the man as someone who, while "seeking a miracle,"[28] refuses to give up.[29] Indeed, despite being seen as a person who in his possessed state was associated with wishing to "hold on to his

---

have caused others to go insane. They didn't want him around their children" (A from Reading Group Three, April 17, 2006).

23. B from Reading Group Three, April 17, 2006.

24. E from Reading Group One, April 11, 2006.

25. Facilitator: "What does this man need?" A: "A life." B: "That's it." A: "Like everybody else." B: "Maybe he needed somebody just to listen to him and just to care" (from Reading Group One, April 11, 2006).

26. "Probably in the conversation before, he had told him how his life was, he probably just wanted to be with Jesus. He knew if he was he would be taken care of" (B from Reading Group One, April 11, 2006).

27. "Maybe they might have meant that there were other people that were there. They were too afraid to come out—'I'm standing here, speaking for everyone'—a lot who were left out because they were a little different" (C from Reading Group One, April 11, 2006).

28. "Troubled. Seeking a miracle in life from the Lord. He's going through hard times and needs a good miracle. He really needs something good to happen to him" (B from Reading Group One, April 11, 2006).

29. A: "It shows the swine—an animal—and they don't go to heaven, but the man who had demons in him didn't kill himself, he lived with it, he knew he had an immortal soul. You would say swine don't have an afterlife. A person should not give up in suffering." B: "Absolutely yeah. And he was prepared to do more, and when he saw Jesus he could let him go" (from Reading Group Two, April 11, 2006).

illness,"[30] he was also associated with the hope inherent in "clinging to the promise of healing."[31] And when readers considered the man's response to Jesus, after being restored to his "right mind" he was seen as a "new priest,"[32] called to agency, "trusting himself to make decisions without the crutch of another,"[33] "bearing witness,"[34] and "planting seeds"[35] for the one who healed him.

Thus whether seen as a man who wants to be taken care of (see n. 26) or as one who wishes to represent the needs of others (see n. 27), a consistent theme that group readers offered was that the man among the tombs is a person who has endured. He has refused to give up; despite his possessed condition he enters the scene in 5:1–20, according to the view offered by group readers, as one who is able to exercise agency.

---

30. B: "I read it like the man is begging Jesus not to send his legions out of his body. The country is like his body, which is like his country." A: "Maybe I do relate to that, I hold on to my illness." B: "I know for me, if you think you have special power, or special … maybe you think you have something. I can relate to OCD [obsessive-compulsive disorder] like you have a magical power and so rituals to fix things and if you give up special powers to fix things. Even if you want the truth, you don't want to give up the ritual. If I think a thought, if I don't like it, I think another thought and cancel it out—a special power, a magical power." A: "It's giving up the control." B: "You dare to let go, like the OCD, you dare to be mediocre" (from Reading Group Three, April 17, 2006).

31. "Also there's a sense of authority, a sense that God allowed him to be in this state. What else will he do? 'Don't torment me anymore.' He doesn't realize God is ready to heal him. Just last night I asked, 'God, what do you want from me?' The good thing is he gets healed in the end, so let me cling to that promise" (B from Reading Group Three, April 17, 2006).

32. "He was kind of a new priest, because it wouldn't have served any purpose to go with Christ. He gave him a challenge. We know that Jesus had enemies and many were martyred for the cause of Jesus. Christ was asking him to be a witness to his power" (A from Reading Group Two, April 11, 2006).

33. "People who believe Jesus is the living Christ and lives in a person, he never leaves or forsakes you, so in a way it's a beginning. I relate to that begging of Jesus, to stay with me, I've written a song about it; and part of my illness is not trusting myself to make decisions when he gave me a mind and heart to make decisions" (B from Reading Group Three, April 17, 2006).

34. "Christ was asking him to be a witness to his power" (A from Reading Group Two, April 11, 2006).

35. "It would have been good for him to follow, but things don't happen outright. Planting the seed and seeing what it grows into, I guess" (C from Reading Group Two, April 11, 2006).

6. DIALOGUE AND MUTUALITY

The significance of this emphasis on the man as one who has endured and still exercises agency was made apparent by group readers in their explicit associations between the man's plight and his subsequent refusal to give up, and their own experiences of living with poor mental health. One of the ways in which this was manifest was in questioning whether the man was being punished by God—"Suffering. He seems like he's worthless. I relate—when I'm tormented by my thoughts I have a tendency to say, 'What do you want from me, God? Why are you doing this?'"[36]—and then viewing his endurance through it in a positive light: "Was this God's punishment for the man then?" "Yes. He has to take up his cross. Every good Catholic is required to take up his cross."[37] Indeed, the man among the tombs was likened to "a saint," or at least one who was "heading that way."[38] For other readers, though, while the man's condition was one of desolation and anguish—"like mental illness"[39]—his suffering was considered as a "cleansing" and as a "way of growth."[40]

Thus the expansive view that group readers' various interpretations offered of this text was that this man has suffered and survived and is able to initiate a healing episode with Jesus. These are more than just interesting exegeses of the pericope—they are interpretations that have an interest in this sort of trajectory for the story. For whether the readers' comments are associated with divine punishment, define a way of redemptive anguish, reflect parallels to crucifixion, or are seen as ways of cleansing and growth, the fundamental conceptual shift that group readers offered the interpretation of this text was to see it as a recovery story.[41] Contrary to Morna Hooker's interpretation, which sees the man as wishing to destroy himself (1991,

---

36. B from Reading Group Three, April 17, 2006, when asked the question: "What do you think of the fact that he was bruising himself with stones?"

37. A from Reading Group Two, April 11, 2006.

38. "Many saints do this like that. I know they used to sleep on a concrete slab—like a penance, trying to get it out. He bangs his head, scrapes his head, like he's doing penance in a way. I'm not saying that he was a saint, but he was heading that way maybe" (A from Reading Group Two, April 11, 2006).

39. "It's like there is a piece of him that is aware. He's so broken, so ill that he lives in this desolate existence. Mental illness can be like that. There is a lot of anguish in mental illness" (A from Reading Group Three, April 17, 2006).

40. Facilitator: "Is mental illness a punishment from God?" B: "It's not a punishment. It's a cleansing of the soul." C: "A way of growth" (from Reading Group Two, April 11, 2006).

41. From a different perspective, John Mellon offers a similar emphasis, arguing

142), readers saw him as a man who did not give up on himself; indeed, he was taken as an exemplar of perseverance in the midst of suffering: "It shows the swine—an animal—and they don't go to heaven, but the man who had demons in him didn't kill himself, he lived with it, he knew he had an immortal soul. You would say swine don't have an afterlife. A person should not give up in suffering."[42] He is one who clings onto the promise of healing, the promise of re-membering his fragmented identity and of re-membering the pieces of right relating within a fractured and amnesic community. As one reader put it: "I think we have to ask how he is constructing the narrative. I would imagine it to be a recovery story. I was lost, I was insane, hanging out with the dead. Jesus brought me back to life."[43] This shift was particularly resonant with readers for whom the associations of going through "the hell" of "being out of your mind" were all too well known.[44]

The other fundamental opening of the text that readers offered was of the significance of dialogue in the story in enabling that recovery. While one group reader asserted that Jesus' first concern was to get the man "out of a rut,"[45] another reader stated that Jesus wanted to know the man,[46] and in extending this desire into conversation, Jesus was able to open up space for the man to show that he is normal:

> C: Jesus was talking to him. Jesus started talking, "You are not possessed no more, keep it down."
> B: I think it shows great compassion for the man, and I also think that it was proof that he had done the miracle since the man was clearly okay.
> A: They were resting together.
> E: Talking to him.
> A: Yeah exactly.
> E: Showed that he is normal now.

---

that the pericope depicts alcoholism as a force seeking to destroy the world, its power proportionate to the number of victims it claims (1995, 191).

42. A from Reading Group Two, April 11, 2006.
43. A from Reading Group Three, April 17, 2006.
44. Facilitator: "It says he was howling at night. What do you think that is about?" C: "Going out of his mind." A: "Going through hell. It could be the work of the devil too, you know" (from Reading Group One, April 11, 2006).
45. "His heart broke for the man. First he wants to get him out of the rut. It's the character of God to love his people. He doesn't want them to suffer. Then he has a conversation" (B from Reading Group Three, April 17, 2006).
46. "Jesus was an obvious believer in truth and wanted to know this man" (B from Reading Group Two, April 11, 2006).

C: Might have been talking about life, if he had a wife, if he had kids, what he used to do before he lost his mind to those demons.[47]

Furthermore, in that dialogue, the man was able to remember his forgotten identity[48] and demonstrate his transformation: "That he was screaming, naked, beating himself, lonely—now he is okay, I think that to me is no joke. I pray for that every day."[49]

Group readers' interpretations, then, offer a reimagining of the play of power in this pericope. While group readers made little direct reference to the colonial context of the story or to its suggestive vocabulary, they did offer interpretations that resonated with the postcolonial theorists' penchant for ambiguity of identity and agency. More than that, though, group readers pushed at the boundary of other readings of this text in their emphases on the struggles of this man, punctuated both by suffering and his refusal to give up. Through their association of this man's suffering with their own experiences, a story of possession and exorcism was read also as a story of survival and recovery. In this final section, I consider how these themes expand the interpretive frame of this text, and specifically how dialogue acts as an emancipatory tool for recovery.

6.1.4. "They Were Resting Together": Dialogue as an Emancipatory Tool[50]

Group readers' interpretations focused on the radical alterity of the man among the tombs. Rather than brushing over the profoundly othered societal location of this man, group readers strongly emphasized it. The significance of this is not only in how group readers offered a closer reading of the suffering the man endured, it is also in their emphasis on how, given this suffering, the man did not give up. In their view, it is a survivor of dead ends that Jesus encounters in 5:1–20.[51] Furthermore, group readers' noted emphatically that Jesus chooses to engage the man in dialogue, sug-

---

47. From Reading Group One, April 11, 2006.
48. A: "It depends if he was going to remember what he experienced in his life before." B: "He must remember in some way." A: "He remembers in a rough shape" (from Reading Group Three, April 17, 2006).
49. B from Reading Group Three, April 17, 2006.
50. A from Reading Group One, April 11, 2006.
51. Such a view of the man links to Nancy Eiesland's theology of disability that presents Jesus Christ as the "disabled God," one who is not the "overcomer God" but is "God as survivor." Furthermore, in another interesting parallel, "the disabled God

gesting that the actions of Jesus toward the man are not necessarily actions that seek only to reduce or remove the man's condition. Indeed, Jesus does not delay dialogically engaging the man until he is "in his right mind" (5:15). Just as Elly Elshout argues for a reading of the Bible that might give persons with disabilities back the power to imagine the self differently and craft a reality that more accurately reflects the talent of surviving (1999, 440), so group readers' interpretations suggested that this pericope be interpreted not as the negation of the unclean by the clean, but as the opening of an opportunity for the man in 5:1–20 to articulate his own talent for surviving.

Given this emphasis, the central point that I wish to make concerning this pericope is that it is only when the man is reengaged in the story, through the praxis of mutuality exercised between the man and Jesus, that healing is made possible. Indeed, whether the man's "possession" is interpreted politically,[52] as part of a cosmic struggle between Jesus and Satan (Gundry 1993, 252–55), or even as a part of the parabolic teaching of the evangelist about how to be good soil in the kingdom Jesus ushers in (Tolbert 1989, 265), the textual fact of the matter is that a man whom others had left in the place of the dead, chained, and unheard, acts to dialogically engage with Jesus. While group readers reflected that the experience of poor mental health is one where others often fail to see what is "holding them back,"[53] one group reader argued that the encounter with Jesus "brought a sense of clarity" to the man's speech.[54] Thus this man, who according to John Davies and John Vincent had kept up a "violent monologue with himself" (1986, 56), is able to move toward the re-membering of his fragmented identity.

The form this reengagement and re-membering takes is through a conversation,[55] which begins with the man running toward Jesus and shouting at the top of his voice (5:2, 6–7). Thus it is the man among the

---

is God for whom interdependence is not a possibility to be willed from a position of power, but a necessary condition for life" (1994, 102–3).

52. See Myers 1988, 191; Sugirtharajah 2002, 92; Waetjen 1989, 116; Horsley 2001, 50.

53. A from Reading Group Two, April 11, 2006.

54. A from Reading Group Three, April 17, 2006.

55. Stuart Rochester (2011) argues that Mark's Gospel overall serves as a "transformative discourse" that aims to change its readers, just as the man who runs to Jesus is changed from a "distorted" to a "restored" state.

tombs, so often written out of any significant role in this pericope, who initiates the process of reengagement that ultimately leads to his healing. While some group readers associated the struggles of the man in 5:1–20 with divine punishment, the character who encounters Jesus is no passive victim of divine or indeed any other form of retribution. Rather, he is, as many group readers stressed, a survivor. He is one who has endured, and when he sees the opportunity for healing arrive in the person of Jesus, he seizes the moment and begins to negotiate his healing in dramatic fashion.

The dialogue between the man and Jesus begins with two acts of naming, both enunciated by the man: Jesus, named as Son of the Most High God (5:7), and the man, named as Legion (5:9). Van Iersel states that the naming of the man acts as a form of surrender (1998, 199). What sort of surrender, though, is this? Gundry argues that it is the surrender of the cosmic powers of Satan to the lordship of Jesus (1993, 249–51). One set of group readers offered another insight: the man is surrendering control. Beginning with the offering of a name, the man once possessed is daring to let go of that which had caused him suffering yet had given him power:

> A: Maybe I do relate to that, I hold onto my illness.
> B: I know for me, if you think you have special power, or special … maybe you think you have something. I can relate to OCD [obsessive-compulsive disorder] like you have a magical power and so rituals to fix things and if you give up special powers to fix things. Even if you want the truth, you don't want to give up the ritual. If I think a thought, if I don't like it, I think another thought and cancel it out—a special power, a magical power.
> A: It's giving up the control.
> B: You dare to let go, like the OCD, you dare to be mediocre.[56]

At the heart of this pericope, then, is the mutual act of surrender that the praxis of mutuality in dialogue represents. That is, it is a dialogue wherein each participant begins to recognize the other fully as a person. This simple act of dialogue thus addresses one of the fundamental relational deficits in colonial societies between colonizer and colonized: "'talking therapy' … was hardly a feature of colonial psychiatry, since talking was itself a problem between the ruler and the ruled" (Vaughan 1991,

---

56. From Reading Group Three, April 17, 2006.

125). The man and Jesus practice dialogue as a form of emancipation. They recognize one another and, by dialogically engaging one another, opportunity is opened up for the man to articulate his own talent for surviving. For despite being chained and removed from the possibility of relational engagement, he has managed to break that which binds him and thus is already a survivor. As one of the group readers stated: "To me the image is powerful—breaking chains."[57]

Given the opportunity, then, the man indicates to Jesus the means of his own transformation (5:12). Put another way: the man tells how he should be healed. In opening himself up to the relational encounter he has with the man, Jesus also remains open to being corrected in the art of transforming a tortured soul. In other words, it is in his receptiveness to the man's agency in dialogue that Jesus clears the way for healing to occur, such that, from Jesus' command narrated in 5:8 for the unclean spirit to come out of the man, the man realigns Jesus' approach toward two thousand nearby pigs (5:11).

From this reading it is clear that while the people of the nearby city need to keep the man in chains, Jesus does not.[58] The dialogue between the man and Jesus undermines the destructive power of the value system that chained the man up in the first place (Maluleke 2002, 553). While chained, the man is denied mutual relating. Furthermore, he is denied the opportunity to break free from his amnesic identity, and the community remains forgetful of him and their responsibility to him. Much like persons who experienced poor mental health in the eighteenth century, he is shuffled off the horizon of societal concern (Foucault 2001, 45) and confined to his alterity. Even broken free from his chains, he is now chained by the silence of being unheard (248). Yet Jesus breaks that silence; he "wanted to know" the man.[59]

Perhaps it should not be surprising, then, that when the people who had once chained him come to see how their chains had been broken (both

---

57. A from Reading Group Three, April 17, 2006, in response to the facilitator's question: "Is the man powerful or powerless, would you say?"

58. Indeed, as Hamerton-Kelly points out, that they chained him in the first place shows how much they needed him as a scapegoat for their violence. They want him to remain in the "shadows of the cemetery" as a guarantee of their complacency and, indeed, their complicity with the system that chains him (1994, 93).

59. "Jesus was an obvious believer in truth and wanted to know this man" (B from Reading Group Two, April 11, 2006).

6. DIALOGUE AND MUTUALITY

literally and figuratively), they are both, afraid (5:15), and keen for Jesus to leave (5:17). For what is revealed in the dialogical engagement between the man among the tombs and Jesus is the potential power of the praxis of mutuality as an agency for the reimagination of hegemonic relational dynamics. Thus the man whose radical alterity was emphasized by group readers is reimagined as a partner in the act of his own healing. Furthermore, this reimagining is only possible through the praxis of mutuality that had for so long been denied him. The man among the tombs is not, therefore, the passive recipient of a healing bestowed upon him by Jesus; he is one who joins with Jesus in the mutual space their dialogue opens up.

Moreover, as Jeffrey Staley argues in exploring the reasons why the townspeople might be afraid of the sight of the man clothed and in his right mind, it is possible to conjecture that the man is now more of a threat to them than before. Claiming that changes in clothing reflected changes in social status in ancient cultures, Staley suggests that the clothing of the man among the tombs might represent a form of colonial mimicry, threatening both to colonizer and colonized (2006, 324).

However, if the analysis remains at this point of the narrative—of the man sitting, clothed, and "in his right mind" (5:15)—the full significance of the encounter between Jesus and the man will be missed, for a further feature of this encounter is a commissioning. Having been healed, the man asks Jesus if he can follow him on the way. Rather than permitting him to do so, Jesus sends the man back home and beyond to the ten cities of the Decapolis "to tell how much the Lord has done for you" (5:19).

From the perspective of the praxis of mutuality, this refusal on Jesus' part might look like a limit that Jesus is placing on the extent of mutuality between himself and the now restored man. Indeed, Fernando Belo argues that Jesus' commissioning of the man speaks more to Jesus' own needs to avoid danger than the man's needs, such that in the Gentile territory in which the story is set, there is no command from Jesus for secrecy; rather, in the absence of danger for Jesus, the man is encouraged to "broadcast the news" of his transformation (1981, 130). An alternative explanation is offered by Painter, who argues that the man is not allowed to follow Jesus because he is a Gentile: "being healed did not qualify a person to become a member of Jesus' mission" (1997, 92). However, such an explanation is hard to reconcile with the fact that Jesus does commission the man in 5:19b, or with the confession of the Roman centurion at the cross in 15:39.

I contend that at the heart of this refusal is that Jesus has confidence in the capability of the man to carry out his work beyond his supervision as "one who does the will of my Father" (3:35). However, this is more than the commissioning of a man who has had his symptoms dealt with. While some group readers interpreted Jesus' refusal to have the man follow him on the way (5:19a) as a recognition of the man's primary duty as a new adherent to "preach the gospel" (5:19b),[60] one might argue that the refusal acts as a recognition of the man's primary need to attempt to restore the praxis of mutuality in the community that had previously denied it. He is sent "home" (5:19a) to be, as Sharyn Dowd asserts, no longer among the dead but among the living (2000, 56), now to serve as a reminder not only to friends and those at "home," but presumably also to those who may have moved to chain him in the first place, of their attempts at subjugation and silencing and their failure to succeed. He is, then, sent back to reengage in the art of dialoguing with the violence done to him and furthermore with the violence he had done to himself (5:5), in the form of, as Robert Hamerton-Kelly puts it, the "reintegrated victim."[61]

There is also a more personal significance to the commissioning of the man. Mary Ann Tolbert argues that Jesus' refusal of the man's wish to follow him is an indication that "good soil" does not need the nurturing of "the farmer" (1989, 265). Similarly, Davies and Vincent argue that Jesus denies the man's request because he does not want the man to become a dependent adherent by adopting Jesus as his alter ego (1986, 57). The refusal that Jesus gives the man, then, might be interpreted as a prompt for the man to continue to articulate his own survival. It is a prompt for the man to cling no longer, neither to that which had bound him, nor to the one whom he might erroneously perceive he should surrender his agency to. In his refusal and commissioning of the man, Jesus is asking him not to surrender his agency but to exercise it through the transformed identity that their encounter, and the praxis of mutuality within it, opened up for him. Perhaps the begging of the man (5:18) reflects the fear that such a

---

60. B: "He wanted this man to preach the gospel. Whatever it is, the people he goes to will see that he is in his right mind—not in the cemetery—he is preaching the word of God, being a witness to Jesus." A: "He was kind of a new priest, because it wouldn't have served any purpose to go with Christ. He gave him a challenge. We know that Jesus had enemies and many were martyred for the cause of Jesus. Christ was asking him to be a witness to his power" (from Reading Group Two, April 11, 2006). See also van Iersel 1998, 201.

61. Hamerton-Kelly 1994, 94. Indeed, some have argued that the individual person and the community have a "dialogic relationship" through which a model community or *familia/communidad* is reflected. See Gonzales 2004, 75.

participation elicits, for his encounter with Jesus had been an encounter punctuated by fear and unknowing (5:7, 15, 18). Yet, as I have maintained, it is also an encounter readers might find is imbued with hope: "I relate to that begging of Jesus, to stay with me, I've written a song about it; and part of my illness is not trusting myself to make decisions when he gave me a mind and heart to make decisions. Jesus encourages the man that you can do it on your own."[62]

The significance of this reimagining of the man in 5:1–20, who is reengaged in the praxis of mutuality through dialogue, lies in its readership. For, in focusing on the debilitated condition and radical alterity of the man, and the subsequent reengagement, dialogue, and commissioning the encounter narrates, the group readers prompt a reimagining of the man not as a symbol of despair and depravity but as a representative of survival and of the possibility of counterdiscourse. As one of the readers points out, "healing comes in a lot of forms."[63] At its core, 5:1–20 is a story about resisting dead ends and the recognition that the reengagement of dialogue is a profoundly emancipatory act.

The final of the six pericopae paints the opposite sort of picture. Here the dialogical confrontation of questions about identity leads not to emancipation but ultimately to the closure of dialogue.

6.2. Mark 15:1–5

> 1 As soon as it was morning, the chief priests held a consultation with the elders and scribes and the whole council. They bound Jesus, led him away, and handed him over to Pilate. 2 Pilate asked him, "Are you the King of the Jews?" He answered him, "You say so." 3 Then the chief priests accused him of many things. 4 Pilate asked him again, "Have you no answer? See how many charges they bring against you." 5 But Jesus made no further reply, so that Pilate was amazed.

6.2.1. Introduction: Where Is the Good News? Power, Identity, and the Failure of Dialogue

In this final pericope, Jesus is seen in a subordinate position as he faces the embodiment of colonial power in his hearing before Pilate. Much scholar-

---

62. B from Reading Group Three, April 17, 2006.
63. B from Reading Group Three, April 17, 2006.

ship that considers the relational dynamics of the pericope focuses on how the dialogical exchange between Jesus and Pilate serves in a number of different ways as a conduit for other textual, intertextual, and theological agendas to be played out. Yet, when one attends more closely to the dialogue between the two men in its own right, the brevity of the exchange is complicated by the debated significance of power and silence. Below, through the particular lenses of group readers' experiences both of this text and of encounters akin to being bound and led away, the roles of power and silence are explored. Specifically, silence within dialogical exchange is assessed as a strategic form of resistance that may interact with the praxis of mutuality in more ways than one.

6.2.2. The Significance of Dialogue in the Interpretation of 15:1–5— Scholars' Perspectives

The question, "Who do you say that I am?" (9:29), is one that reverberates throughout Mark, with allusions in almost every chapter of the Gospel.[64] In this final pericope (15:1–5), this question returns to its interlocutor in a dramatic climax of the theme of Jesus' identity, with Pilate's question, "Are you the King of the Jews?" (15:2), paralleling the preceding question of the high priest, "Are you the Messiah, the Son of the Blessed One?" (14:61b).

My own interest within the encounter between Jesus and Pilate narrated in 15:1–5 is how dialogue is employed in the negotiation of the relational dynamics of the meeting. Standing as the pericope does at a dramatic point in the Markan narration of Jesus' journey to the cross, the brief exchange of 15:1–5 assumes significance for scholars from a diverse set of theological and textual perspectives. Primarily, the attention to the dialogue in 15:1–5 is subordinated to an interest in various postulated identities of Jesus. According to Herman Waetjen, the designation of Jesus' identity as "insurrectionist"[65] has determined that Pilate, as a symbol of the imperial oppressors of Rome, is one who seeks to suppress any attempt at subversion and who is guilty of "flagrant abuses of power" (1989, 7). Alternatively, the designation of Jesus' identity as "religious dissident/blasphemer" determines that it is not the Roman but the Jewish (religious) leaders who

---

64. See Mark 1:7, 11, 24, 37, 45; 2:7, 18; 3:11, 35; 4:41; 5:7, 19; 6:51; 7:28, 36; 8:11, 27–38; 9:7, 17, 30–32, 38, 41; 10:17–18, 32–34, 38–45, 47–51; 11:3, 10, 28; 12:6, 32, 35–37; 13:26–27, 32; 14:14, 21–24, 36, 41, 45, 61–62, 71; 15:2, 18, 26, 32, 34, 39; 16:6.

65. See, e.g., W. Campbell 2004, 290; Horsley 2001, 100; Waetjen 1989, 226–27.

6. DIALOGUE AND MUTUALITY

are to be viewed as negative characters in the text. Pilate emerges from this sort of reading as merely an instrument by which the Sanhedrin's sentence is carried out (Hooker 1991, 366). The characters, then, of 15:1–5 are not read as agents having a genuine dialogical exchange in the text, but more as ciphers in a gruesome theological or political end game.

The subordination of the role of dialogue in the text is also seen to result from the presumed importance of intra- and intertextual levels of analysis. Intratextually, some think that the actions of Jesus and those encountering him in 15:1–5 follow a pattern of repetition and fulfillment. In terms of repetition, while the significance of the preceding hearing/trial scene in 14:53–64 is emphasized, so too is the repetition of Jesus' silence—interpreted as the absence of dialogue in the two hearings/trials (Hooker 1991, 368; Gundry 1993, 924). Others assert that 14:53–64 and 15:1–5 are juxtaposed to highlight the similarities between the two scenes (e.g., Myers 1988, 378), contrary to scholars who posit that the parallel construction highlights their differences (e.g., Humphrey 2003, 75). In terms of fulfillment, much is made of the way in which the encounter narrated in 15:1–5 is predetermined by intratextual predictions of the passion. For instance, Gundry argues that the "handing over" of Jesus to Pilate (15:1) fulfills the prediction of 10:33: the "Son of Man" is to be handed over to the Gentiles.[66]

Similar arguments along a fulfillment theme are postulated as interpretive lenses intertextually. Jesus' silence in response to the charges made against him by the chief priests (15:3–5) is argued to evoke images both of Pss 38:13–15 and 39:9 (Marcus 1992, 173), and also of the "suffering servant" of Isa 53:7–9, 11–12 (van Iersel 1998, 460). For instance, Eckhard Schnabel asserts that while in the preceding narratives of the Gospel Jesus almost always answers his opponents in some way,[67] he remains silent here because he knows that he will not be able to make himself understood as his accusers will not be able to grasp the "true nature of his claims"—what

---

66. Gundry 1993, 923. Also see Painter, who argues that Jesus' refusal to clearly answer Pilate's question in 15:2 ("Are you the King of the Jews?") might be because in the mouth of the Roman procurator, the title meant "something more overtly political and military than the reality of his messiahship … but for Mark the 'King of the Jews' legitimately reveals the crucified one" (1997, 199).

67. Schnabel 1999, 205. See, e.g., Jesus' clarification of his pronouncements (e.g., 9:12–13; 10:11–12); his explanation of his power to exorcise (e.g., 9:25); his response to "unclean spirits," even if only to silence (e.g., 1:25); and his quoting of Scriptures to interlocutors who oppose him (e.g., 2:25–26; 7:6–10; 10:7–8).

Schnabel calls Jesus' "divine dignity"—and because he knows his death is inevitable (1999, 256). Some also argue that other characters' actions and responses in the pericope follow a pattern of prophetic fulfillment. For instance, Joel Marcus suggests that Pilate's amazement at Jesus' silence (15:5) echoes Isa 52:15 (1992, 187–88).

A similar textually driven reading of 15:1–5 is seen in those who postulate that 15:2 (Jesus' ambiguous reply to Pilate's question) and 15:5 (Jesus' silence following Pilate's asking if he has anything more to say following the accusations made against him) form the first two parts of a Markan triad. The questioning narrated in 15:2 and 15:5 is followed by a third line of questioning in 15:8–14 that centers on the dialogue between Pilate and the crowds. According to this view, Jesus' silence in 15:5 serves compositionally to reduce the impact of the first two questions and to emphasize the significance of the final, third question, thus switching the focus from Jesus on trial to Pilate and the people, who in a sense are now on trial (so Broadhead 2001, 123).

Scholars also pay particular attention to the issue of power in the pericope. Indeed, Hamerton-Kelly describes the pericope as "the roll call of the powers of this world" (Roman and Jewish), within which Jesus is interpreted as the victim of a struggle for dominance (1994, 54). Some contend that Jesus is a character who has little choice and maintain that Pilate holds the power of choice in the pericope (Derrett 1985b, 260). Others suggest that the Jewish authorities already have negated the opportunities for Pilate to make a choice by presenting Jesus to him already bound (Bammel 1984, 415). Arguing along this second trajectory, Ernst Bammel posits that presenting Jesus bound before Pilate demonstrates that the Sanhedrin consultation had already sealed Jesus' fate,[68] with Pilate taking up the finding of the previous hearing from the outset (15:2).[69]

---

68. This argument is based on the establishment that the charge of the first hearing/trial (14:61b, "Are you the Messiah, the Son of the Blessed One?") is the same and not different from the charge in the second in (15:2, "Are you the King of the Jews?"). See Myers 1988, 378, who contends that the two questions and structures of the episodes serve to emphasize their sameness. Conversely, Humphrey (2003, 75) asserts that the parallels highlight their differences, not similarities. See also Santos 2003, 251, for a detailed textual comparison of the two episodes.

69. Such an interpretation is not without potential problems. One is that the assumption that the Jewish authorities had such powers of persuasion over the Roman procurator is not an opinion all scholars share (see, e.g., Waetjen 1989, 7), although within the text alone the persuasive power both of the Sanhedrin and the crowd is sig-

6. DIALOGUE AND MUTUALITY

In each case, the choices Jesus may or may not be able to make are subjugated textually by the necessity for the outcome of the hearing/trial to be a sentence of death. Whether from a reading of prophetic fulfillment or from political powerlessness, Jesus is interpreted as a character who is lacking the opportunity within the context of 15:1–5 to exercise power. Indeed, textually, Dowd (2000, 156) notes that he is framed within a vocabulary of binding and being handed over (15:1, 7, 15). This Jesus, who accepts the inevitability of his death, is the passive, powerless victim of his dire circumstances, yet fulfilling his cosmic purpose.[70] In this role he is also a model for such passive acceptance by others who suffer persecution. For example, Ben Witherington argues that the binding and handing over of Jesus to the authorities must have recalled for a Gentile audience their own handing over to authorities, and furthermore that "Mark shows his audience how to behave by the example of Jesus" (2001, 389; see also Santos 2003, 253). Similarly, for some, Jesus is portrayed in this pericope primarily as the servant of others (Kingsbury 1989, 49–50; Tannehill 1980, 81) who receives willingly and silently the accusations of religious authorities (15:1), the shouts of the crowds (15:13), the release of Barabbas (15:7), the sentence by Pilate (15:15), and the mistreatment he suffers at the hands of Roman soldiers (15:19), with all of the above taken to exemplify true servanthood (Santos 2003, 253).

It is rather ironic, given the predominance and indeed preeminence of Jesus as a participant in dialogical engagement in the Gospel, that the significance of Jesus' dialogical contributions in 15:1–5 are so readily written out of the act of interpretation by so many.[71] However, not all scholars agree that Jesus is powerless in this narrative's encounter with Pilate. Many look to the practice of dialogue for an alternative under-

---

nificant (15:11, 13–15). A second problem is the assumption that the Jewish authorities had the power to perform an execution, whether by stoning or not. This has been a highly contentious issue in the history of interpretation, particularly given the charges of deicide that have been placed before Jewish people in centuries passed (see, e.g., Winter 1974, 18).

70. See Lane 1974, 552, who writes that the reader of 15:1–5 senses in Jesus' passivity and silence "that the Sovereign Lord of history is accomplishing his mysterious purposes to which even the Son of Man must be submissive."

71. Derrett 1985b, 260; Lane 1974, 552; Bammel 1984, 415; Brown 1986, 29; O'Neill 1969, 165; Schnabel 1999, 255–56; Marcus 1992, 187–88; Cárdenas Pallares 1986, 98; Hamerton-Kelly 1994, 54–55.

standing of the relational dynamics of the text. Scholars who assess more directly the dialogical exchange between Jesus and Pilate argue from a number of perspectives. Some focus on Pilate's question to Jesus in 15:2 ("Are you the King of the Jews?"), which is read variously as a dangerous accusation (given who is making it and the consequences for opposing Rome's hegemony in Jerusalem; see van Iersel 1998, 459), as sarcasm (ibid.), and as filled with contempt (Myers 1988, 378; Hooker 1991, 367). Pilate's decision to inquire about the titular "King of the Judeans" and not "King of Israel" is seen as a deliberate reminder that Judeans were not sovereign in their own land (Myers et al. 1996, 196). Alternatively, some contend that Pilate's question to Jesus is more directly concerned with a political reality of the day. That is, as Belo asserts, Pilate's concern may be to ascertain whether Jesus is in some way connected with the Zealot movement, which would be perceived as a threat, or at least as an irritant to Roman power in Jerusalem (1981, 224). From another perspective, José Cárdenas Pallares maintains that Pilate's question is a deliberate maneuver to make it more difficult for him to hand down a "not guilty" verdict for Jesus (1986, 95).

Other scholars focus on Jesus' response to Pilate's question. Richard France thinks that Jesus' answer to Pilate in 15:2b constitutes some sort of attempt to open dialogue in that it affirms Jesus to be the "King of the Jews," but not as Pilate understands it (1990, 91). William Campbell suggests, rather differently, that Jesus' answer is a genuine attempt to open the dialogical space to questions and answers rather than to dismiss Pilate with an enigmatic reply. He argues that faced with hegemonic circumstances, Jesus chooses to practice a three-form strategy of resistance: engagement, disengagement, and obstruction (2004, 283). The central claim Campbell makes, contrary to the interpretation of Jesus as a passive victim, is that Jesus acquiesces neither to the end he potentially faces nor to the circumstances that might lead to it. That is, 15:1–5 and the surrounding texts do not paint the picture of a man who refuses to defend himself at trial, willingly enduring his arrest, trials, persecutions, and crucifixion. Rather, the picture painted is one of resistance.

According to Campbell, however, this is not the resistance of a man who is bent on defiance and disdain for the procedure before him, as Myers contends (1988, 378), nor of one who is contemptuous of his interlocutor, as Hooker states in her claim that the emphatic "you" both in Pilate's question and Jesus' response is an expression of their mutual contempt for each other (1991, 367). Campbell's point is that Jesus chooses to dialogically engage with Pilate with his enigmatic response in 15:2b. He argues that while Jesus disavows the attribution of being "King of the Jews," he does signal a willingness in his answer to continue in dialogue; as Campbell states, his reply "cries out for a follow-up."[72]

However, the problem with Campbell's framing of Jesus' response as a genuine attempt to open up dialogue is that it is couched in such ambiguous terms that providing a response in a publicly charged setting would be risky indeed. It is not surprising, then, that other scholars prefer to focus on the diffusion of meaning and invitation to dialogue rather than its opening up. For instance, some view the exchange as laced with irony, wherein the further the dialogue attempts to proceed the more implicated the characters who end up negotiating Jesus' death sentence seem to appear.[73] Similarly, others see the irony in that it is Pilate, Rome's representative, who accords Jesus with his rightful political status, only to execute him on grounds of sedition (Myers 1988, 378).

While the scholars sampled above do attend to the relational dynamics of the encounter between Jesus and Pilate, the function of power, choice, dialogue, and silence as expressions of agency is not altogether clear. I now turn to group readers' interpretations whose readings of the text focus on these themes and bring to the pericope particular experiences that might offer fresh insights into the relational dynamics of the encounter narrated.

6.2.3. "It Has to Do with People Wanting Power"—Group Readers' Perspectives[74]

At the forefront of group readers' varied interpretations of 15:1–5 is the question of autonomy. Focusing on Jesus' lack of freedom,[75] the "cruel

---

72. W. Campbell 2004, 289. From a more political reading of the text, Theodore Jennings makes a similar point, asserting that Jesus' answer to Pilate is so phrased as to "throw the responsibility back to Pilate," such that Pilate now either has to "acknowledge Jesus' authority as the legitimate ruler or he must deny this authority" (2003, 276).

73. See Tolbert 1989, 278, who maintains that all dialogue after 15:2b to 15:34 is ironical, "further implicating them as the wicked tenants."

74. A from Reading Group Two, May 2, 2006.

75. "I don't like the idea of him being bound up because he's not free anymore, he's captured" (A from Reading Group One, May 2, 2006).

and unusual punishment" he suffered,[76] and the "torture" he endured,[77] Jesus was read as a character whose power to choose within the context of 15:1–5 was severely attenuated: "He did not have the ability to overcome the things before him. He was unable to speak for himself in that he wanted to save the world. We learn to grow, to love, to hope, even though he could not help himself physically because he was not well enough."[78] Another reader saw Jesus' lack of choice through a theological lens: "God made his choice; Jesus had no choice."[79] In either case, the group readers identified a certain lack of control on Jesus' part.

The interpretations of group readers were personal and often associated with some of their own experiences of losing autonomy. They likened the experience of being bound (15:1) to being locked up in "the [psychiatric] ward"[80] or being threatened that this would happen if behavior did not improve.[81] Central to this experience was a loss of autonomy suffered by those who are "bound" or locked up: "I haven't been locked up except on the wards. It's pretty hard to be taken from your house."[82] In addition, readers elaborated on the loss of autonomy in their associations with Jesus being led away (15:1). Here it was not only the physical restraining that was highlighted—"Actually, they put one of my friends in restraints, I didn't like that"[83]—it was also the psychological restraining that was seen to be doubly hegemonic: "Yeah, I didn't like being hospitalized. They put me in 'human resources' instantly. Something about it tortured my mind. Well, I had dreams that I cut my wrists with razors. I had a dream, thinking I was beautiful."[84]

---

76. "It's cruel and unusual punishment. I think they were jealous, that this man was actually saying to him in his own way he was just as good or better than Pilate and he saw Jesus as a threat to his relationship to Rome" (A from Reading Group Two, May 2, 2006).

77. "What they did was torture him. That is torturing, binding someone like that" (B from Reading Group Two, May 2, 2006).

78. B from Reading Group Two, May 2, 2006.

79. B from Reading Group Two, May 2, 2006.

80. Facilitator: "Have you ever been led away to a place you didn't want to go to?" C: "Yes." B: "Locked up in the ward" (from Reading Group One, May 2, 2006).

81. "No freedom. Can't get out, can't go nowhere. Staff at the house … 'If you do this one more time, you will be locked up'" (C from Reading Group One, May 2, 2006).

82. B from Reading Group One, May 2, 2006.

83. C from Reading Group Two, May 2, 2006.

84. B from Reading Group Two, May 2, 2006.

6. DIALOGUE AND MUTUALITY

Finally, the handing over of Jesus to Pilate (15:1) resonated with one reader's experience of being moved from residence to residence.[85] Another reader's experience associated the loss of autonomy in being "taken" and "locked up" with a loss of knowing: "In a way that's happened to me. It was the middle of the night and I was trying to get better in hospital. They took me bodily and put me in a hot shower. I didn't know what to do. I don't know why they did it; I felt frightened by that."[86]

These group readers interpreted Jesus, and with him themselves, as one who is disempowered by his circumstances. He is one who was seen to be utterly limited by his lack of choice: "I don't think anybody likes being out away where they have no choice."[87]

However, this was not the only way Jesus was seen in this pericope. When readers were asked more directly about the nature of the negotiation between Jesus and Pilate, the questions of choice, autonomy, and power were less clear-cut than the associations described above might suggest. For instance, while one group reader saw Pilate's question in 15:2 as an act of sarcasm, or as "poking fun" at Jesus,[88] thus confirming the picture of powerlessness, other readers wondered whether Pilate was in some way afraid for Rome.[89] Focusing on the notion that the two men were trading jibes with each other, one group reader interpreted Jesus' response to Pilate in 15:2 ("You say so") as Jesus "rebutting the whole group,"[90] or as another reader put it: "Jesus hit him back."[91] Another reader saw Jesus' response as mockery: "He's been laughed at by Jesus."[92]

---

85. "I've been that way, from residence to residence and home. The part of LA [Los Angeles] I came from they give you a place, an apartment, though you have to go through all kinds of heck. I'm not against Massachusetts, it just takes awhile to do things" (C from Reading Group One, May 2, 2006).

86. A from Reading Group Two, May 2, 2006.

87. B from Reading Group One, May 2, 2006.

88. "I think he was probably trying to poke fun at him. He asked it, almost sarcastically" (B from Reading Group One, May 2, 2006).

89. "Well, I think Pilate was seeking to find a way to accuse him of trying to take over the city of Jerusalem. He was really afraid; he was gaining more control, more and more people. He was afraid he might overthrow the Roman Empire. So they scapegoated him instead" (B from Reading Group One, May 2, 2006).

90. "I think it's a brief way of rebutting that whole group of people. He was angry at this point" (B from Reading Group One, May 2, 2006).

91. "Jesus hit him back" (A from Reading Group One, May 2, 2006).

92. A from Reading Group Two, May 2, 2006.

What, then, did group readers make of the nature of the power differential in the pericope in relation to the silence employed by Jesus? One reader stated that even if "the words were good" that Jesus used, he still had no power in the situation.[93] Another reader saw the encounter as hopelessly skewed in Pilate's favor, and in not telling Pilate what to do—in remaining silent—Jesus demonstrates how he was "overwhelmed."[94] Some readers elaborated on these sorts of interpretations in an association of silence with the quality of relating they perceived themselves to have with staff members at the day centers they had experience of:

> A: Silence and subjection. It's submission, humility. We're subservient to the staff, we take advice and protection but we have to help them to wash dishes and. ...
> C: We help them out because they help us. One of the greatest things is to be a servant.
> A: What they say counts.[95]

Or as another reader put it: "Sometimes the most you can say is nothing."[96]

Jesus' silence in 15:1–5 was interpreted by most group readers as a sign of Jesus' lack of power in the encounter. However, for some readers, Jesus did have power in the situation and this was interpreted more in line with the theological tone of some scholars' perspectives on the pericope: "I place my hope in you, Father, because of what you say, not I."[97] Similarly, other readers focused on the designation of Jesus as being from a power beyond the one being represented before him in Pilate, such that, "He [Jesus] didn't need a show of power,"[98] and he had "abilities Pilate never dreamt of."[99] Moreover, others felt that his silence took on a more

---

93. "It's good, the words were good, it's just he has no power" (D from Reading Group One, May 2, 2006).

94. "Pilate has power; he's an elected official. They really make a show court out of it. He did not tell Pilate what to do. He was overwhelmed" (C from Reading Group Two, May 2, 2006).

95. From Reading Group Two, May 2, 2006.

96. A from Reading Group Two, May 2, 2006.

97. B from Reading Group Two, May 2, 2006.

98. "He didn't have to impress anybody. He didn't need a show of power, they made him a little lower than the angels" (E from Reading Group One, May 2, 2006).

99. "Because the king is like Pilate and Pilate is like the pope. If Jesus is king, then he may be greater than the representative of the emperor. He has abilities Pilate

combative role as a sign of his refusal to "dignify all this with a reply,"[100] and also an act of engaging Pilate only to condemn him.[101] Indeed, one group reader focused on the fact that even in the face of the seemingly complete absence of power at his disposal, Jesus "has the power to choose not to answer."[102] Furthermore, as another reader speculated, in that moment "Jesus might have given power to Pilate deliberately so Pilate could do his job."[103]

Whether Jesus was interpreted to have power or to lack it, what the group readers' interpretations do suggest is a picture of power in the pericope that is far from clear: "I think at first power is to Pilate. He's the big shot, but as Jesus doesn't answer him it slips away and slips right back to Jesus."[104] Through the role of silence, group readers variously saw the play of power that 15:1–5 narrates as being complicated. What the group readers' interpretations presented was a lack of consensus regarding the agency exercised within the text. It is this very agonism, left unresolved in the reading groups, that I now wish to probe in returning to the text and asking how Jesus practices his own resistive agency in speech and in silence and how this agency relates to the praxis of mutuality.

6.2.4. Silent Agency: The Choice for Silence and Mutuality

Group readers' interpretations of this pericope, especially of the themes of power, dialogue, and silence, reveal the same sort of heterogeneity that scholars' interpretations do. Jesus, in particular, was read by some as a person who remains silent in the encounter, confident in "abilities Pilate never dreamt of" (see n. 100), yet was read by others as not offering a reply to Pilate's question in 15:4 ("Have you no answer? See how many charges they bring against you") because he is "overwhelmed" (see n. 95). The roles of silence and dialogue in this pericope thus remain unclear.

---

never dreamt of, he has a power beyond description" (C from Reading Group Two, May 2, 2006).

100. "Well, I think he's preached so much to people, he doesn't think he should dignify all this with a reply" (B from Reading Group One, May 2, 2006).

101. "Frustrated. He's been laughed at by Jesus. His silence condemns Pilate" (A from Reading Group Two, May 2, 2006).

102. B from Reading Group One, May 2, 2006.

103. A from Reading Group Two, May 2, 2006.

104. A from Reading Group One, May 2, 2006.

That said, there is one set of emphases that remained peculiar to group readers in their interpretations of this pericope: the strong associations made between the narrated experience of Jesus in the story and their own real life experiences. Not only were associations made between Jesus' experience of being bound (see n. 81), being led away,[105] and being handed over (see n. 86), associations were also made with silence. Silence was associated by one reader with "subjection," "submission," and subservience,[106] while another stated, "Sometimes the most you can say is nothing."[107] These two sets of associations—of being bound, led away, and handed over, and of the place of silence in the lives of persons with poor mental health—when taken together, suggest a way of probing this pericope that asks how silence might operate as a postcolonial praxis.

The possibility that I explore below is that Jesus' decision to be silent rather than speak—and that this is not an indication that he is one who seeks to side with the oppressed (Cárdenas Pallares 1986, 98), nor that he is one who passively endures his cosmic fate (Lane 1974, 552)—is an indication that silence might function in this pericope as a dialogical strategy. William Campbell already makes this point that Jesus' silence is an act of disengagement in the face of the testimony of the chief priests in 15:3, and a strategy that amazes his previous interlocutor, Pilate, in 15:5 (2004, 290). Similarly, José Cárdenas Pallares asserts that the religious authorities of Israel no longer fully recognized Jesus as a person, such that "Jesus cannot speak to them in a language they are willing to use." Jesus' silence, continues Cárdenas Pallares, serves to unmask the "farce" of his so-called trial (1986, 98). Contrary to these interpretations, I wish to explore the possibility that the employment of silence by Jesus is an act of dialogical engagement with Pilate.

That silence was used as a strategy during legal proceedings in antiquity is suggested by a number of scholars. For example, Campbell cites how in Philostratus (*Vit. Apoll.* 8.2), Apollonious refers to silence as the "fourth excellence in a court of law," highlighting Socrates as a model (2004, 286). Similarly, Ernst Bammel cites Josephus's report that Jesus, son of Ananias,

---

105. "Actually, they put one of my friends in restraints, I didn't like that" (C from Reading Group Two, May 2, 2006).

106. "Silence and subjection. It's submission, humility. We're subservient to the staff, we take advice and protection but we have to help them to wash dishes" (A from Reading Group Two, May 2, 2006).

107. A from Reading Group Two, May 2, 2006.

was acquitted after refusing to offer a defense before Jewish and Roman authorities (1984, 422). Jesus' silence in 15:3–5 also can be considered to resonate with the theological principle advocated in 13:11: "when they bring you to trial and deliver you up, do not be anxious beforehand what you are to say; but say whatever is given to you in that hour for it is not you who speak, but the Holy Spirit" (W. Campbell 2004, 289).

How, then, might Jesus' silence be interpreted textually as a strategy of engagement with Pilate? One possibility is to interpret Jesus' silence as opening up a shared dialogical space in order to affirm the potential of Pilate to act within that space. John Keenan suggests that Jesus' silence reveals who he is by mirroring the presence of Abba in his broken humanity, "standing unprotected before the plans and machinations of deluded minds" (1995, 373). What, though, if Jesus' silence was not an attempt to engage Pilate's "deluded mind," but to affirm his potential to act?[108] Jesus' emptying of the dialogical space between himself and Pilate, and by extension between himself and the assembled crowd, clears the way for Pilate, the crowds, and by an even further extension the reader, to choose to answer the preeminent Markan question: "Who do you say that I am?" (8:29).

Jesus can be interpreted in 15:3–5 to withdraw as a speaking dialogue partner in order to allow the other agents in the text to exercise agency at the critical moment of the encounter: the ethical moment of life and death. Through the lens of mutuality as a postcolonial praxis, this strategy of engagement is one that seeks to reimagine a postcolonial space of relating into being at the very site of colonial power. This is not, though, sly civility that Jesus presents in the face of power, and it is certainly not the passivity of the suffering servant. This is an open attempt to reimagine colonial discourse as it occurs.

Yet as a postcolonial praxis that might invite others into the reimagining of hegemonic relational dynamics, the extent to which silence can operate as a praxis of mutuality is limited by the ambiguity of its operation in 15:1–5. On one hand, one could argue that Jesus' silence in the encounter stands as an invitational praxis that seeks to draw Pilate into a dialogical exchange beyond the charges of the chief priests and into a space where

---

108. The notion that silence might be interpreted as a dialogical strategy of engagement resonates with arguments in pastoral theology about the need to foster "more mature" models of human adequacy "in relation to God" that move beyond human infantile dependency and God as super-father figure; see Woodruff 1978, 26.

hegemonic and colonial relational dynamics are not only resisted, but through the agency of the colonial power par excellence—Pilate—have the potential to be transformed. In this sense, Pilate may say anything of his choosing within the dialogical space that Jesus' silence opens up. In some ways, then, the role of silence as a postcolonial praxis might be likened to the invitational praxis of mutuality in 3:1–6 in Jesus' word to the man with the withered hand to "come forward" (3:3). In 15:1–5 it is Pilate to whom the invitation to "come forward" is made. Indeed, keeping in mind the question that Jesus poses to those who were watching in the synagogue in Capernaum—"Is it lawful to do good or do harm on the sabbath, to save life or to kill?" (3:4)—and the response of those to whom it is put—"But they were silent" (3:4)—one might see 15:1–5 as a mirror image of that earlier encounter, with the same question of the lawfulness of saving a life still hanging over Jesus' ministry. Here it is Pilate, seen through the lens of an invitational praxis of mutuality that seeks the transformation of the life-denying relational dynamics of the scene, who is challenged to come up with a definitive answer.

On the other hand, one could argue that the role of silence in 15:1–5 is limited to a praxis of mutuality that is only resistive and does not aspire to transformation. That is, Jesus could have used a strategy of silence in order to reassert his identity as a person who still retains at least some power in his encounter with Pilate: "I think at first power is to Pilate. He's the big shot, but as Jesus doesn't answer him it slips away and slips right back to Jesus."[109] Thus one might see the operation of silence in this pericope to function similarly to the way the ambiguity used by Jesus in 3:19b–35 functions: as a strategy through which Jesus sought to distance himself from the charges being brought before him. Yet silence does not operate in a way that enables the transformation of the relational dynamics Jesus is faced with. Indeed, it is striking how Jesus' ambiguous silence here follows charges that are made against him by the chief priests (15:3) just as his ambiguous binarism in 3:19b–35 follows charges also brought by religious leaders (the scribes who "came down from Jerusalem," 3:22).

While the extent to which silence as a postcolonial praxis operates as a praxis of mutuality is difficult to ascertain, the effectiveness of the strategy is not. With the teleology of 15:1–5 in mind—Jesus' execution—the strategy of silence that Jesus employs in the encounter with Pilate and the

---

109. A from Reading Group One, May 2, 2006.

crowd is a failed one. For whether intended by Jesus to be invitational or intentionally ambiguous, Pilate does not respond positively to the silence he encounters in Jesus, other than being amazed (15:5).

To view silence as a strategy of engagement and resistance that attempts to call forth the agency of others might be in the light of the group readers' perspectives a rather utopian notion of the significance of silence in dialogical relating. However, as I have already discussed, struggles within hegemonic relational dynamics should not be seen as agencies that necessarily lead to a utopian transformation of hegemonic relational dynamics. Indeed, perhaps it is the inevitability of Jesus' sentence to death that reveals the utility of the praxis of silence. For what silence affords is a space of dignity within relational dynamics that seek to deny such a place for the "other." This praxis thus enables a sense of mutuality within the self when all other hopes for mutual relation are lost. Silence, then, might be seen as a praxis that undermines colonial power in circumstances where open resistance is clearly a lost cause, not in the hope of toppling colonial rule, but in the hope of finding solace in the face of that power's inevitable reach. If it is the case, then, as one reader proposed, that "sometimes the most you can say is nothing,"[110] perhaps silence ends up saying a great deal, even if the subaltern voicing of such silent speech is most often irretrievable.

With the other texts in mind, the above exploration of the dialogical function of silence need not be limited to this pericope. For instance, one reader commented in relation to the attack on Jesus' character in 3:19b–35: "Even so-called regular people, if you say the truth, people let you have it. Even regular people have to shut up. Jesus had to keep his mouth shut sometimes. That's the way of society."[111] Similar interpretations of the absence of speech were suggested about the man with the withered hand in 3:1–6, who some group readers thought was hiding and "cowering in a corner,"[112] "afraid."[113] Likewise, one group reader saw the woman with

---

110. A from Reading Group Two, May 2, 2006.
111. A from Reading Group One, April 4, 2006.
112. "He's hiding, cowering in the corner. They wouldn't have wanted him to get help just because it was that day" (D from Reading Group Two, March 21, 2006).
113. "Could be afraid to for societal reasons. The fact that they wanted to destroy the man who healed him—I can see he would be afraid they were going to destroy him too, he would be petrified" (B from Reading Group Two, March 21, 2006).

hemorrhages in 5:21–43 as crawling on the ground due to an inability to speak openly with Jesus.[114]

Thus, while silence is explored here in the analysis of 15:1–5, it was a prevalent feature of group readers' interpretations across the different pericopae, especially in their interpretations of so-called subaltern characters in the text. One might think that what these interpretations constitute as a collection of insights is the strand of postcolonial biblical criticism that attempts to "resurrect lost voices" that have been distorted or silenced in the canonized text (Sugirtharajah 1999b, 4). Here, though, what is being heard are lost "voices" of silence, heard in multiple ways and in multiple settings. This exploration of the role of silence does not seek to reify the agency of the oppressed in a suggestion that somehow silence is a more significant agency than it actually is in the text; rather it seeks to serve as a reminder of the struggles that living within hegemonic relational dynamics might entail.

This emphasis on silence also links back to this work's societal location as a piece of contextual biblical criticism and the significance of silence in the lived experience of poor mental health in North Atlantic societies. In chapter 1 I mentioned that Foucault's genealogical exploration of poor mental health sees silence as a prominent feature of the societal landscape of persons with poor mental health,[115] and Sander Gilman argues that the exclusionary societal practices related to language have tended to reduce persons with poor mental health to silence.[116]

---

114. "She knew she had to struggle with herself. Had to crawl on the ground to get to that cloth and when she touched, she knew" (D from Reading Group Four, April 25, 2006).

115. "Madness, which for so long had been overt and unrestricted, which had for so long been present on the horizon, disappeared. It entered a phase of silence from which it was not to emerge for a long time; it was deprived of its language; and although one continued to speak of it, it became impossible for it to speak of itself" (Foucault 1976, 68); "All the rest is reduced to silence … the silence of mental disease, as it would develop in the asylum, would always only be of the order of observation and classification. It would not be dialogue" (Foucault 2001, 59); "Delivered from his chains, he is now chained by silence" (248).

116. "One does not even have to wait for the insane to speak. The mentally ill are instantly recognizable" (Gilman 1988, 48).

6.3. Conclusion

What, then, should be made of dialogue in these pericopae? In terms of 15:1–5, dialogue is a process, even in silence, that always has the potential to collapse into monologue. Jesus' agency fails because as soon as his silence attempts to open up space for another's agency in that relational encounter, the execution cries of the crowd (15:13–14) and Pilate's sentence (15:15) collapse all chances for dialogue to continue. Jesus remains bound, led away, and handed over, and his condition only worsens until his own breaking of his silence in his cry of dereliction from the cross (15:34). The praxis of dialogue, such as it operates in this pericope, is exercised within a thin space of hope.

In this vein, the dialogical agency of the man among the tombs in 5:1–20 also is exercised within a thin space of hope, yet with quite different results. For, while Jesus' encounter with Pilate foreshadows death, the man who lived among the tombs had already managed to survive amid the dead. Moreover, the man not only survives dead ends, but also, through the praxis of mutual dialogue, he recovers from them. Thus 5:1–20 is a recovery story, where dialogue is an effective emancipatory tool leading not only to the man's recovery from that which possessed him, but also to the recovery of the possibility of mutual relating in the town from which he had come.

In terms of the praxis of dialogue, what clearly separates these two stories is that while in 5:1–20 dialogue is enabled by the praxis of mutuality between Jesus and the man among the tombs, in 15:1–5 there is little room at all given to such praxis even if Jesus' strategy of silence is understood as one that sought out the transformation of a hegemonic relational dynamic. In the end Jesus' praxis of mutuality is not reciprocated. Without mutuality, dialogue as a tool of emancipation and transformation, as presented in these texts at least, is a lost cause.

I will address more of the role and efficacy of the praxis of mutuality in chapter 7. With this, what I will ask of these readings is how such explorations of biblical texts might speak to everyday relational dynamics of persons with poor mental health and the discourses that shape those dynamics.

7
MUTUALITY AND MARK:
REFLECTIONS TEXTUAL AND CONTEXTUAL

In this work I have explored the extent to which mutuality might be an effective form of resistive and transformative postcolonial praxis. In this final chapter, I assess this possibility to ascertain what has emerged by placing perceptions of the lived experience of poor mental health into conversation with the biblical texts. My primary interest lies in assessing the operation of mutuality as a postcolonial praxis within the Markan texts analyzed. Specifically, I explore below how this praxis operates within the agonisms of power differentials, how the praxis of mutuality might delineate according to gender and according to an axis of hidden versus open agency, and how mutuality acts as an enabler of other postcolonial praxes. Considering these features, I ask how effective mutuality is as a praxis with the potential to be both resistive and transformative of relational power dynamics, and I assess its significance as a praxis that is supplemental. Following this, I suggest how this work of contextual biblical criticism might offer expansions for interpretation and hermeneutics in biblical scholarship. I also explore various methodological limitations that future work might seek to address.

7.1. MUTUALITY AS A POSTCOLONIAL PRAXIS: QUALITIES AND EFFICACIES WITHIN TEXTUAL RELATIONAL DYNAMICS

As I argued in chapter 2, to see mutuality as both a resistive *and* a transformational praxis is to push at the boundaries of what counts as postcolonial agency, that is, beyond praxis only as reactive survival operating from within the assumption of hegemony. I explored the effectiveness of mutuality as an agency that might hold the potential both to resist hegemonic discourses and to some extent to begin to transform those discourses.

As a piece of contextual biblical criticism, this work has followed the classic pattern of moving from context to text and then back again to context. It has related to context through the analysis of the relational dynamics of textual encounters between Jesus and other characters in Mark, informed by the readership of persons who have experienced the societal contexts of poor mental health. I should state clearly here that this work has never intended to offer a biblically generated prescriptive model for context. Relational dynamics of ancient Near Eastern texts cannot simply and unproblematically be translated into twenty-first-century contexts; the praxis of mutuality and indeed the other forms of postcolonial praxes analyzed in these Markan texts are not suggested as options for real life acts of relating. Rather, I offer this work as a correlative to possible lived experiences of mental health in contemporary society, to offer heuristics for relational encounters with persons with poor mental health. Such a stance acknowledges that while ancient biblical texts cannot simply be superimposed onto modern-day contexts, they may well inform such contexts. The practice of reading from context to text, and back from text to context, can be valuable if the status of such a correlation remains heuristic and not pedagogical or prescriptive.

In making this full circle back to context, it is informative to locate the interpretations of this work within recent developments in mental health services and the literature related specifically to the recovery of people who have experienced seasons of poor mental health and the agency of such persons in that recovery. This focus is important as the agency of characters in the Gospel of Mark in their "recoveries" was one of the central emphases of middle chapters of this work. The significance of dialogue as part of therapeutic encounters with persons with poor mental health has come to the forefront over the past twenty years. Central to this attempt has been a reconsideration of the agency of persons with poor mental health in their ability to make choices. For instance, William Anthony, a leading advocate of the recovery movement in psychiatric discourse, contends that whereas historically choice had been taken away from persons with poor mental health under the belief that they could not make useful choices for themselves, longitudinal research has found that listening to people who seek to recover from episodes of poor mental health is crucial to the success of that recovery (2003, 24). Anthony asserts that much present medical practice takes choice away from users such that so-called recovery programs are mandated and not cooperative, with providers neglecting to acknowledge complicity when users fail to attend sessions or fail to recover (25). It is in this vein that the centrality of dialogue is highlighted again and again in the literature:[1] "I'm

---

1. See, e.g., J. Green 2003, 3; Faulkner and Layzell 2000, 2; Wright 2001, 35.

tired of being talked about, treated as a statistic, pushed to the margins of human conversation, I want someone who will have time for me" (Gilbert and Nicholls 2003, 1). Indeed, Sarah Wright argues that it is not simply the fact of relationship and dialogue that is significant, but, predictably, it is the quality of the same (2001, 14).

A further correlation between text and context in recovery work is the recognition that individuals with poor mental health are more than mere descriptions of their pathology. Disregard for this leads to a skewed power dynamic from the outset of a relational encounter (Anthony 1993, 536); as one group reader testified: "You think misdiagnosis—label—say, schizophrenic, and you really aren't one … and we might feel inferior."[2] This recognition of users as participants in their medical treatment has most significantly been demonstrated by the emergence of the "user-led" movement (see, e.g., J. Green 2003; Faulkner and Layzell 2000). This movement contends that users of mental health services need to be able to develop their own strategies for treatment and so forge their own path—articulate their own way—to recovery and healing (Faulkner and Layzell 2000, 3). Indeed, Jim Green suggests that the very concept of recovery requires that people with poor mental health take control and that models of best practice make the move away from a medical model of the person as patient and toward a user-led model of the person as survivor (2003, 2–3). Anthony states that the professional should no longer be seen as the provider of treatment but as the facilitator of recovery (1993, 531). In an interesting parallel to my own dialogical method, the need for psychiatry (Spaniol 2001, 169), and perhaps more widely for discourse on mental health, to "listen to the stories" of persons with poor mental health is expressed with increasing volume and acceptance (Chavez 2000).

In several ways these contextual developments that focus on recovery correlate with the interpretive insights of this project. The agency of individuals to make choices, the centrality of listening to people such that this might lead to their recovery, the importance of give and take in dialogue and the quality of the relationship between dialogue partners, the movement toward a user-led understanding of recovery whereby individuals might articulate their own ways to healing, and the conception of professionals as facilitators in the recovery process are all features that relate to

---

2. C from Reading Group Three, April 3, 2006.

the operation of mutuality in the relational dynamics of Markan texts as illumined in my work with group readers.

Beyond these general correlations, in multiple ways the core concept of the praxis of mutuality offers heuristics for the lived societal experience of poor mental health that I argue below present an expansion to these contextual developments. These heuristics are made explicit in interpretations of the textual relational dynamics of Mark. The first heuristic is that mutuality operates within and not beyond the structures of discursive power. From a Foucauldian perspective, this might look like a statement of the obvious. However, I need to stress again that, quite different from the theological and hermeneutical teleologies of liberation hermeneutics and its motif of liberation from the margins, the praxis of mutuality operates within the agonisms of relational power, seeking to resist the tendency in biblical interpretation to move to sublation or resolution.

A striking example of mutuality operating within the structures of discursive power proceeds from the analysis of 5:1–20, the man who lives among the tombs. This pericope narrates only the partial transformation of what binds the man—his "unclean spirits." However, the townspeople, who supposedly had bound him in the first place, also held power over the man and are still present at the end of the pericope as troubling purveyors of power. There is no sense in this story that the man is to be liberated from this continued presence of discursive power by being granted his request to follow Jesus onto the boat and out of the relational tension that surrounds him. Rather, he is commissioned to go back to the people who had denied his own power for self-survival and mutual relationship. This aspect of domination is neither sublated nor resolved in the passage, and hence one can see 5:1–20 as only the beginning of a struggle for mutual relating.

Similarly, at the end of 3:1–6, the power structures still remain and emerge as threatening after the physical transformation of the "man with the withered hand." The somewhat enigmatic "they," introduced in 3:2, are not included in the relational dynamics of the transformation they witnessed inside of the synagogue, yet "they," named as the Pharisees at the end of the pericope, displace the seemingly liberatory nature of that space by their gathering with the Herodians outside the synagogue to seek ways to destroy Jesus (3:6). Therefore, Jesus' invitation and the man's choosing to respond to it do not render the relational dynamics of this scene liberated from exclusion and dominating power. Rather, with the supposed threat that such an act of transformation presented to religious authorities, struggles with those authorities were imagined to have continued. For Jesus, the struggle beyond this encounter points forward into Mark forebodingly all the way to the cross. As for the man, the reader is left to speculate as to how his open struggle to renegotiate identity and power leaves him within the discourse of religious/theological and political power of Capernaum. While his physical recovery might be celebrated, his societal status is far from secured. Indeed, as one group reader put it: "They might cut off his head."[3]

Structures of power are also retained in the struggles for survival and transformation in the two encounters Jesus has with women. Drawing on the emphases of group readers and feminist critiques of 5:21–43 and 7:24–30, I do not see Jesus as one who breaks the bonds of gendered and ethnic domination; rather, to an extent he colludes with them. In 5:21–43, unlike the male protagonist in the story (Jairus) who openly negotiates his daughter's healing, the woman is forced to take healing and power from Jesus surreptitiously, and ultimately her gendered alterity is not surpassed in the pericope. Similarly, in 7:24–30 the woman faces the pejorative structures of power wherein ethnically charged difference is retained in the story such that while healing is gained for her daughter, the woman is humiliated in the process. Perhaps nowhere in the six pericopae more than in 15:1–5 are the structures of hegemonic power retained. Here no amount of incitement to reimagine power via the spacious silence of Jesus is enough to transcend structures of power and death that seem to run with dramatic inevitability throughout the Gospel to this point.

Thus, from the readings of the pericopae studied, the praxis of mutuality clearly operates within the retention of power differentials. This conclusion is significant for the recovery movement within mental health, particularly keeping in mind the movement's emphasis on partnership and dialogue. This work offers the point that "recovery" takes place for these textual characters within the struggles of hegemonic relational dynamics. On one hand, this emphasis simply reinforces a key proposition of pastoral care practitioners who utilize a liberation hermeneutics paradigm: the relational dynamics of poor mental health are set within a social structure of power that is in ways hegemonic (Pattison 1994, 94). On the other hand, it offers a crucial development: encounters with persons with poor mental health exercising agencies of recovery are encounters that expect

---

3. A from Reading Group Two, March 21, 2006.

the agonisms of societal power to remain largely intact for such persons, and not give way to a liberative site of the resolution of those agonisms. Viewed through a textual lens, various degrees and forms of hegemonic societal power might be seen as constants in the emergence of recovery.

A second heuristic drawn from this work is that mutuality operates in these texts according to gender-specific delineations of power. This can be demonstrated in analyzing the axis of open versus hidden forms of agency, as alluded to above. In chapter 2 I raised the question of the potential hiddenness of postcolonial agency. In considering the work of James Scott (1990) I asked whether mutuality might be seen to operate in Markan texts as an open or as a more hidden form of postcolonial praxis. In terms of the readings of the pericopae, the results are split almost entirely along lines of gendered differentiation. For instance, in 5:21–43 the agency of the woman with hemorrhages is seen to be an intentionally hidden and liminal act of survival. Similarly, the confrontation that the Syrophoenician woman initiates in 7:24–30, as direct as it might be, takes place in the privacy, or hiddenness, of a home. Interestingly, group readers did not interpret either of these encounters to be one wherein mutual relating was present much at all. Even if the movement within each pericope toward greater intimacy is taken as evidence of the praxis of mutuality, it is seen to operate more as a by-product of other agencies rather than as a praxis that was intended from the outset of the encounter. Thus what might distinguish the instances of more hidden postcolonial praxes of resistance and transformation is that where the praxis of mutuality does seem to become augmented, it is pushed into the situation more than invited.

For instance, the Syrophoenician woman is seen to renegotiate the terms of colonial relational dynamics and thus possibly bring Jesus to a more mutual form of praxis via the use of rhetorical mimicry. The mutuality of the encounter, if one accepts that it is there, serves as a corollary of mimicry, not an enabler of it. Similarly, the debated greater mutuality that emerges between Jesus and the woman with hemorrhages in 5:33–34 is a result of the surreptitious nature of her agency being made public. Mutual relating is not sought at the outset. Jesus does not, at first, notice the woman; she has to stretch out to reach him.

By contrast, a male, Jairus, who in 5:21–43 negotiates a healing for his daughter in public, stands as a clear example of open agency. Such open acts of resistive praxis are seen with the other males of the pericopae, such as the man among the tombs in 5:1–20 who runs toward Jesus in full view; the man in the synagogue in 3:1–6 whose decisive action was open and public, literally in the middle of relational space in the synagogue at Capernaum; and finally Jesus himself as interpreted in 15:1–5 to offer an open yet silent moment of mutual relating, albeit one that ultimately fails.

The praxis of mutuality is not a more hidden form of postcolonial agency by nature. Rather, this praxis delineates along lines of gender identity. As a praxis operating within hegemonic relational dynamics, the embodied double othering of females is played out through the perceived operation of mutuality, such that the subaltern females of these texts are seen to exercise a hiddenness in their praxes. This is the reverse of Carter Heyward's notion of relational power as the mutuality that might be expected to exist between persons (1999, 3). For these women apparently expected that mutuality would be absent, not present, thus necessitating more hidden forms of agency. For males acting within colonial relational contexts, open displays of mutual relating were demonstrated as not only permissible but beneficial.

Not only is the openness of the praxis of mutuality in these pericopae gender specific, a third heuristic drawn from this work is that male praxis of mutuality opens the way to transformative encounters not as a by-product of other praxes but as an enabler of them. For instance, in 5:1–20 Jesus and the man among the tombs are both characters whose identities and agencies in the text are subversive of hegemonic relational power. Their praxis is successful as an emancipatory tool due to the relative presence of mutuality in dialogue. By contrast, Jesus' binaristic rhetoric in 3:19b–35, which is shrouded in ambiguity, is marked by a profound absence of mutuality in its full form. While it is resistive, it is not aspiring of a positive transformation of relational dynamics he shares with his biological family or with the scribes from Jerusalem. Indeed, the strategy of ambiguity that I stated Jesus employs in 3:19b–35 is one that does not succeed effectively to resist the hegemonic acts of labeling he faces, let alone work to transform those relational dynamics. In fact, as I presented in chapter 4, the absence of the fuller praxis of mutuality serves as a prelude to the souring of relations between his family and the scribes as the Gospel narrative goes on.

Where there was a relative absence of the praxis of mutuality, effective resistance was present, but the transformation of hegemonic relational dynamics was less so. In the two pericopae in which I explored the agency of females—5:21–43 and 7:24–30—the relative absence of mutuality in those relational encounters did not mean that agency was entirely ineffective in those instances. Fundamentally, these pericopae are stories about the desire for healings, both of which successfully occur. The relative absence of the praxis of mutuality in these encounters does not undermine the notion that mutuality serves as an enabler of other praxes; it merely points to the conclusion that other postcolonial praxes can operate successfully without the aid of mutual relating as forms of resistance, but they do not operate as successfully as praxes that facilitate the transformation of hegemonic relational dynamics.

This role of mutuality as an enabler of other praxes corresponds to what I have maintained about the potential of mutuality as a praxis that works in conjunction with other postcolonial praxes. In chapter 2 I posited that the postcolonial praxes of hybridity, mimicry, ambiguity, sly civility, and other such incremental and supplemental forms of agency might be present and interact with the praxis of mutuality in the relational dynamics between characters in the selected Markan texts. Yet I also argued for a crucial delineation between these postcolonial praxes and mutuality, such that mutuality is a praxis that is both resistive and aspiring of the transformation of hegemonic relational dynamics and thus, in its full form, is inherently a more positive and hopeful praxis than its counterparts are.

How hopeful has the praxis of mutuality in these textual relational dynamics been? While I never contended that the praxis of mutuality was likely to tell "tall tales" of the overthrow of colonial structures, given these conclusions above about the operation of mutuality in the relational dynamics of Mark's Gospel, I might state that the high hope that mutuality as a postcolonial praxis could push at the boundaries of postcolonial notions of agency has not altogether been realized. For as it operates in these Markan texts, mutuality is discernible as a praxis that remains tied to structures of colonial power in general, and to gender in particular.

Is it the case, then, that mutuality in the end emerges more as an effective praxis of resistive survival than of transformation? When the pericopae are considered again, it is truly only in the story of the man among the tombs (5:1–20) that the praxis of mutuality opens the way for the relational dynamics of the man's life to be transformed. This man who had elicited the fear of others to the point where he was chained up and left among the dead (5:3–4), through the mutual praxis of dialogue about the man's way to healing between Jesus and the man among the tombs, ends the pericope leaving the very people who had shunned him amazed (5:20). In no other pericope is such a transformation of relational dynamics witnessed. For while in 15:1–5 Pilate is also "amazed" at Jesus' potentially invitational praxis of mutuality in silence (15:5), the outcome of that exchange is not the transformation of hegemonic relational dynamics but the execution of the silent man. In 3:1–6, a pericope in many ways demonstrating the efficacy of mutuality to enable another praxis of resistance and transformation, in this case hybridity, the foreboding ending to the story ("The Pharisees went out and immediately conspired with the Herodians against him, how to destroy him," 3:6) leaves a question mark over the extent of the transformation of the relational dynamics of the man with the withered/divine hand, even if his physical transformation is clear. Similarly, the relational dynamics of 3:19b–35 reveal no transformation of the rift narrated in the pericope between Jesus and his family and some scribes from Jerusalem.

It is tempting, therefore, to view the operation of mutuality in its full form of aspiring transformation as limited within the relational dynamics of these texts. However, in cases where the praxis of mutuality is seen to operate at least to some extent, its effect on the dynamics of power is such that although power dynamics are not overcome, they are rendered more diffuse. For instance, in 3:1–6 the dynamics of power held in tension between Jesus and those watching him, through the praxis of mutuality, appear to become diffused as that dynamic opens to include the hybrid power of the man with the withered/divine hand. Similarly, in both 5:21–43 and 7:24–30, women othered by power differentials of gender, economics, and ethnicity, while not interpreted to transform hegemonic relational dynamics, do offer those relational contexts what Homi Bhabha has called a "supplemental position" to or "slight alteration" of such dynamics (1995, 82).

One might easily overlook this potential of the praxis of mutuality to render power dynamics more diffuse. However, I contend that this operates as more than just an instance of resistive survival, but serves as a beginning for a change in hegemonic relational dynamics operating as a transient form of praxis. For, in returning to the Foucauldian understanding of how counterdiscourses might be articulated, one might see the praxis of mutuality as an ad hoc counterdiscourse to hegemonic discourses that by necessity must be exercised again and again in the reimagining of power (Foucault 1982, 221). The question remains as to how the textual exploration of this final heuristic drawn from this work of a supplemental and incremental form of postcolonial agency might correlate with praxes in context. As I argued in chapter 2 regarding the supposed efficacy of third space praxes of resistance, Scott's work on the hidden nature of resistance suggests that the presence and effectiveness of mutuality as a supplemental and incremental praxis in context will be difficult to assess.[4] Yet perhaps it is this heuristic that might be most effective of all in the operation of mutuality as a postcolonial praxis of resistance and transformation. Indeed, as Bhabha argues, incremental and often liminal praxes of "slight alterations and displacements" are "often the most significant elements in a process of subversion and transformation" (1995, 82).

Such then are the correlative heuristics of my reading of the relational dynamics of six Markan pericopae. To conclude that the most that is seen of mutuality in terms of a praxis that might lead to the transformation of hegemonic relational dynamics is a supplemental and incremental form of agency seems to offer very little. Yet with the multiple and generally consistent emphases of group readers on the struggle of the characters of these texts, and their associations with their own lived experiences of struggle, such a thin space of hope is significant. Indeed, I would herald these interpretations of textual instances of resistance, and the beginnings of the transformation of hegemonic relational dynamics to postcolonial ones, as the most significant achievements of this work. For in them the difference that this perceived alterity embodies is not overcome, nor is it sublated; rather it is an avenue for survival and even hope. Such insights into these biblical texts have become possible because of the partners in reading that were engaged in this work. It is to an assessment of that hermeneutical decision that I now turn.

7.2. Mutuality and Mark: Hermeneutical Achievements and Limitations

In terms of this work's location within biblical criticism, one of the key components is its use of a dialogical reading method. One of the central achievements of this approach is that group readers offered an expansion of the interpretation of the relational dynamics of the texts in question. This occurred in several ways. First, group readers related their own struggles to those of the characters in the pericopae. For instance, the struggles interpreted by group readers to be present described feelings

---

4. "Unless one can penetrate the official transcript of both subordinates and elites, a reading of the social evidence will almost always represent a confirmation of the status quo in hegemonic terms" (Scott 1990, 90).

of unworthiness,[5] "prejudice,"[6] name-calling,[7] and as reflecting personhood that is "different,"[8] hidden,[9] "cursed,"[10] "alienated,"[11] a "project" and an "experiment,"[12] rejected,[13] and even "guilty."[14] Indeed, beyond this pericope, readers questioned whether characters in relational encounters felt stupid and wondered if they were "normal,"[15] begging,[16] requiring

---

5. "It is said in the Bible, Jesus said go and sin no more. That part always scares me. Somehow sin is attached to affliction. I struggle with that sin leads to punishment. There are different schools of thought that mental illness is possession or spiritual warfare" (C from Reading Group Three, April 3, 2006).

6. A: "Yeah. It's called prejudice. They don't understand, they hate them automatically. They make up stories. Our Lord never had prejudice. He tried to help as many people as possible." B: "They were probably afraid that sometimes they might find it, might call it an illness in the hand. People are afraid of the mentally ill." D: "You think so?" B: "Yeah" (from Reading Group One, March 21, 2006).

7. "They call you names—loony, crazy" (B from Reading Group Two, March 21, 2006).

8. "Yes, I feel that when you are different you stand out. Everybody watches him and is seeing what you are going to do about him" (B from Reading Group One, March 21, 2006).

9. "He hid out. He wasn't accepted, he was different" (B from Reading Group Two, March 21, 2006).

10. "Maybe he had a family but when he got disabled, they said, 'You got yourself cursed, get out of here'" (C from Reading Group Three, April 3, 2006).

11. "When Jesus was going about teaching and preaching these people were so obsessed with the law. When you were struck with leprosy at that time there was no cure. They were alienated from normal people" (B from Reading Group Four, April 4, 2006).

12. "He became a project—he was used, like an experiment" (B from Reading Group Four, April 4, 2006).

13. "The crowd rejects him the same reason they reject Jesus. They don't want to identify with Jesus" (C from Reading Group Four, April 4, 2006).

14. "I think he was probably ambivalent. He wanted to be healed but he felt guilty. We know how that is. Guilty that he didn't go to Jesus of his own will" (C from Reading Group Four, April 4, 2006).

15. B: "Stupid. Because he is just standing there. His hand is not like anyone else's. He's wondering if he is normal." C: "The man feels responsible." A: "He can't help it, although I think some of the people are wondering how he had it." D: "He might be nervous or afraid, in the spotlight. Before he was not in the spotlight, now everybody can see him" (from Reading Group One, March 21, 2006).

16. "She had humility. I beg to people sometimes, well yeah, if I'm asking for forgiveness or I don't want to be punished. Like with the staff at the home—be merciful, have mercy" (C from Reading Group One, April 25, 2006).

mercy,[17] trusting people they did not know,[18] and taking risky actions out of desperation.[19]

The fundamental expansion that group readers offered, and this was seen across reading groups, was the emphasis on the profound alterity that biblical characters were perceived to inhabit. This made relational encounters much less straightforward than some of the staid subject locations often presented in biblical scholarship of characters: Jew and Gentile (5:1–20), male and female (7:24–30), Jesus and "the Pharisees" (3:1–6), and so on. What group readers added was a thicker description of the imagined personal nature of the colonial landscape. Thus they saw encounters as "upsetting" experiences,[20] so much so that "sometimes the most you can say is nothing."[21] When encounters were read to be more hopeful in their emancipatory possibilities, such hopefulness was often set in relief to a more existentially rich backdrop. For instance, in the case of the man among the tombs in 5:1–20, despite being described as a person who was "troubled,"[22] punished,[23] a "loser" whom nobody liked,[24] and so on, such a relational encounter was still seen as a possibility for hope and

---

17. "For her forgiveness, she needs to be forgiven" (A from Reading Group One, April 25, 2006).

18. A: "Could be, opening up to someone you don't really know." B: "Where he comes from it is." A: "It shows trust. I myself wouldn't trust in doing it like that" (from Reading Group Two, April 25, 2006).

19. "Well, it seems to me that she's kind of desperate. Her daughter has a demon or whatever. She doesn't quite know what to do about it. She's probably tried numerous things without getting anything out of it. So she's looking to somebody to help the situation she has" (A from Reading Group Two, April 25, 2006).

20. "It would be upsetting. I would feel disillusioned, not know what to say, or say I didn't think you were like this … I think some people have this mental constitution to react in that way [referring to the Syrophoenician woman's reaction to Jesus in 7:28] but … mental health problems can overlap with problems with hating yourself, feeling depressed and getting really high and manic" (A from Reading Group Three, April 24, 2006).

21. A from Reading Group Two, May 2, 2006.

22. "Troubled. Seeking a miracle in life from the Lord. He's going through hard times and needs a good miracle. He really needs something good to happen to him" (B from Reading Group One, April 11, 2006).

23. "It's a kind of punishment. Maybe they thought they were protecting him" (D from Reading Group One, April 11, 2006).

24. "He might have seemed a loser, might not have liked him. No one wanted to have anything to do with him" (C from Reading Group One, April 11, 2006).

transformation, of "giving up the control" and daring to "let go."[25] Indeed, the breaking of chains[26] and becoming "okay" were profoundly significant images for certain readers.[27] Fundamentally, group readers did not overlook, rather they probed as an important aspect of biblical interpretation, the profundity of human struggle when set within contexts where mutual relating is deficient.

I have also argued that another significant hermeneutical feature that pursuing a dialogical form of postcolonial biblical criticism would enable is the resistance of the tendency to elevate the identity and agency of Jesus, and to relegate the identity and agency of so-called minor characters. However, what occurred was a fairly consistent pattern of interpretations across reading groups that elevated Jesus' status, often at times beyond the text's narration (e.g., Jesus was described as "our Lord" who "never had prejudice,"[28] as one who is "divine" and who "didn't make mistakes like human beings,"[29] and as the "all-powerful God" who "doesn't need to play games with anybody").[30] In addition, though, so-called minor characters were seen as significant agents in the relational spaces they shared with Jesus (e.g., from the man in 3:1–6 who demonstrates belief[31] and holds on to hope,[32] to the woman in 5:21–43 who "takes something" from

---

25. A: "It's giving up the control." B: "You dare to let go, like the OCD, you dare to be mediocre" (from Reading Group Three, April 17, 2006).

26. "To me the image is powerful—breaking chains" (A from Reading Group Three, April 17, 2006, in response to the facilitator's question: "Is the man powerful or powerless, would you say?").

27. "That he was screaming, naked, beating himself, lonely—now he is okay, I think that to me is no joke. I pray for that every day" (B from Reading Group Three, April 17, 2006).

28. "Yeah. It's called prejudice. They don't understand, they hate them automatically. They make up stories. Our Lord never had prejudice. He tried to help as many people as possible" (A from Reading Group One, March 21, 2006).

29. "Jesus was divine, he didn't make mistakes like human beings" (D from Reading Group One, April 4, 2006).

30. "I think Christ is an unassuming man. He doesn't need to play games with anybody. He is the all-powerful God" (B from Reading Group Two, April 18, 2006).

31. "He played a big part. He had to believe" (C Reading Group One, March 21, 2006).

32. "He accepted what had happened to him and he did not try to deny them because he went and accepted them. He tried to hold on to hope and he got better" (E from Reading Group Two, March 21, 2006).

Jesus[33] and heals herself).[34] In this vein, it is not the agency of Jesus, nor the agency of textual "others," but the dynamics of power between these characters that is stressed.

This emphasis on the dynamics between characters relates to the place that this work's reflections on Mark have in postcolonial biblical criticism in two specific ways. One is that in this work Jesus and the characters he encounters are not interpreted to act either as simply pro- or anticolonial agents. Rather, what emerges is an interpretation more akin to Simon Samuel's notion of characters as operating along an axis of both antagonism and affiliation to colonial discourse (2007, 156). For instance, on one hand, Jesus undermines hegemonic praxis, such as in his recognition of and dialogical engagement with the man among the tombs in 5:1–20, or in his subversion of the authority of those who watch him in 3:1–6 in his invitation for the man with the withered hand to come forward. On the other hand, Jesus also colludes with the structures of hegemonic relational dynamics such as in his ethnocentric othering of the Syrophoenician woman in 7:24–30. Indeed, as I maintained in chapter 5, in 5:21–43 the woman with hemorrhages exercises agency liminally, expecting Jesus to act in complicity with hegemonic gradations of gendered power; and by the same token, Jairus acts under the same assumption, but to his favor, by exercising agency openly.

The importance of agency and the view of encounters between characters in Mark as negotiations with power resonate with the other connection to postcolonial biblical criticism that I sought to explore: the attempt to "resurrect lost voices" in the hope that "the once-colonised" might produce "knowledge of their own" (Sugirtharajah 1999b, 4). This is exactly what I argue does occur in these pericopae in the central role that characters have in negotiating the dynamics of relational power within the hegemonic structures of their situation. Radical alterity, postcolonial agency,

---

33. "The crowd thinks she's ripped off this situation. She takes something from him. He was going to see someone else" (B from Reading Group Two, April 18, 2006).

34. Facilitator: "What part do you feel each person plays in their own healing?" B: "A major role: they heal themselves. It's just the way it happens, you have to do certain things." Facilitator: "And in the story?" D: "An important role. Not sure if it is small or large. I hope it would be large. You have to take care of the situation you are in. There was not much knowledge about medication, so there was a lot of self-healing" (from Reading Group Two, April 18, 2006).

and the possibilities of hopeful counterdiscourse all offer expansions of how the Markan texts might be read. These are articulations of lost voices.

Yet the significance of the dialogical method in postcolonial biblical criticism extends beyond the text alone to the act of inclusion that this method represents. As a practical attempt to answer Gayatri Spivak's challenge regarding subaltern speech (1995), the voices of those who have variously described what it is to know struggles within the hegemonic relational dynamics of poor mental health serve as a reminder to biblical studies of the significance of the colonial experience beyond the communal/structural level of analysis, and at the interpersonal level wherein the structures of power are felt. This simple yet profound emphasis should not be overlooked in how it correlates with the lived contexts of mental health today.

In this work, mutuality served as a heuristic for developing a dialogical reading space. The hope inherent in this methodology was that no single interpretive approach or conclusion was valued or validated over another, and that readers were encouraged to retain the tensions of different interpretations of the texts as they emerged in reading. Reflecting on the practice of this methodology, tensions, by and large, were retained. In part this was the product of pursuing a flatter reading relationship between readers and myself as facilitator, as discussed in chapter 3. Of course, it is difficult to assess how well this "flatness" was achieved. On one hand, the readings offered here are testament to the relative success of the model. For instance, one reader stated in the middle of an exchange between himself and another reader: "We all have our opinions here, right D?"[35] I might hope that this was a function of the sort of interpretive space that I endeavored to nurture during readings.

On the other hand, the success of this dialogical model was in the end limited in part by the challenge faced in numerous reading groups to remain focused on the act of reading. Such distractibility sometimes resulted in readings that look disparate and even incoherent. While this is a fair criticism, it should be qualified. While for some of the readers the ability, or indeed the desire, to focus on one task in the company of others was limited, this is also where the gift of these interpretations was

---

35. Facilitator: "What role does Jesus have in this?" C: "Nothing, Jesus had no role in it." B: "He's the savior." D: "I think Jesus cast the demon out." C: "I think the devil has to leave. We all have our opinions here, right D?" (from Reading Group One, April 25, 2006).

found: the unexpected and unlikely interpretations of these biblical stories by these group readers.

That said, it is clear that my practice of a dialogical form of postcolonial biblical criticism is also open to further critiques. One is that despite engaging with a reading population that was hitherto underrepresented in biblical studies, an area for future research might be to probe more extensively the significance of intercultural differences in reading insights. Although the reading groups included Caucasian, African American, and Latino readers, the groups were not as culturally diverse as those of other dialogical projects (see de Wit 2004b, 32), nor was there any attempt to probe such cultural diversity as a measure of interpretation. Indeed, it would be an invaluable asset for biblical studies within the area of mental health to be expanded by the vast diversity of global perspectives on reading texts in contexts beyond the ones this work explored.[36]

Another limitation of this work and an area for future research is the relationship between Bible reading and its impact on social structures.[37] While such a research concern is beyond conventional biblical criticism, it does invite an interdisciplinary approach to reading biblical texts that this book's contextually driven work at least points toward. Indeed, one of the most significant shortcomings is the absence of directly related engagement in praxis in relation to mental health. Gerald West is clear that the work of his own contextual Bible study consortium is not work done for the sake of research alone, but is done to effect change. Future work might take up West's challenge and attempt to embed academic work into the daily contexts of persons who experience poor mental health (West 2004a, 211). That said, it would be remiss to entirely discount the practical impact that the dissemination of ideas in the form of the written word can have in North Atlantic societies. For instance, some contend that one practical impact that may lead to a change in the praxis of readers is "perspective transformation," the idea that through acts of reading participants alter

---

36. See, e.g., de Wit's intercultural reading project that highlighted the significance of liturgical framings of reading experiences (de Wit and Kool 2004, 58) as well profoundly varied contextual locations (see, e.g., a reading group from El Salvador who experience "violence on the streets, in homes, in school, and between rival gangs. People in former war zones have been traumatized. Others experience oppression, daily hunger, and homelessness" (ibid.).

37. See de Wit 2004b, 42, who argues that very little is still known about the exact nature of this relationship.

their views of one another and of the issues that the reading highlights (Schipani and Schertz 2004, 440).

A further limiting factor is that the texts were selected by me before reading with groups began, indeed before I even met the readers. While I decided that the highly varied population of group members from week to week in each reading location necessitated the preselection of texts and the questions attached to those texts, future research might wish to embed more closely within a reading community, enabling such communities both to select texts and to generate more of their own questions regarding those texts, particularly before the Bible studies occur. Indeed, that the texts were biblical I had also decided beforehand, and thus reflects a limitation that future work might wish to address by exploring extrabiblical texts that readers themselves might wish to explore.

Beyond group readers not selecting texts and questions for the textual studies beforehand, another limitation of this work is in how undeveloped the relationship was between group readers' and trained scholars' interpretations. I chose to offer no information to group readers about the historical background to texts or about the varying interpretations of scholars concerning the relational dynamics of the particular stories. I avoided this in order to offset a strong division in expertise between myself as facilitator and the group readers. Thus the ways in which these differing interpretations of group readers and trained scholars were held in tension was something that I did unilaterally as the author of this work. That is, in the end this aspect of the project lacked mutuality; mutuality hit its limit.

A further limitation that also relates to the interpretive insights of group readers is that such readers' insights into biblical texts were solicited but no critiques of the same were offered. In organizing group readers' interpretations, what I looked for was consistent with the sampling methodology that I employed in reviewing scholars' perspectives. That is, I highlighted certain tendencies and emphases that I saw in the group readers' interpretive work.

That said, I believe that the decision not to offer any critique of readers during the Bible study process is justified for two reasons. First, to have offered critiques of group readers' perspectives in the course of the Bible studies may have threatened the hermeneutic pursued, which sought to maintain as flat a reading relationship as possible. One could argue that some critique may have produced a genuine dialogue about the differences between the readers' interpretations and the critique. However, critique also would have run the risk, at best, of encouraging group readers only to offer the sort of interpretations that they believed the facilitator wished to hear, and at worst, of shutting people down from contributing anything at all. This last possibility is no small thing for persons with poor mental health who might find themselves in other settings in the presence of experts who offer corrective visions of their insights.

Second, it would have been nonsensical to take insights from group readers, offered spontaneously and without edit, and after the act of reading was over to apply the same sort of critiques that are applied to biblical scholars whose work has been developed over the course of many years of training. Not only would this inhabit a certain level of dishonesty and nonmutuality—by offering no critique in the presence of group readers, only to offer it when they are no longer present to hear it—it would miss the point about the significance of these group readers' contribution to biblical interpretation. Group readers offer fresh insights and expansions of textual interpretations freed from some of the tried and tested trajectories and theological teleologies often in operation in biblical scholarship. To then apply those trajectories to such expansions without the platform to have those criticisms returned would potentially set up group readers' contributions for failure from the outset.

This tension within this project between so-called trained and untrained interpretive work begs the question as to the place within the rigor of academic dialogue that readers such as the group readers of this work have. Indeed, given this work's core concept of the praxis of mutuality, how much can dialogical biblical studies truly be mutual? The challenges of keeping focus, and at times keeping individuals engaged in the reading process in any coherent way at all, were significant in this work. As I mentioned above, the possibility of embedding within the life of a community over a long-term period might offer various benefits. It might be more possible for the same group readers to engage in the initial reading process in dialogue with one another, subsequently to come into dialogue, via the facilitator, with the insights of trained biblical scholarship in general, and then perhaps even with the facilitator in particular. This, of course, runs the risk of changing the relationship between group readers and facilitator, but if the aim of such an approach is to develop an organic intellectual reading relationship with group readers, then perhaps change in that relationship is what is desired. This work's reading population, with its transient attendance at the locations reading groups met, would not allow for such a development. However, work not dissimilar to this has been done in Hans de Wit's intercultural reading project, wherein reading groups exchange communal interpretations with global partners and then respond to the same, enabling both groups to see the text through the eyes of another group's interpretation (2004b, 5).

In terms of future research, three further areas of interest might relate well to mutuality. The first lies within the developing field of postcolonial theologies (see Keller et al. 2004) and specifically the Korean concept of *jeong* presented by Anne Joh: "Jeong connotes agape, eros, and filial love with the compassion, empathy, solidarity, and understanding that emerges between connected hearts," blurring boundaries between self and other (2004, 152–53). Yet jeong also captures the sense of struggle that relational dynamics inhabit, emerging "out of relationships that are not always based on mutuality" (153). Despite the commonalities between my own work and Joh's presentation of jeong, her interpretation of Jesus sees him blur and transgress the boundary between oppressor and oppressed through the jeong of compassion and empathy. However, exactly how such a transgression is manifest in the Gospels, especially where the praxis of Jesus looks to be much less in the spirit of jeong (such as in 3:19b–34 and 7:24–30), is unclear.

The second area of interest for future research lies within disability studies. Beyond the work of Nancy Eiesland, future research might relate the concept of mutuality as a postcolonial praxis to theologies of disability that have a Trinitarian theological grounding. One such theological approach to disability is offered by Jennie Weiss Block, who proposes a theological interplay between the church and the disability rights movement (2002, 21; cf. Reinders 2008, 181–90) via the notion that the "true human being" finds itself in a Trinitarian grounded communion with others where inclusion is found within the "copious host," Jesus Christ. Humans then act as cohosts of that Christ in being present to the other. For Block, this cohosting can take place only when persons with disabilities are also present (2002, passim; Reinders 2008, 181–90). On one hand, this sort of mandate to recognize the previously othered subaltern is a relatively common theme in the textual interpretations of this work, in which the initial manifestation of the praxis of mutuality was often seen as an agency that sought recognition. For the man with the withered hand (3:1–6), Jesus recognizes the already-present man with disability. For the man among the tombs (5:1–20), it is the man's running toward Jesus that demands recognition that he is a capable agent present within relational dynamics. For the woman with hemorrhages (5:21–43), her reaching out to touch Jesus was the demand that her very body be recognized as being present in the midst of the business of healing being transacted between Jesus and Jairus. On the other hand, when Block's notion of the Christ of the Trinity as "copious host" is considered, my reading of 7:24–30 immediately comes to mind as an agonistic conversation partner for such a theological prolegomenon, where Jesus' hosting involves the throwing of food (metaphorically at least) and insults.

The third and final word concerning possible future directions for this work should go to Stanley Hauerwas. In his own work, Hauerwas decided to stop writing on the subject of intellectual disability, stating that if one is really to care "about" such individuals then one cannot write *about* them, only *with* them (1998, 143–56). In other words, there is an ethical imperative to know such people lest writing not refer to actual people but merely be about the memory of persons (144). There is a spectral or phantasmal presence in the pages of this book, and indeed all biblical scholarship that seeks to be contextual, which demands that such work does not fall prey, as Hans Reinders has warned, to using other people for our own purposes (2008, 205). It remains, then, an open question and critique of this work, as well as an invitation for future scholarship, as to how much persons with poor mental health have been encountered and known in any sort of mutual relationship through the course of this work. Indeed, as Reinders urges, there is a theological necessity for friendship with persons with intellectual disabilities, and by extension persons with poor mental health, that no level of accrual of civil rights can secure (43) but must be received first as a gift (225). It is in this hope for friendship that I desire that debate should be provoked by this work, not only from within the corridors and studies of the academy but in the thin spaces of struggle persons with poor mental health, such as the group readers of this work, live with everyday. It is here that I wish for the debate to be most real and most incisive, for it is here that academic production of the sort I offer here will count, or in the end, it will count nowhere at all.

Appendix: Reading Group Transcripts

Mark 3:1–6

1 Again he entered the synagogue, and a man was there who had a withered hand. 2 They watched him to see whether he would cure him on the sabbath, so that they might accuse him. 3 And he said to the man who had the withered hand, "Come forward." 4 Then he said to them, "Is it lawful to do good or to do harm on the sabbath, to save life or to kill?" But they were silent. 5 He looked around at them with anger; he was grieved at their hardness of heart and said to the man, "Stretch out your hand." He stretched it out, and his hand was restored. 6 The Pharisees went out and immediately conspired with the Herodians against him, how to destroy him.

Questions

Verse 1
- Who was this man "with a withered hand"?
- What might it feel like to be him?
- Where is he to be found and how is he to be recognized?
- What do we learn about this man?
- Where are his friends?
- What do you think he is doing in the synagogue?

Verse 2
- Who are "they"?
- What do they know about Jesus?
- What does Jesus know about them?
- Why do you think "they" are watching Jesus?

Verse 3

- "Come forward." What does this sound like to you? A command? A request?
- Has anyone asked for help?
- What is the "man with the withered hand" coming forward for?
- Where was he? Can you picture where he might have been? Was he hidden?
- Have you ever been asked to "come forward"?
- Who asked you?
- What did it feel like?
- Who or what is the focus at this point? Jesus? The man with the withered hand? The withered hand, without much attention given to the man? "Them"? A teaching about the Sabbath? Something else?

Verse 4

- Who gets to speak in this passage as a whole?
- Why do you think there isn't much of a conversation?
- What do you feel about that?
- Do you ever feel like you don't get to speak?
- What is Jesus most concerned about in this passage as a whole, healing the man or having an argument?
- What do you think he should be concerned about?
- Why do "they" remain silent?
- Why do you think "they" aren't named from the start?
- What sort of conversation would you describe this as? A good one? A bad one?
- Have you ever been in a situation like this, where people don't answer?

Verse 5

- Jesus is angry. How does that make you feel? Do you think he should be angry?
- Is anyone else angry?
- How do you think that "the man with the withered hand" feels? How would you feel if you were him?
- "Stretch out your hand." How do you think Jesus might have said this? Could you say it in the tone of voice you think he might have used?

- How does the man with the withered hand feel now? Do you think that he has any choice in what is happening?
- What about "them," how do you think they feel?
- What part does the man play in his own healing?
- Did it cost him anything?
- What do you think "they" think of the man now? How do you think "they" will treat him?
- What is the most important thing to you about this episode?
- What kind of relationship is shared between the parties? Do you feel happy or not as happy about the quality of the relationships between the people involved?

Verse 6
- Now "they" are named. Why are they named now, at the end?
- How do you feel toward them?
- Why do you think they reacted the way they did and planned how to destroy Jesus?
- What do you think "destroy" might mean?
- Have you ever felt like someone was trying to destroy you?
- Where is Jesus now and where is the man? What is the nature of their relationship now?
- Do you think this episode was intended to solve problems or to cause them?
- Have you ever felt like any of these characters, or have you been in a situation like this before?

Reading Group One, March 21, 2006[1]

A: Is it near the crucifixion? Are they ready to kill him? It's amazing how he can be so good to people all the time when the Pharisees were going against him.

F: *Who was this man "with a withered hand"? What might it feel like to be him?*

---

1. The letters A, B, C, D, and E refer to members of the reading group; F refers to me in my role as facilitator.

A: A profound moment in his life. He saw the Lord in person. He heard him defend himself to the Pharisees. He was probably there to make a sacrifice in the temple. Jesus put it to them squarely.

B: I think that he [the man with the withered hand] was sad, upset. In those days there was not much hope for the handicapped.

C: Everybody else in the place had a good hand.

D: Difficult to make a living. It didn't sound like he wanted to get help.

A: Just that Jesus was there, a coincidence.

B: He was just standing there.

F: *Where is he to be found and how is he to be recognized? Would people have noticed him?*

E: No. I don't know. There is so much evil in the world now.

B: Some of the crowd would call him names, making fun of it, because that's the way things are in the world.

A: Yes.

C: Others were feeling pity for him.

E: The crowd was making fun of him. Making fun of Jesus too, because he is trying to cure sick people. Maybe they thought he was a doctor; he was the Son of God.

B: Yes, I feel that when you are different you stand out. Everybody watches him and is seeing what you are going to do about him.

E: He without sin throw the first stone, so everybody is different.

F: *Different?*

A: Yeah. It's called prejudice. They don't understand, they hate them automatically. They make up stories. Our Lord never had prejudice. He tried to help as many people as possible.

F: *Where are his friends?*

B: They were probably afraid that sometimes they might find it, might call it an illness in the hand. People are afraid of the mentally ill.

D: You think so?

B: Yeah.

D: Some people, not all.

F: *Why?*

B: They don't know how to behave toward them.

E: They think we're crazy. We're not sick. This is not our home, we don't live here.

F: *What might it feel like to be this man?*

B: Could be embarrassed. All the people were looking at his hand.

D: Maybe he's been praying for a cure. Nobody really hears him. But Jesus hears him and Jesus repairs his hand.

F: *Would you have liked to have known more about him?*

B: I would like to hear how he accepts it from the people, how he thought he [Jesus] looked at him. His whole hand was deformed probably.

C: Diabetes.

A: If his hand was crooked.

B: How he felt.

F: *Does Jesus understand how he feels?*

B: No.

A: Yes. Maybe he already knew what the man was thinking.

F: *Why didn't Jesus ask him if he wanted help?*

A: Because he was the Son of God. He already knew the facts about it.

F: *Who are "they"?*

D: Pharisees.

F: *Why do you think "they" are watching Jesus?*

D: To see what he would do next.

C: Curious.

A: They already hated Jesus no matter what. They knew something was going to happen.

B: Maybe they thought he was a fake. They wanted to argue with him.

F: *"Come forward." What does this sound like to you? A command? A request?*

B: I think he was asking him.

A: A command. More of a command. Just by the way he said it, more of a command.

F: *Has anyone asked for help?*

D: He was praying for it for a long time.

A: We all ask for help now and again.

F: *Why did he come forward?*

C: I don't know.

D: He believed.

F: *Where was he? Can you picture where he might have been? Was he hidden?*

B: He might have been in a corner, in the crowd.

A: Jesus could still see him.

B: Something different always stands out in the crowd.

A: That's true.

E: He was very different.

B: Yes.

F: *Have you ever been asked to come into the middle?*

C: I'd avoid it, because I usually mind my own business.

B: Always avoid those people.

F: *Was he under pressure?*

B: Yes.

A: He was embarrassed. Coming to the middle of the temple.

D: He was the focus. Everyone found a man with a withered hand. But then everyone was focused on Jesus, what he was going to do.

F: *"He said to them": Who gets to speak in this passage as a whole?*

A: It sounds like to me that Jesus is in command of the whole situation. He always knows how to defeat plans with a good saying.

D: The Pharisees were temporarily defeated. That's why they are so quiet.

F: *"Is it lawful to do good or to do harm ...": What is Jesus most concerned about in this passage as a whole, healing the man or having an argument?*

C: Not to kill.

A: The healing of the man. Because he can stand out in the crowd Jesus wanted to do a lot for him and wanted them to understand because they didn't get it because they remained silent.

D: Because Jesus is Jesus, and Jesus is superior.

B: Maybe they didn't know how to reply to him.

A: Proving a point. It is because this is a forerunner to the crucifixion and he knows he will save the life of all.

F: *"But they were silent": Why do "they" remain silent?*

C: Couldn't give him a good answer.

D: If they answer one way, there can be no answer. They would look bad either way.

B: We don't know what they're thinking.

F: *"He looked around at them with anger": Jesus is angry. How does that make you feel? Do you think he should be angry?*

D: He gets angry with them, they don't give him a straight answer.

A: He very rarely gets angry. If he does it was in the synagogue. They have it in their hearts to do away with him.

C: They were very picky. He wanted to establish new laws of his Father.

B: He ran out of patience.

C: Oh sure, why not? He was only human. Once in a while we can see his human side.

F: *How do you think that "the man with the withered hand" feels? How would you feel if you were him?*

B: Stupid. Because he is just standing there. His hand is not like anyone else's. He's wondering if he is normal.

C: The man feels responsible.

A: He can't help it, although I think some of the people are wondering how he had it.

D: He might be nervous or afraid, in the spotlight. Before he was not in the spotlight, now everybody can see him.

F: *"He looked around at them with anger": Jesus is angry. Is anyone else angry?*

D: They [the Pharisees] should have been more compassionate.

F: *"Stretch out your hand": How does the man with the withered hand feel now? Do you think that he has any choice in what is happening?*

B: I think you always have a choice.

A: I think he was trying to show the Pharisees something more important than the Mosaic law: the law of Christ.

D: Jesus didn't ask because the man had already said so many prayers to Jesus and he had already heard him that Jesus already knew his [the man's] answer. So the man has got faith.

F: *"The Pharisees ... conspired with the Herodians ... how to destroy him": Why do you think they reacted the way they did and planned how to destroy Jesus?*

A: They were very angry, always getting angry with Jesus.

D: They wanted to destroy him.

A: Yes.

F: *"He stretched it out and his hand was restored": What part does the man play in his own healing?*

C: He played a big part. He had to believe.

A: He saw the Son of God and knew he could help him.

F: *How does the man feel now?*

A: Happy.

B: Grateful, relieved.

D: His belief got stronger.

F: *Did it cost him anything?*

A: A little embarrassment.

B: But for what he received, surely he would have forgot all about that.

C: They [the Pharisees] might have felt that he was in cahoots with Jesus, that he was a fake.

E: They are not good.

D: Jealous because they couldn't do that.

F: *"The Pharisees … conspired with the Herodians … how to destroy him": How do you feel toward them?*

D: They're always biased against Jesus. It proved that they can't do all his miracles.

A: They're terrible people to me. It's hurtful when someone wants to kill you.

C: They want Jesus to just go away.

F: *What is the most important thing to you about this episode?*

A: Jesus is the center of attention. Helping this man he got more followers.

D: The man with the withered hand had a problem and Jesus wanted to solve it.

F: *Have you ever felt like someone was trying to destroy you?*

A: My own conflicts, yes, but I don't recall.

B: Sometimes I get angry with what people say if they don't know the truth about what is going on with me.

A: I can see Jesus being very angry about the Pharisees.

Reading Group Two, March 21, 2006

A: Jesus was a good guy.

B: He helped a lot of people.

A: Back in those days, things were so different. Hard.

B: They were trying to trick Jesus.

F: *Why?*

B: Because they. …

A: Didn't believe in him.

C: Didn't know who he was, didn't trust him.

D: No evidence.

B: He [the man with a withered hand] probably searched high and low to find hope.

E: A friend turned to God in her own way, read from the Bible, addressed her disputes.

F: *Who was this man "with a withered hand"? What might it feel like to be him?*

B: He hid out. He wasn't accepted, he was different.

E: My friend, she found out she is not alone. She has trouble feeling good inside.

F: *Where are his friends?*

C: None. He was handicapped.

B: Sometimes when people are handicapped, people shun them, like the mentally ill, some people shun you. They think that you're crazy.

C: Some people don't understand.

A: Some do.

E: They shouldn't do that. Wouldn't wish it on anyone.

B: They call you names—loony, crazy.

F: *What might it feel like to be him?*

C: Scared.

E: Depressed.

F: *What is he scared of?*

C: What's going to happen to him.

E: Mental anguish, pain.

B: Sometimes you don't know what is going to happen.

F: *What do you think he is doing in the synagogue?*

E: He went to pray.

A: Maybe he hoped to get cured. He heard what Jesus was doing. It spread.

E: Maybe he wants to understand how he feels. He's going to the synagogue to help him understand, to try to cope.

D: It may be difficult for that person. Helps him feel better.

F: *Who are "they"?*

B: The Pharisees. They didn't trust him. What is he up to?

D: Discouraged, insulted. They didn't trust him, didn't believe in him.

E: They thought they were better. Personally, I think they looked down on Jesus. You wonder whether they are ill. There are a lot of people like that, unfortunately.

D: You never know what's going to happen in the future.

F: *"Come forward". What does this sound like to you? A command? A request?*

A: Telling him.

C: They wanted to have hope. He tried to help.

F: *Why come to the front?*

B: He wanted to be cured, so he wouldn't be victimized anymore. He believed Jesus could cure him.

C: He was hiding.

D: He feels a bit embarrassed because they had ridiculed him.

A: Triumphant.

B: Nervous but hopeful.

E: He accepted what had happened to him and he did not try to deny them because he went and accepted them. He tried to hold on to hope and he got better.

F: *Who are "they"? Why do you think "they" are watching Jesus?*

A: They wanted to see what he could do, if he could really perform miracles.

E: He believed so much in his faith of a tiny mustard seed.

B: There's always a reason why they think the way they do.

D: Sometimes the Pharisees turned to God and didn't get a response.

C: Sometimes you feel people are against you. Whispering. They don't like you. You have a stigma.

B: Stigma.

E: Many people in the Catholic faith have the rosary, ten Hail Marys five times. …

B: It's upsetting. Can't always accept how I feel.

F: *What is most important in this passage: the man's healing or Jesus teaching a lesson to the Pharisees?*

D: The man's healing. Because he wanted to be whole again.

C: I feel it is important to have all your faculties so you can work.

F: *"He looked around at them with anger": Jesus is angry. How does that make you feel? Do you think he should be angry?*

E: It may not explain how he felt and he went ahead and accepted.

APPENDIX: READING GROUP TRANSCRIPTS

B: He said, "This is the way I see it."

E: He didn't mean to be unkind.

B: Yes.

C: That showed him that people didn't believe in him.

E: He wanted to help them but they didn't allow it.

F: *"Stretch out your hand": How does the man with the withered hand feel now? Do you think that he has any choice in what is happening?*

E: Stop this fighting over me, I don't want any more fighting.

F: *"He stretched it out and his hand was restored." What part does the man play in his own healing?*

E: He played a very important part. He showed he believed. As tiny as a mustard seed, just a small amount.

B: He had nothing to lose.

F: *"The Pharisees … conspired with the Herodians … how to destroy him." Why do you think they reacted the way they did and planned how to destroy Jesus?*

C: They were jealous of him.

A: He had power, they wanted that power.

E: Perhaps we learn from our beliefs.

F: *How does the man feel now?*

D: He probably feels so much for Jesus because he helped him.

A: Worried for himself.

D: He may be a little afraid of the Herodians.

A: They might cut off his head.

F: *Have you ever felt like someone was trying to destroy you?*

E: He found those he trusted and they hurt him. They did not want him to think of himself as perfect. These people were his people. Not fair to single this one out as not worthy. Some of them did not feel worthy.

B: Made me feel how I was treated in school.

Reading Group Three, April 3, 2006

F: *Who was this man "with a withered hand"? What might it feel like to be him?*

A: Frustrating.

B: Difficult back then to be crippled. I just imagine the awkward attention toward a man with a physical impairment. People might have been a lot less welcoming and friendly and nice.

C: "I desire mercy, not sacrifice." Makes me think of my own life and how God does want to heal me even if I don't deserve it. Maybe even makes me think I should pray to God. I forget about God and that he wants me to have healing.

A: Perhaps the people were more concerned about Jesus and not the man—of sticking to the letter of the law.

B: It's hard, today there is medical knowledge and research and nursing assistance. Back then it was not known. Imagine how that added mystery and questions in the mind of how a person got that way.

C: Why God would have created them that way.

B: It's counterintuitive that people would not have wanted him to get helped.

C: I struggle with God's prestige, so my mind doesn't work, but is it spiritual blindness or physical blindness? They may have heard that he was punished by God. But Jesus says if your eye causes you to [do] wrong then pull it out.

B: Values versus laws.

F: *Where is he to be found and how is he to be recognized?*

A: Back, asked to come forward, into the middle.

B: He's an outcast. He's back, pushed there because of his disability or maybe he's ashamed.

C: In the middle, well … yeah, the center of attention.

D: He's hiding, cowering in the corner. They wouldn't have wanted him to get help just because it was that day.

C: He didn't want to be judged or be different because of something.

B: I think the people, the priests, and the congregation were unconscious of the man. I think that probably explains why Jesus says come forward, not to be afraid to approach him and be known.

F: *Who are "they"?*

A: Pharisees.

C: People who were doubting that this was the Son of God ... people who doubted.

A: It's named the Pharisees.

B: Not clear. "They" could have referred to a whole lot of people who were skeptical.

F: *What do you think "they" care about the man?*

B: They don't care about him at all. They are more concerned with gathering evidence against Jesus. It says at the end how they planned to destroy him. I am assuming "destroy" means Jesus. And they were silent when a question was asked. Although it is clear from the second verse they are watching to see what is going to happen, although that part doesn't necessarily mean that they completely despised him, although later on when he asks them in verse four, I don't know, he could be teaching them or could he be defending his actions? I see that ambiguity.

A: I don't see Jesus feels the need to explain himself.

C: Jesus brings radical love to a people whose hardness of heart is against him, telling people to love people who hate you. I am sure there were people who demonstrated what love really is, and mercy. ... I don't have mercy on myself more than anybody else. Even people who don't like me probably would be more merciful to me.

B: Yes.

C: I think that it's not necessarily the case from this. It is not that they have forgotten about mercy but it could be based on ways to act at that time. That reminds me of society today as a whole where people of all positions and different kinds of responsibility think that it is a good thing to do but can't do it right now. It could be about an insecurity instead of helping people. They want to make more money. Many people think they can't behave in a caring way because of this reason.

B: I think it's psychologically normal for people at times to do things outrageous or provocative.

F: *Where are his friends?*

A: Maybe he doesn't have any.

C: Maybe he had a family but when he got disabled, they said, "You got yourself cursed, get out of here."

B: If you read the last sentence of this thing during the healing on the Sabbath, if someone is capable of killing someone, then they are capable of ostracizing this guy not just because he is a cripple, but because it means something to them.

C: It wasn't an attitude of some people who sinned. It is said in the Bible, Jesus said go and sin no more. That part always scares me. Somehow sin is attached to affliction. I struggle with that; sin leads to punishment. There are different schools of thought that mental illness is possession or spiritual warfare.

A: I just think that life's not fair, like only bad things happen to bad people. I say that bad things happen to good people.

C: It's just tough to understand different Scriptures, that it rains on the good and the bad. No one is righteous, we are all in the same boat.

F: *"Come forward." What does this sound like to you? A command? A request?*

B: With authority.

D: Probably in an encouraging tone of voice. Loving.

B: Yeah, lots of things discourage being there in the first place but a benevolent tone of voice. …

F: *Has anyone asked for help?*

B: Could be afraid to for societal reasons. The fact that they wanted to destroy the man who healed him—I can see he would be afraid they were going to destroy him too, he would be petrified.

C: Yeah, bleeding woman. ...

B: I wanted to say something. The meaning of a person being crippled has a deeper significance. I think I see. I think that this applies to not only people who suffer, but applies to different religions and how they treat each other. Regardless of the state of the person who is blaspheming. I guess I'm reading meaning far more into it. I see a lot of people assigning deeper meaning to a lot of other people, and often they make conclusions about the attitude of the people being judged and then God judges them. It may be a healthy prosperous nation they are saying is bad off because of this or that deeper meaning.

C: Kind of, most people already have to strike the balance that this way of doing things is correct and in the process they can write other peoples' beliefs off as crazy or not favored by God.

B: I think the religious form of this problem is a prominent form of this.

C: I think very often, more a feeling or knowing and a willingness and desire to take responsibility of judging. In my own view mental health professionals as a group can be judgmental to greater extents than some others.

B: Because they have some knowledge that they didn't give up. People who go into the field want to help with "diagnosis." I think that when a person decides to devote their life to that kind of thing. ...

C: They have issues ... [laughs].

B: I think they'll encounter some arguing, some hostility even, and also the nature of the idea of a psychological illness is a very significant collection of beliefs. Persons with issues have different labels, reasons why their judgment might be this way, they might feel like they are not being reasonable or normal.

C: It's hard not to feel patronized and it's tough not to feel stymied.

A: And not to blame individuals who go into the field because it's part of how it is taught.

B: It's a problem of great complexity. People read too much into things.

C: You think misdiagnosis—label—say, schizophrenic, and you really aren't one.

A: I think it is a name of something. It is useful when someone like us walks into an office there may be a whole lot of reasons why our judgment might be off.

C: And we might feel inferior to the person.

B: You can feel invalidated.

C: It's difficult, you always know it is a professional argument. It's really tough, learning how to live with it and in the midst of it. I can be paranoid.

B: It's almost like a caste system of your brain. Technically I can't judge my teachers.

C: They take us back.

A: That can be one really positive aspect, you can be forgiven because they understand you're dealing with a lot.

B: I don't want you to say that I can't judge them, it's just you don't have the same education as they do.

A: I think there's healthy judgments.

C: Sometimes judgments are off. Sometimes they see things you are not seeing.

F: *In this passage, is Jesus primarily concerned with teaching a lesson here and so using the man, or is his primary concern healing?*

D: I hope it is about healing.

A: Why couldn't he have said, "Let's go into that corner," and heal him?

B: I can see how he was trying to help this man. Not just physically if we consider he was outcast, shunned. He encountered him, calling him publicly. Basically through the people, Pharisees, and the crowd he's healing him right in front of them and defends that action. In fact, that may not be the most important thing he's doing. The most important thing might be the way he is doing it. Healing is the operative thing. If he was using the guy to make a point, then I think that would be going in the direction of the people he is saying this to, and I think one of the huge points is that he is completely different in important ways. There's no way he's embodying objectifying. To the Pharisees their relation to the law was more important than whether this guy is suffering. The most obvious thing in this passage: Jesus feels different.

A: Basically, could not Jesus wait a day?

B: Why would he do that? Maybe he's taking the opportunity to teach something rather than setting out to do so.

C: He was angry too. Don't forget all these people who wanted to destroy him. It's to his advantage to be as public as possible. It is far less effective to do it privately.

F: *"But they were silent": Why do "they" remain silent?*

D: They didn't have any answer.

B: Nothing in the rules spelled out an answer. In the moment they were stuck.

C: They were waiting for him to make a mistake so that he might have need of them.

F: *"Stretch out your hand": How does the man with the withered hand feel now?*

D: Fearful.

B: Exposed. Confronted.

A: Embarrassed.

C: Reminds me of the woman at the well. She was confronted with what Jesus already knew about her.

B: Vulnerable.

A: Not safe.

C: Well, if he was the Son of God it has an effect on people. Did he have doubts and then he believed? Jesus has an effect on him.

Reading Group Four, April 4, 2006

F: *Who was this man "with a withered hand"? What might it feel like to be him?*

A: Embarrassed.

B: Painful.

C: Mad, angry, because he has a crippled hand and can't use it. Everyone was laughing at him.

B: I had a hand like that with radial nerve palsy. The man felt a bit like, I didn't want to be a spectacle. But he was willing to do it, probably had faith that Jesus could heal his hand back.

D: The Pharisees were scared when they saw that, they had just met God and so they were afraid. They knew that God was going to judge them for their hardness of heart. They were afraid.

A: It is like a setup. It says that they watched him. Like a setup—premeditated to trap Jesus.

B: When Jesus was going about teaching and preaching, these people were so obsessed with the law. When you were struck with leprosy at that time there was no cure. They were alienated from normal people.

A: Jesus had to contend with them.

E: This man was brought as a witness.

D: Why would he have to witness to that which he created?

E: The Sabbath day was the holiest of days and a man with a withered hand—Jesus needed to show the true miracles of God.

F: *Where are his friends?*

A: He is held against his will. They grabbed him—do this.

B: He became a project—he was used, like an experiment.

D: Sounds like he was visible right when Jesus walked in.

C: He looked like he didn't belong there. You could tell there was something different about him.

A: Forced to go there.

C: The crowd rejects him [for] the same reason they reject Jesus. They don't want to identify with Jesus.

A: The man is not only embarrassed, but angry with the fact that he's brought forward. It was so grotesque then.

B: I have a picture of the synagogue. A circle. In the middle, empty, and everyone can be a witness. That way it's like a stage.

E: They knew he would heal him on the Sabbath. Their concern was the Sabbath.

F: *"Come forward": What does this sound like to you? A command? A request?*

B: A request.

A: Command.

D: Oh yeah, not a command as we say, but Jesus has nothing but love—soothing. It probably just shocked the whole room. We wonder why the whole room was still. Jesus was silent, just the Holy Ghost speaking through the Father.

C: The same way a mother would tell a four-year-old to put a seat belt on: a statement made with love.

F: *What is the man with the withered hand coming forward for?*

C: I think Jesus knew exactly what was going on. What their intentions were.

A: He [Jesus] was probably making a point. They were trying to have some evidence to accuse him of wrongdoing. You Pharisees are looking to kill and on the Sabbath.

D: Because this being is used of God, he probably wanted to be healed of his deformity. He couldn't even offer things to God because of his deformity.

F: *In this passage, is Jesus primarily concerned with teaching a lesson here and so using the man, or is his primary concern healing?*

D: In his sovereignty everything is efficient. It doesn't become a matter of what is most important. This one act will heal and demonstrate how wicked they are, right?

A: I think he wanted to heal the man, he heals in front of the Pharisees [so that] they would see his way. They were not going to believe anyway.

F: *Was this man with the withered hand used by Jesus to make his point?*

A: Yes.

C: I think he was probably ambivalent. He wanted to be healed but he felt guilty. We know how that is. Guilty that he didn't go to Jesus of his own will.

D: These people were seeking to accuse the Father himself. That was the true fight—it was a fight to accuse the Father. The authority that Jesus had was so unbelievable, he could feel God's grace as well as the pain.

F: *"But they were silent": Why do "they" remain silent?*

B: Because it took them a minute to figure out the significance. They realized they were totally uncovered—how could he know our thoughts.

C: Maybe they were silent because they realized that what they were doing was just as bad as harm. By this setup, they felt foolish. When he asked them a question, he just saw through them.

A: He felt sorry for them.

C: That's a trip, we'd want to kick them in the face.

F: *"Stretch out your hand": How does the man with the withered hand feel now? Do you think that he has any choice in what is happening?*

D: He knew he was going to be used of Jesus. He did so understanding that he would be the one.

B: Just a spectacle. He didn't understand, he was just grieved.

C: Maybe he felt Jesus had such authority, he felt like a child, he just obeyed him.

B: Unworthy, right.

A: Unworthy.

D: It was a fight against good and evil.

Mark 3:19b–35

19b Then he went home; 20 and the crowd came together again, so that they could not even eat. 21 When his family heard it, they went out to restrain him, for people were saying, "He has gone out of his mind." 22 And the scribes who came down from Jerusalem said, "He has Beelzebul, and by the ruler of the demons he casts out demons." 23 And he called them to him, and spoke to them in parables, "How can Satan cast out Satan? 24 If a kingdom is divided against itself, that kingdom cannot stand. 25 And if a house is divided against itself, that house will not be able to stand. 26 And if Satan has risen up against himself and is divided, he cannot stand, but his end has come. 27 No one can enter a strong man's house and plunder his property without first tying up the strong man; then indeed the house can be plundered."

28 "Truly I tell you, people will be forgiven for their sins and whatever blasphemies they utter; 29 but whoever blasphemes against the Holy Spirit can never have forgiveness, but is guilty of an eternal sin"—30 for they had said, "He has an unclean spirit."

31 Then his mother and his brothers came; and standing outside, they sent to him and called him. 32 A crowd was sitting around him; and they said to him, "Your mother and your brothers and sisters are outside, asking for you." 33 And he replied, "Who are my mother and my brothers?" 34 And looking at those who sat around him, he said, "Here are my mother and my brothers! 35 Whoever does the will of God is my brother and sister and mother."

Questions

Verse 20
- Can you imagine Jesus' home?
- What is it like?
- Is it a place of comfort for him?
- And at this point in the story, is it a place of comfort?
- What kind of people are in "the crowd"?
- What do they want?
- Where does Jesus find nourishment?
- What is it like to be him?

Verse 21
- What had Jesus' family heard?
- Why are they so worried?
- Who are they worried for?
- How might they "restrain him"?
- Have you ever felt "restrained"?
- Can you imagine Jesus "out of his mind"?
- If he were, would "restraining" him help?

Verse 22
- Why do you think the scribes have come from Jerusalem?
- What are they hoping for?
- How might Jesus "have" Beelzebul? Who is in control of whom?
- What do you imagine Beelzebul to be?
- And demons, what do you imagine those to be?
- What have these got to do with Jesus' mind?

Verse 23
- Why does Jesus call to them?
- How do you think he might have called? With what tone of voice? And with what gestures?
- And why speak in parables?
- Does Jesus think they are accusing him of being Satan?
- Has Jesus got it right or wrong?
- How do we know Jesus wasn't Satan?
- Who is Satan anyway?

Verses 24–25
- What does a house divided make you think of?
- Is a divided kingdom any different?
- Could you live in a divided house?
- Are there aspects of your life that are divided, even your own house?
- What might this have to do with Jesus' mind?

Verse 26
- What do you feel about Satan?
- Do you think his "end will come"?

Verse 27
- ▸ Who do you think the strong man is?
- ▸ Who is tying him up?
- ▸ Is there anything wrong with plundering? Are you comfortable with what Jesus seems to be advocating here?

Verses 28–30
- ▸ Who needs forgiveness of sins in this passage?
- ▸ What is blasphemy to you?
- ▸ Why "blasphemes against the Holy Spirit"?
- ▸ What is an eternal sin? Is it different from other sins?
- ▸ What answer can be given to Jesus here when he says that "they" have blasphemed against the Holy Spirit?
- ▸ Who do you think "they" might be?
- ▸ Who has said the worst thing? The scribes who said to Jesus: "He has Beelzebul"? The people who said: "He has gone out of his mind"?

Reading Group One, April 4, 2006

F: *Can you imagine Jesus' home? What is it like? Is it a place of comfort for him?*

C: No idea.

D: A place to rest, comfortable for him.

B: He's home but the crowd is eager to seize him. He's tired, couldn't get any rest.

A: Jesus needs a place to get away.

C: Satan was an angel or I think separate from God because I just think so.

F: *What had Jesus' family heard?*

A: People were saying he's gone out of his mind.

B: Everybody was exhausted.

D: They wanted to protect him from the crowd.

C: It's all good.

F: *How might they "restrain him"?*

C: To stop him from doing things.

D: First tell him, then touch him. He might have told his family he could do it and they said no.

C: What was Jesus? Couldn't have been human. What was he? A superhuman? Batman or Hercules?

F: *What do you think?*

A: He is God; just God.

C: Lots of people think this is hell. This is life, the eternal everlasting universe.

F: *Can you imagine Jesus "out of his mind"?*

C: Gone crazy. Saying things that can't be true.

B: Things he does, the way he talks. Thought he could do this, do that.

A: They didn't understand what he was trying to do. They wouldn't believe what he had done. He keeps doing these strange things, they couldn't understand him so they told him that he was out of his mind.

C: Anybody could be not trusted. God could make a spectacle. He [Jesus] could be drunk on beer or wine and go crazy that way too.

A: Well that's a problem with me, to me if he did he wouldn't have been able to preach. Maybe he was just tired.

D: Jesus was divine, he didn't make mistakes like human beings.

F: *Why do you think the scribes have come from Jerusalem?*

D: May have been that they came to catch him making a mistake.

B: To uphold the law, to see if he was going to break the law.

A: They were always trying to catch him during his whole life with their "itty-bitty" laws.

F: *Were those laws important?*

A: Not as important as his laws.

C: Not important. I believe the Lord has his own space. The modern day Lord, he flies in a UFO in space.

F: *How might Jesus "have" Beelzebul? Who is in control of whom?*

C: That he is doing everything the wrong way. Satan has control over him, that is, he is doing all his miracles.

D: An accusation, not a fact.

F: *Can you imagine Jesus "out of his mind"?*

A: Even in the case where Jesus throws out seven demons from a man, he has to argue with them over the law.

B: I hope not.

A: I hope not either.

C: We are all complicated because everyone has to get along. We would have to be constantly wary of these spirits and they would be pretty bad.

F: *Have you ever known someone to be out of their mind?*

B: Heard a few stories about possession and people trying to get hold of them. But it was sort of jumbled in their mind. Wondered if it was real or not.

F: *"And he called to them": Why does Jesus call to them?*

C: Maybe out of curiosity and to find out why they are that way.

A: Because he sought to teach them again what was important and what was not important. He wanted to teach them the difference between fake and God. He couldn't let them go on by.

B: You have to defend yourself somehow. Have to say something. They will walk all over you and you believe all these stupid things about yourself and you lose yourself for a while. It's very difficult for you.

F: *"A kingdom/house divided against itself": What does a "house divided" make you think of?*

A: Everybody arguing with one another. You don't achieve anything.

B: I think it's something about yourself. A soul divided into pieces cannot function properly. It's hard to believe it's a real house.

D: A soul divided against itself, given over to sin and personal pressures. Before you know it, it is all messed up.

C: Every day I'm called that. They said it was an inner conflict.

F: *"Binding the strong man": Who do you think the strong man is?*

B: God or Jesus.

C: Hard to say. Have to figure out who the strong man is. A man with a good soul and the devil comes and ties him up and his whole person would be ravaged.

F: *Who needs forgiveness of sins in this passage?*

A: The crowd, because they accused him of all those problems he didn't have.

F: *Does Jesus' family need forgiveness?*

D: Not really. Well … this was their son, they tried to protect him.

F: *Who has said the worse thing? The scribes who said to Jesus: "He has Beelzebul," or the people who said: "He has gone out of his mind"?*

C: No idea, Simon.

B: Well, we don't have this horrible thing where they say devils on you like they had in the Bible, I think the worse thing is saying you are out of your mind.

A: Cruel.

B: Yes I think so. I most certainly do.

A: It's never easy to defend yourself against the Pharisees and the scribes. Always trying to trap you.

C: It's worse being called crazy. It's unfair.

A: Yeah, that's right.

C: Sometimes people suffer for real. Sometimes I suffer so much I don't see reality and I don't realize what people are doing. When I finally get through I find that people are just living. It's all a racket. You've got to even pay to die. It's not worth it. If you really think about being in the world today you go nuts. You go off the deep end. When a person has faith, these people don't think about these things. It is the small things that put you over. You can't think over and over about the same thing.

A: Oh yeah, I see that.

B: I get that a lot.

A: Even so-called regular people, if you say the truth, people let you have it. Even regular people have to shut up. Jesus had to keep his mouth shut sometimes. That's the way of society.

C: We have to live and act like we are a separate category of people.

D: Oh no we shouldn't.

C: It's just the way of life, that's all.

Reading Group Three, April 10, 2006

F: *Can you imagine Jesus' home? What is it like? Is it a place of comfort for him?*

A: A place of comfort for him.

F: *How might they "restrain him"?*

A: It definitely sounds like a physical word.

B: I don't know … no, I mean it's the text, it leaves it up in the air.

F: *Does it sound protective to you or repressive?*

B: We don't know the rest of society to know how crazy or not he is to lock him up.

F: *What do you think it felt like to be Jesus with his family trying to restrain him?*

A: Completely let down.

C: Frustrating.

B: At the same time they might want to protect him and keep him quiet.

A: I think they might want the criticism to go away.

F: *Can you imagine Jesus "out of his mind"?*

A: Yeah, depending on what it means. I feel like it's a strong psychological temptation to be megalomaniac, where you consider yourself to be really great. I imagine Jesus to be a really good teacher. It's plausible that hearing the crowd this could go to his head. He could convince himself that he could do more than he really could, more than just an ordinary man.

F: *Were the family justified in what they did?*

B: I don't have enough detail about the story. It could be Jesus was humble and saw himself totally accurately. It could be the opposite end and that he is unrealistic. Even then, restraint is something that … an extreme measure. If he wasn't going to hurt anybody or himself.

F: *Why do you think the scribes have come from Jerusalem? What are they hoping for?*

B: They might have been concerned that they were losing popularity. They wanted to maintain power.

A: They might have been worried about passing on the tradition and ensuring that the Messiah could come eventually.

F: *How do you feel about them labeling Jesus?*

B: It depends on the person. He does a good job of thinking of something to say.

F: *Do you think we should ignore labels or resist them?*

B: There's a woman I know with bipolar. She has a guy friend who tells her that she is a manic depressive. She left, sat in the car, and cried. Then she went back and said, "Go to hell." Then she left, she didn't want to give him more fuel. I think she wanted to represent herself and all people with bipolar in a positive light. If she had stayed to argue she might have got angry in the heat of the moment and wouldn't have helped this guy to see mental illness in a positive light.

F: *"And he called to them": Why does Jesus call to them?*

A: Well, I mean it is no longer the religious authorities who are deciding. He has flipped the power relation and he is teaching to students.

B: He's calm.

F: *Who has said the worse thing? The scribes who said to Jesus: "He has Beelzebul," or the people who said: "He has gone out of his mind"?*

B: Out of his mind.

A: I agree. I think being possessed is not really true, but in my perception there is mass possession if you lose your mind. Not that mental illness is that but that can be an ingredient.

F: *Can you imagine Jesus "out of his mind"?*

B: I think you can have a person who is completely out of his mind at a certain time. Someone who is deluded about certain things. There is a spectrum from fully sane to insane.

C: People like to label, it's convenient.

A: And especially when a person is troubling you but you don't want to argue with them. It's easy to say he is an idiot. Then deep down I need to be in conflict with myself about those things he is saying.

F: *Should you resist this?*

A: No. No fighting. You need it, not to create any more tension.

B: Show, don't teach. He can say he is not a disciple of Satan until he is blue in the face. He demonstrates it. He shows he is not controlled by evil.

F: *Is it hard to shake a label off?*

B: I guess for me it's not as much about the label than how well I'm doing. Am I safe? Am I in touch with reality? Are my moods stable or not? I don't know that people respect me or consider me mentally ill.

A: I have no problem with labels.

B: Labels can be useful, giving people an idea of what history might be there, what symptoms to look for with family and friends. Really getting a sense of the problems I've been facing.

F: *How do you feel about the situation at the end of the reading concerning Jesus' family?*

C: It's sad for him, there's a wall between them.

A: I don't know, it's sort of like his followers were his family, that could be part of this radical love thing—love as if they were your family.

B: I don't know, it sort of seems he usually forgives them. What you've done proves you're not on my side, so get this, this is my real family.

A: It's hard.

Reading Group Four, April 11, 2006

F: *Can you imagine Jesus' home? What is it like? Is it a place of comfort for him?*

A: Chaos.

B: No comfort. It's no surprise to him. He was doing everything. He was breaking all the laws. He didn't respect the Sabbath. He claimed to be the Messiah. They were waiting for another Messiah. They were all thinking that he was demented, he's a nut.

F: *What kind of people are in "the crowd"? What do they want?*

A: Eternal life.

C: They wanted, expected, Jesus to lead them against the Romans. When he didn't do that they saw he wasn't about to gather an army like the forty years in the desert, he just preached to love your enemies.

F: *What had Jesus' family heard?*

A: That he was a lunatic.

B: They wanted to see a miracle. They didn't want to believe, they wanted to see something concrete.

A: They didn't believe.

F: *Why do you think they wanted to restrain him?*

C: They were afraid something might happen to him.

A: If it was your child, you'd want to.

B: They were trying to protect him.

A: To take him out of there.

B: It was more like a request, because Mary already knew who she was dealing with.

F: *How do you imagine Jesus feels about this?*

C: Sad, he came here to teach so the world could be saved. He loves us like we love our child. We teach children fear. They feared him.

F: *Why do you think the scribes have come from Jerusalem?*

B: The scribes were sent by their superiors. Jesus posed a threat to them, discrediting them for all the things they were doing.

A: Threatening their tradition.

C: Jesus goes against the law of Moses.

F: *Who has said the worse thing? The scribes who said to Jesus: "He has Beelzebul," or the people who said: "He has gone out of his mind"?*

B: They were saying he is of Satan, that is more damaging because Satan is Satan, he wants to destroy everything he's teaching.

A: Satan existed in those days.

B: The devil is the antithesis of what he is trying to teach. "Out of his mind" is a physical model. Satan, that's spiritual, not physical.

F: *What about you?*

B: I'm not out of my mind.

A: Not nice.

B: I know if they said I had Satan I'd rather say I was nuts.

C: It's tough, words are worse than the sword emotionally. I faced a family member head on, straight to the matter, who said I was crazy, "You've been smoking too much crack." I had to surrender right there. But for Jesus it was different; he knew exactly what was going on.

F: *Is mental illness a punishment?*

C: I talk like that, because of all the stuff I have done.

B: I'm a firm believer that Jesus will not give up on me. I've seen work in my life I really believe is of God. Only be taught as a child. When you are subject, then there is freedom to rationalize it and continue to do something wrong. I knew that I was enslaved to my disease. When I used to get high I was a devil. The walking dead. Trying to use self-defeating thoughts to be my excuses.

C: I fell out of consciousness one time. It was the first time she, my girlfriend, saw fear in my eyes. That changes you.

Mark 5:21–43

21 When Jesus had crossed again in the boat to the other side, a great crowd gathered around him; and he was by the sea. 22 Then one of the leaders of the synagogue named Jairus came and, when he saw him, fell at his feet 23 and begged him repeatedly, "My little daughter is at the point of death. Come and lay your hands on her, so that she may be made well, and live." 24 So he went with him.

And a large crowd followed him and pressed in on him. 25 Now there was a woman who had been suffering from hemorrhages for twelve years. 26 She had endured much under many physicians, and had spent all that she had; and she was no better, but rather grew worse. 27 She had heard about Jesus, and came up behind him in the crowd and touched his cloak, 28 for she said, "If I but touch his clothes, I will be made well." 29 Immediately her hemorrhage stopped; and she felt in her body that she was healed of her disease. 30 Immediately aware that power had gone forth from him, Jesus turned about in the crowd and said, "Who touched my clothes?" 31 And his disciples said to him, "You see the crowd pressing in on you; how can you say, 'Who touched me?'" 32 He looked all around to see who had done it. 33 But the woman, knowing what had happened to her, came in fear and trembling, fell down before him, and told him the whole truth. 34 He said to her, "Daughter, your faith has made you well; go in peace, and be healed of your disease."

35 While he was still speaking, some people came from the leader's house to say, "Your daughter is dead. Why trouble the teacher any further?" 36 But overhearing what they said, Jesus said to the leader of the synagogue, "Do not fear, only believe." 37 He allowed no one to follow him except Peter, James, and John, the brother of James. 38 When they came to the house of the leader of the synagogue, he saw a commotion, people weeping and wailing loudly. 39 When he had entered, he said to them, "Why do you make a commotion and weep? The child is not dead but sleeping." 40 And they laughed at him. Then he put them all outside, and took the child's father and mother and those who were with him, and went in where the child was. 41 He took her by the hand and said to her, "Talitha cum," which means, "Little girl, get up!" 42 And immediately the

girl got up and began to walk about (she was twelve years of age). At this they were overcome with amazement. 43 He strictly ordered them that no one should know this, and told them to give her something to eat.

Questions

Verse 21
- How might it feel to be Jesus at this point?
- What is the crowd gathering around him for?
- What sort of atmosphere do you imagine there being?

Verses 22–24
- What sort of man is Jairus?
- What does the crowd think of him falling at Jesus' feet?
- What does Jesus think of Jairus falling at his feet?
- How do you imagine Jairus begging?

Verse 23
- What sort of hope does Jairus have?
- Have you wanted to have or have you had that sort of hope?
- Do you think that Jesus' hands can make people well?
- Why do you think Jairus believes this?

Verse 24
- What makes Jesus go with Jairus? Because he is a powerful man? Because he begged?
- And how does the crowd feel about all of this?

Verses 25–26
- Where do you think this woman is to be found?
- How do you imagine she has "suffered"?
- What do you think she might have endured?
- Do you know how she feels to have endured much at the hands of doctors?
- How has this left her?
- How important do you think this woman is?
- What do you think it is like after all that treatment to get worse, not better?
- What do you think the crowd thinks of a woman like this?

Verses 27–28
- ▸ What do you imagine she had heard about Jesus?
- ▸ Why do you think she comes up behind him and not in front of him?
- ▸ How do you think she feels to be doing this?
- ▸ What do you make of her hope in Jesus that after all these years of treatment that if she only touches his cloak she will be healed?
- ▸ Could you imagine yourself thinking like that?

Verses 29–30
- ▸ Why do you think that her bleeding stopped so suddenly?
- ▸ How did she know she was healed?
- ▸ How do you think Jesus knew, immediately, that "power had gone forth from him"?
- ▸ Is the woman in sight?

Verse 30
- ▸ "Who touched my clothes?" In what tone of voice does Jesus say this?
- ▸ Why do you think he wants to know?

Verses 31–32
- ▸ Why do the disciples question Jesus here?
- ▸ How do you think they feel about the crowd?
- ▸ What do you think Jairus is making of all of this?
- ▸ Do you think the disciples are concerned about what Jairus thinks?
- ▸ Do you think Jesus is concerned about what Jairus thinks of all this?
- ▸ "He looked all round to see who had done it": Why is Jesus persisting in looking for the person who had touched his clothes?
- ▸ How do you think the woman feels about Jesus' persistence?

Verses 33–34
- ▸ Why does the woman come in fear and trembling?
- ▸ Do you imagine her falling at Jesus' feet in the same way as you imagine Jairus falling at his feet?
- ▸ Why does Jesus call her daughter?
- ▸ What will give her greatest peace now?

APPENDIX: READING GROUP TRANSCRIPTS

Verses 35–36
- Is it trouble for Jesus to do what he does?
- Who do you think lacked faith at this point?
- How do you think Jairus felt when Jesus asked him not to fear?
- Can you imagine yourself in that situation?
- How does it feel to be told your daughter is dead and at the same time that you should not fear?

Verses 37–40
- Why do you think he only allowed Peter, James, and John to follow him to Jairus's house?
- How do you think the other disciples felt about this?
- Why was there such a commotion?
- Do you think this concerned Peter, James, and John at all?
- What do you think the crowds might have been expecting?
- How do you feel about the people laughing at Jesus? Would you have laughed?
- Do you think Jairus laughed?
- Do you think the disciples laughed?
- Why do you think he only allowed a few with him to see the child?

Verses 41–43
- How important is touch in this whole passage, 5:21–43?
- How do you imagine Jesus' voice saying, "Talitha cum"?
- Who do you think was overcome with amazement?
- Why do you think Jesus wanted this to be a secret?

Reading Group One, April 18, 2006

F: *What sort of man is Jairus?*

D: Better off than others, not rich but not poor.

B: I think the crowd were amazed, one of the most prominent members. It's very impressive to the crowds.

F: *What does Jesus think of Jairus falling at his feet?*

B: Well, along his ministry there were great crowds, many miracles. Jairus was overcoming his pride, he was desperate for his daughter.

F: *Does Jairus care what people think?*

A: He is only thinking about his child.

B: That's right.

F: *Why do you think he wants Jesus to lay his hands on his daughter?*

C: His powers.

D: To make the child well, from hearing about all the other miracles he'd performed.

F: *Have you ever wished this? To be made well by the laying on of hands?*

A: I wish.

B: Oh yeah, he certainly was hopeful. In fact he knew enough to ask Jesus to help him, oh yeah. He had heard about other people being helped. If my daughter was dying I'd do anything.

F: *"So he went with him": What makes Jesus go with Jairus? Because he is a powerful man? Because he begged?*

B: Because the man shows such great faith—come lay hands on her—he assumed our Lord's powers.

F: *Is faith important?*

E: Oh yes, because if you have faith, you believe that the Spirit of God is in three persons when they try to heal you. They can do what doctors can't do.

B: That's right, Jesus can do this, doctors can't.

F: *And how does the crowd feel about all of this? Jesus going with Jairus, I mean.*

D: Shock. The fact that he begged. Mixed feelings I guess.

B: They were curious to see if our Lord would actually cure his daughter.

F: *"Now there was a woman …": Where do you think this woman is to be found?*

A: On the street with the crowd.

C: Just wandering anywhere, even though she had that. That wouldn't stop here from doing anything, just uncomfortable.

A: She has to be pretty near him to get his attention for five minutes.

D: Pushing through the crowd to catch up: "she came from behind."

F: *What do you make of her hope in Jesus that after all these years of treatment that if she only touches his cloak she will be healed?*

B: She asked the Lord to help her, praying to the Lord, asking Jesus to heal her.

A: When doctors make mistakes I make them pay.

D: She was helpless and hopeless at this point, and sure I would be hoping for something to happen so she could stop bleeding. She was desperate for a cure, like Jairus.

E: It must be a beautiful feeling to have a real bad disease and then be cured by the Lord—all gone.

F: *Of Jairus's daughter and the woman, who is worse off?*

C: They're both in the same boat. Equal.

A: It says the young girl was twelve years old on her deathbed. This lady had it for twelve years.

D: I think the little girl is in worse shape. She actually passes away.

B: I'd say the little girl because right there she is at the point of death but doesn't. The lady with the hemorrhages is not at the point of death.

F: *How important is this woman?*

A: Not that important really, probably nobody really cares about her.

D: Rich. She had spent all her money on doctors.

C: An everyday woman.

F: *What do you think the crowd thinks of a woman like this?*

B: Some might have thought, "How dare she touch him."

C: Just sometimes how people think.

E: He questioned: "Who touched me?" They thought nothing happened to them when they bumped into him.

F: *Why do you think she comes up behind him and not in front of him?*

D: Maybe she couldn't get to the front of the crowd.

B: Either she was afraid of something, that he wouldn't cure her and not do a miracle for her.

A: She's humble. She knew just the clothes would do it.

C: Maybe the Lord made her do that. Just the way he wanted her to walk. No need really.

A: It was just she was so desperate she did it as a last resort. Maybe somehow … or she could feel his power and she was captivated by that.

B: Her faith was that strong.

E: No one ever failed to get healed.

F: "Who touched my clothes?" *Why do you think he wants to know?*

D: Maybe he wanted to see with his own eyes who had that much faith that even if I touch him I'd be healed. To see if the person will come forth, "Yeah, I did it."

F: *In what tone of voice does Jesus say this?*

D: Not angry. A normal tone, he just asked the question.

F: *What do you think the disciples and the crowd think here?*

A: They probably want him to get moving to the girl's house. There were a lot of people pressing on him.

F: *And Jairus?*

A: Hurry up!

B: Very upset at this point to think that our Lord would help a woman who was bleeding but not dying, wishing Jesus to come to his house right away.

F: "But the woman … came in fear and trembling": *Why does the woman come in fear and trembling?*

APPENDIX: READING GROUP TRANSCRIPTS

D: Because Jesus asked, "Who touched me?" She knows it was her, like she did something wrong.

C: Maybe she thought it wasn't Jesus. She had to tell him the whole truth who did that. Maybe she had doubts. Looks like she had doubts.

B: Don't forget our Lord had a magnificent presence. People were attracted to him and his charisma.

A: I think that the woman is so impressed by him and so afraid, and now healed she feels a lot different—standing in the presence of the God who healed her.

C: Unless it was a beautiful blessing. She didn't think one person could get rid of it all.

F: *Why does Jesus call her "daughter"?*

C: Just a figure of speech—"How you going, son?"—like that. Someone you don't even know.

D: He knew that she was somebody's daughter. By her faith she became Jesus', God's daughter.

C: I don't know about that.

A: I always thought of this woman as being an older woman. She could have been even younger than Jesus.

F: *"Why trouble the teacher anymore?" How do you think Jairus felt when Jesus asked him not to fear?*

D: Extremely hurt and crushed. But then I guess Jesus reassured him, because in the beginning he was going on his belief, on faith, so Jesus told him don't let your faith go away, just believe.

F: *"He took her by the hand": How important is touch in this whole passage, 5:21–43?*

E: Who Jesus was, in motion, blessed motions, he could knock on a door and you would know it was him.

D: Jesus had a certain touch to him.

E: I think touch is important even now, a sign of affection, or consolation. But when Jesus touched people his divine power was ever present. It could change a person of a terrific nature—bringing people back from the dead.

F: *What part do the characters play in their own healing?*

D: I think the young girl played no role. Her father did. The other lady, her faith played a big role in it: if she laid hands on Jesus she would be saved.

C: They're just there, ordinary people on the streets, down the marketplace, seeing Jesus. They just need help and see Jesus walking by and say "Hi" if he's walking by.

B: From the text they recognize our Lord, fall at his feet, and the bleeding woman who told the truth had both the protagonist's role and recognized a great leader and that somehow he could cure her.

Reading Group Two, April 18, 2006

F: *What sort of man is Jairus?*

A: Probably protective. He wanted to see what was going on. He had a job to perform.

C: He is a leader, makes sure the tradition is being upheld—a responsibility for what was happening.

B: I guess Jairus, maybe he was a small-time religious person. He knew Jesus could perform miracles. He didn't have any qualms. Being a religious person he would know humility, because he recognized the magnitude of the kingdom of God. He had justification.

D: He was desperate, fearful because of his daughter.

F: *How do you imagine Jairus begging?*

E: He is just taken over with emotions.

B: Emotions taken over by their desperation, his desperation and love for her. He wanted the cry of right. He wanted to bring back something that he cherished tremendously.

F: *"Come lay your hands on her": What sort of hope does Jairus have?*

D: That she get well. That she is healed.

B: That's self-evident, but the point is Jairus says my daughter is at the point of death. But he doesn't know. He is not a physician.

C: Christ can see everything

B: Maybe he is telling Jairus he has conflicting views. Maybe he heals Jairus of the fact that it is not good to play double games on whether or not the kind of power you have.

F: *Is Jairus trying to trick Jesus, you mean?*

B: He may be.

F: *"So he went with him": What makes Jesus go with Jairus?*

D: Because Jairus is a good man, well, maybe a good man. Jesus felt he deserved to be helped. His daughter being so young needed to be helped too.

E: What's Jesus going to do anyway?

B: I think Christ is an unassuming man. He doesn't need to play games with anybody. He is the all-powerful God. "I have come here to teach you to love." He's concerned about the man's little girl. He's concerned about the man's concern. He wants everything to be foolproof, and the greater the trial, the stupider the man.

F: *Are you saying that Jairus is somehow to blame for his daughter's condition?*

B: No, not at all. It was preordained she would be ill.

E: Usually there is a reason why someone is like they are.

F: *Was the woman with hemorrhages to blame for her state?*

A: No.

B: She led a disordered life. She became straggly and bitchy.

C: It's not her fault. I don't think she is to blame.

B: Imperfection is disease. When does the world begin to die?

C: No one's perfect.

F: *Do you know how she feels to have endured much at the hands of doctors?*

B: Like the blind leading the blind. Dark doctors don't see the light.

D: Scary, frustrating. It hurts, it's hateful.

B: For every antagonism, there is an equal antagonism.

C: I'd be afraid of not getting the help I needed, of not getting better again.

A: A little hopeful that I'd heal.

E: She gave up.

F: *What do you think it is like after all that treatment to get worse, not better?*

D: It complicates it even more.

B: You get angry, pissed off, disgusted, every time you try you end up with a problem. You have no hope anymore. Sorrow and tears and despair.

F: *Why do you think she comes up behind him and not in front of him?*

D: She's scared.

C: Embarrassed. She's a woman and he's a man. This way she doesn't have to deal with his discovering about the problem as a woman.

E: Hopeless.

F: *What do you make of her hope in Jesus that after all these years of treatment that if she only touches his cloak she will be healed?*

B: She feels his clothes are magical, representative of him, because at that time if a boy was missing they'd grab his clothes and remember. They think clothes have some living part of him. That is miraculous.

F: *Could you imagine yourself thinking like that?*

D: That would be good.

B: No. It goes from black to blue, yellow, white. Always travel through what it means. That is why it is always a master and a student. That is what this is.

F: *Is mental health like that?*

C: You have to know. You have to have some idea of what is going on to tell somebody else.

A: Better than reading it in a book.

C: To actually explain it, not unless it is happening to them.

D: Sometimes I wonder if anyone really knows anything anymore. The world is dying, killing itself.

F: *What do you think the crowd is making of all this?*

E: Crazy, maybe afraid for her.

B: The crowd thinks she's ripped off this situation. She takes something from him. He was going to see someone else.

C: She did get healed.

D: I think maybe the crowd knew it took place, they could see it on her face. They wanted a piece of the action too. They wanted something to be healed.

F: *"But the woman ... came in fear and trembling": Why does the woman come in fear and trembling?*

B: He's powerful and beautiful—his manifestation. She's afraid. She's only a woman and does not have any ability to say she was a good woman, a happy woman. Unable to be working, unable to get rid of the malady which scorned her—a bit of a devil. Unable to show herself as a true person.

C: The sole purpose of a woman was to bear children. She hasn't been able to do it—she's childless—and the fact that she touched his clothes, she gets herself saved.

B: Maybe she's shy and sly and distraught. A shady woman.

F: *Why does Jesus call her "daughter," do you think?*

C: She is born again. A son or a daughter of God.

B: He is the Son of God, everybody believes. It adds validity to himself of what was being said of this Son of God.

F: *What do you make of the phrase, "your faith has made you well"?*

D: She knew she had to struggle with herself. Had to crawl on the ground to get to that cloth, and when she touched, she knew.

F: *Was it her faith that healed her?*

C: God knows that he heals, but he wants her to know when you have faith in what I am, your faith heals you.

F: *"Why trouble the teacher anymore?": How do you think Jairus feels right now?*

D: He feels very few who make it know they are healers. Jairus is seeing all these people gathering around and my daughter dies. Will he be able to bring her back? Is the time gone?

C: Did I lose my opportunity?

B: He is groping and grasping to get his daughter help. So the news is a devastating blow to his whole purpose.

A: Maybe he has hope, some. "I want you to see her. Show me what needs to be done. Even though I didn't get along with these people and they don't listen to me." Maybe he holds this against the people.

F: *How do you think Jairus felt when Jesus asked him not to fear but only believe?*

B: He already knew, Jesus is self-fulfilled.

A: He was trying to eliminate the emotion from this and just believe.

B: He is saying, "There is nothing more accurate to say than this—do not fear, only believe." It doesn't hurt his belief. No part of him at all. I'm not going to tell you that she's not dead, but he's a king, majesty.

F: *What do you learn from that?*

B: You are free from duality, free from death.

F: *How do you feel about the people laughing at Jesus? Would you have laughed?*

C: I don't know, Christ is all knowing.

D: What a relief, only sleeping!

F: *Who do you think needed healing the most?*

B: It's self-evident, the woman receives a blessing, the child is secondary, or it wouldn't be that way. Things accordingly happen in the story.

F: *What part do you feel each person plays in their own healing?*

B: A major role: they heal themselves. It's just the way it happens, you have to do certain things.

F: *And in the story?*

D: An important role. Not sure if it is small or large. I hope it would be large. You have to take care of the situation you are in. There was not much knowledge about medication, so there was a lot of self-healing.

A: There are a range of healing techniques. It is hard to come by the holistic approach.

C: I think they did. People who wanted to know Jesus and love him, they wanted him to set them free from a bondage and wanted to be happy.

B: Treat the problem. There is no way to direct every goddamn problem there is because God demands it.

Reading Group Four, April 25, 2006

F: *How might it feel to be Jesus at this point?*

B: He probably feels he's back in the lion's den.

D: He probably feels he can't let the fame go to his head. All the people pushing around saying, "Lord, Lord." He had to keep his mind open so he wouldn't become prideful. His position in life meant that he couldn't look at himself fully until he was glorified.

C: He's humble.

D: He is humble but people are still following him. We can't comprehend the goodness of Jesus. Imagine having people begging you for life. I just can't imagine being in that position. But he didn't show any pride. He wanted people to understand how he loved them: most powerful and most humble.

F: *What sort of man is Jairus?*

A: Emotional to start with. He ignored his power. His emotions had gone beyond his position in life. He was just a human being and caring about his daughter.

B: He believes in Jesus and in asking for his help somehow he believes he is superior to him.

F: *Do you think Jesus pays more attention to Jairus because of his status?*

A: I don't think so. He's not trying to prove a point, he is just being a servant of God.

D: He wasn't looking for publicity. He was just doing things in the simplest terms.

C: Jesus was a respected person. He healed one of the Roman centurion's slaves.

F: *What does the crowd think of him falling at Jesus' feet?*

A: They didn't want to leave Jesus. I don't think they thought it out of the ordinary. I know I would never have left his side.

D: Well, his disciples might have thought, "I don't know." I just think that Jesus, in his goodness, encouraged everyone around him. No darkness at all was able to exist around him. The Shekinah of God. The glory of God.

F: *"Come lay your hands on her": What sort of hope does Jairus have?*

C: He's a believer. He doesn't say, "Do something," he says, "Lay on your hands." He believes Jesus can do it.

A: Jairus must have seen him before. He saw what Jesus did. He knew no one could do these things unless they were from God.

F: *Have you wanted to have or have you had that sort of hope?*

C: I guess so, yeah, but I accept my lot in life. I've reaped what I've sown.

A: My mother had a stroke, my sister is in a coma. What's to be is God's will. It's God's will.

F: *Why do you think Jairus believes this?*

A: He is responsible for a lot of people. He has a large following himself. By making her better, Jesus would pass the word along. He did not want to convince this guy, but to show God's love to Jairus and Jairus will show that to his congregation. What better than the leader of the community? Jairus didn't pick Jesus out. Jesus picked out Jairus.

B: He never backed down.

C: He could have just said the word, "Your daughter is healed." I wonder why he goes with Jairus and not with the centurion. Could it be he just felt like going?

F: *What do you think the crowd is thinking?*

C: Why is he going so far out of his way for the people who are against him? Why raise the daughter of a leader who hates him? Bald-faced hypocrites.

B: They wanted to see it.

A: Curiosity.

B: They all know.

F: *"Now there was a woman …": How do you imagine her?*

A: Desperate. She knows she's tried everything she could. Maybe not just one, not just local, and at that time there probably weren't more than one doctor in a town. She had sought help from other places. Spent all she had. She had a lot of money to do that, but now she has no money left, and there's no recovery for herself, and plus, she is getting worse. She couldn't even keep her stasis.

F: *Do you know how she feels to have endured much at the hands of doctors?*

A: You're drowning.

D: Or if all the drugs are sucking the life out of you, you try to touch that hem.

B: It's because you are trying that you are desperate.

C: Yeah, there was a point in my life, two years ago, a situation in my life. I tried everything. My expectations were unrealistic, because I wasn't looking for God. I tried to do it my way, but to no avail. When weakness came, I gave in straightaway. I had played both roles: a father and a very active drug addict. It depends on how you are trying. She tried all those physicians.

A: She had an awful lot of faith.

B: She saw what he was doing.

F: *How do you picture her coming toward Jesus?*

D: I see her just going forward. Her faith overcoming everything. Jesus already knows. Her faith is beyond that obstacle, somehow she is going to get there and she does. She's not thinking, "Am I able?"

B: She's on a mission.

F: *How important is this woman?*

D: Just a pauper, a beggar ... whatever, a common person.

C: A commoner.

A: But she had money to spend. She wasn't poor.

D: She didn't use to be.

B: There were no HMOs!

F: *What do you think "the crowd" thinks of a woman like this?*

D: I think the crowd thinks she is insignificant. They couldn't feel what Jesus feels. There was something more to that touching. The crowd was indifferent to this woman, still Jesus turns around.

C: Just one of many.

D: She touched him in a certain way. In a way that through him she was healed, through his power.

B: She had so much faith.

A: All through the crowd, quite a few touched his clothes, but he knew what had happened. He wanted her to come forward.

D: Like the armor of God. Someone touched his divinity and it went out from him.

F: *Why did Jesus say, "your faith has made you well"?*

C: Because she believed through him.

D: She believed so much that she touched Jesus' divinity, his knowing goodness, his true clothes.

F: *Do you think that the woman contaminated Jesus?*

D: No, not at all. That woman was just like his disciples, following him for the rest of his life.

C: No, because she was faithful.

F: *What role does the woman play in her own healing?*

A: She was desperate, looking for help.

C: She felt guilty. Knowing what had happened, she was afraid. Maybe she felt guilty because she stood out there—not good enough for Jesus to come to her. Afraid Jesus thought she was sneaky or something.

B: She'd done something wrong.

F: *Is that true?*

D: No, she didn't do something wrong.

A: I don't think she thought she did anything wrong.

D: I don't know, she was a little bit overwhelmed with everything. Jesus felt her faith, he felt everything about her. Her faith was too much for her to think she was doing something wrong. She knew that he was the Messiah.

A: She knew it was God.

D: Yeah, exactly. Her faith told her what this person is going to say. Not wrong, not in fear because she knows she is touching God.

C: She was a sinner—"he's going to look through me and see me a sinner."

F: *Did she heal herself?*

A: Yeah.

B: Yeah.

D: No, hold on.

B: Jesus said, "Your faith has made you well."

C: She doesn't know it's her faith that's healed her. She has faith but at the moment she is not thinking about anything: "I've just gotta touch him."

B: She's hoping.

F: *Why does Jesus call her "daughter," do you think?*

C: 'Cause he's God.

D: She's one of God's children.

A: He has accepted her into his family.

B: But why "daughter" when others are "friends"?

D: Putting the Father's words on Jesus' lips reveals the Word of God himself.

F: *How is Jairus feeling while this is happening, do you think?*

D: Just attentive. Just listening, letting the guy do his thing.

B: He wants Jesus to hurry up. "Let's go." To him that time is an eternity.

F: *Is he giving up hope?*

D: No, not giving up hope.

C: He's so confident in Jesus. The crowd couldn't leave Jesus.

A: Jairus is fearful he will lose his daughter. On the other hand he has just seen a miracle and that gives him confidence. He feels both at the same time. Fear and a reaffirmation that this Jesus will help his daughter.

F: *Did Jairus's daughter want to be healed?*

C: Yeah, if she believed, yeah. But if she had no faith, then she wanted to die instead of suffering.

B: She's still a child, she's immature.

A: How can we even speculate, the first time we hear, she is at the point of death.

B: For her, being so sick, she didn't realize what was going on.

F: *Why do you think Jesus wanted this to be a secret?*

C: He wasn't ready to … this was big, and I think he knew the people were already planning something for him. This would go over the limit and they would use it against him.

D: He was ready to be that famous. Jesus was never unready. He just knew his time, all planned out.

A: With him being the humble person he was, he didn't want to make this into a publicity event. He didn't want her to become notorious for this. In a way, she had an ally when he walked out of the house. Others would say he did it on purpose, to make it happen for fame. Jesus did it from his heart. He did it privately.

F: *Who needed healing the most in this passage?*

C: Hard to say ... I think the woman. She's older, she had sinned more. She needed more healing.

A: The child was innocent—only twelve years old. The woman needed more healing when you look beyond the hemorrhages and everything. Maybe she wasn't an adulterous person, but she committed sins. So for that, yeah, she needed more healing.

B: Outwardly, the girl who was dying more than the woman. She [the woman] could live. She could live even though it was a bit messy.

Mark 7:24–30

24 From there he set out and went away to the region of Tyre. He entered a house and did not want anyone to know he was there. Yet he could not escape notice, 25 but a woman whose little daughter had an unclean spirit immediately heard about him, and she came and bowed down at his feet. 26 Now the woman was a Gentile, of Syrophoenician origin. She begged him to cast the demon out of her daughter. 27 He said to her, "Let the children be fed first, for it is not fair to take the children's food and throw it to the dogs." 28 But she answered him, "Sir, even the dogs under the table eat the children's crumbs." 29 Then he said to her, "For saying that, you may go—the demon has left your daughter." 30 So she went home, found the child lying on the bed, and the demon gone.

Questions

Verse 24
- Where is Jesus now?
- Why didn't he want anyone to know where he was?
- How do you think Jesus is feeling here?
- How do you think he felt knowing that he could not hide even if he wanted to?

Verse 25
- How do you think it was possible that the Syrophoenician woman immediately heard about Jesus?
- Who told her?
- Why do you think she comes and bows at Jesus' feet?
- Was there anything odd about this?
- How do you think Jesus felt about her doing that?

Verse 26
- What significance is it, do you think, that the Syrophoenician woman was a Gentile?
- Why does she beg?
- What do you think she believes about Jesus?
- Can you imagine yourself in her position, begging?

Verse 27
- Who are the "children" that Jesus refers to?
- Why should they be fed first?
- Who are the "dogs"?
- Why should they have their food thrown to them?
- Which do you mostly associate with: the children or the dogs?
- How do you feel about Jesus using the word *dog* to describe another person?

Verse 28
- How do you feel about her answering Jesus back?
- Has Jesus said something wrong that the Syrophoenician woman needs to correct him?
- Why do you think she calls Jesus "Sir"?
- Why should the dogs only get crumbs to eat?
- Does the Syrophoenician woman expect too little?
- Should she also have a place at the table?
- Who do you most associate with in this story?

Verse 29
- What do you think Jesus means when he says, "For saying that …"?
- Did the Syrophoenician woman say something wrong?
- How does Jesus feel at this point?

- Was the Syrophoenician woman free to leave before now?
- How do you think she feels just at this point? Has she pushed Jesus too far?
- What do you think has made the demon leave her daughter?

Verse 30
- How has the girl been all this while?
- Was she something to be bargained over?
- How do you think the woman feels now?
- Is she one of the "children" now or still a "dog"?
- How about Jesus? How do you think he feels now?
- Did Jesus learn anything from this encounter?

Reading Group One, April 25, 2006

C: Everybody has their place, even the birds.

F: *Where is Jesus now? Why didn't he want anyone to know where he was?*

B: Might have been tired, wanted to rest.

D: He didn't want his enemies to know where he is.

F: *How do you think he felt knowing that he could not hide even if he wanted to?*

A: Maybe he wanted personal space.

C: Paranoid. We always think that people were after him, yeah, he had a persecution complex.

F: *What does it feel like when you don't manage it?*

D: Probably maybe frustrated and aggravated.

C: I think he was relieved that someone found him, someone he could talk to.

B: Love the one you're with. If you can't be with the one you love—God—love people you are with.

F: *How do you think it was possible that the Syrophoenician woman immediately heard about Jesus?*

B: He was probably doing a lot of miracles, so he was just in the next town. They were probably following him. I'm sure he didn't walk in the house all by himself.

F: *Why do you think she comes and bows at Jesus' feet?*

D: She has faith that he is the Messiah.

B: She saw the Lord, she was astonished.

C: She had humility. I beg to people sometimes, well yeah, if I'm asking for forgiveness or I don't want to be punished. Like with the staff at the home—be merciful, have mercy.

A: For her forgiveness, she needs to be forgiven.

F: *How do you think Jesus felt about her doing that?*

A: Merciful.

C: He probably said, "You don't have to keep crying all the time," otherwise she might go into a frenzy and go mentally ill.

A: She could have been in danger of losing her mind.

C: Sure they had mental illness, even in those days.

F: *Was it significant that she is a woman begging?*

C: I don't think so.

A: A woman is more likely to beg to a man than another man.

B: Jesus is Lord, there is no sexual connection to the woman.

C: A man still has pride.

D: A woman is more emotional.

A: Some men just can't get over their egos and be just as spiritual with Jesus as the women are.

D: A man can be just as humble as a woman, I changed my mind.

F: *Is she an outsider?*

B: Well, I think Jesus found her very interesting, to figure out how she found him since she is an outsider.

D: Since she was an outsider she took a risk going to see him.

A: I think it took courage to beg, to be humble.

F: *How does she feel, begging, do you think?*

D: She went to Jesus to get the demon out of her daughter. She is very confident he can do it.

B: I think she is thinking about herself and her daughter. When somebody dies you feel sorry for yourself too. She doesn't want to feel sad, or lonely.

A: They belong to each other—her daughter and her—a special bond.

F: *Who are the "children" that Jesus refers to?*

C: The children of the neighborhood, I guess.

D: The Jewish people.

F: *And the "dogs"?*

A: People who don't have any food.

D: Or the people who don't believe.

B: Well, the dogs are the people whom Jesus doesn't recognize as part of his people.

C: Doesn't sound too good, no, when he calls them dogs. Those are people beneath him, he doesn't recognize them as equal.

F: *And how do you feel about them having their food thrown to them?*

C: No good either, doesn't have any manners.

F: *How would you feel if you were called a "dog"?*

A: I would feel humiliated.

C: I would ask him to change his view in the way he was looking at the daughter.

B: What is he referring to? Is he saying that the daughter is a dog?

A: Sounds like it.

D: She's possessed by a demon.

C: I think the devil can take it out, God can't.

D: I disagree with that.

B: I think he could be referring to the demons as dogs—throwing food to dogs—talking to the demons.

F: *Do you think that "dog" might refer to the woman?*

C: No. I don't think she can know the dog in the devil, talking about the demons under the table.

D: It's just a figure of speech.

A: Everyone needs a chance sometimes.

F: *Does this seem like a negotiation to you?*

C: Yes, to fix the daughter, to be well, to get him to rid the demon, the devil.

F: *"But she answered him …": How do you feel about her answering Jesus back?*

A: Well, she's not like him, so he's really afraid of what she says.

F: *Why's that?*

C: Because I think she's stronger than him, because she comes from another area, and the area she comes from is probably very powerful.

F: *So she's not afraid to answer back?*

C: No.

F: *Does the Syrophoenician woman expect too little? Should she also have a place at the table?*

A: She should have said, "I have a place at the table too," that's the best answer.

C: Well, maybe she wants him to be with her, so that she can help him, and he could help her. Maybe she's looking for a mate.

D: I think she's humbling herself even more, she's showing she has faith too.

F: *How has the girl been all this while?*

C: Like in the exorcist.

B: Sick.

F: *Would you have liked to have known more about her?*

A: Yes.

D: Why was she possessed in the first place?

C: Well, what caused her to be possessed? That would help figure out a way to get rid of the demons, how to go about it.

F: *How do you think Jesus feels when she answers back?*

A: Surprised, well he. …

B: I don't think he was angry.

C: It doesn't say Jesus got the demon out, all it says is that the demon left her. It would have said, "Jesus took the demon out."

F: *What do you think made the demons leave?*

C: The demon himself left.

F: *Why?*

C: I don't know, Simon.

F: *Does the woman push Jesus too far?*

A: I think she wants to see how far she can push him, what he's able to do.

C: I don't think Jesus had enough power to get rid of the demon. I think the demon had to leave by himself.

D: I don't think so, not too far.

B: I don't think she pushed him too far because the demon finally left.

C: God and the devil are separate from each other. God does his work and the devil does his work.

D: Don't you think the devil only has the power you give him?

C: I don't know "D," it's all a feeling, a feeling, you know.

F: *What do you think has made the demon to leave her daughter?*

B: I think the mother's faith.

D: I think that the mother prayed that the demon would leave.

F: *What role does Jesus have in this?*

C: Nothing, Jesus had no role in it.

B: He's the savior.

D: I think Jesus cast the demon out.

C: I think the devil has to leave. We all have our opinions here, right D?

F: *Do you think we could say that the girl was bargained over?*

A: She was auctioned, a bargained thing.

B: If it was a bargain, the lady got what she wanted, but what did the Lord get out of it?

F: *What do you think?*

C: He probably did get something. She didn't believe before, now she believes.

F: *How do you think the woman feels now? Like a woman, a child, a dog?*

A: I think she thinks of herself as a child now, 'cause I think after this she changed her life around.

C: She felt like a dog, because of what happens to her. She's been treated like a dog.

D: I think she's well off and humbled herself—changed her life around.

C: Well, I don't know. Yeah. ...

Reading Group Two, April 25, 2006

F: *How do you think Jesus is feeling here?*

A: Not sure. Jesus was caring for people. Difficult not to be unnoticed. I'm not too sure why it would bother him.

F: *Why do you think she comes and bows at Jesus' feet?*

A: I'd rather she didn't, but maybe a male and female greeted one another. Hard to say. Customs at that time.

F: *Was it significant that she was a woman?*

A: Possibly might have made a difference. I don't know if a male would do the same thing, he might, I don't know.

F: *Was she an outsider?*

B: Like two ships meeting in the ocean, the story as it's told or whoever's telling the story set it up that way.

A: Possibly. Seems like the first time they met, first time.

F: *Is it risky to behave that way, to beg on your knees to a complete stranger?*

A: Could be, opening up to someone you don't really know.

B: Where he comes from it is.

A: It shows trust. I myself wouldn't trust in doing it like that.

F: *Why does she beg?*

A: Well, it seems to me that she's kind of desperate. Her daughter has a demon or whatever. She doesn't quite know what to do about it. She's probably tried numerous things without getting anything out of it. So she's looking to somebody to help the situation she has.

F: *Who are the "children" that Jesus refers to?*

A: The hungry, basically those who don't have as much as you do.

F: *And the "dogs"?*

B: Unbelievers.

F: *How do you feel about Jesus' terms?*

B: Where it was and the time it was appropriate. People could relate better to what he was saying.

A: I wouldn't be very happy about it. Just the fact that the language he used wouldn't seem right, wouldn't seem [like] the sincerity I expect him to have.

F: *How would you react to it?*

B: Who the hell does this guy think he is?

A: I would probably let him elaborate on his answer and try and get more of an answer from him.

F: *Is this anything like how you are encountered having mental health problems today?*

A: A major problem is that you don't know what it going on with a person having problems. They don't notice.

F: *Does the way the woman answers back work as a way of resisting the label Jesus offers?*

B: You might end up with a fight on your hands.

A: If you wanted a fight, I presume it would be fine to do that.

B: Could be verbal or physical.

A: It could happen.

F: *Is it a risk then to answer back?*

B: Yeah.

F: *How do you feel about her answering Jesus back?*

A: She was expressing a certain amount of truth—kids eat, they drop food, somebody else eats it. It just keeps going.

F: *Is she correcting him, do you think?*

A: Yeah, but I don't know if I'd call it correcting, but just elaborating on the sentence before.

F: *Does the Syrophoenician woman expect too little? Should she also have a place at the table?*

A: She puts herself at a certain level when she calls him "sir." I'm not too sure. …

F: *Who is in control of this encounter, do you think?*

A: I think Jesus is trying to exhibit control by saying, "You may go now."

B: There's no round up to see the daughter. A person can say things. People say many things. There's no way to validate if this is true, so in some ways he has the upper hand.

F: *Has she pushed Jesus too far?*

B: They both push each other too far.

F: *Do you think the woman's role was significant?*

A: Yes. I am not too sure that Jesus knows this about the daughter until she mentions it to him, but she has been experiencing this for some time.

F: *Would you have liked to have had more focus in the story on the girl?*

A: Yes, just to validate the statement that the two are making—just go in faith on what they say.

F: *Do you think we could say that the girl was bargained over?*

B: Initially, it seem more like bargaining, but eventually he was like the counselor or a head shrink, asking her questions or giving her assurance.

F: *Does he do that in the right way?*

A: Yes I think so.

F: *Even with the terms he uses?*

A: Well, I'm not too sure there.

F: *How do you think the woman feels now? Like a woman, a child, a dog?*

A: Hard to say

B: Wouldn't take it. Sorry, see you later.

Reading Group Three, April 24, 2006

All answers for this session are provided by reader "A," who asked for the session to be short.

F: *Why do you think she comes and bows at Jesus' feet?*

Just she probably thought he was extremely holy, a saving person, maybe even something beyond that—an angel or a god.

F: *Was it out of respect?*

More respect, it could be desperation too. The text leaves it open.

F: *How do you think Jesus feels about this?*

I don't know. It could be a kind of grandiose thing, like it assumes that the historical Jesus was a regular person, but no special connection to the divine. Because of actions due to people like this he developed a problem: a God complex.

F: *Do you think it is about Jesus' power?*

I remember a psychiatrist when starting would always have his head above mine. I've never felt that kind of thing with people I am working with now. Although I do remember trying to get into a certain living situation and my caseworker was holding the reigns.

F: *Why does she beg?*

That is strange, because if somebody like Jesus has the power to heal people and is a pretty benevolent person, it should not require begging. It may be more about her desperation. She may not know much about Jesus and just knows that he heals. She doesn't know if he is a benevolent person or wants to heal.

F: *Who are the "dogs"?*

It's enigmatic. It's metaphorical. She's asking him for something, he is throwing an aphorism at her. It doesn't really make sense to me. It's definitely open to interpretation, that he is calling her a dog. It's disturbing. It's not a compassionate, loving thing to do.

F: *How would you feel?*

It would be upsetting. I would feel disillusioned, not know what to say, or say, "I didn't think you were like this."

F: *Is her response realistic if imagined for a person who lives with the social experience of poor mental health?*

I think some people have this mental constitution to react in that way, but to the extent that mental health problems can overlap with problems with hating yourself, feeling depressed, and getting really high and manic—yeah, this part just feels like a story, it doesn't feel like something that could really have happened.

F: *Is there a way to resist this sort of label?*

Well, one way is just not to associate with that person anymore, or give them a label to write off whatever they say.

F: *A label to "write them off"?*

Labeling back: because of this label I feel confident writing off anything you say. Just give me a crumb.

F: *Are labels important?*

Depends on the person you are reaching out to. With regard to that stuff, we've made some progress historically from the time before when there were asylums—everyone outside is safe, the insane as criminals at the same time. There's a lot more willingness [now] to see us as people too.

F: *Does the Syrophoenician woman expect too little? Should she also have a place at the table?*

I don't know. Her kid gets cured. It seems that this is all she is asking for in the first place.

F: *Who is in control of this situation?*

Definitely I think Jesus. It seems almost like he's saying aphorisms, it's like he's throwing something at her, something small and profound for her to think about. I guess Jesus … but it depended on her saying the right thing.

F: *Who has power?*

I think both have some power; I can't say who has more.

F: *Would you have liked to have learned more about the daughter?*

She matters. It would be nice to get a comparison between what she is like before and after the spirit [demon]. Even the individual will have a very muddy perception of themselves, depending on the situation. It's good to keep that person in the know. You can't make generalizations without having some individual personal story. Individual stories might be useful in general for advancing scientific knowledge, but they are personal stories of infinite value. It's about honoring every individual human life.

F: *What makes the demon leave?*

You could definitely read it, because the woman said the response to Jesus, he did, but Jesus decided. It's not clear. Maybe the woman, maybe without Jesus' action, made the demon leave. I would say, though, it is Jesus, I think it makes more sense.

F: *Who would you like it to be?*

I guess the woman. It's cooler if she makes it happen just by saying that.

Mark 5:1–20

1 They came to the other side of the sea, to the country of the Gerasenes. 2 And when he had stepped out of the boat, immediately a man out of the tombs with an unclean spirit met him. 3 He lived among the tombs; and no one could restrain him any more, even with a chain; 4 for he had often been restrained with shackles and chains, but the chains he wrenched apart, and the shackles he broke in pieces; and no one had the strength to subdue him. 5 Night and day among the tombs and on the mountains he was always howling and bruising himself with stones. 6 When he saw Jesus from a distance, he ran and bowed down before him; 7 and he shouted at the top of his voice, "What have you to do with me, Jesus, Son of the Most High God? I adjure you by God, do not torment me." 8 For he had said to him, "Come out of the man, you unclean spirit!" 9 Then Jesus asked him, "What is your name?" He replied, "My name is Legion; for we are many." 10 He begged him earnestly not to send them out of the country. 11 Now there on the hillside a great herd of swine was feeding; 12 and the unclean spirits begged him, "Send us into the swine; let us enter them." 13 So he gave them permission. And the unclean spirits came out and entered the swine; and the herd, numbering about two thousand, rushed down the steep bank into the sea, and were drowned in the sea.

14 The swineherds ran off and told it in the city and in the country. Then people came to see what it was that had happened. 15 They came to Jesus and saw the demoniac sitting there, clothed and in his right mind, the very man who had had the legion; and they were afraid. 16 Those who had seen what had happened to the demoniac and to the swine reported it. 17 Then they began to beg Jesus to leave their neighborhood. 18 As he was getting into the boat, the man who had been possessed by demons

begged him that he might be with him. 19 But Jesus refused, and said to him, "Go home to your friends, and tell them how much the Lord has done for you, and what mercy he has shown you." 20 And he went away and began to proclaim in the Decapolis how much Jesus had done for him; and everyone was amazed.

Verses 1–2
- At what sort of pace is the story at just now?
- What does it feel like to Jesus?
- Why do you think he has no place to get away from the crowds?

Verses 3–5
- What sort of existence has the man with the demons had?
- What does the fact that he lived "among the tombs" say to you about him and his life?
- Who do you think had been restraining him with chains and shackles?
- Why do you think he was so strong?
- What would it feel like to be that man?
- Can you imagine what it might feel like to be restrained?

Verse 6
- Why do you think he runs to Jesus?
- And why bow?
- How do you think this makes Jesus feel?
- What do the swineherds think about this?
- And the disciples, do you think they are around?

Verses 7–8
- What do you make of his question: "What have you to do with me?"
- Who does he recognize Jesus as?
- Do you think that Jesus would or should torment the man?
- Who is doing the speaking here?
- Who is Jesus speaking to?

Verse 9
- What do you make of Jesus asking his name then and not before?

- And what about the name "Legion"? What does that make you think of?

Verse 10
- Why is there so much anxiety about being sent out of the country?
- Where might that be, do you think?

Verses 11–13
- How do you feel about the pigs being drowned?
- Why do you think the unclean spirits wanted to go into them?
- What do you think the pig herders thought about that?
- Do you think Jesus had any concern for the animals or the pig herders' livelihood?

Verse 14
- Why do you think the herders ran off? What was their aim?
- How do you think the crowds in the city and country reacted?

Verse 15
- What has happened in the meantime?
- How long do you think the man and Jesus have been together?
- Are they alone?
- Do you think they were talking to one another? What might they have been talking about?
- Why were the people afraid?
- Who were they afraid of, do you think?

Verses 16–17
- Who is reporting to whom?
- How do you think that report was received?
- Why do you think they beg Jesus to leave?

Verses 18–20
- In what frame of mind do you think Jesus got back into the boat?
- Had it been a good trip?
- Why is the man begging again?
- How do you feel about him still being someone who begs?

- How do you feel about Jesus refusing him?
- Is his advice to the man good advice? If so, how so?
- What do you take the word *amazed* to mean at the end of this passage?

Reading Group One, April 11, 2006

F: *What sort of existence has the man with the demons had?*

B: Troubled. Seeking a miracle in life from the Lord. He's going through hard times and needs a good miracle. He really needs something good to happen to him.

C: Looks like it. Same old grind every day. He needs a "pick me up."

F: *Who do you think had been restraining him with chains and shackles?*

A: How barbaric. Who chained him up? Why would they pick on him? Why was he elected to be chained? There must have been a reason—like a prisoner is in jail.

D: Maybe to the crowd, they thought he was going out of his mind, so they chained him up all this time.

F: *Does that sound fair to you?*

C: No, it's not fair.

E: Living next to the cemetery, nobody to talk to. Nobody likes to wake up in the morning and see a bunch of dead people.

D: It's a kind of punishment. Maybe they thought they were protecting him.

F: *What did it feel like to be that man?*

B: Kind of tough. That's why he fought it all the time and so got so powerful that they couldn't restrain him anymore.

C: I wouldn't want to be him.

D: It doesn't say why he was restrained. I'd like to know.

F: *It says he was howling at night. What do you think that is about?*

C: Going out of his mind.

A: Going through hell. It could be the work of the devil too, you know.

F: *What does this man need?*

A: A life.

B: That's it.

A: Like everybody else.

B: Maybe he needed somebody just to listen to him and just to care.

F: *Why do you think he runs to Jesus?*

D: Because Jesus is beautiful, he's God. Jesus is an absolutely beautiful human being. He was happy. He decided he was good. I'm pretty sure if we saw God we'd bow down to him too you know.

F: *What do you think the disciples thought about this?*

C: They might have felt the same way as the man … I don't know, they felt bad for him.

A: They might have taken his chains off.

E: Well, I read the Bible. The disciples are always very protective of Jesus and usually try to hold off the crowd.

C: I don't think they got out of the boat this time.

D: Put it this way: if one of us saw Jesus, we'd run to him too.

B: That's right.

C: Definitely.

A: He's astonished.

F: *What do you make of his question: "What have you to do with me?"*

C: He said that to the Lord because the Lord could do anything, he could change his mind. God can also torment too. You can get afraid of the Lord. The Lord can go haywire, just like someone who has too many drinks.

F: *Do you think he was afraid of Jesus then?*

C: Might have been.

A: I think it's a conflict of witches, and those under the spell speak through the man.

D: He recognizes him as the Most High God, but he also wants nothing to do with him.

E: We don't know who's speaking, the man or the demons.

C: The legions of hell.

F: *Do you think that Jesus would torment someone?*

C: He could. Jesus could do anything.

D: I think he's more afraid than anything, because Jesus is so good, he has all sorts of problems and thought he might be punished by God for having demons in him.

F: *Is mental illness a condition of being punished by God?*

A: I don't go that far.

B: It's just a disease.

F: *And what about the name "Legion"? What does that make you think of?*

C: That's his name. That's his name, that's all.

D: I think it means an army of evil spirits.

F: *Could it refer to the Romans?*

E: I don't know, it doesn't sound like Romans.

C: Maybe they might have meant that there were other people that were there. They were too afraid to come out—"I'm standing here, speaking for everyone"—a lot who were left out because they were a little different.

F: *Why is there so much anxiety about being sent out of the country?*

C: They send them away if they don't do your hygiene. "Get away, get away, you stink."

B: I don't understand this. Maybe he thought. ...

E: Maybe he thought what Jesus thought, that he should push them out too.

C: He might have seemed a loser, might not have liked him. No one wanted to have anything to do with him.

F: *How do you feel about the pigs being drowned?*

A: Kind of rough.

F: *What do you think was the biggest story the herders ran off and told: that the man had been healed or that the pigs had run off the cliff?*

A: Yes, the pigs.

D: You have to think, this was their livelihood.

C: What about both could happen?

B: I think they lost livelihood and told people Jesus drowned two thousand pigs.

F: *Why did the crowds come?*

D: They were amazed.

C: To praise the pigs.

B: Some might have come to get healed themselves.

D: They would have been angry.

A: Jesus has created a stir.

F: *What has happened in the meantime? Do you think they were talking to one another? What might they have been talking about?*

C: Jesus was talking to him. Jesus started talking, "You are not possessed no more, keep it down."

B: I think it shows great compassion for the man, and I also think that it was proof that he had done the miracle since the man was clearly okay.

A: They were resting together.

E: Talking to him.

A: Yeah, exactly.

E: Showed that he is normal now.

C: Might have been talking about life, if he had a wife, if he had kids, what he used to do before he lost his mind to those demons.

F: *Why were the people afraid?*

E: Of the pains of life.

D: Might have been afraid because of what just happened with the pigs.

C: I think Jesus might have given off bad vibrations, because they were afraid he could do something wrong they backed off a little. Afraid of his power, that if you do something wrong you could … well, you know, you could be in trouble.

B: I think some were afraid because he killed the swine, some might be angry I'm sure, that is what they had to eat.

F: *Why do you think they beg Jesus to leave?*

D: Maybe they were scared, what would happen next.

C: Getting bad vibrations.

F: *And the man?*

A: They were probably afraid of him too.

B: Yeah I think so too. He had changed so much in such a [short] space of time.

D: Maybe they overlook him, they forget about him. It seemed a small thing in comparison. It was overshadowed.

F: *In what frame of mind do you think Jesus got back into the boat?*

C: "Same old baloney! Perform a miracle and this is the thanks I get. I don't know!"

D: I think he was feeling good because he helped somebody. A good trip.

B: I think he thought a lot of his work. It was wonderful how he helped this poor man and bring him back to normal life. It shows the power the Lord has to change peoples' lives.

F: *How do you feel about him [the man] still being someone who begs and how do you feel about Jesus refusing him?*

D: I think he knew that Jesus was the Son of God. He wanted to be near him.

B: Probably in the conversation before, he had told him how his life was, he probably just wanted to be with Jesus. He knew if he was he would be taken care of.

Reading Group Two, April 11, 2006

F: *What sort of existence has the man with the demons had?*

A: Many saints do this like that. I know they used to sleep on a concrete slab—like a penance, trying to get it out. He bangs his head, scrapes his head, like he's doing penance in a way. I'm not saying that he was a saint, but he was heading that way maybe.

B: They wanted to separate the man from other people. Probably they had a belief in the afterlife. It must have had some meaning to them. He wants to get rid of the demon. The only person who could do it for him was Jesus.

F: *Can you imagine what it might feel like to be restrained?*

A: Hard to say. I don't know how he feels. It's just that in that situation you don't know what to do about it.

C: Yes, it's desperate.

F: *Why do you think he runs to Jesus?*

B: Because he believes in the afterlife and because Jesus is the promised Messiah and probably he heard people talk about him. I think he realizes that Jesus is the only one who can get rid of the demons.

A: It's like mentally ill people. Some people can't see what is bothering them and holding them back. I think he [Jesus] knew. Maybe God had this suffering for him to do and he accepted it.

B: It just goes to show the power of Satan, he could break out of shackles.

F: *Was this God's punishment for the man then?*

A: Yes. He has to take up his cross. Every good Catholic is required to take up his cross.

C: Sounds like the psychiatrist. Because Jesus would listen to the man and give various advice and could ask questions. People need answers too.

F: *What do you make of his question: "What have you to do with me?"*

C: Probably wants an answer.

A: I think he says, "It's up to you, Jesus." Does Jesus think he should continue suffering or should Jesus have the demons taken out of him? I think it goes with the theology of our Catholic church, each one has our cross to bear.

B: It's God's will you have to go by. We have to do it. Not our will but yours.

F: *Is mental illness a punishment from God?*

B: It's not a punishment. It's a cleansing of the soul.

C: A way of growth.

A: You don't have to do something wrong. Life can just be unfair. I took a positive view: if you are suffering and you seem to be suffering more than others, maybe God has a plan for you ultimately.

F: *Do you think Jesus would torment someone?*

A: Jesus had mercy, he saw his suffering.

C: The easy way out. He was looking for this, and wanted the answers there and then and Jesus wasn't going to give him what he wanted.

F: *Why?*

A: Just a learning lesson that he had to go through. Everyone has to go through certain things.

F: *What do you make of Jesus asking his name then and not before?*

C: He doesn't know this. It was a searching process all the way around for Jesus and the man.

B: Well, I think with unclean spirits Jesus was saying, "After, if you want, you can go. You aren't a follower of mine."

F: *And what about the name "Legion"? What does that make you think of?*

B: An army soldier, like a great soldier.

A: The Roman Empire. In the Roman army, lots of people, maybe symbolic wisdom. Many people were afflicted by demons. He saw himself as one of many. It was Christ, he could take out everyone. He called him by his first name, Legion, a lot of people who have demons. I think it's a way for Jesus to conjure up the devil, and this man has wisdom. He does have wisdom, put the demons in the swine and they drowned, so he cured a lot of people. It's symbolic of many people who are being cleansed by this. This is a reason for suffering.

F: *How do you feel about the pigs being drowned?*

C: What a waste of life, yeah.

B: Demons aren't very smart basically.

A: It shows the swine—an animal—and they don't go to heaven, but the man who had demons in him didn't kill himself, he lived with it, he knew he had an immortal soul. You would say swine don't have an afterlife. A person should not give up in suffering.

B: Absolutely yeah. And he was prepared to do more, and when he saw Jesus he could let him go.

F: *What do you think was the biggest story the herders ran off and told: that the man had been healed or that the pigs had run off the cliff?*

C: The agricultural disaster. That's the way they made their life and then say goodbye!

A: It was different for different herders. It depended on what their faith was like. Jesus was also a human and Jewish. Maybe the pigs were symbolic, unclean, like the demons.

B: I would normally say the pigs but it was an apocalyptic time with lots of excitement about Jesus. They might have been just as interested in Jesus as anyone else. Jesus had followers and enemies. Jesus symbolically saw swine as unclean, showing that the devil has an end. He has dominion over the devil. He can put an end to them.

F: *Why do you think Jesus remains with the man?*

C: To claim credit for the miracle. Whatever it is they could see that they were amazed by that.

B: Jesus was an obvious believer in truth and wanted to know this man.

A: I don't know if they begged him to leave, but the man begs him to stay.

F: *Why do you think Jesus refuses to allow the man to follow him?*

B: He wanted this man to preach the gospel. Whatever it is, the people he goes to will see that he is in his right mind—not in the cemetery—he is preaching the word of God, being a witness to Jesus.

A: He was kind of a new priest, because it wouldn't have served any purpose to go with Christ. He gave him a challenge. We know that Jesus had enemies and many were martyred for the cause of Jesus. Christ was asking him to be a witness to his power.

C: It would have been good for him to follow, but things don't happen outright. Planting the seed and seeing what it grows into, I guess.

Reading Group Three, April 17, 2006

F: *What sort of existence has the man with the demons had?*

A: Very dirty, not changing clothes, scavenging, living off whatever he can get.

B: Pretty desperate.

F: *What does the fact that he lived "among the tombs" say to you about him and his life?*

B: Close to the spirit world. He's probably unconscious of that being a taboo. He feels he belongs. That means that he belongs with the dying.

F: *And the chains?*

A: They might have had the assumption that someone with insanity would be polluting for them to be among the rest of society. They might have thought it would have caused others to go insane. They didn't want him around their children.

F: *What do you think of the fact that he was bruising himself with stones?*

B: Suffering. He seems like he's worthless. I relate—when I'm tormented by my thoughts I have a tendency to say, "What do you want from me, God? Why are you doing this?"

A: It's like there is a piece of him that is aware. He's so broken, so ill, that he lives in this desolate existence. Mental illness can be like that. There is a lot of anguish in mental illness.

B: Is it a physical or a spiritual oppression?

A: Sure, it is hard to separate one from the other.

F: *What's most troubling to you about his context?*

B: In bondage, trapped in his suffering. No one can help him. He can't help himself.

A: Helpless, he's howling.

B: If he's oppressed, it reminds me of [the movie] *The Passion of Christ*, how they depicted Judas going crazy seeing things 'til he finally hung himself. He feels almost punished … I'm not sure. It also reminds me of whether or not he brought it upon himself or was it sin? Or both? It reminds me of the thief on the cross: even though guilty of sin God still had mercy on him in his last hour. It's really hard to see beyond the behavior and opinions and see the child of God, not these who they are. Not to pass judgment, like some pastors.

F: *Why do you think he runs to Jesus?*

A: Maybe he felt like if Jesus is there in the opposite direction to the demons he ran away to safety.

B: Also there's a sense of authority, a sense that God allowed him to be in this state. What else will he do? "Don't torment me anymore." He doesn't realize God is ready to heal him. Just last night I asked, "God, what do you want from me?" The good thing is he gets healed in the end, so let me cling to that promise.

F: *And why bow?*

B: Imagine if you met Jesus like that. Well, it says a lot because even in the midst of his torment, his presence must have been so holy he fell at his feet. I don't have that kind of humility, especially when I'm suffering—I get really mad.

F: *Was this reverence then and not fear?*

A: Fear of something worse. If that was the case he was aware of his condition, otherwise he would be out of it. Jesus almost brought a sense of clarity to speech. "What do you want with me?" He knew who he was. Even the demons. I was hoping he was talking to him, not just the demons.

F: *And the disciples, what do they think of all this?*

B: Well, I'm beginning to think they have remained open to him begging the Son of God. They've seen this character of God at work and how it changes people. God's presence. When God shows up it's not, … I mean, these disciples lives' have changed forever.

F: *Do they see this man positively or negatively?*

A: I guess positively.

B: Could be protective, but maybe they are getting the gist.

F: *"He shouted at the top of his voice …"?*

A: I assume it's the guy.

B: It's so painful, this story.

F: *Who is Jesus talking to?*

B: The demons.

A: I don't know.

B: His heart broke for the man. First he wants to get him out of the rut. It's the character of God to love his people. He doesn't want them to suffer. Then he has a conversation.

F: *And what about the name "Legion"? What does that make you think of?*

A: It's not like he has multiple personalities. He believes his psyche consists of thousands of soldiers.

B: There is war inside of him battling it out. He gets left in the corner with all the voices.

F: *Is the man powerful or powerless, would you say?*

A: To me the image is powerful—breaking chains.

B: I imagine inside is a legion, all on the same side. All very well organized to combat whatever enemy.

F: *Could Jesus be that enemy?*

A: An enemy he is surrendering to?

F: *Why is there so much anxiety about being sent out of the country?*

B: He didn't want to let it go. The demons begged him.

A: I don't know.

B: I read it like the man is begging Jesus not to send his legions out of his body. The country is like his body, which is like his country.

A: Maybe I do relate to that, I hold on to my illness.

B: I know for me, if you think you have special power, or special … maybe you think you have something. I can relate to OCD [obsessive-compulsive disorder] like you have a magical power and so rituals to fix things and if you give up special powers to fix things. Even if you want the truth, you don't want to give up the ritual. If I think a thought, if I don't like it, I think another thought and cancel it out—a special power, a magical power.

A: It's giving up the control.

B: You dare to let go, like the OCD, you dare to be mediocre.

F: *What do you think was the biggest story the herders ran off and told: that the man had been healed or that the pigs had run off the cliff?*

A: If people are more concerned with economics they would obviously care more about the pigs. If they are interested in religion and spirituality then the greater significance is the human part of the story.

B: That he was screaming, naked, beating himself, lonely—now he is okay, I think that to me is no joke. I pray for that every day.

F: *What do you think people make of the scene? Why are they afraid?*

B: It revealed to them their own sin. They realized this wasn't just some guy, this was somebody who was significant.

A: Maybe they thought Jesus was a devil, helping this guy and maybe got him dressed up, speaking clearly—like a Trojan horse. Make it seem like he was normal again.

F: *What had happened in the meantime? Do you think they were talking to one another? What might they have been talking about?*

A: It depends if he was going to remember what he experienced in his life before.

B: He must remember in some way.

A: He remembers in a rough shape.

F: *How do you feel about Jesus refusing to allow him to follow him?*

B: He was one of the first missionaries in the Bible.

A: Also, go back to your friends. He has people to go back to.

F: *How do you feel about him still being someone who begs?*

A: The fact that he begs and doesn't ask, to me connotes a desperation.

B: It's spiritual, he feels he needs Jesus.

A: It's intense.

F: *Is he fully healed if he still needs to beg?*

B: Well, maybe he is moved by the compassion of the love of Jesus, begging him to be with him. Yes he's healed, he's just thankful. He didn't want him to go. It reminds me how Jesus is the man through whom God teaches us about relationships. He really knows this.

F: *Is this the beginning of a relationship?*

B: He doesn't want this to end.

A: Maybe he felt he can't do this without him and he wanted assurance that he would be okay. If the therapist goes on vacation, and it's too much of a crutch.

B: People who believe Jesus is the living Christ and lives in a person, he never leaves or forsakes you, so in a way it's a beginning. I relate to that begging of Jesus, to stay with me, I've written a song about it; and part of my illness is not trusting myself to make decisions when he gave me a mind and heart to make decisions. Jesus encourages the man that you can do it on your own. More of the illness and not the relationship, I think.

F: *What did the man say to people that made them amazed?*

A: I think we have to ask how he is constructing the narrative. I would imagine it to be a recovery story. I was lost, I was insane, hanging out with the dead. Jesus brought me back to life.

B: The love of God had mercy on me. His terms are always right. Right now is a real dark time for me. God uses those times. What I wondered is will the demons get thrown into slavery or prison? My story would be love of God. He wished it for divine reasons and had the mercy to heal me. I have fought with God. Why? She prayed for healing in her life. Her life changed people. She was healed in special ways. My story would be like that: healing comes in a lot of forms. I know God is healing me.

Mark 15:1–5

1 As soon as it was morning, the chief priests held a consultation with the elders and scribes and the whole council. They bound Jesus, led him away, and handed him over to Pilate. 2 Pilate asked him, "Are you the King of the Jews?" He answered him, "You say so." 3 Then the chief priests accused him of many things. 4 Pilate asked him again, "Have you no answer? See how many charges they bring against you." 5 But Jesus made no further reply, so that Pilate was amazed.

Verse 1
- What do you imagine the chief priests, elders, scribes, and whole council held a consultation about?
- What do you imagine the mood to be like?
- What do you think they want?
- How do you feel about Jesus being bound?
- Have you ever felt bound?
- Have you ever been led away to a place you didn't want to go to?
- Have you ever felt "handed over"?

APPENDIX: READING GROUP TRANSCRIPTS

Verse 2
- "Are you the King of the Jews?": What does Pilate mean by this?
- Is this a label that Jesus wants?
- Why do you think Pilate asks this question?
- What do you make of Jesus' answer?
- Who is "you" here?
- Do you think this is a good answer to offer?
- Is it clear what Jesus does think from this answer?

Verse 3
- What do you imagine they accused him of?
- How do you think Jesus feels at this point?
- Have you ever been accused of many things?
- Do you think that Jesus had any chance to defend himself?
- How would you defend yourself in this situation?
- How have you defended yourself when you have been accused?

Verse 4
- Why do you think Pilate asks him again?
- How do you imagine Pilate to be feeling right now?
- How about Jesus, how does he feel?
- "Have you no answer?": Now how do you imagine Pilate feels?
- What do you imagine Jesus' accusers are hoping for now?
- Do you think that Jesus should speak up here?
- Would you speak up in this situation?

Verse 5
- Why do you think Jesus remains silent at this point?
- Have you ever felt like you have been reduced to silence?
- Do you think Jesus' accusers are disappointed?
- "Pilate was amazed": Why do you think Pilate was amazed here?
- Do you think anybody else was amazed?
- What do you think the other people gathered thought of Jesus now?
- What do you think the other people gathered thought of Pilate now?
- What do you think of Jesus now?
- Who do you think has power in this encounter?
- Who do you think is in control of this conversation in the end?

- How important do you think silence is to this passage?

Reading Group One, May 2, 2006

F: *What do you imagine the chief priests, elders, scribes, and whole council held a consultation about?*

C: They're there to find out if he is King of the Jews. They're just talking.

D: A big meeting about what they were going to do with Jesus.

B: Jesus must be becoming quite popular with the people, and the chief priests were against him all along and probably talking about how to get rid of him.

E: They were probably holding talks. Jesus was talking to the Father and there was no answer from the Lord whether he is or not.

F: *What do you imagine the mood to be like?*

B: I think they are very happy that they are going to be getting rid of him.

A: They might have been very angry, loud, some of them might have been scared.

C: The consultation might be coming up with something, leading up to something.

D: Some might have seen what he did, but they were scared to speak out, scared that if they didn't follow they'd be next.

F: *How do you feel about Jesus being bound?*

A: I don't like the idea of him being bound up because he's not free anymore, he's captured.

C: What, with rope?

A: Yeah, with ropes.

C: Why would they do that to him?

B: They're going to crucify him.

C: Ah!

F: *Have you ever been led away to a place you didn't want to go to?*

C: Yes.

B: Locked up in the ward.

F: *Why?*

C: No freedom. Can't get out, can't go nowhere. Staff at the house ... "If you do this one more time, you will be locked up. ..."

E: No, well I think the other way. It could be prophesised he could be sacrificed.

B: I haven't been locked up except on the wards. It's pretty hard to be taken from your house.

E: Jesus knew this was going to happen.

B: I don't think anybody likes being out away where they have no choice.

F: *Have you ever felt "handed over"?*

C: I've been that way, from residence to residence and home. The part of LA [Los Angeles] I came from they give you a place, an apartment, though you have to go through all kinds of heck. I'm not against Massachusetts, it just takes awhile to do things.

F: *"Are you the King of the Jews?": What does Pilate mean by this?*

C: Just what it says: "Are you the King of the Jews?"

E: It's leading up to the crucifixion.

F: *Does it seem an odd question to you?*

C: If the Lord says, "Yes," Pilate says, "Remarkable," and walks off.

F: *Do you think Pilate felt threatened?*

D: No, I don't think he felt threatened.

B: I think he was probably trying to poke fun at him. He asked it, almost sarcastically.

F: *"Are you the King of the Jews?": Is this a label that Jesus wants?*

D: I don't think he wanted any label or to label himself.

F: *Why?*

D: He was the Son of God. He was confident in who he was. He really didn't need a label or title or anything.

C: I don't know ... I wouldn't want to be called "King of the Jews." I don't know ... It's like being the leader of the pack; I wouldn't want to be leader of the pack. I'd rather be the underdog than be the king ... I don't know.

B: Well, I think Pilate was seeking to find a way to accuse him of trying to take over the city of Jerusalem. He was really afraid; he was gaining more control, more and more people. He was afraid he might overthrow the Roman Empire. So they scapegoated him instead.

F: *"You say so": What do you make of Jesus' answer?*

D: I think he said that because they were saying that, not Jesus himself. He never said that.

A: Jesus hit him back.

C: There are a couple of ways. It could be a question or returning it back to him, "He [Pilate] says so."

F: *Who is "you" here, do you think?*

E: I think "you" is Pilate, the chief priests, the elders—all of them.

A: Jesus wasn't afraid. I'd bet we'd be afraid.

F: *You think Jesus wasn't afraid?*

E: No, Jesus wasn't afraid. His deity and his power would have been shown.

D: I don't think he was afraid.

F: *"You say so": Do you think this is a good answer to offer?*

D: Yes.

C: I don't think it's good. He could have said, "Yes I am," or, "If you think I am, you have a right." Three words aren't clear enough.

B: I think it's a brief way of rebutting that whole group of people. He was angry at this point.

F: *Is it clear what Jesus does think from this answer?*

A: No, it's a quizzical reply.

C: I don't think it is.

F: *"Accused him of many things": What do you imagine they accused him of?*

C: I don't know.

B: I think one of the charges is blasphemy. To say you are the Son of God was unheard of. The chief priests were looking for ways to do away with him or at least ways to stop his power.

F: *Do you think that Jesus had any chance to defend himself?*

A: Probably not without all the apostles.

D: I think no matter what he has said, they would have tried to turn it on him.

F: *"Pilate asked him again": How do you imagine Pilate to be feeling right now?*

D: He might have got frustrated.

B: I think Pilate became incredibly curious why this heroic figure made no reply. Not even a word to say for himself. It was strange to a person used to trials and trying people.

E: They wanted him to take care of it.

F: *"But Jesus made no further reply": Why do you think Jesus remains silent at this point?*

E: He didn't have to impress anybody. He didn't need a show of power, they made him a little lower than the angels.

C: Maybe he thought he was proud. I think Jesus was really stuck up or proud.

B: Well, I think he's preached so much to people, he doesn't think he should dignify all this with a reply.

F: *Have you ever felt like you have been reduced to silence?*

B: Well, I say to myself, just shut up, if you don't have nothing to say. Just be quiet.

C: Yeah I do, yeah. When I go to smoke. I like to be by myself. I don't say that much.

F: *Who do you think has power or control in this encounter?*

C: I don't think anybody does.

B: I think Jesus does. He has the power to choose not to answer, it frustrated the guy.

A: I think at first power is to Pilate. He's the big shot, but as Jesus doesn't answer him it slips away and slips right back to Jesus.

D: I don't think anybody has power. It's kind of a plain episode.

C: Not too exciting.

D: It's good, the words were good, it's just he has no power.

Reading Group Two, May 2, 2006

A: I think Jesus was showing his innocence. If Jesus believed he had guilt he would have told Pilate.

B: Pilate crucified him anyway.

F: *What do you imagine the chief priests, elders, scribes, and whole council held a consultation about?*

A: Sounds like a lawyer and a jury, trying to find out if Jesus really was the King of the Jews or just a phony person.

F: *What do you imagine the mood to be like?*

A: They want to find out the truth. First they want to find out if he deserves a higher authority, if he is King of the Jews, ruler of Jerusalem.

B: If Jesus says yes, then Jesus has a chance of being made king.

A: Sometimes people just subject to their priests.

C: But I think he may have been pompous with Jesus.

B: What they put Jesus through, partly because he was innocent. He didn't realize that, that they were trying to help him, not hurt him.

F: *How do you feel about Jesus being bound?*

A: It's cruel and unusual punishment. I think they were jealous, that this man was actually saying to him in his own way he was just as good or better than Pilate and he saw Jesus as a threat to his relationship to Rome.

F: *A threat?*

C: Because the king is like Pilate and Pilate is like the pope. If Jesus is king then he may be greater than the representative of the emperor. He has abilities Pilate never dreamt of, he has a power beyond description.

B: Maybe he was scared he would get violent.

A: It has to do with people wanting power; Jesus was unable to say anything.

F: *Have you ever been led away to a place you didn't want to go to?*

A: This is a bit different. I had a dream I couldn't lift my leg—a dream I used to have.

B: Yeah, I didn't like being hospitalized. They put me in "human resources" instantly. Something about it tortured my mind. Well, I had dreams that I cut my wrists with razors. I had a dream, thinking I was beautiful.

C: I didn't want to go to the hospital, I knew it was run down, the other one was good. Actually, they put one of my friends in restraints, I didn't like that. It was a place of a lot of tragedies. Some people started to believe things about themselves.

F: *Have you ever felt "handed over"?*

A: In a way that's happened to me. It was the middle of the night and I was trying to get better in hospital. They took me bodily and put me in a hot shower. I didn't know what to do. I don't know why they did it; I felt frightened by that.

F: *"Are you the King of the Jews?": What does Pilate mean by this?*

B: Why not, he was head priest there, but I think Jesus wanted to save the world.

A: Maybe one thing led to another and they planned this. They saw Jesus was getting more popular.

B: Like I said, he believed Jesus had a higher power, or at least partially, or he wouldn't have asked it.

F: *Was Pilate being sarcastic?*

C: No.

B: No, the people crowned him with thorns, they wanted him to die upon a cross: it wasn't a fun-and-games thing.

A: He may have been testing him.

B: What they did was torture him. That is torturing, binding someone like that.

F: *"Are you the King of the Jews?": Is this a label that Jesus wants?*

C: Not at all. He did not know want they would do to him.

B: I think he did. Well, if he did believe it he would have answered Pilate's question. If he was innocent he could be king as he knows how to rule.

F: *"You say so": What do you make of Jesus' answer?*

A: He's accepting the people in government there. He was accepting he was brought to trial.

C: What will the other people think? The people in Jerusalem, they might say to Pilate, "You're wrong."

B: I guess he's telling Pilate to tell him if he is or isn't.

F: *Do you think this is a good answer to offer?*

B: I think he is a humble man. He didn't want to say anything about it.

A: Jesus decided to be poor rather than rich.

B: They mocked him when they put the crown of thorns on his head.

C: Why did Jesus suffer all of that? Why would somebody do that?

A: I have no idea.

C: People were making fun of him.

B: God made his choice; Jesus had no choice.

C: I'd kick him [Pilate] in the shins.

APPENDIX: READING GROUP TRANSCRIPTS

A: I would say, "I've done nothing wrong. All the accusations are fake."

B: He did not have the ability to overcome the things before him. He was unable to speak for himself in that he wanted to save the world. We learn to grow, to love, to hope, even though he could not help himself physically because he was not well enough.

F: *"Pilate asked him again": How do you imagine Pilate to be feeling right now?*

A: Frustrated. He's been laughed at by Jesus. His silence condemns Pilate.

C: I don't think so. I think he's amazed and he couldn't get over his abilities and things of that nature.

A: Do you like Pilate, you're sticking up for him?

C: No, no. He may have been amazed at Jesus. He may not know he was a sacred person.

F: *"Have you no answer?": Do you think that Jesus should speak up here?*

C: I think sooner or later he will. I don't think he can keep silent forever.

A: I think he should remain silent, because if he did speak the world would be shocked.

C: You wonder why so many people worship Jesus when he had a fate worse than death.

A: Jesus preferred to cry than laugh.

B: I place my hope in you, Father, because of what you say, not I.

F: *Have you ever felt like you have been reduced to silence?*

B: It's probably very understandable, the Father must have known.

A: Silence and subjection. It's submission, humility. We're subservient to the staff, we take advice and protection but we have to help them to wash dishes and. ...

C: We help them out because they help us. One of the greatest things is to be a servant.

A: What they say counts.

C: That may be a way of feeling; we can learn from thoughts.

A: My roommate doesn't speak at all. Well, if we watch TV and we're trying to talk, she won't even acknowledge me. She barely speaks a word.

C: Sometimes people want to keep something from you.

A: I get silent when I realize you are right.

B: They scourged him and crowned him with thorns, and I am trying to express, whoever may receive, that this is kind and good and an amazingly accepting thing.

F: *Who do you think has power and control in this encounter?*

B: Well, it might not be quite what it seems. He had his apostles and tried to do the Father's work and this entailed all he was and did.

A: Jesus might have given power to Pilate deliberately so Pilate could do his job, to be a big shot.

B: Remember Jesus with the loaves and fish: he fed a group of people.

C: Pilate has power; he's an elected official. They really make a show court out of it. He did not tell Pilate what to do. He was overwhelmed.

A: Some people need to be authoritative. Jesus wanted Pilate to have a good self-image.

F: *Should Jesus have said more?*

A: He may have no knowledge of his wrongdoings. He could not say more.

C: Sometimes it's hard to say, "I don't know." It's hard to say that. It's easier to remain silent.

A: Sometimes the most you can say is nothing.

B: He was humiliated and hurt. Why are people so angry about that? They made fun of him and mocked him.

A: They certainly did.

C: Sometimes when you say, "I don't know," it's really an affirmation.

Bibliography

Ahearne-Kroll, Stephen P. 2001. "Who Are My Mother and My Brothers?" Family Relations and Family Language in the Gospel of Mark. *Journal of Religion* 81:1–25.

Aichele, George. 1999. Jesus' Uncanny "Family Scene." *JSNT* 74:29–48.

Aichele, George, et al. 1995. *The Postmodern Bible: The Bible and Culture Collective*. New Haven: Yale University Press.

Althaus-Reid, Marcella. 1998. The Hermeneutics of Transgression. Pages 251–71 in *Liberation Theologies on Shifting Grounds: A Clash of Socio-economic and Cultural Paradigms*. Edited by Georges de Schrijver. Leuven: Leuven University Press.

———. 2000. *Indecent Theology: Theological Perversions in Sex, Gender and Politics*. London: Routledge.

Althaus-Reid, Marcella, Ivan Petrella, and Luis Carlos Susin, eds. 2007. *Another Possible World*. Liberation Theology Series. London: SCM.

Anderson, Hugh. 1976. *The Gospel of Mark*. New Century Bible. London: Oliphants.

Anthony, William A. 1993. Recovery from Mental Illness: The Guiding Vision of the Mental Health Service System in the 1990s. *Psychosocial Rehabilitation Journal* 16:521–38.

———. 2003. The Decade of the Person and the Walls That Divide Us. *Behavioral Healthcare Tomorrow* 12, no. 2:23–30.

Antonio, Edward. 2007. Black Theology. Pages 79–104 in *The Cambridge Companion to Liberation Theology*. Edited by Christopher Rowland. 2nd ed. Cambridge: Cambridge University Press.

Anum, Eric. 2004. Unresolved Tensions and the Way Forward. Pages 176–95 in *Through the Eyes of Another: Intercultural Reading of the Bible*. Edited by Hans de Wit, Louis Jonker, Marleen Kool, and Daniel Schipani. Elkhart, Ind.: Institute of Mennonite Studies.

Apostola, Nicholas K. 1998. Mutual Accountability and the Quest for Unity. *Ecumenical Review* 50:301–6.

Aristotle. 1962. *Nicomachean Ethics*. Translated by Martin Ostwald. New York: Macmillan.

Ashcroft, Bill, Gareth Griffiths, and Helen Tiffin. 2000. *Post-colonial Studies: The Key Concepts*. London: Routledge.

Ateek, Naim S. 2006. A Palestinian Perspective: Biblical Perspectives on the Land. Pages 227–34 in *Voices from the Margin: Interpreting the Bible in the Third World*. Edited by R. S. Sugirtharajah. 3rd ed. Maryknoll, N.Y.: Orbis.

Avotri, Solomon K. 2000. The Vernacularization of Scripture and African Beliefs: The Story of the Gerasene Demoniac among the Ewe of West Africa. Pages 311–25 in *The Bible in Africa: Transactions, Trajectories, and Trends*. Edited by Gerald O. West and Musa W. Dube. Leiden: Brill.

Bammel, Ernst. 1984. The Trial before Pilate. Pages 415–52 in *Jesus and the Politics of His Day*. Edited by Ernst Bammel and C. F. D. Moule. Cambridge: Cambridge University Press.

Barham, Peter, and Robert Hayward. 1996. The Lives of Users. Pages 226–37 in *Mental Health Matters: A Reader*. Edited by Tom Heller, Jill Reynolds, Roger Gomm, Rosemary Muston, and Stephen Pattison. New York: Palgrave Macmillan.

Barta, Karen A. 1991. "She Spent All She Had ... But Only Grew Worse": Paying the price of paternalism. Pages 24–36 in *Where Can We Find Her? Searching for Women's Identity in the New Church*. Edited by Marie-Eloise Rosenblatt. New York: Paulist Press.

Bauman, Zygmunt. 1987. *Legislators and Interpreters: On Modernity, Postmodernity, and Intellectuals*. Ithaca, N.Y.: Cornell University Press.

Beavis, Mary Ann. 1988. Women as Models of Faith in Mark. *BTB* 18:3–9.

———. 2010. The Resurrection of Jephthah's Daughter: Judges 11:34–40 and Mark 5:21–24, 35–43. *Catholic Biblical Quarterly* 72:46–62.

Beck, Robert R. 1996. *Nonviolent Story: Narrative Conflict Resolution in the Gospel of Mark*. Maryknoll, N.Y.: Orbis.

Belo, Fernando. 1981. *A Materialist Reading of the Gospel of Mark*. Translated by Matthew J. O'Connell. Maryknoll, N.Y.: Orbis.

Benjamin, Chris. 2006. What Do You Have to Do with Us, Son of the God Most High? Mark 5:1-20. Pages 129–34 in *Preaching Mark's Unsettling Messiah*. Edited by David Fleer and David Bland. St. Louis: Chalice.

Berg, Temma F. 1989. Reading in/to Mark. *Semeia* 48:187–206.

Bernstein, Richard J. 1994. Foucault: Critique as a Philosophical Ethos.

Pages 211–41 in *Critique and Power: Recasting the Foucault/Habermas Debate* . Edited by Michael Kelly. Cambridge: MIT Press.
Best, Ernest. 1990. *The Temptation and the Passion: The Markan Soteriology.* 2nd ed. SNTSMS 2. Cambridge: Cambridge University Press.
Betcher, Sharon. 2004. Monstrosities, Miracles, and Mission: Religion and the Politics of Disablement. Pages 79–99 in *Postcolonial Theologies: Divinity and Empire.* Edited by Catherine Keller, Michael Nausner, and Mayra Rivera. St. Louis: Chalice.
Bhabha, Homi. 1990. The Third Space: Interview with Homi Bhabha. Pages 207–21 in *Identity: Community, Culture, Difference.* Edited by Jonathan Rutherford. London: Lawrence and Wishart.
———. 1994. *The Location of Culture.* London: Routledge.
———. 1995. Translator Translated: W. J. T. Mitchell Talks with Homi Bhabha. *Artforum International* 33, March:80–83, 110–19.
———. 1997. Front Lines/Border Posts. *Critical Inquiry* 23:431–59.
Bhabha, Homi, and John Comaroff. 2002. Speaking of Postcoloniality, in the Continuous Present: A Conversation. Pages 15–46 in *Relocating Postcolonialism.* Edited by David Theo Goldberg and Ato Quayson. Oxford: Blackwell.
Bhugra, D. 1989. Attitudes toward Mental Illness: A Review of the Literature. *Acta Psychiatrica Scandinavica* 80:1–12.
Bird, Lisa. 1998. The Prevalence of Mental Health Problems in the Prison Setting. *Updates* (London: Mental Health Foundation) 1, no. 3:1–4.
Block, Jennie Weiss. 2002. *Copious Hosting: A Theology of Access for People with Disabilities.* New York: Continuum.
Bomford, Rodney. 2010. Jairus, His Daughter, the Woman and the Saviour: The Communication of Symmetric Thinking in the Gospel of Mark. *Practical Theology* 3:41–50.
Bowman, John. 1965. *The Gospel of Mark: The New Christian Jewish Passover Haggadah.* Leiden: Brill.
Broadhead, Edwin K. 2001. *Mark.* Sheffield: Sheffield Academic Press.
Brock, Rita N. 1988. *Journeys by Heart: A Christology of Erotic Power.* New York: Crossroads.
Brockington, Ian F., Peter Hall, Jenny Levings, and Christopher Murphy. 1993. The Community's Tolerance of the Mentally Ill. *British Journal of Psychiatry* 162:93–99.
Brooks, James A. 1991. *Mark.* New American Commentary 23. Nashville: Broadman.

Brown, Raymond E. 1986. *A Crucified Christ in Holy Week: Essays on the Four Gospel Passion Narratives.* Collegeville, Minn.: Liturgical Press.

Brown, Raymond E., Karl P. Donfried, Joseph A. Fitzmyer, and John Reumann, eds. 1978. *Mary in the New Testament.* Philadelphia: Fortress.

Budesheim, Thomas L. 1971. Jesus and the Disciples in Conflict with Judaism. *ZNW* 62:190–209.

Butin, Dan W. 2003. If This Is Resistance I Would Hate to See Domination: Retrieving Foucault's Notion of Resistance within Educational Research. *Educational Studies* 32, no. 2:157–76.

Camery-Hoggatt, Jerry. 1992. *Irony in Mark's Gospel: Text and Subtext.* SNTSMS 72. Cambridge: Cambridge University Press.

Campbell, John M. 2003. *Being Biblical: How Can We Use the Bible in Constructing Ethics Today?* London: United Reformed Church Press.

Campbell, William Sanger. 2004. Engagement, Disengagement and Obstruction: Jesus' Defense Strategies in Mark's Trial and Execution Scenes (14:53–64; 15:1–39). *JSNT* 26:283–300.

Cardenal, Ernesto. 1976–1982. *The Gospel in Solentiname.* Translated by Donald D. Walsh. 4 vols. Maryknoll, N.Y.: Orbis.

Cárdenas Pallares, José. 1986. *A Poor Man Called Jesus: Reflections on the Gospel of Mark.* Translated by Robert R. Barr. Maryknoll, N.Y.: Orbis.

Chavez, Nelba. 2000. *Participatory Dialogues: A Guide to Organizing Interactive Discussions on Mental Health Issues among Consumers, Providers, and Family Members.* U.S. Department of Health and Human Services, Substance Abuse and Mental Health Services Administration, Center for Mental Health Services. Consumer Information Series 3. Online: http://download.ncadi.samhsa.gov/ken/pdf/SMA00-3472/SMA00-3472.pdf.

Connolly, William E. 1985. Taylor, Foucault, and Otherness. *Political Theory* 13:365–76.

Corrigan, P. W. 2000. Mental Health Stigma as Social Attribution: Implications for Research Methods and Attitude Change. *Clinical Psychology Scientific Practice* 54:48–67.

Corrigan, Patrick W., and Amy C. Watson. 2002. Understanding the Impact of Stigma on People with Mental Illness. *World Psychiatry* 1:16–20.

Cotter, Wendy. 2001. Mark's Hero of the Twelfth-Year Miracles: The Healing of the Woman with the Hemorrhage and the Raising of Jairus's Daughter (Mark 5:21–43). Pages 54–78 in *A Feminist Companion to*

Mark. Edited by Amy-Jill Levine with Marianne Blickenstaff. Sheffield: Sheffield Academic Press.
Crain, Margaret Ann, and Jack L. Seymour. 1996. The Ethnographer as Minister: Ethnographic Research in Ministry. *Religious Education* 91:299–315.
Crossan, John Dominic. 1994. *Jesus: A Revolutionary Biography*. San Francisco: HarperCollins.
———. 1999. Mark and the Relatives of Jesus. Pages 52–84 in *The Composition of Mark's Gospel: Selected Studies from Novum Testamentum*. Edited by David E. Orton. London: Brill.
Cruikshank, Barbara. 1999. *The Will to Empower: Democratic Citizens and Other Subjects*. Ithaca, N.Y.: Cornell University Press.
D'Angelo, Mary Rose. 1999. Gender and Power in the Gospel of Mark: The Daughter of Jairus and the Woman with the Flow of Blood. Pages 83–109 in *Miracles in Jewish and Christian Antiquity: Imagining Truth*. Edited by John C. Cavadini. Notre Dame, Ind.: University of Notre Dame Press.
Davies, John Dudley, and John J. Vincent. 1986. *Mark at Work*. London: Bible Reading Fellowship.
Dawson, Andrew. 2007. The Origins and Character of the Base Ecclesial Community: A Brazilian Perspective. Pages 139–58 in *The Cambridge Companion to Liberation Theology*. Edited by Christopher Rowland. 2nd ed. Cambridge: Cambridge University Press.
Deakin, Simon, et al. 2008. *The Governance of Mutuality*. Centre for Business Research, University of Cambridge.
Deibert, Richard I. 1999. *Mark*. Interpretation Bible Studies. Louisville: Geneva.
Derrett, J. Duncan M. 1979. Contributions to the Study of the Gerasene Demoniac. *JSNT* 3:2–17.
———. 1984. Christ and the Power of Choice in Mark 3:1–6. *Bib* 65:168–88.
———. 1985a. *From Jesus' Baptism to Peter's Recognition of Jesus as the Messiah*. Vol. 1 of *The Making of Mark: The Scriptural Bases for the Earliest Gospel*. Shipston-on-Stour: Drinkwater.
———. 1985b. *From the Transfiguration to the Anastasis*. Vol. 2 of *The Making of Mark: The Scriptural Bases for the Earliest Gospel*. Shipston-on-Stour: Drinkwater.
———. 1986. Mark's Technique: The Haemorrhaging Woman and Jairus' Daughter. Pages 30–61 in *Midrash, the Composition of Gospels, and Discipline*. Vol. 4 of *Studies in the New Testament*. Leiden: Brill.

Dewey, Joanna. 1980. *Markan Public Debate: Literary Techniques, Concentric Structure and Theology in Mark 2:1–3:6*. SBLDS 48. Chico, Calif.: Scholars Press.

Dews, Peter. 1987. *Logics of Disintegration: Post-structuralist Thought and Claims of Critical Theory*. London: Verso.

Donahue, John R., and Daniel J. Harrington. 2002. *The Gospel of Mark*. Sacra Pagina 2. Collegeville, Minn.: Liturgical Press.

Donaldson, Laura E. 1996. Postcolonialism and Biblical Reading: An Introduction. *Semeia* 75:1–14.

———. 2005. Gospel Hauntings: The Postcolonial Demons of New Testament Criticism. Pages 97–113 in *Postcolonial Biblical Criticism: Interdisciplinary Intersections*. Edited by Stephen D. Moore and Fernando F. Segovia. London: T&T Clark.

Doughty, Darrell J. 1983. The Authority of the Son of Man (Mk 2:1–3:6). *ZNW* 74:161–81.

Dowd, Sharyn Echols. 1988. *Prayer, Power, and the Problem of Suffering: Mark 11:22–25 in the Context of Markan Theology*. SBLDS 105. Atlanta: Society of Biblical Literature.

———. 2000. *Reading Mark: A Literary and Theological Commentary on the Second Gospel*. Macon, Ga.: Smyth & Helwys.

Dube, Musa W. 2000. *Postcolonial Feminist Interpretation of the Bible*. St. Louis: Chalice.

Eiesland, Nancy L. 1994. *The Disabled God: Toward a Liberatory Theology of Disability*. Nashville: Abingdon.

Ekblad, Bob. 2003. Preaching outside the Lines: A Just Paradigm for Preaching That Empowers Just Action. Pages 195–206 in *Just Preaching: Prophetic Voices for Economic Justice*. Edited by André Resner Jr. St. Louis, Mo.: Chalice.

———. 2004. Jesus's Surprising Offer of Living Cocaine: Contextual Encounters at the Well with Latino Inmates in U.S. jails. Pages 131–41 in *Through the Eyes of Another: Intercultural Reading of the Bible*. Edited by Hans de Wit, Louis Jonker, Marleen Kool, and Daniel Schipani. Elkhart, Ind.: Institute of Mennonite Studies.

Ellison, M. M. 1996. *Erotic Justice: A Liberating Ethic of Sexuality*. Louisville: Westminster John Knox.

Elshout, Elly, facilitator. 1999. Roundtable Discussion: Women with Disabilities—A Challenge to Feminist Theology. Pages 429–58 in *Women in the Hebrew Bible: A Reader*. Edited by Alice Bach. London: Routledge.

Falzon, Christopher. 1998. *Foucault and Social Dialogue: Beyond Fragmentation*. London: Routledge.
Fanon, Frantz. 1963. *The Wretched of the Earth*. Translated by Constance Farrington. New York: Grove.
———. 1967. *Black Skin, White Masks*. Translated by Charles Lam Markmann. New York: Grove.
Faulkner, Alison, and Sarah Layzell. 2000. *Strategies for Living: A Report of User-Led Research into People's Strategies forLliving with Mental Distress*. London: Mental Health Foundation.
Fearday, Frederick L., and Anita L. Cape. 2004. A Voice for Traumatized Women: Inclusion and Mutual Support. *Psychiatric Rehabilitation Journal* 27:258–65.
Fendler, Lynn. 2004. Praxis and Agency in Foucault's Historiography. *Studies in Philosophy and Education* 23:445–66.
Fisher, Pamela. 2007. Experiential Knowledge Challenges "Normality" and Individualised Citizenship: Towards "Another Way of Being." *Disability and Society* 22:283–98.
Fortune, Marie M. 1995. *Love Does No Harm: Sexual Ethics for the Rest of Us*. New York: Continuum.
Foucault, Michel. 1970. *The Order of Things: An Archaeology of the Human Sciences*. New York: Random House.
———. 1972. The Discourse on Language. Pages 215–37 in *The Archaeology of Knowledge and the Discourse on Language*. New York: Pantheon.
———. 1976. *Mental Illness and Psychology*. Translated by Alan Sheridan. Rev. ed. Berkeley: University of California Press.
———. 1978–1986. *History of Sexuality*. Translated by Robert Hurley. 3 vols. New York: Vintage.
———. 1980. Two Lectures. Pages 78–108 in *Power/Knowledge: Selected Interviews and Other Writings, 1972–1977*. Edited by Colin Gordon. Translated by Colin Gordon et al. New York: Pantheon.
———. 1982. The Subject and Power. Pages 208–26 in *Michel Foucault: Beyond Structuralism and Hermeneutics*. Edited by Hubert L. Dreyfus and Paul Rabinow. Chicago: University of Chicago Press.
———. 1991. *Discipline and Punish: The Birth of the Prison*. London: Penguin.
———. 1997a. The Hermeneutic of the Subject. Pages 93–106 in *Ethics: Subjectivity and Truth*. Edited by Paul Rabinow. Translated by Robert Hurley et al. Essential Works of Michel Foucault, 1954–1984, vol. 1. New York: New Press.

———. 1997b. Michel Foucault: An Interview by Stephen Riggins. Pages 121–33 in *Ethics: Subjectivity and Truth*. Edited by Paul Rabinow. Translated by Robert Hurley et al. Essential Works of Michel Foucault, 1954–1984, vol. 1. New York: New Press.

———. 1997c. Polemics, Politics, and Problematizations: An Interview with Michel Foucault. Pages 111–19 in *Ethics: Subjectivity and Truth*. Edited by Paul Rabinow. Trans Essential Works of Michel Foucault, 1954–1984, vol. 1. New York: New Press.

———. 1997d. Psychiatric Power. Pages 39–50 in *Ethics: Subjectivity and Truth*. Edited by Paul Rabinow. Translated by Robert Hurley et al. Essential Works of Michel Foucault 1954–1984, vol. 1. New York: New Press.

———. 1997e. Sexuality and Solitude. Pages 175–84 in *Ethics: Subjectivity and Truth*. Edited by Paul Rabinow. Translated by Robert Hurley et al. Essential Works of Michel Foucault, 1954–1984, vol. 1. New York: New Press.

———. 1998. Nietzsche, Genealogy, History. Pages 369–91 in *Aesthetics, Method, and Epistemology*. Edited by James D. Faubion. Translated by Robert Hurley et al. Essential Works of Michel Foucault, 1954–1984, vol. 2. New York: New Press.

———. 2001. *Madness and Civilization: A History of Insanity in the Age of Reason*. Routledge Classics Edition. London: Routledge.

———. 2002. *The Archaeology of Knowledge*. Routledge Classics Edition. London: Routledge.

Fowler, Robert M. 1989. The Rhetoric of Direction and Indirection in the Gospel of Mark. *Semeia* 48:115–34.

———. 1991. *Let the Reader Understand: Reader-Response Criticism and the Gospel of Mark*. Minneapolis: Fortress.

Fox, Nicholas J. 1999. *Beyond Health: Postmodernism and Embodiment*. London: Free Association.

France, Richard T. 1990. *Divine Government: God's Kingship in the Gospel of Mark* London: SPCK.

Freire, Paulo. 1996. *Pedagogy of the Oppressed*. Translated by Myra Bergman Ramos. 1970. Repr., London: Penguin.

Gandhi, Leela. 1998. *Postcolonial Theory: A Critical Introduction* .New York: Columbia University Press.

Garroway, Joshua. 2009. The Invasion of a Mustard Seed: A Reading of Mark 5:1–20. *JSNT* 32:57–75.

Geyer, Douglas W. 2002. *Fear, Anomaly, and Uncertainty in the Gospel of Mark.* Lanham, Md.: Scarecrow.

Gilbert, Peter, and Vicky Nicholls. 2003. *Inspiring Hope: Recognising the Importance of Spirituality in a Whole Person Approach to Mental Health.* London: National Institute for Mental Health in England.

Gill, LaVerne McCain. 2000. *Daughters of Dignity: African Women in the Bible and the Virtues of Black Womanhood.* Cleveland: Pilgrim.

Gilman, Sander L. 1988. *Disease and Representation: Images of Illness from Madness to AIDS.* Ithaca, N.Y.: Cornell University Press.

Glancy, Jennifer A. 2010. Jesus, the Syrophoenician Woman, and Other First Century Bodies. *BibInt* 18:342–63.

Gnanadason, Aruna. 2001. Jesus and the Asian Woman: A Post-colonial Look at the Syro-Phoenician Woman/Canaanite Woman from an Indian Perspective. *Studies in World Christianity* 7:162–77.

Goldberg, David Theo. 2000. Heterogeneity and Hybridity: Colonial Legacy, Postcolonial Heresy. Pages 72–86 in *A Companion to Postcolonial Studies.* Edited by Henry Schwarz and Sangeeta Ray. Oxford: Blackwell.

Goldstein, Jan, ed. 1994. *Foucault and the Writing of History.* Oxford: Blackwell.

Gonzales, Michelle A. 2004. Who Is American/o? Theological Anthropology, Postcoloniality, and the Spanish-Speaking Americas. Pages 58–78 in *Postcolonial Theologies: Divinity and Empire.* Edited by Catherine Keller, Michael Nausner, and Mayra Rivera. St. Louis: Chalice.

Graham, Larry K. 1992. *Care of Persons, Care of Worlds: A Psychosystems Approach to Pastoral Care and Counseling.* Nashville: Abingdon.

Gready, Paul. 2003. *Writing as Resistance: Life Stories of Imprisonment, Exile, and Homecoming from Apartheid South Africa.* Lanham, Md.: Lexington.

Green, Jim. 2003. User-centred Initiatives: Guiding Lights—beyond User Involvement. *Updates* (London: Mental Health Foundation) 4, no. 13:1–4.

Green, Laurie. 1987. *Power to the Powerless: Theology Brought to Life.* London: Marshall Pickering.

Grey, Mary. 2007. Feminist Theology: A Critical Theology of Liberation. Pages 105–22 in *The Cambridge Companion to Liberation Theology.* Edited by Christopher Rowland. 2nd ed. Cambridge: Cambridge University Press.

Guardiola-Sáenz, Leticia A. 1997. Borderless Women and Borderless Texts: A Cultural Reading of Matthew 15:21–28. *Semeia* 78:69–81.

Gudorf, Christine E. 1994. *Body, Sex, and Pleasure: Reconstructing Christian Sexual Ethics*. Cleveland: Pilgrim.

Guelich, Robert A. 1989. *Mark 1–8:26*. WBC 34A. Dallas: Word Books.

Gundry, Robert H. 1993. *Mark: A Commentary on His Apology for the Cross*. Grand Rapids: Eerdmans.

Gutiérrez, Gustavo. 1988. *A Theology of Liberation*. 15th anniversary ed. Maryknoll, N.Y.: Orbis.

Gutiérrez, Gustavo. 2007. The Task and Content of Liberation Theology. Translated by Judith Condor. Pages 19–38 in *The Cambridge Companion to Liberation Theology*. Edited by Christopher Rowland. 2nd ed. Cambridge: Cambridge University Press.

Haber, Susan. 2003. A Woman's Touch: Feminist Encounters with the Hemorrhaging Woman in Mark 5:24–34. *JSNT* 26:171–92.

Habermas, Jürgen. 1990. *The Philosophical Discourse of Modernity*. Cambridge: MIT Press.

Hacking, Ian. 1986. The Archaeology of Foucault. Pages 27–40 in *Foucault: A Critical Reader*. Edited by David Couzens Hoy. Oxford: Blackwell.

Hagerty, Bonnie M. K., Judith Lynch-Sauer, Kathleen L. Patusky, and Maria Bouwsema. 1993. An Emerging Theory of Human Relatedness. *IMAGE: Journal of Nursing Scholarship* 25:290–96.

Hamerton-Kelly, Robert G. 1994. *The Gospel and the Sacred: Poetics of Violence in Mark*. Minneapolis: Fortress.

Hamre, Per, Alv A. Dahl, and Ulrik F. Malt. 1994. Public Attitudes to the Quality of Psychiatric Treatment, Psychiatric Patients, and Prevalence of Mental Disorders. *Norwegian Journal of Psychiatry* 4:275–81.

Hanson, James S. 2000. *The Endangered Promises: Conflict in Mark*. SBLDS 171. Atlanta: Society of Biblical Literature.

Hare, Douglas R. A. 1996. *Mark*. Westminster Bible Companion. Louisville: Westminster John Knox.

Harrison, Beverly Wildung. 1983. *Our Right to Choose: Toward a New Ethic of Abortion*. Boston: Beacon.

Hart, Lawrence D. 2010. The Canaanite Woman: Meeting Jesus as Sage and Lord: Matthew 15:21–28 and Mark 7:24–30. *ExpTim* 122:20–25.

Hauerwas, Stanley. 1998. *Sanctify Them in the Truth: Holiness Exemplified*. Nashville: Abingdon.

Hedelin, B., and I. Jonsson. 2003. Mutuality as Background Music in

Women's Lived Experience of Mental Health and Depression. *Journal of Psychiatric and Mental Health Nursing* 10:317–32.

Heil, John Paul. 1992. *The Gospel of Mark as a Model for Action: A Reader-Response Commentary.* New York: Paulist Press.

Hentrich, Thomas. 2007. Masculinity and Disability in the Bible. Pages 73–87 in *This Abled Body: Rethinking Disabilities in Biblical Studies.* Edited by Hector Avalos, Sarah J. Melcher, and Jeremy Schipper. SemeiaSt 55. Atlanta: Society of Biblical Literature.

Heyward, Carter. 1979. Coming Out: Journey without Maps. *Christianity and Crisis* 39:153–56.

———. 1982. *The Redemption of God: A Theology of Mutual Relation.* New York: University Press of America.

———. 1989. *Coming out and Relational Empowerment: A Lesbian Feminist Theological Perspective.* Stone Center for Developmental Services and Studies 38. Wellesley, Mass.: Stone Center.

———. 1994. Boundaries or Barriers? *Christian Century* 111, no. 18:579–80.

———. 1999. *Saving Jesus from Those Who Are Right: Rethinking What It Means to Be Christian.* Minneapolis: Fortress.

Hiebert, D. Edmond. 1994. *The Gospel of Mark: An Expositional Commentary.* Greenville, S.C.: Bob Jones University Press.

Hiers, Richard H. 1974. Satan, Demons, and the Kingdom of God. *SJT* 27:35–47.

Hilton, James L., and William von Hippel. 1996. Stereotypes. *Annual Review of Psychology* 47:237–71.

Hinga, Teresia M. 1996. "Reading With": An Exploration of the Interface between "Critical" and "Ordinary" Readings of the Bible: A Response. *Semeia* 73: 277–84.

Hollenbach, Paul W. 1981. Jesus, Demoniacs, and Public Authorities: A Socio-historical Study. *Journal of the American Academy of Religion* 49:567–88.

Holmlund, Christine Anne. 1991. Displacing Limits of Difference: Gender, Race, and Colonialism in Edward Said and Homi Bhabha's Theoretical Models and Marguerite Duras's Experimental Films. *Quarterly Review of Film and Video* 1:1–22.

Hooker, Morna D. 1991. *The Gospel according to St. Mark.* BNTC. London: Black.

Horsfall, J. 2003. Consumers/Service Users: Is Nursing Listening? *Issues in Mental Health Nursing* 24:381–96.

Horsley, Richard A. 1993. The Imperial Situation of Palestinian Jewish Society. Pages 395–407 in *The Bible and Liberation: Political and Social Hermeneutics Political and Social Hermeneutics*. Edited by Norman K. Gottwald and Richard A. Horsley. Rev. ed. Maryknoll, N.Y.: Orbis.

———. 1998. Submerged Biblical Histories and Imperial Biblical Studies. Pages 152–73 in *The Postcolonial Bible*. Edited by R. S. Sugirtharajah. Sheffield: Sheffield Academic Press.

———. 2001. *Hearing the Whole Story: The Politics of Plot in Mark's Gospel*. Louisville: Westminster John Knox.

Hoy, David Couzens. 1986. Power, Repression, Progress: Foucault, Lukes, and the Frankfurt School. Pages 123–48 in *Foucault: A Critical Reader*. Edited by David Couzens Hoy. Oxford: Blackwell.

Hultgren, Arland J. 1979. *Jesus and His Adversaries: The Form and Function of the Conflict Stories in the Synoptic Tradition*. Minneapolis: Augsburg.

Humphrey, Robert L. 2003. *Narrative Structure and Message in Mark: A Rhetorical Analysis*. Lewiston, N.Y.: Mellen.

Hyler, Steven E., Glen O. Gabbard, and Irving Schneider. 1991. Homicidal Maniacs and Narcissistic Parasites: Stigmatization of Mentally Ill Persons in the Movies. *Hospital Community Psychiatry* 42:1044–48.

Iersel, Bas M. F. van. 1998. *Mark: A Reader-Response Commentary*. JSNTSup 164. Sheffield: Sheffield Academic Press.

Ingleby, Jonathan. 2006. Hybridity or The Third Space and How Shall We Describe the Kingdom of God. *Encounters Mission Ezine* 11:1–10.

Ionita, Viorel. 1997. One Gospel and Diverse Cultures: Towards an Intercultural Mutuality. *International Review of Mission* 86:53–56.

Isenberg, Bo. 1991. Habermas on Foucault: Critical Remarks. *Acta Sociologica* 34:299–308.

Iverson, Kelly R. 2007. *Gentiles in the Gospel of Mark: Even the Dogs under the Table Eat the Children's Crumbs*. London: Continuum.

JanMohamed, Abdul R. 1985. The Economy of Manichean Allegory: The Function of Racial Difference in Colonialist Literature. Pages 78–106 in *"Race," Writing, and Difference*. Edited by Henry Louis Gates Jr. Chicago: University of Chicago Press.

Jefferess, David. 2008. *Postcolonial Resistance: Culture, Liberation, and Transformation*. Toronto: University of Toronto Press.

Jennings, Stephen C. A. 2007. "Ordinary" Reading in "Extraordinary" Times: A Jamaican Love Story. Pages 49–62 in *Reading Other-Wise: Socially Engaged Biblical Scholars Reading with Their Local Communi-*

ties. Edited by Gerald O. West. SemeiaSt 62. Atlanta: Society of Biblical Literature.

Jennings, Theodore W. 2003. *The Insurrection of the Crucified: The "Gospel of Mark" as Theological Manifesto.* Chicago: Exploration Press.

Jeon, Yun-Hee. 2004. Shaping Mutuality: Nurse-Family Caregiver Interactions in Caring for Older People with Depression. *International Journal of Mental Health Nursing* 13:126-34.

Jinkins, M. 2003. Mutuality and Difference: Trinity, Creation and the Theological Ground of the Church's Unity. *SJT* 56:148-71.

Joh, W. Anne. 2004. The Transgressive Power of Jeong: A Postcolonial Hybridization of Christology. Pages 149-63 in *Postcolonial Theologies: Divinity and Empire.* Edited by Catherine Keller, Michael Nausner, and Mayra Rivera. St. Louis: Chalice.

Johnson, Sherman E. 1960. *A Commentary on the Gospel according to St Mark.* BNTC. London: Black.

Jones, David W. 1996. Families and the Experience of Mental Distress. Pages 97-104 in *Mental Health Matters: A Reader.* Edited by Tom Heller, Jill Reynolds, Roger Gomm, Rosemary Muston, and Stephen Pattison. New York: Palgrave Macmillan.

Jones, Linda. 1996. George III and Changing Views of Madness. Pages 121-33 in *Mental Health Matters: A Reader.* Edited by Tom Heller, Jill Reynolds, Roger Gomm, Rosemary Muston, and Stephen Pattison. New York: Palgrave Macmillan.

Jonker, Louis. 2007. On Becoming a Family: Multiculturality and Interculturality in South Africa. *ExpTim* 118:480-87.

Jordan, Mark D. 2002. *The Ethics of Sex.* Oxford: Blackwell.

Joy, David. 2005. Markan Subalterns/the Crowd and Their Strategies of Resistance: A Postcolonial Critique. *Black Theology: An International Journal* 3:55-74.

———. 2008. *Mark and Its Subalterns: A Hermeneutical Paradigm for a Postcolonial Context.* London: Equinox.

Juel, Donald H. 1999. *The Gospel of Mark.* Nashville: Abingdon.

Kahl, Werner. 2007. Growing Together: Challenges and Chances in the Encounter of Critical and Intuitive Interpreters of the Bible. Pages 147-58 in *Reading Other-Wise: Socially Engaged Biblical Scholars Reading with Their Local Communities.* Edited by Gerald O. West. SemeiaSt 62. Atlanta: Society of Biblical Literature.

Kapoor, Ilan. 2003. Acting in a Tight Spot: Homi Bhabha's Postcolonial Politics. *New Political Science* 25:561-77.

Kee, Howard Clark. 1968. The Terminology of Mark's Exorcism Stories. *NTS* 14:323–46.

———. 1977. *The Community of the New Age: Studies in Mark's Gospel.* Philadelphia: Westminster.

Keenan, John P. 1995. *The Gospel of Mark: A Mahayana Reading.* Maryknoll, N.Y.: Orbis.

Keller, Catherine, Michael Nausner, and Mayra Rivera, eds. 2004. *Postcolonial Theologies: Divinity and Empire.* St. Louis: Chalice.

Kelly, B. D. 2005. Structural Violence and Schizophrenia. *Social Science and Medicine* 61:721–30.

Kessler, Rainer. 2004. From Bipolar to Multipolar Understanding: Hermeneutical Consequences of Intercultural Bible Reading. Pages 452–59 in *Through the Eyes of Another: Intercultural Reading of the Bible.* Edited by Hans de Wit, Louis Jonker, Marleen Kool, and Daniel Schipani. Elkhart, Ind.: Institute of Mennonite Studies.

Kim, Yung Suk. 2006. "In Christ" as a Hermeneutical Key for Diversity. *Journal of Biblical Studies* 6:35–54.

Kingsbury, Jack D. 1989. *Conflict in Mark: Jesus, Authorities, Disciples.* Minneapolis: Fortress.

Kinukawa, Hisako. 1994. *Women and Jesus in Mark: A Japanese Feminist Perspective.* Maryknoll, N.Y.: Orbis.

———. 2004. Mark. Pages 367–78 in *Global Bible Commentary.* Edited by Daniel Patte. Nashville: Abingdon.

Kramer-Dahl, Anneliese. 1996. Reconsidering the Notions of Voice and Experience in Critical Pedagogy. Pages 242–62 in *Feminisms and Pedagogies of Everyday Life.* Edited by Carmen Luke. Albany: State University of New York Press.

Kuthirakkattel, Scaria. 1990. *The Beginning of Jesus' Ministry according to Mark's Gospel (1:14–3:6): A Redaction Critical Study.* Rome: Pontifical Biblical Institute.

Kwok, Pui-lan. 1995. *Discovering the Bible in the Non-biblical World.* Maryknoll, N.Y.: Orbis.

———. 1996. Response to *Semeia* Volume on Postcolonial Criticism. *Semeia* 75:211–17.

———. 2005. *Postcolonial Imagination and Feminist Theology.* Louisville: Westminster John Knox.

Lambrecht, Jan. 1999. The Relatives of Jesus in Mark. Pages 85–102 in *The Composition of Mark's Gospel: Selected Studies from Novum Testamentum.* Edited by David E. Orton. London: Brill.

Lane, William L. 1974. *The Gospel according to St. Mark.* New International Commentary on the New Testament. Grand Rapids: Eerdmans.

Lanser-van der Velde, Alma. 2004. Making Things in Common: The Group Dynamics Dimension of the Hermeneutic Process. Pages 288–303 in *Through the Eyes of Another: Intercultural Reading of the Bible.* Edited by Hans de Wit, Louis Jonker, Marleen Kool, and Daniel Schipani. Elkhart, Ind.: Institute of Mennonite Studies.

Lategan, Bernard C. 1996. Scholar and Ordinary Reader—More Than a Simple Interface. *Semeia* 73:243–55.

Leech, Kenneth. 1999. *The Eye of the Storm: Spiritual Resources for the Pursuit of Justice.* Repr., London: DL&T.

Lees, Janet. 2007a. Enabling the Body. Pages 161–71 in *This Abled Body: Rethinking Disabilities in Biblical Studies.* Edited by Hector Avalos, Sarah J. Melcher, and Jeremey Schipper. SemeiaSt 55. Atlanta: Society of Biblical Literature.

———. 2007b. Remembering the Bible as a Critical "Pedagogy of the Oppressed. Pages 73–85 in *Reading Other-Wise: Socially Engaged Biblical Scholars Reading with Their Local Communities.* Edited by Gerald O. West. SemeiaSt 62. Atlanta: Society of Biblical Literature.

Levi, Jerome M. 1999. Hidden Transcripts among the Rarámuri: Culture, Resistance, and Interethnic Relations in Northern Mexico. *American Ethnologist* 26:90–113.

Liew, Tat-siong Benny. 1999. *Politics of Parousia: Reading Mark Inter(con)textually.* Leiden: Brill.

———. 2002. Ambiguous Admittance: Consent and Descent in John's Community of "Upward" Mobility. Pages 193–224 in *John and Postcolonialism: Travel, Space and Power.* Edited by Musa W. Dube and Jeffrey L. Staley. Sheffield: Sheffield Academic Press.

———. 2006. Tyranny, Boundary, and Might: Colonial Mimicry in Mark's Gospel. Pages 206–23 in *The Postcolonial Biblical Reader.* Edited by R. S. Sugirtharajah. Oxford: Blackwell.

Link, Bruce G. 1987. Understanding Labeling Effects in the Area of Mental Disorders: An Assessment of the Effects of Expectations of Rejection. *American Sociological Review* 52:96–112.

Liu, Rebekah. 2010. A Dog under the Table at the Messianic Banquet: A Study of Mark 7:24–30. *Andrews University Seminary Studies* 48:251–55.

Loew, Patty. 1997. Hidden Transcripts in the Chippewa Treaty Rights Struggle: A Twice Told Story Race, Resistance, and the Politics of Power. *American Indian Quarterly* 21:713–28.

Logan, Finlay. 2008. Authorial Ambiguity: Lecture. *The Daily Gazette.* Online: http://daily.swarthmore.edu/2008/2/4/authorial-ambiguity-lecture.
Lopez, Edgar Antonio. 2004. Intercultural Bible Reading by Catholic Groups in Bogotá. Pages 142–60 in *Through the Eyes of Another: Intercultural Reading of the Bible.* Edited by Hans de Wit, Louis Jonker, Marleen Kool, and Daniel Schipani. Elkhart, Ind.: Institute of Mennonite Studies.
MacLaurin, E. C. B. 1978. Beelzeboul. *NovT* 20:156–60.
Mack, Burton L. 1988. *A Myth of Innocence: Mark and Christian Origins.* Philadelphia: Fortress.
Madianos, M. G., D. Madianou, J. Vlachonikolis, and C. N. Stefanis. 1987. Attitudes toward Mental Illness in the Athens Area: Implications for Community Mental Health Intervention. *Acta Psychiatrica Scandinavica* 75:158–65.
Malbon, Elizabeth Struthers. 1986. Disciples/Crowds/Whoever: Markan Characters and Readers. *NovT* 28:104–30.
———.1988. *Narrative Space and Mythic Meaning in Mark.* San Francisco: Harper & Row.
———. 1995. Galilee and Jerusalem: History and Literature in Markan Interpretation. Pages 253–68 in *The Interpretation of Mark.* Edited by William Telford. 2nd ed. Edinburgh: T&T Clark.
———. 2000. *In the Company of Jesus: Characters in Mark's Gospel.* Louisville: Westminster John Knox.
Maldonado-Torres, Nelson. 2005. Liberation Theology and the Search for the Lost Paradigm: From Radical Orthodoxy to Radical Diversality. Pages 39–61 in *Latin American Liberation Theology: The Next Generation.* Edited by Ivan Petrella. Maryknoll, N.Y.: Orbis.
Maluleke, Tinyiko Sam. 2002. Bible Study: The Graveyardman, the "Escaped Convict" and the Girl-Child: A Mission of Awakening, an Awakening of Mission. *International Review of Mission* 91:550–57.
Mann, C. S. 1986. *Mark.* AB 27. Garden City, N.Y.: Doubleday.
Marchal, Joseph A. 2005. Mutuality Rhetorics and Feminist Interpretation: Examining Philippians and Arguing for Our Lives. *The Bible and Critical Theory* 1, no. 3:17-1–16.
Marcus, Joel. 1992. *The Way of the Lord: Christological Exegesis of the Old Testament in the Gospel of Mark.* Louisville: Westminster John Knox.
———. 2000. *Mark 1–8.* AB 27. New York: Doubleday.

Marshall, Christopher D. 1989. *Faith as a Theme in Mark's Narrative.* SNTSMS 64. Cambridge: Cambridge University Press.

Martin, Jack K., Bernice A. Pescosolido, and Steven A. Tuch. 2000. Of Fear and Loathing: The Role of "Disturbing Behavior," Labels, and Attributions in Shaping Public Attitudes toward People with Mental Illness. *Journal of Health and Social Behavior* 41:208–23.

Martín-Baró, Ignacio. 1994. Toward a Liberation Psychology. Pages 17–32 in *Writings for a Liberation Psychology.* Edited by Adrianne Aron and Shawn Corne. Cambridge: Harvard University Press.

Masoga, Mogomme Alpheus. 2000. *Weeping City, Shanty Town Jesus: Introduction to Conversational Theology.* Cape Town: Salty Print.

———. 2002. Redefining Power: Reading the Bible in Africa from the Peripheral and Central Positions. Pages 95–109 in *Reading the Bible in the Global Village: Cape Town.* Edited by Justin S. Ukpong. Global Perspectives on Biblical Scholarship 3. Atlanta: Society of Biblical Literature.

———. 2007. "Dear God! Give Us Our Daily Leftovers and We Will Be Able to Forgive Those Who Trouble Our Souls": Some Perspectives on Conversational Biblical Hermeneutics and Theologies. Pages 19–27 in *Reading Other-Wise: Socially Engaged Biblical Scholars Reading with Their Local Communities.* Edited by Gerald O. West. SemeiaSt 62. Atlanta: Society of Biblical Literature.

McAllister, N. 2004. Different Voices: Reviewing and Revising the Politics of Working with Consumers in Mental Health. *International Journal of Mental Health Nursing* 13:22–32.

McCarthy, Thomas. 1994. The Critique of Impure Reason: Foucault and the Frankfurt School. Pages 243–82 in *Critique and Power: Recasting the Foucault/Habermas Debate.* Edited by Michael Kelly. Cambridge: MIT Press.

McClintock, Anne. 1995. *Imperial Leather: Race, Gender and Sexuality in the Colonial Contest.* New York: Falmer.

McCloughry, Roy, and Wayne Morris. 2002. *Making a World of Difference: Christian Reflections on Disability.* London: SPCK.

McGovern, Arthur F. 1993. The Bible in Latin American Liberation Theology. Pages 74–85 in *The Bible and Liberation: Political and Social Hermeneutics.* Edited by Norman K. Gottwald and Richard A. Horsley. Rev. ed. Maryknoll, N.Y.: Orbis.

Melcher, Sarah J. 2007. With Whom Do the Disabled Associate? Metaphorical Interplay in the Latter Prophets. Pages 115–29 in *This Abled*

Body: Rethinking Disabilities in Biblical Studies Edited by Hector Avalos, Sarah J. Melcher, and Jeremy Schipper. SemeiaSt 55. Atlanta: Society of Biblical Literature.

Mellon, John C. 1995. *Mark as Recovery Story: Alcoholism and the Rhetoric of Gospel Mystery.* Chicago: University of Illinois Press.

Meredith, P. 1998. Hybridity in the Third Space: Re-thinking Bi-cultural Politics in Aotearoa/New Zealand. Paper presented to Te Oru Rangahau Maori Research and Development Conference 7-9 July 1998, Massey University, Aotearoa/NewZealand. Online: http://lianz.waikato.ac.nz/PAPERS/paul/hybridity.pdf.

Mesters, Carlos. 1993. The Use of the Bible in Christian Communities of the Common People. Pages 3–16 in *The Bible and Liberation: Political and Social Hermeneutics.* Edited by Norman K. Gottwald and Richard A. Horsley. Rev. ed. Maryknoll, N.Y.: Orbis.

Miguez, Nestor. 2004. Reading John 4 in the Interface between Ordinary and Scholarly Interpretation. Pages 334–47 in *Through the Eyes of Another: Intercultural Reading of the Bible.* Edited by Hans de Wit, Louis Jonker, Marleen Kool, and Daniel Schipani. Elkhart, Ind.: Institute of Mennonite Studies.

Mitchell, David, and Sharon Snyder. 2007. "Jesus Thrown Everything off Balance": Disability and Redemption in Biblical Literature. Pages 173–83 in *This Abled Body: Rethinking Disabilities in Biblical Studies.* Edited by Hector Avalos, Sarah H. Melcher, and Jeremy Schipper. SemeiaSt 55. Atlanta: Society of Biblical Literature.

Mitchell, David T., and Sharon L. Snyder, eds. 1997. *The Body and Physical Difference: Discourses of Disability.* Ann Arbor: University of Michigan Press.

Mitchell, Joan L. 2001. *Beyond Fear and Silence: A Feminist-Literary Approach to the Gospel of Mark.* New York: Continuum.

Moore, Stephen D. 2006a. Mark and Empire: "Zealot" and "Postcolonial" Readings. Pages 193–205 in *The Postcolonial Biblical Reader.* Edited by R. S. Sugirtharajah. Oxford: Blackwell.

———. 2006b. *Postcolonialism and the New Testament.* Sheffield: Sheffield Phoenix Press.

Moore-Gilbert, Bart. 1997. *Postcolonial Theory.* London: Verso.

———. 2000. Spivak and Bhabha. Pages 451–66 in *A Companion to Postcolonial Studies.* Edited by Henry Schwarz and Sangeeta Ray. Oxford: Blackwell.

Morris, Wayne. 2006. Does the Church Need the Bible? Reflections on the Experiences of Disabled People. Pages 162–72 in *Education, Religion and Society: Essays in Honour of John M. Hull*. Edited by Dennis Bates, Gloria Durka, and Friedrich Schweitzer. London: Routledge.

Mosala, Itumeleng J. 1989. *Biblical Hermeneutics and Black Theology in South Africa*. Grand Rapids: Eerdmans.

Moss, Candida R. 2010. The Man with the Flow of Power: Porous Bodies in Mark 5:25–34. *JBL* 129:507–19.

Mulackal, Shalini. 2010. The Power of the Bleeding Woman: A Rereading of Mark 5:21–34. *Jeevadhara* 40:204–16.

Myers, Ched. 1984. A Socio-literary Reading of Mark 1–3. MA diss. Graduate Theological Union Library, Berkeley, California.

———. 1988. *Binding the Strong Man: A Political Reading of Mark's Story of Jesus*. Maryknoll, N.Y.: Orbis.

———. 1993. The Ideology and Social Strategy of Mark's Community. Pages 428–52 in *The Bible and Liberation: Political and Social Hermeneutics*. Edited by Norman K. Gottwald and Richard A. Horsley. Rev. ed. Maryknoll, N.Y.: Orbis.

Myers, Ched, Marie Dennis, Joseph Nangle, Cynthia Moe-Lobeda, and Stuart Taylor. 1996. *"Say to This Mountain": Mark's Story of Discipleship*. Edited by Karen Lattea. Maryknoll, N.Y.: Orbis.

Nations, Marilyn K., Chizuru Misago, Walter Fonseca, Luciano L. Correia, and Oona M. R. Campbell. 1997. Women's Hidden Transcripts about Abortion in Brazil. *Social Science and Medicine* 44:1833–45.

Nausner, Michael. 2004. Homeland as Borderland: Territories of Christian Subjectivity. Pages 118–32 in *Postcolonial Theologies: Divinity and Empire*. Edited by Catherine Keller, Michael Nausner, and Mayra Rivera. St. Louis: Chalice.

Nkwoka, Anthony O. 1989. Mark 3:19b–21: A Study of the Charge of Fanaticism against Jesus. *Bible Bhashyam* 14:205–21.

Oakman, Douglas E. 1988. Rulers' Houses, Thieves, and Usurpers: The Beelzebul Pericope. *Foundations and Facets Forum* 4:109–23.

O'Neill, J. C. 1969. The Silence of Jesus. *NTS* 15:153–67.

Ottermann, Monika. 2007. '"How Could He Ever Do That to Her?" Or, How the Woman Who Anointed Jesus Became a Victim of Luke's Redactional and Theological Principles. Pages 103–16 in *Reading Other-Wise: Socially Engaged Biblical Scholars Reading with Their Local Communities*. Edited by Gerald O. West. SemeiaSt 62. Atlanta: Society of Biblical Literature.

Owen, David. 1995. Genealogy as Exemplary Critique: Reflections on Foucault and the Imagination of the Political. *Economy and Society* 24:489–506.

Pailin, David A. 1992. *A Gentle Touch: From a Theology of Handicap to a Theology of Human Being.* London: SPCK.

Painter, John. 1997. *Mark's Gospel: Worlds in Conflict.* London: Routledge.

Parry, Benita. 1995. Problems in Current Theories of Colonial Discourse. Pages 36–44 in *The Post-colonial Studies Reader.* Edited by Bill Ashcroft, Gareth Griffiths, and Helen Tiffin. London: Routledge.

Pattison, Stephen. 1994. *Pastoral Care and Liberation Theology.* Cambridge: Cambridge University Press.

Perkinson, Jim. 1996. A Canaanitic Word in the Logos of Christ; or the Difference the Syro-Phoenician Woman Makes to Jesus. *Semeia* 75:61–85.

Peterson, Dwight N. 2000. *The Origins of Mark: The Markan Community in Current Debate.* Leiden: Brill.

Peterson-Iyer, Karen. 1998. Prostitution: A Feminist Ethical Analysis. *Journal of Feminist Studies in Religion* 14, no. 2:19–44.

Petrella, Ivan, ed. 2005. *Latin American Liberation Theology: The Next Generation.* Maryknoll, N.Y.: Orbis.

———. 2008. The Global Material Context of the Liberation Theologian: The Poverty of the Majority. Pages 5–44 in *Beyond Liberation Theology: A Polemic.* Reclaiming Liberation Theology. London: SCM.

Phelan, Jo C., Bruce G. Link, Ann Stueve, and Bernice A. Pescosolido. 2000. Public Conceptions of Mental Illness in 1950 and 1996: What Is Mental Illness and Is It to Be Feared? *Journal of Health and Social Behavior* 41:188–207.

Pixley, George V., and Clodovis Boff. 2006. A Latin American Perspective: The Option for the Poor in the Old Testament. Pages 207–16 in *Voices from the Margin: Interpreting the Bible in the Third World.* Edited by R. S. Sugirtharajah. 3rd ed. Maryknoll, N.Y.: Orbis.

Plaatjie, Gloria Kehilwe. 2001. Toward a Post-apartheid Black Feminist Reading of the Bible: A Case of Luke 2:36–38. Pages 114–42 in *Other Ways of Reading: African Women and the Bible.* Edited by Musa W. Dube. Atlanta: Society of Biblical Literature.

Porter, Roy. 2002. *Madness: A Brief History.* Oxford: Oxford University Press.

Queller, Kurt. 2010. "Stretch out Your Hand!" Echo and Metalepsis in Mark's Sabbath Healing Controversy. *JBL* 129:737–58.

Rabinow, Paul. 1997. Introduction. Pages xi– xlii in *Ethics: Subjectivity and Truth.* Edited by Paul Rabinow. Translated by Robert Hurley et al. Essential Works of Michel Foucault, 1954–1984, vol. 1. New York: New Press.

Rabkin, Judith G. 1974. Public Attitudes toward Mental Illness: A Review of the Literature. *Psychology Bulletin* 10:9–33.

Rahman, Aminur. 2001. *Women and Microcredit in Rural Bangladesh: An Anthropological Study of Grameen Bank Lending.* Boulder, Colo.: Westview.

Rawlinson, A. E. J. 1949. *St Mark.* 7th ed. Westminster Commentaries. London: Methuen.

Reinders, Hans S. 2008. *Receiving the Gift of Friendship: Profound Disability, Theological Anthropology, and Ethics.* Grand Rapids: Eerdmans.

Riches, John. 1996. Interpreting the Bible in African Contexts: Glasgow Consultation. *Semeia* 73:181–88.

———. 2004. Intercultural Hermeneutics: Conversations across Cultural and Contextual Divides. Pages 460–76 in *Through the Eyes of Another: Intercultural Reading of the Bible.* Edited by Hans de Wit, Louis Jonker, Marleen Kool, and Daniel Schipani. Elkhart, Ind.: Institute of Mennonite Studies.

Rieger, Joerg. 2001. *God and the Excluded: Visions and Blind Spots in Contemporary Theology.* Minneapolis: Augsburg Fortress.

———. 2004. Liberating God-Talk: Postcolonialism and the Challenge of the Margins. Pages 204–22 in *Postcolonial Theologies: Divinity and Empire.* Edited by Catherine Keller, Michael Nausner, and Mayra Rivera. St. Louis: Chalice.

Ringe, Sharon H. 2001. A Gentile Woman's Story, Revisited: Rereading Mark 7:24–31a. Pages 79–100 in *A Feminist Companion to Mark.* Edited by Amy Jill Levine with Marianne Blickenstaff. Sheffield: Sheffield Academic Press.

Robb, Carol S. 1995. *Equal Value: An Ethical Approach to Economics and Sex.* Boston: Beacon.

Robbins, Vernon K. 1994. *New Boundaries in Old Territory: Form and Social Rhetoric in Mark.* New York: Peter Lang.

Rochester, Stuart T. 2011. *Good News at Gerasa: Transformative Discourse and Theological Anthropology in Mark's Gospel.* New York: Peter Lang.

Roman, P. M., and H. H. Floyd Jr. 1981. Social Acceptance of Psychiatric Illness and Psychiatric Treatment. *Social Psychiatry* 16:16–21.

Rorty, Richard. 1980. *Philosophy and the Mirror of Nature*. Oxford: Blackwell.

———. 1986. Foucault and Epistemology. Pages 41–50 in *Foucault: A Critical Reader*. Edited by David Couzens Hoy. Oxford: Blackwell.

Rosenhan, David L. 1996. On Being Sane in Insane Places. Pages 70–78 in *Mental Health Matters: A Reader*. Edited by Tom Heller, Jill Reynolds, Roger Gomm, Rosemary Muston, and Stephen Pattison. New York: Palgrave Macmillan.

Rowland, Christopher, and John Vincent, eds. 2001. *Bible and Practice*. British Liberation Theology Series 4. Sheffield: Urban Theology Unit.

Sabourin, Leopold. 1975. The Miracles of Jesus (III): Healings, Resuscitations, Nature Miracles. *BTB* 5:146–200.

Said, Edward. 1986. Foucault and the Imagination of Power. Pages 149–56 in *Foucault: A Critical Reader*. Edited by David Couzens Hoy. Oxford: Blackwell.

Sakenfeld, Katharine Doob. 2008. Whose Text Is It? *JBL* 127:5–18.

Samuel, Simon. 2002. The Beginning of Mark: A Colonial/Postcolonial Conundrum. *BibInt* 10:405–19.

———. 2007. *A Postcolonial Reading of Mark's Story of Jesus*. London: T&T Clark.

Santos, Narry F. 2003. *Slave of All: The Paradox of Authority and Servanthood in the Gospel of Mark*. JSNTSup 237. Sheffield: Sheffield Academic Press.

Scheff, Thomas J. 1996. Labelling Mental Illness. Pages 64–69 in *Mental Health Matters: A Reader*. Edited by Tom Heller, Jill Reynolds, Roger Gomm, Rosemary Muston, and Stephen Pattison. New York: Palgrave Macmillan.

Schipani, Daniel, and Mary Schertz. 2004. Through the Eyes of Practical Theology and Theological Education. Pages 437–51 in *Through the Eyes of Another: Intercultural Reading of the Bible*. Edited by Hans de Wit, Louis Jonker, Marleen Kool, and Daniel Schipani. Elkhart, Ind.: Institute of Mennonite Studies.

Schipper, Jeremy. 2007. Disabling Israelite Leadership: 2 Samuel 6:23 and Other Images of Disability in the Deuteronomistic History. Pages 103–13 in *This Abled Body: Rethinking Disabilities in Biblical Studies*. Edited by Hector Avalos, Sarah J. Melcher, and Jeremy Schipper. SemeiaSt 55. Atlanta: Society of Biblical Literature.

Schnabel, Eckhard J. 1999. The Silence of Jesus: The Galilean Rabbi Who

Was More Than a Prophet. Pages 203–58 in *Authenticating the Words of Jesus*. Edited by Bruce Chilton and Craig A. Evans. Leiden: Brill.

Schüssler Fiorenza, Elisabeth. 1989. *Rhetoric and Ethic: The Politics of Biblical Studies*. Minneapolis: Fortress.

———. 1993. *But She Said: Feminist Practices of Biblical Interpretation*. Boston: Beacon.

Scott, James C. 1990. *Domination and the Arts of Resistance: Hidden Transcripts*. New Haven: Yale University Press.

Scull, Andrew. 1993. *The Most Solitary of Afflictions: Madness and Society in Britain, 1700–1900*. New Haven: Yale University Press.

Segovia, Fernando F. 1999. Notes toward Refining the Postcolonial Optic. *JSNT* 75:103–14.

———. 2000a. Interpreting beyond Borders: Postcolonial Studies and Diasporic Studies in Biblical Criticism. Pages 11–34 in *Interpreting beyond Borders*. Edited by Fernando F. Segovia. Bible and Postcolonialism 3. Sheffield: Sheffield Academic Press.

———. 2000b. Reading-across: Intercultural Criticism and Textual Posture. Pages 59–83 in *Interpreting beyond Borders*. Edited by Fernando F. Segovia. Bible and Postcolonialism 3. Sheffield: Sheffield Academic Press.

Selvidge, Marla J. 1990. *Woman, Cult, and Miracle Recital: A Redactional Critical Investigation on Mark 5:24–34*. London: Associated University Presses.

Shoenberg, Elizabeth. 1980. Therapeutic Communities: The Ideal, the Real and the Possible. Pages 64–71 in *The Therapeutic Community*. Edited by Elly Jansen. London: Croom Helm.

Shumway, David R. 1989. *Michel Foucault*. Boston: Twayne.

Sibeko, Malika A., and Beverley G. Haddad. 1997. Reading the Bible "with" Women in Poor and Marginalized Communities in South Africa. *Semeia* 78:83–92.

Silva, Silvia Regina de Lima. 2005. From within Ourselves: Afrodescendant Women on Paths on Theological Reflection in Latin America and the Caribbean. Pages 62–74 in *Latin American Liberation Theology: The Next Generation*. Edited by Ivan Petrella. Maryknoll, N.Y.: Orbis.

Smith, Stephen H. 1994. Mark 3:1–6: Form, Redaction and Community Function. *Bib* 75:153–74.

Snoek, Hans. 2004. Biblical Scholars and Ordinary Readers Dialoguing about Living Water. Pages 304–14 in *Through the Eyes of Another: Intercultural Reading of the Bible*. Edited by Hans de Wit, Louis Jonker,

Marleen Kool, and Daniel Schipani. Elkhart, Ind.: Institute of Mennonite Studies.

Socall, Daniel W., and Thomas Holtgraves. 1992. Attitudes toward the Mentally Ill: The Effects of Label and Beliefs. *Sociology Quarterly* 33:435–45.

Spaniol, LeRoy. 2001. Recovery from Psychiatric Disability: Implications for Rehabilitation Counselling Education. *Rehabilitation Education* 15, no. 2:167–75.

Spargo, R. C. 1999. Jesus Unbound: The Correction of Jesus's Intentions in Mark 5–8. *Religion and the Arts* 3:303–34.

Sperberg, Elizabeth D., and Sally D. Stabb. 1998. Depression in Women as Related to Anger and Mutuality in Relationships. *Psychology of Women Quarterly* 22:223–38.

Spivak, Gayatri. 1995. Can the Subaltern Speak? Pages 24–28 in *The Postcolonial Studies Reader.* Edited by Bill Ashcroft, Gareth Griffiths, and Helen Tiffin. London: Routledge.

Staley, Jeffrey L. 2006. "'Clothed in Her Right Mind": Mark 5:1–20 and Postcolonial Discourse. Pages 319–28 in *Voices from the Margins.* Edited by R. S. Sugirtharajah. 3rd ed. Maryknoll, N.Y.: Orbis.

Stocker, Susan S. 2001. Disability and Identity: Overcoming Perfectionism. *Frontiers: A Journal of Woman Studies* 22, no. 2:154–73.

Sugirtharajah, R. S. 1986. The Syrophoenician Woman. *ExpTim* 98:13–15.

———. 1999a. *Asian Biblical Hermeneutics and Postcolonialism.* Sheffield: Sheffield Academic Press.

———. 1999b. A Brief Memorandum on Postcolonialism and Biblical Studies. *JSNT* 73:3–5.

———. 1999c. Vernacular Resurrections: An Introduction. Pages 11–17 in *Vernacular Hermeneutics.* Edited by R. S. Sugirtharajah. Bible and Postcolonialism 2. Sheffield: Sheffield Academic Press.

———. 2001. *The Bible and the Third World: Pre-Colonial, Colonial, and Postcolonial Encounters.* Cambridge: Cambridge University Press.

———. 2002. *Postcolonial Criticism and Biblical Interpretation.* Oxford: Oxford University Press.

———. 2003. *Postcolonial Reconfigurations: An Alternative Way of Reading the Bible and Doing Theology.* London: SCM.

———. 2005. *The Bible and Empire: Postcolonial Explorations.* Cambridge: Cambridge University Press.

———, ed. 2006a. *The Postcolonial Biblical Reader.* Oxford: Blackwell.

———, ed. 2006b. *Voices from the Margin: Interpreting the Bible in the Third World*. 3rd ed. Maryknoll, N.Y.: Orbis.
———, ed. 2008a. *Still at the Margins: Biblical Scholarship Fifteen Years after Voices from the Margin*. London: T&T Clark.
———. 2008b. *Troublesome Texts: The Bible in Colonial and Contemporary Culture*. Sheffield: Sheffield Phoenix Press.
———, ed. 2009. *Caught Reading Again: Scholars and Their Books*. London: SCM.
Sun, Poling. 2010. Naming the Dog: Another Asian Reading of Mark 7:24–30. *Review and Expositor* 107: 389.
Sung, Jung Mo. 2005. The Human Being as Subject: Defending the Victims. Pages 1–19 in *Latin American Liberation Theology: The Next Generation*. Edited by Ivan Petrella. Maryknoll, N.Y.: Orbis.
Swidler, Leonard. 1971. Jesus Was a Feminist. *South East Asia Journal of Theology* 13, no. 1:102–10.
Swinton, John. 1999. The Politics of Caring: Pastoral Theology in an Age of Conflict and Change. *Scottish Journal of Healthcare Chaplaincy* 2:25–30.
———. 2005. *Healing Presence*. Center for Christian Ethics at Baylor University. Online: http://www.baylor.edu/christianethics/SufferingarticleSwinton.pdf.
Tannehill, Robert C. 1980. The Gospel of Mark as Narrative Christology. *Semeia* 16:57–95.
———. 1995. The Disciples in Mark: The Function of a Narrative Role. Pages 169–96 in *The Interpretation of Mark*. Edited by William Telford. 2nd ed. Edinburgh: T&T Clark.
Taylor, Charles. 1986. Foucault on Freedom and Truth. Pages 69–102 in *Foucault: A Critical Reader*. Edited by David Couzens Hoy. Oxford: Blackwell.
Taylor, Mark Lewis. 2004. Spirit and Liberation: Achieving Postcolonial Theology in the United States. Pages 39–55 in *Postcolonial Theologies: Divinity and Empire*. Edited by Catherine Keller, Michael Nausner, and Mayra Rivera. St. Louis: Chalice.
Taylor, Vincent. 1966. *The Gospel according to St. Mark: The Greek Text with Introduction, Notes, and Indexes*. 2nd ed. London: Macmillan.
Telford, William R. 1999. *The Theology of the Gospel of Mark*. Cambridge: Cambridge University Press.
Theissen, Gerd. 1991. *The Gospels in Context: Social and Political History in the Synoptic Tradition*. Minneapolis: Fortress.

Thomson, Rosemarie G. 1997. *Extraordinary Bodies: Figuring Physical Disability in American Culture and Literature*. New York: Columbia University Press.

Toensing, Holly Joan. 2007. "Living among the Tombs": Society, Mental Illness, and Self-Destruction in Mark 5:1–20. Pages 131–43 in *This Abled Body: Rethinking Disabilities in Biblical Studies*. Edited by Hector Avalos, Sarah J. Melcher, and Jeremy Schipper. SemeiaSt 55. Atlanta: Society of Biblical Literature.

Tolbert, Mary Ann. 1989. *Sowing the Gospel: Mark's World in Literary and Historical Perspective*. Minneapolis: Fortress.

———. 1995. Reading for Liberation. Pages 263–76 in *Social Location and Biblical Interpretation in the United States*. Vol. 1 of *Reading from This Place*. Edited by Fernando F. Segovia and Mary Ann Tolbert. Minneapolis: Fortress.

Torres, Sergio, and Virginia Fabella, eds. 1978. *The Emergent Gospel: Theology from the Underside of History*. Maryknoll, N.Y.: Orbis.

Tremain, Shelley. 2005. Foucault, Governmentality, and Critical Disability Theory. Pages 1–26 in *Foucault and the Government of Disability*. Edited by Shelley Tremain. Ann Abor: University of Michigan Press.

Vaughan, Megan. 1991. *Curing Their Ills: Colonial Power and African Illness*. London: Polity.

———. 1994. Colonial Discourse Theory and African History, or Has Postmodernism Passed Us By? *Social Dynamics: A Journal of African Studies* 20, no. 2:1–23.

Vuola, Elina. 2002. *Limits of Liberation: Feminist Theology and the Ethics of Poverty and Reproduction*. Sheffield: Sheffield Academic Press.

Waetjen, Herman C. 1989. *A Reordering of Power: A Sociopolitical Reading of Mark's Gospel*. Minneapolis: Fortress.

———. 1995. Social Location and the Hermeneutic Mode of Integration. Pages 75–93 in *Social Location and Biblical Interpretation in the United States*. Vol. 1 of *Reading from This Place*. Edited by Fernando F. Segovia and Mary Ann Tolbert. Minneapolis: Fortress.

Wahl, Otto F., ed. 2003. *Media Madness: Public Images of Mental Illness*. Repr., New Brunswick, N.J.: Rutgers University Press.

Wallace, David L., and Helen Rothschild Ewald. 2000. *Mutuality in the Rhetoric and Composition Classroom*. Carbondale, Ill.: Southern Illinois University Press.

Walshe, Peter. 1987. The Evolution of Liberation Theology in South Africa. *Journal of Law and Religion* 5:299–311.

Warrior, Robert Allen. 2006. A Native American Perspective: Canaanites, Cowboys, and Indians. Pages 235–41 in *Voices from the Margin: Interpreting the Bible in the Third World*. Edited by R. S. Sugirtharajah. 3rd ed. Maryknoll, N.Y.: Orbis.

Watson, Jean. 1999. *Postmodern Nursing and Beyond*. Toronto: Churchill Livingstone.

Watson, Robert A. 2007. Ready or Not, Here I Come: Surrender, Recognition, and Mutuality in Psychotherapy. *Journal of Psychology and Theology* 35:65–73.

Watts, Rikki E. 1997. *Isaiah's New Exodus in Mark*. Grand Rapids: Baker.

Weaver, Jace. 1996. From I-Hermeneutics to We-Hermeneutics: Native Americans and the Post-Colonial. *Semeia* 75:153–76.

Weems, Renita J. 1993. Reading *Her* Way through the Struggle: African American Women and the Bible. Pages 31–50 in *The Bible and Liberation: Political and Social Hermeneutics*. Edited by Norman K. Gottwald and Richard A. Horsley. Rev. ed. Maryknoll, N.Y.: Orbis.

West, Gerald O. 1991. The Relationship between Different Modes of Reading (the Bible) and the Ordinary Reader. *Scriptura* 39:87–110.

———. 1994. Difference and Dialogue: Reading the Joseph Story with Poor and Marginalized Communities in South Africa. *BibInt* 2:152–70.

———. 1999a. *The Academy of the Poor: Towards a Dialogical Reading of the Bible*. Sheffield: Sheffield Academic Press.

———. 1999b. Local Is Lekker, but Ubuntu Is Best: Indigenous Reading Resources from a South African Perspective. Pages 37–51 in *Vernacular Hermeneutics*. Edited by R. S. Sugirtharajah. Bible and Postcolonialism 2. Sheffield: Sheffield Academic Press.

———. 2004a. Artful Facilitation and Creating a Safe Interpretive Site: An Analysis of Aspects of a Bible Study. Pages 211–37 in *Through the Eyes of Another: Intercultural Reading of the Bible*. Edited by Hans de Wit, Louis Jonker, Marleen Kool, and Daniel Schipani. Elkhart, Ind.: Institute of Mennonite Studies.

———. 2004b. Explicating Domination and Resistance: A Dialogue between James C. Scott and Biblical Scholars. Pages 173–94 in *Hidden Transcripts and the Arts of Resistance: Applying the Work of James C. Scott to Jesus and Paul*. Edited by Richard A. Horsley. Leiden: Brill.

———. 2006. Contextual Bible Reading: A South African Case Study. *Analecta Bruxellensia* 11:131–48.

———. 2007a. (Ac)claiming the (Extra)ordinary African "Reader" of the Bible. Pages 29–47 in *Reading Other-Wise: Socially Engaged Biblical*

Scholars Reading with Their Local Communities. Edited by Gerald O. West. SemeiaSt 62. Atlanta: Society of Biblical Literature.

———. 2007b. The Bible and the Poor: A New Way of Doing Theology. Pages 159–82 in *The Cambridge Companion to Liberation Theology.* Edited by Christopher Rowland. 2nd ed. Cambridge: Cambridge University Press.

———. 2007c. Reading Other-Wise: Socially Engaged Biblical Scholars Reading with Their Local Communities: An Introduction. Pages 1–6 in *Reading Other-Wise: Socially Engaged Biblical Scholars Reading with Their Local Communities.* Edited by Gerald O. West. SemeiaSt 62. Atlanta: Society of Biblical Literature.

West, Gerald, and Ujamaa Centre Staff. 2007. *Doing Contextual Bible Study: A Resource Manual.* The Ujamaa Centre for Biblical and Theological Community Development and Research. Online: http://www.ukzn.ac.za/sorat/ujamaa/ujam123.pdf.

Wielenga, Bastiaan. 2007. Liberation Theology in Asia. Pages 55–78 in *The Cambridge Companion to Liberation Theology.* Edited by Christopher Rowland. 2nd ed. Cambridge: Cambridge University Press.

Wilhelm, Dorothee. 1999. Roundtable Discussion: Women with Disabilities—A Challenge to Feminist Theology. Pages 433–36 in *Women in the Hebrew Bible: A Reader.* Edited by Alice Bach. London: Routledge.

Wilkin, P. E. 2001. From Medicalization to Hybridization: A Postcolonial Discourse for Psychiatric Nurses. *Journal of Psychiatric and Mental Health Nursing* 8:115–20.

Williamson, Lamar. 1983. *Mark.* Interpretation Bible Commentary. Atlanta: John Knox.

Wink, Walter. 1980. *Transforming Bible Study.* London: SCM.

Winter, Paul. 1974. *On the Trial of Jesus.* Berlin: de Gruyter.

Wit, Hans de. 2004a. Intercultural Bible Reading and Hermeneutics. Pages 477–92 in *Through the Eyes of Another: Intercultural Reading of the Bible.* Edited by Hans de Wit, Louis Jonker, Marleen Kool, and Daniel Schipani. Elkhart, Ind.: Institute of Mennonite Studies.

Wit, Hans de. 2004b. Through the Eyes of Another: Objectives and Backgrounds. Pages 1–53 in *Through the Eyes of Another: Intercultural Reading of the Bible.* Edited by Hans de Wit, Louis Jonker, Marleen Kool, and Daniel Schipani. Elkhart, Ind.: Institute of Mennonite Studies.

Wit, Hans de, and Marleen Kool. 2004. Tableaux Vivants. Pages 54–85 in *Through the Eyes of Another: Intercultural Reading of the Bible.* Edited by Hans de Wit, Louis Jonker, Marleen Kool, and Daniel Schipani. Elkhart, Ind.: Institute of Mennonite Studies.

Wit, Hans de, Louis Jonker, Marleen Kool, and Daniel Schipani, eds. 2004. *Through the Eyes of Another: Intercultural Reading of the Bible*. Elkhart, Ind.: Institute of Mennonite Studies.

Wit, Hans de, and Gerald O. West, eds. 2008. *African and European Readers of the Bible in Dialogue: In Quest of a Shared Meaning*. Leiden: Brill.

Witherington, Ben, III. 2001. *The Gospel of Mark: A Socio-rhetorical Commentary*. Grand Rapids: Eerdmans.

Woodruff, C. Roy. 1978. Toward a Theology of Maturity in Pastoral Care. *Pastoral Psychology* 27: 26–38.

Wright, Sarah. 2001. *"Is Anybody There?" A Survey of Friendship and Mental Health*. London: Mental Health Foundation.

Wright, Sarah, and Paul De Ponte. 2000. Pull Yourself Together! A Survey of the Stigma and Discrimination Faced by People Who Experience Mental Distress. *Updates* (London: Mental Health Foundation) 2, no. 4:1–4.

Wynn, Kerry H. 2007. The Normate Hermeneutic and Interpretations of Disability within the Yahwistic Narratives. Pages 91–101 in *This Abled Body: Rethinking Disabilities in Biblical Studies*. Edited by Hector Avalos, Sarah J. Melcher, and Jeremy Schipper. SemeiaSt 55. Atlanta: Society of Biblical Literature.

Yee, Gale A. 1995. The Author/Text/Reader and Power: Suggestions for a Critical Framework for Biblical Studies. Pages 109–18 in *Social Location and Biblical Interpretation in the United States*. Vol. 1 of *Reading from This Place*. Edited by Fernando F. Segovia and Mary Ann Tolbert. Minneapolis: Fortress.

Yoder, John H. 1990. The Wider Setting of "Liberation Theology." *Review of Politics* 52:285–96.

Young, Robert J. C. 2001. *Postcolonialism: An Historical Introduction*. Oxford: Blackwell.

Index of Ancient Sources

Hebrew Bible

Exodus
- 3:7–10 — 26
- 6:6 — 105
- 14:21 — 105
- 14:26–28 — 170
- 14:27 — 105
- 14:28 — 170 n. 8
- 22:31 — 152
- 23:31b–33 — 26

Leviticus
- 12 — 134
- 12:6–8 — 134
- 15 — 134
- 15:11 — 134 n. 9
- 15:29–30 — 134
- 20 — 134

Numbers
- 5:1–4 — 134 n. 9
- 19:11–21 — 133

Deuteronomy
- 4:34 — 105
- 5:15 — 105
- 7:1–2 — 26, 28
- 33:17 — 170 n. 8

Judges
- 11:34–40 — 136

1 Kings
- 8:42 — 105

2 Kings
- 17:36 — 105

Isaiah
- 6:10 — 107
- 50:2 — 105
- 52:15 — 188
- 53:7–9 — 187
- 53:11–2 — 187
- 65:4 — 170

Jeremiah
- 7:25 — 25
- 31:8 — 107

Ezekiel
- 20:6 — 25
- 20:33–34 — 105

Hosea
- 11:1 — 25

Amos
- 2:10 — 25

Zephaniah
- 3:19 — 107

Psalms
- 38:13–15 — 187
- 39:9 — 187
- 95:5 — 170 n. 8

2 Chronicles
- 6:32 — 105

New Testament

Matthew
  15:21–28   154

Mark
  1:7   186 n. 64
  1:9–11   69
  1:11   186 n. 64
  1:12–13   112
  1:15   145
  1:21–28   170
  1:24   170, 186 n. 64
  1:25   187 n. 67
  1:37   186 n. 64
  1:45   186 n. 64
  2:1–3:5   92 n. 4
  2:7   186 n. 64
  2:13–22   134 n. 9
  2:15–17   103
  2:18   186 n. 64
  2:18–20   103
  2:23–27   103
  2:23–28   92 n. 5
  2:25–6   187 n. 67
  3:1–6   6, 11, 16 n. 1, 67, 82, 89–93, 102, 105, 107–8, 110, 127–28, 165, 198–99, 206, 208, 211, 214–16, 221
  3:2   90–91, 102, 206
  3:3   105, 198
  3:3–5   92
  3:4   91–2, 95, 103, 198
  3:5   70, 102, 105, 107
  3:6   91 n. 4, 103, 105 n. 71, 106, 108, 128, 206, 211
  3:8   157
  3:11   186 n. 64
  3:13–19   111
  3:19b–21   111 n. 84
  3:19b–35   6, 11, 67, 89, 109–10, 110 n. 80, 116–17, 119, 121, 121 n. 119, 122, 125–28, 164 n. 83, 198–99, 209, 211
  3:20   120, 120 n. 114
  3:20–35   130 n. 1
  3:21   110–11, 120, 124
  3:22   110–11, 120, 125, 198
  3:22–30   111
  3:23   123
  3:23–25   110
  3:28–30   120
  3:31   120, 125
  3:31–34   111
  3:33   120
  3:35   120, 184, 186 n. 64
  4:35–41   170
  4:37   170
  4:39   170
  4:41   186 n. 64
  5:1–20   6, 13, 67, 70, 135, 166–73, 176, 179–81, 185, 201, 206, 208–10, 214, 216, 221
  5:2   180
  5:3–4   210
  5:3–5   168–70, 173–74
  5:5   184
  5:6–7   180
  5:7   170, 181, 185, 186 n. 64
  5:8   171, 182
  5:9   171
  5:11   182
  5:12   182
  5:13   150
  5:15   170, 180, 183, 185
  5:17   183
  5:18   184–85
  5:19   183, 186 n. 64
  5:19a   184
  5:19b   183–84
  5:20   210
  5:21–43   6, 12, 67, 129–30, 130 n. 1, 131–32, 132 n. 6, 133, 134 n. 9, 135–37, 142–43, 146–48, 165, 168 n. 1, 200, 207–9, 211, 215–16, 221
  5:22   131–33, 143
  5:23   132, 144
  5:24   132
  5:24–34   134
  5:24b   143
  5:25   132

5:26	131, 144, 148	8:38–9:1	69
5:28	133, 147	9:2–8	69
5:29	145	9:7	186 n. 64
5:29–34	147	9:12–13	187 n. 67
5:30	143, 146–47	9:17	186 n. 64
5:31	143	9:25	187 n. 67
5:33	133, 143, 147–48	9:29	186
5:33–34	137	9:30–32	186 n. 64
5:34	70, 144, 147–48	9:38	186 n. 64
5:35	144	9:41	186 n. 64
5:36	144 n. 42	10:2–9	92
5:37	133	10:7–8	187 n. 67
5:38	133, 144	10:11–2	187 n. 67
5:38–40	144	10:17–18	186 n. 64
5:41–42	70	10:29–30	125
5:42	132–33	10:32–34	186 n. 64
5:43	144	10:33	125, 187
6:1–6	124	10:38–45	186 n. 64
6:2b	50	10:47–51	186 n. 64
6:3	118, 124	11:3	186 n. 64
6:3b	124–25	11:10	186 n. 64
6:4	125	11:12–26	130
6:6	125	11:14	150
6:7–32	130 n. 1	11:15	150
6:11	125	11:18	126
6:34–44	153	11:21	150
6:51	186 n. 64	11:27–28	126
7:1–23	134 n. 9	11:28	50, 186 n. 64
7:1–24	152	12:6	69, 186 n. 64
7:6	150	12:8	126
7:6–10	187 n. 67	12:9–11	69
7:19	152	12:12	126
7:24–30	6, 12, 67, 129, 149–55, 157–59, 161–64, 164 n. 83, 165, 207–9, 211, 214, 216, 222	12:24–34	126
		12:32	186 n. 64
		12:35–37	186 n. 64
7:25	165	12:36	69
7:27	150–53, 160	12:38	126
7:28	153, 157, 162, 186 n. 64	12:40	126
7:29	70, 156, 162	13:1–2	69
7:30	163	13:11	197
7:36	186 n. 64	13:12	125
8:1–10	153	13:24–27	68 n. 7
8:11	186 n. 64	13:26	69
8:27–38	186 n. 64	13:26–27	186 n. 64
8:33	150	13:32	186 n. 64

Mark (cont.)

14:1	126
14:1–11	130 n. 1
14:10–25	130 n. 1
14:14	186 n. 64
14:21–24	186 n. 64
14:36	186 n. 64
14:41	186 n. 64
14:43	126
14:44	125
14:45	186 n. 64
14:50	125
14:53	126
14:53–64	187
14:54–72	130 n. 1
14:61–62	69, 186 n. 64
14:61b	186, 188 n. 68
14:71	125, 186 n. 64
15:1	126, 189, 191–93
15:1–5	6, 13, 67, 166–67, 185–89, 189 n. 70, 190–92, 194–95, 197–98, 200–1, 207, 209–10
15:2	186, 186 n. 64, 187 n. 66, 188, 188 n. 68, 190, 193
15:2b	190–91
15:2b–15:34	191 n. 73
15:3	196, 198
15:3–5	187, 197
15:4	195
15:5	188, 199, 210
15:7	189
15:8–14	188
15:11	189 n. 69
15:13	189
15:13–14	201
15:13–15	189 n. 69
15:15	189, 201
15:18	186 n. 64
15:19	189
15:26	186 n. 64
15:32	126, 186 n. 64
15:34	186 n. 64, 201
15:39	69, 183, 186 n. 64
15:40–41	125
16:6	186 n. 64

Romans

3:25	135

1 Corinthians

10:20	170

APOCRYPHA AND PSEUDEPIGRAPHA

1 Enoch

19:1	170 n. 8
99:7	170 n. 8

Jubilees

1:11	170 n. 8
10:7ff.	112 n. 87

Tobit

8:3	112 n. 87

SECOND TEMPLE LITERATURE

Dead Sea Scrolls

1QpHab 6.3ff.	170 n. 8
11Q19 49.16–17; 50.10–14	133 n. 8
1QM 14.2–3	133 n. 8

Josephus, *Antiquities of the Jews*

4.81	133 n. 8
14.450	172 n. 13
17.271, 274	113

Josephus, *Jewish War*

4.486–490	172 n. 13

Philo, *Special Laws*

3.205–209	133 n. 8

GRECO-ROMAN TEXTS

Philostratus, *Vita Apollonii* 8.2	196

RABBINIC TEXTS

Tosefta Parah

3.14; 10.2; 5.6; 7.4	133 n. 8

Index of Modern Authors

Ahearne-Kroll, Stephen P.   112, 124–25
Aichele, George   9 n. 8, 120 n. 116, 121
Althaus-Reid, Marcella   25 n. 11, 28, 30 n. 19
Anderson, Hugh   86 n. 42, 91 n. 4, 103 n. 64, 121 n. 118, 169
Anthony, William A.   204–5
Antonio, Edward   30
Anum, Eric   83 n. 28
Apostola, Nicholas K.   44–5
Ashcroft, Bill   54 n. 10, 122
Ateek, Naim   24 n. 9
Avotri, Solomon   86 n. 41
Bammel, Ernst   188, 189 n. 71, 196
Barham, Peter   19
Barta, Karen A.   131 n. 2
Bauman, Zygmunt   40
Beavis, Mary Ann   131, 136
Beck, Robert R.   132 n. 5, 152
Belo, Fernando   86 n. 38, 183, 190
Benjamin, Chris   169
Bernstein, Richard   36
Best, Ernest   111 n. 81, 120 n. 117
Betcher, Sharon   163
Bhabha, Homi   5, 12, 43, 52–53, 53 n. 9, 54, 54 n. 11, 55–56, 56 n. 15, 57–58, 58 n. 16, 59–61, 65, 67, 106, 122, 127, 148, 160–61, 211–12
Bhugra, D.   17
Bird, Lisa   20
Block, Jennie Weiss   221–22
Boer, Ronald   65
Boff, Clodovis   25
Bomford, Rodney   132 n. 7
Bowman, John   110 n. 80
Broadhead, Edwin K.   86 n. 42, 110 n. 80, 120 n. 114, 170, 188
Brock, Rita N.   145 n. 47
Brockington, Ian F.   17
Brooks, James A.   86 n. 42, 144 n. 44, 151–52, 169 n. 6
Brown, Raymond E.   125, 189 n. 71
Budesheim, Thomas L.   91 n. 2
Butin, Dan   38
Camery-Hoggart, Jerry   86 n. 37, 169 nn. 3–4, 170
Campbell, John M.   88
Campbell, William Sanger   186 n. 65, 190–91, 196–97
Cape, Anita L.   36
Cardenal, Ernesto   71, 86 n. 41, 91, 112 n. 85
Chavez, Nelba   205
Comaroff, John   53 n. 9, 127, 148
Connolly, William E.   40
Corrigan, P. W.   17, 19
Cotter, Wendy   86 n. 40, 131 n. 3
Crossan, John Dominic   120 n. 115, 171
Cruikshank, Barbara   40
D'Angelo, Mary Rose   131 n. 2
Davies, John Dudley   180, 184
Dawson, Andrew   72
De Ponte, Paul   20
Deakin, Simon   45 n. 1
Deibert, Richard   86 n. 42, 169
Derrett, J. Duncan M.   93 n. 6, 102, 105, 134–35, 169 n. 3, 170 n. 8, 171, 171 n. 12, 188, 189 n. 71
Dewey, Joanna   91 n. 2
Dews, Peter   37

Donaldson, Laura E. 163
Doughty, Darrell 91 n. 2, 92
Dowd, Sharyn Echols 110, 120 n. 115, 133, 135, 152–53, 169 n. 2, 169 n. 4, 184, 189
Dube, Musa W. 154–55
Eiesland, Nancy 4–6, 21 n. 5, 43, 45, 47–8, 51, 57, 59, 179 n. 51, 221
Ekblad, Bob 72 n. 15, 78 n. 23, 84 nn. 30–31, 85 n. 33
Ellison, M. M. 48
Elshout, Elly 93, 104 n. 68, 180
Ewald, Helen Rothschild 44
Fabella, Virginia 22, 65 n. 5
Fanon, Frantz 56 n. 14, 172 n. 14
Faulkner, Alison 204 n. 1, 205
Fearday, Frederick L. 46
Fendler, Lynn 35 n. 23, 36, 39
Fisher, Pamela 46
Fortune, Marie M. 48
Foucault, Michel 4, 15, 17, 31, 32–35, 35 n. 23, 36–37, 37 n. 24, 38, 38 n. 25, 39–41, 43–44, 46, 49–50, 52, 54 n. 11, 60, 66, 69, 114, 118 n. 108, 182, 200, 200 n. 115, 206, 211
Fowler, Robert M. 81, 86, 121 n. 119
Fox, Nicholas J. 57
France, Richard T. 190
Gandhi, Leela 81
Garroway, Joshua 172
Gilbert, Peter 205
Gill, LaVerne McCain 151 n. 49, 152, 160 n. 78, 161 n. 79
Gilman, Sander 18–19, 97, 200, 200 n. 116
Glancy, Jennifer A. 154 n. 53
Gnanadason, Aruna 150
Goldberg, David Theo 55, 57
Goldstein, Jan 36 n. 23
Gonzales, Michelle, A. 184 n. 61
Graham, Larry 23–24
Gready, Paul 122 n. 120
Green, Jim 204 n. 1, 205
Green, Laurie 22 n. 6, 24 n. 9, 25 n. 10, 204 n. 1

Grey, Mary 30
Guardiola-Sáenz, Leticia 163
Gudorf, Christine E. 48
Guelich, Robert A. 93, 110 n. 80, 111 n. 84
Gundry, Robert H. 86 n. 42, 120 n. 115, 131 n. 3, 169, 169 n. 3, 174, 180–81, 187
Gutiérrez, Gustavo 21
Haber, Susan 86 n. 40, 131 n. 2, 133, 133 n. 8, 134 n. 9
Habermas, Jürgen 38–39
Haddad, Beverly G. 24 n. 9, 77, 77 n. 23
Hagerty, Bonnie, M. K. 45
Hamerton-Kelly, Robert G. 68, 120, 169 n. 3, 182 n. 58, 184, 188, 189 n. 71
Hamre, Per 17
Hare, Douglas R. A. 86 n. 42, 91 n. 2, 110 n. 80
Harrison, Beverly Wildung 48
Hart, Lawrence D. 153
Hauerwas, Stanley 222
Hayward, Robert 19
Hedelin, B. 46 n. 3
Heil, John Paul 86 n. 36, 103 n. 64, 110 n. 80
Hentrich, Thomas 105 n. 69
Heyward, Carter 5–6, 43, 45, 49–51, 53, 56–57, 59, 105, 105 n. 69, 146, 209
Hiebert, D. Edmond 86 n. 42, 91 n. 2, 93, 111, 111 n. 83, 120 n. 117
Hiers, Richard H. 111 n. 81, 112, 112 n. 87, 120 n. 117, 121
Hilton, James 17
Hinga, Teresia M. 75 n. 20
Hippel, William von 17
Holmlund, Christine Anne 55
Hollenbach, Paul W. 172, 172 n. 14, 173
Holtgraves, Thomas 19
Hooker, Morna D. 86 n. 42, 91 n. 2, 135, 151, 174, 177, 187, 190
Horsley, Richard 64 n. 1, 68, 86 n. 38, 92 n. 5, 113, 113 n. 88, 134 n. 9, 145, 151, 171, 171 n. 9, 180 n. 52, 186 n. 65
Hoy, David Couzens 36

INDEX OF MODERN AUTHORS

Hultgren, Arland J. 92
Humphrey, Robert L. 187, 188 n. 68
Hyler, Steven 18
Iersel, Bas M. F. van 86 n. 36, 91, 91 n. 3, 131 n. 3, 134, 152 n. 51, 169, 181, 184 n. 60, 187, 190
Ionita, Viorel 44–45
Isenberg, Bo 39
Iverson, Kelly R. 154, 169 n. 5
JanMohamed, Abdul R. 55
Jauss, Hans Robert 9 n. 8
Jefferess, David 122 n. 120
Jennings, Stephen 75 n. 20
Jennings, Theodore 72, 191
Jeon, Yun-Hee 45
Jinkins, M. 44
Joh, Anne W. 107 n. 74, 221
Johnson, Sherman E. 120 n. 115
Jonker, Louis 77
Jonsson, I. 46 n. 3
Jordan, Mark D. 48
Joy, David 154
Juel, Donald H. 86 n. 42, 131 n. 3, 134
Kahl, Werner 80 n. 26
Kapoor, Ilan 54
Keenan, John P. 121 n. 119, 132, 145, 197
Keller, Catherine 65 n. 5, 104, 106 n. 72, 221
Kelly, B. D. 20
Kessler, Rainer 82
Kingsbury, Jack D. 189
Kinukawa, Hisako 86 n. 40, 133–34, 146, 160, 160 n. 77, 169 n. 3, 174
Kool, Marleen 218 n. 36
Kramer-Dahl, Anneliese 74
Kuthirakkattel, Scaria 91 n. 2
Kwok, Pui-lan 65, 71 n. 12, 161
Lambrecht, Jan 120 n. 115
Lane, William L. 189 nn. 70–71, 196
Lanser-van der Velde, Alma 83
Lategan, Bernard 80
Layzell, Sarah 204 n. 1, 205
Leech, Kenneth 29
Lees, Janet 72 n. 15, 74, 74 n. 18
Levi, Jerome M. 56 n. 13

Liew, Benny, 2 n. 4, 6, 65, 67–8, 68 nn. 7–8, 69, 69 n. 9, 70, 86 n. 39, 107, 110 n. 80, 119 n. 113, 122 n. 120, 147–48, 164 n. 83
Link, Bruce G. 17
Liu, Rebekah 151
Loew, Patty 56 n. 13
Logan, Finlay 122
MacLaurin, E. C. B. 111 n. 81, 120 n. 117
McAllister, N. 45
McCarthy, Thomas 37
McClintock, Anne 55
McCloughry, Roy 22
McGovern, Arthur 24
Madianos, M. G. 17
Maldonado-Torres, Nelson 31 n. 20
Maluleke, Tinyiko Sam 182
Mann, C. S. 70, 86 n. 42, 91 n. 2, 93, 111, 111 n. 82, 120 n. 117
Marchal, Joseph A. 48
Marcus, Joel 86 n. 42, 91 n. 2, 111–12, 187–88, 189 n. 71
Marshall, Christopher D. 130 n. 1, 131, 133, 144–45
Martin, Jack K. 19
Martín-Baró, Ignacio 23 n. 8
Masoga, Mogomme Alpheus 24 n. 9, 77, 77 n. 22, 84 n. 30
Melcher, Sarah J. 107 n. 77
Mellon, John C. 177 n. 41
Meredith, P. 57
Mesters, Carlos 27
Miguez, Nestor 85 n. 35
Mitchell, David 22, 108 n. 78
Mitchell, Joan 161–62
Moore, Stephen D. 52 n. 6, 64, 64 n. 1, 65, 66 n. 6, 68 n. 7, 86 n. 39, 171, 171 n. 11, 172
Moore-Gilbert, Bart 53, 55, 57–8
Morris, Wayne 21, 22, 24 n. 9,
Mosala, Itumeleng J. 22 n. 6, 24 n. 9
Moss, Candida 145 n. 46
Mulackal, Shalini 132 n. 6
Myers, Ched 67, 86 n. 38, 112, 112 n. 88, 113, 135 n. 10, 143, 143 n.

Myers, Ched (cont.)   42, 152, 171, 171 n. 10, 172 n. 13, 180 n. 52, 187, 188 n. 68, 190–91
Nations, Marilyn K.   56 n. 13
Nausner, Micahel   107 n. 74
Nicholls, Vicky   205
Nietzsche, Friedrich   32
Oakman, Douglas   86 n. 38, 113
O'Neill, J. C.   189 n. 71
Ottermann, Monika   28 n. 15
Owen, David   39
Pailin, David   26, 26 n. 12
Painter, John   86 n. 42, 103 n. 64, 110 n. 80, 111, 152 n. 51, 169, 183, 187 n. 66
Pallares, José Cárdenas   86 n. 38, 103 n. 63, 189 n. 71, 190, 196
Parry, Benita   56, 56 n. 14, 100
Pattison, Stephen   21, 21 n. 5, 23, 23 n. 8, 27 n. 14, 207
Perkinson, Jim   86 n. 39, 160–2
Peterson-Iyer, Karen   48 n. 5
Petrella, Ivan   30, 31 n. 22
Phelan, Jo C.   17
Pixley, George   25
Plaatjie, Gloria Kehilwe   24 n. 9, 75 n. 21, 86 n. 40
Porter, Roy   33–35
Queller, Kurt   105
Rabkin, Judith   17
Rahman, Aminur   56 n. 13
Rawlinson, A. E. J.   90
Reinders, Hans   23 n. 7, 221–22
Riches, John   75 n. 20, 83 n. 27
Rieger, Joerg   7 n. 7, 25 n. 10, 29 n. 17
Ringe, Sharon   86 n. 40, 150
Robb, Carol S.   48
Robbins, Vernon K.   135
Rochester, Stuart T.   180 n. 55
Roman, P. M.   17
Rorty, Richard   57
Rosenham, David   18
Rowland, Christopher   24 n. 9
Sabourin, Leopold   91 n. 2, 93, 100, 132
Said, Edward   40, 40 n. 26, 64 n. 3, 65
Sakenfeld, Doob   74 n. 19
Samuel, Simon   6–7, 52 n. 7, 64, 64 nn. 2–3, 68–71, 70 nn. 10–11, 86 n. 39, 216
Santos, Narry F.   188 n. 68, 189
Scheff, Thomas J.   20
Schertz, Mary   219
Schipani, Daniel   219
Schipper, Jeremy   169 n. 1
Schnabel, Eckhard J.   187–88, 189 n. 71
Schüssler Fiorenza, Elisabeth   24 n. 9, 154, 158
Scott, James C.   5, 55, 55 n. 12, 56, 59, 84 nn. 32–33, 113, 122, 122 n. 122, 208, 211, 212 n. 4
Scull, Andrew   35
Segovia, Fernando F.   51–52, 52 n. 7, 64 n. 2, 65 n. 4
Selvidge, Marla J.   131 n. 2
Sheppard, Gerald   74 n. 19
Shoenberg, Elizabeth   35 n. 23
Sibeko, Malika A.   24 n. 9, 77 n. 23
Silva, Silvia Regina de Lima   31 n. 21
Socall, Daniel W.   19
Smith, Stephen H.   105 n. 70
Snoek, Hans   85
Snyder, Sharon L.   22, 108 n. 78
Spaniol, LeRoy   205
Spargo, R. C.   153
Sperberg, Elizabeth, D.   46 n. 3
Spivak, Gayatri   7–8, 52, 59, 65, 87, 217
Stabb, Sally D.   46 n. 3
Staley, Jeffrey L.   183
Stocker, Susan   46
Sugirtharjah, R. S.   22 n. 6, 52, 57 n. 15, 64, 64 n. 3, 66, 66 n. 5, 161, 173, 180 n. 52, 200, 216
Sun, Poling   151
Sung, Jung Mo   31
Swidler, Leonard   131 n. 2
Swinton, John   21 n. 5, 22, 24
Tannehill, Robert C.   189
Taylor, Mark Lewis   27 n. 13
Taylor, Vincent   91, 120 n. 115
Theissen, Gerd   86 n. 38, 150–51, 170 n. 8

Thomson, Rosemarie Garland 93, 102 n. 62
Toensing, Holly Joan 23
Tolbert, Mary Ann 24 n. 9, 131 n. 3, 132 n. 4, 152, 180, 184, 191, 191 n. 73
Torres, Sergio 22 n. 6, 65 n. 5
Vaughan, Megan 57 n. 15, 181
Vincent, John J. 24 n. 9, 180, 184
Vuola, Elina 30
Waetjen, Herman 68, 86 n. 38, 112 n. 86, 120 n. 115, 135 n. 10, 144 n. 45, 180 n. 52, 186 n. 65, 188 n. 69
Wahl, Otto 17–18
Wallace, David L. 44
Walshe, Peter 30
Warrior, Robert Allen 26
Watson, Amy 17
Watson, Jean 57
Watson, Robert 45, 45 n. 2
Watts, Rikki E. 170, 170 n. 7–8
Weems, Renita J. 24 n. 9, 28
West, Gerald 8, 24 n. 9, 25 n. 10, 72, 72 nn. 13–16, 73, 73 n. 17, 74, 74 nn. 18–19, 75, 75 n. 21, 76, 80, 80 n. 25, 83 n. 29, 84, 84 nn. 30–32, 85 n. 33, 218
Wielenga, Bastiaan 30
Wilhelm, Dorothee 78 n. 24, 87
Wilkin, P. E. 57
Williamson, Lamar 91, 131 n. 3, 144 n. 43, 152 n. 51, 169
Wimbush, Vincent 72 n. 15
Winter, Paul 189 n. 69
Wit, Hans de 9 n. 8, 10 n. 9, 72 n. 15, 76, 218, 218 nn. 36–7, 220–21
Witherington, Ben 86 n. 37, 189
Woodruff, C. Roy 197 n. 108
Wright, Sarah 20, 204 n. 1, 205
Wynn, Kerry H. 93, 94 n. 7, 102 n. 62, 107 n. 75, 126
Yee, Gale A. 86 n. 36
Yoder, John H. 30 n. 18
Young, Robert J. C. 52

Index of Subjects

agency, 2, 4–7, 9, 11–13, 15, 17–19, 29 n. 17, 36–41, 43–44, 49, 51–53, 53 n. 9, 56–57, 57 n. 15, 58–61, 63, 67, 69, 71, 79 n. 25, 86–87, 89–90, 92–95, 98–102, 104–8, 113, 116, 119 n. 113, 123–24, 126–33, 135–38, 140–49, 153, 157–58, 160, 162, 164–65, 172, 175–77, 179, 182–84, 191, 195, 197–201, 203–5, 208–12, 215–16, 221
alterity, 1 n. 1, 13, 165, 175, 179, 182–83, 185, 207, 212, 214, 216
ambiguity, 4–5, 7, 11, 27 n. 14, 47, 49–51, 54, 59, 61, 71, 109–10, 118–19, 121–22, 122 nn. 120–21, 123–26, 128, 154, 157, 163, 179, 197, 198, 209–10, 237
anticolonial, 68, 68 n. 7, 70, 70 n. 10, 216
binarism, 30, 31 n. 22, 50, 68, 109–10, 110 n. 80, 112, 122, 128, 198
colonial, 6, 12–13, 51, 52 n. 6, 53–57, 59, 60, 63–64, 66–68, 68 n. 8, 69, 69 n. 9, 70–71, 78, 87, 106, 110 n. 80, 122, 127, 148, 154, 171–73, 179, 181, 183, 185, 197–99, 208–10, 214, 216–17
contextual biblical criticism, 3, 6, 15, 25, 61, 63–64, 73–4, 74 n. 19, 78 n. 24, 86, 200, 203, 218
dialogical hermeneutics, 8–9, 9 n. 8, 11, 14, 63, 67, 71, 71 n. 12, 72, 72 nn. 13–14, 73–77, 77 n. 22, 78, 78 n. 24, 83 nn. 27–28, 84, 84 n. 30, 85–88, 126, 205, 212, 215, 217–18, 220
dialogue, 2, 9, 13, 15, 17–18, 20, 34, 44, 52, 60, 71, 71 n. 12, 76–78, 84, 84 n. 30, 86–87, 103–4, 154, 160–61, 163–64, 167–68, 178–79, 181–83, 185–91, 191 n. 73, 195, 197, 200 n. 115, 201, 204–5, 207, 209–10, 219–20
disability studies, 22–23, 23 n. 7, 26, 221–22
disabled, 1 n. 3, 26 n. 12, 46–7, 93, 98 n. 33, 102 n. 61, 104 n. 68, 107, 108 n. 78, 179 n. 51, 213 n. 10, 238,
discourse, 4, 12, 14, 32, 34–35, 37–40, 43–44, 47, 49, 52, 54, 54 n. 11, 56, 56 n. 14, 57–58, 60, 66–67, 70, 78, 81, 84 n. 32, 111, 122, 128, 146, 148, 161, 165, 185, 197, 201, 203–5, 207, 211, 216–17
dunamis, 50–51, 56, 146
ethnicity, 12, 28 n. 16, 31 n. 20, 52 n. 6, 128–29, 149, 154, 154 n. 53, 158–59, 211
exclusion, 7–8, 11, 24, 47, 55, 102, 108 n. 78, 117, 129, 134, 134 n. 9, 136, 142, 200, 206
facilitator, 8, 28 n. 15, 63, 74 n. 19, 75–76, 78, 78 n. 23, 80–81, 83–84, 84 n. 30, 85, 85 n. 34, 88, 205, 217, 220
female agency, 12, 129, 132–33, 135–36, 146–48, 158, 164, 209
feminist theology, 5, 12, 30, 48, 48 n. 5, 49, 130, 146, 154, 207
form criticism, 93
gender, 10–13, 20, 28 n. 16, 31 n. 20, 52 n. 6, 55, 128–29, 132–34, 136–37, 139 n. 20, 140–43, 146, 148, 154, 154 n. 53, 155, 164–65, 203, 207–11, 216
Gentile, 24, 68, 135, 149–50, 152, 168–69, 169 n. 5, 183, 187, 189, 214
God, 24–25, 27–28, 30–31, 46 n. 2, 49–50,

God (cont.), 54, 65, 68–70, 76, 92–94, 95 n. 14, 95 n. 16, 95 n. 20, 96, 99, 99 n. 45, 100, 100 n. 51, 103, 103 nn. 63 and 66, 105, 105 n. 69, 107, 109, 111–12, 117 n. 107, 118 n. 111, 119 n. 113, 121 n. 118, 126, 132 n. 5, 135–36, 136 n. 11, 137 n. 13, 140 n. 27, 141, 141 n. 32, 142 n. 39, 143 n. 40, 145, 151, 167, 169 n. 5, 172, 174 n. 20, 176 n. 31, 177, 177 n. 40, 178 n. 45, 179 n. 51, 180 n. 51, 181, 184 n. 60, 192, 197 n. 108, 215, 215 n. 30

group reader, 1 n. 1, 9, 9 n. 8, 10, 10 nn. 9–10, 13, 61, 71, 76, 78, 78 n. 23, 79 n. 25, 80, 80 n. 25, 81–3, 83 n. 27, 83 n. 29, 84, 84 n. 30, 85, 85 n. 35, 86–8, 90, 94–104, 108, 110, 113–19, 119 n. 113, 121–24, 128, 131, 136–43, 145–49, 154–60, 162–65, 168, 173–86, 191–96, 199–200, 205–08, 212–15, 217–20, 222

hegemonic, 4–5, 9, 11, 13, 15, 20, 33, 37–39, 43–44, 46, 49, 52, 56–61, 63, 67, 70–71, 87–89, 95, 101, 106, 108, 115, 122–25, 128–29, 133, 146–49, 155, 160–61, 164–65, 168, 172, 183, 190, 192, 197–201, 203, 207–12, 216–17

Herodians, 90–91, 103, 105 n. 71, 108, 206, 211

heuristic, 2, 6, 39, 51, 61, 71, 79, 123, 204, 206, 208–9, 211–12, 217

hidden agency, 6–7, 13, 51, 56, 59, 147, 203, 208, 211

hidden transcripts, 55–56, 113, 122, 172 n. 13,

hybridity, 5, 11, 52 n. 6, 54, 54 nn. 10–11, 55, 57–59

identity, 2, 9, 11, 15, 17, 30, 36, 38, 44, 52–53, 55, 57–59, 63, 71, 76, 87, 89–90, 92, 92 n. 5, 93–94, 96, 98–102, 104–8, 110, 114–19, 121–24, 127–28, 129, 135, 147, 154 n. 53, 168–69, 174, 178–80, 182, 184–86, 198, 207, 209, 215

ideology criticism, 9 n. 8

incremental agency, 5, 12, 57, 60, 210–12
interested reader, 8
Jairus, 6, 12, 67, 129–35, 137, 137 n. 12, 139, 139 nn. 20 and 22, 140, 140 n. 27, 142–47, 207–8, 216, 222

Jesus, 6–7, 9, 11–13, 24, 28 n. 15, 50, 67–68, 68 n. 7, 69–70, 70 n. 10, 71, 77 n. 22, 81–82, 89–91, 91 n. 3, 92, 92 n. 5, 93, 93 n. 6, 94, 94 n. 11–12, 95, 95 nn. 17, 19–20, and 22, 96, 98, 98 nn. 34 and 36–37, 99, 99 n. 42–45, 100, 100 nn. 52–53 and 57, 101–2, 102 n. 61, 103, 103 nn. 63–64, 104–5, 105 nn. 69 and 71, 106–7, 107 n. 74, 108–10, 110 n. 80, 111, 111 n. 83, 112, 112 nn. 85–86, 113–14, 114 n. 91, 115–16, 116 nn. 101–2, 117, 117 n. 107, 118, 118 n. 111, 119, 119 n. 113, 120, 120 nn. 114–17, 121, 121 n. 119, 122–26, 126 n. 124, 127–32, 132 n. 6, 134, 134 n. 9, 135, 135 n. 10, 136, 136 n. 11, 137, 137 n. 13, 138, 138 n. 16, 139 n. 19, 140, 140 nn. 26–27, 141–43, 143 nn. 40 and 42, 144, 144 nn. 43–44, 145, 145 n. 46, 146–52, 152 n. 50, 153, 153 n. 52, 154, 154 n. 53, 155–56, 156 n. 58, 157, 157 n. 67, 158, 158 n. 73, 159–60, 160 n. 78, 161, 161 n. 79, 162–64, 164 n. 83, 165–69, 169 n. 2, 170–71, 171 n. 12, 173–74, 175 nn. 26 and 29, 176, 176 n. 30, 176 nn. 32–33, 177–78, 178 n. 46, 179, 179 n. 51, 180, 180 n. 55, 181–82, 182 n. 59, 183–84, 184 n. 60, 185–87, 187 nn. 66–67, 188–89, 189 n. 70, 190–91, 191 n. 72, 192, 192 n. 76, 193, 193 n. 91, 194, 194 n. 99, 195, 195 n. 101, 196–201, 204, 206–11, 213 nn. 5 and 13–14, 214, 214 n. 20, 215, 215 n. 29, 216, 217 n. 35, 221–22

Jesus, family of, 6, 67, 89, 109, 111, 111 n. 83, 112, 112 n. 85, 118, 120, 120 n. 114, 121, 121 n. 119, 124–25, 127, 147, 164 n. 83, 209, 211

INDEX OF SUBJECTS

label, 1 n. 1, 11, 16, 18–20, 33, 35–6, 74 n. 19, 89, 109–15, 115 n. 98, 116, 116 n. 99, 117–19, 120 n. 117, 121, 121 n. 119, 122–25, 129, 151, 158 n. 73, 205, 209

liberation hermeneutics, 3, 3 n. 6, 4, 15, 21–30, 29 n. 17, 36–37, 39, 40–41, 43–44, 47, 49, 51–52, 54 n. 11, 61, 64–65, 70, 72, 76, 88, 206, 207,

liberation theology, 7 n. 7, 21, 22 n. 6, 26 n. 12, 30–31, 30 n. 19, 31 n. 21, 31 n. 22, 65 n. 5, 72–73,

and the margins, 3, 3 n. 6, 4, 7 n. 7, 15, 24–25, 27–29, 31, 31 n. 21, 36, 39, 41, 47, 206

and pastoral care, 22–24, 23 n. 8, 27 n. 14, 29, 207

liminal, 5, 35, 54, 57, 142, 145, 147–48, 165, 208, 212, 216

man among the tombs, 6, 13, 67, 166–69, 169 nn. 2–3 and 6, 171, 171 n. 12, 172–75, 175 nn. 22 and 25–26, 175 nn. 28–29, 176, 176 nn. 30–35, 177–78, 178 nn. 44–46, 179, 179 nn. 48 and 51, 183, 201, 206, 208–10, 214, 216, 221

man with withered hand, 6, 11, 82, 89, 91, 91 n. 3, 93, 95–96, 98, 100–1, 105–8, 127–28, 165, 198–99, 206, 211, 216, 221

marginalization, 11, 39, 52 n. 6

Mark, Gospel of, 6–7, 9–11, 50, 63, 66–68, 68 nn. 7 and 8, 69, 69 n. 9, 70, 70 n. 10, 82, 86, 88, 111 n. 84, 113 n. 88, 121 n. 119, 124–25, 126 n. 124, 127, 130, 130 n. 1, 131, 131 n. 4, 132 n. 7, 135, 154, 164, 170–71, 171 n. 9, 180 n. 55, 186, 186 n. 64, 187 n. 66, 188, 197, 204, 207

medical model, 22, 46, 204–5

mental illness, 1 nn. 1 and 3, 17, 19, 33–34, 96, 117, 157, 174 n. 20, 177, 177 nn. 39 and 40, 213 n. 5, 238, 252–53, 255, 278, 293, 297, 300

marginalized, the, 28, 74,

mimicry, 5, 12, 52 n. 6, 54–55, 59, 68 n. 8, 69, 71, 150, 161–62, 183, 208, 210

mutuality
and agency, 101–3, 105–9, 159–60
and ambiguity, 47, 49–51, 54, 59, 61, 71, 123–24, 126, 128, 197, 209–10
and dialogical biblical criticism, 71, 78, 85, 220
and dialogue, 103, 147, 168, 180–81, 185, 201, 209
and ethnicity, 12, 128–29, 149, 154, 154 n. 53, 158–59, 211
and feminist theology, 48–49, 48 n. 5
and gender, 12–13, 128–29, 132–34, 136–37, 139 n. 20, 140–43, 146, 148, 154, 154 n. 53, 155, 164–65, 203, 207–10
and hidden agency, 13, 51, 208–9,
and hybridity, 11, 89, 211
and identity, 122–23, 184
and mental health, 45–46, 46 n. 3
and mimicry, 150
and relational dynamics, 12–13, 47, 63, 70, 90, 106, 123, 131, 146–47, 165, 183–84, 197, 203, 206, 210–11
and other postcolonial praxes, 12, 53, 60, 71, 124, 127–28, 208
and postcolonial theology, 221
and silence, 186, 195, 198, 201, 210
and theologies of disability, 221
application to act of reading, 8, 61, 63, 71, 78–84, 87–88, 217, 219
as postcolonial praxis, 57–61, 70, 104–10, 123, 126–28, 146–49, 160, 162, 164, 198, 203–4, 206, 209, 211–12
Carter Heyward's use of, 5, 49–51
concept, 41, 43–6, 44 n. 1,
core thesis, 9
Nancy Eiesland's use of, 47

negotiation, 5, 38, 45, 47, 50, 53, 59, 60, 63, 70, 77–78, 80, 85, 123, 129, 136, 143, 146–47, 160, 164, 186, 216

normate hermeneutics, 93–94, 102 n. 62, 126

ordinary reader, 8, 9 n. 8, 72–74, 74 n. 19, 75, 75 n. 20, 76–77, 83 nn. 27 and 29, 85 n. 35, 87

other, the, 7, 12, 35, 39, 45, 47, 57, 59, 69, 89, 110, 116, 121 n. 119, 134, 139 n. 20, 147, 154, 158–59, 163, 179, 181, 199, 209, 211, 216, 221
pastoral care, 22–24, 27 n. 14, 29,
Pharisees, 6, 67, 90–92, 92 n. 5, 93–95, 95 n. 14, 98, 98 n. 39, 102–3, 103 n. 64, 104, 105 n. 71, 106, 116 n. 105, 127, 134 n. 9, 150, 206, 211, 214
Pilate, 6, 13, 67, 166–67, 185–87, 187 n. 66, 188–91, 191 n. 72, 192 n. 76, 193, 193 n. 89, 194, 194 nn. 94 and 99, 195, 195 n. 101, 196–99, 201, 210
poor mental health, 1, 1 n. 1, 2, 3, 3 n. 6, 4, 9–11, 11 n. 11, 14–15
  identity, 2, 9, 15, 17, 36, 38, 57, 115–17,
  stigma, 17–20, 29, 36, 97–98, 106, 234
postcolonial
  and hybridity, 54, 54 n. 10, 105, 106 n. 72,
  and the Gospel of Mark, 67–71, 164, 171–73
  biblical criticism, 6, 8, 57 n. 15, 63–67, 66 n. 6, 78, 86, 88, 121, 122 n. 120, 126, 200, 215–17
  criticism, 7–8, 51, 55, 56 n. 15, 59, 63, 65, 104, 179
  definition, 52, 52 n. 6
power dynamics, 4, 36, 38–9, 43, 48, 63, 71, 154, 203, 211
power structures, 4–6, 12, 15, 37, 101, 206
praxis, 5, 9, 12–13, 55–61, 63, 77, 85, 87, 101, 106, 108, 110, 122, 122 n. 120, 123–24, 128–29, 150, 154, 162, 168, 196–99, 203–4, 208–12,
  and theology, 65 n. 5, 107, 107 n. 74,
public agency, 12, 51, 140, 142–44, 164–65, 191, 208–9
reader-response criticism, 9, 9 n. 8, 22 n. 6, 80–81, 86, 126 n. 124,
recovery, 13, 46, 138 n. 17, 168, 177–79, 201, 204–5, 207–8
relational dynamics, 2–3, 3 n. 6, 4–6, 8–9, 12–13, 15, 17, 20–21, 24, 27–31, 36–41, 43–44, 44 n. 1, 46–8, 50–53, 57, 59–61, 63, 66–67, 70, 81–82, 86–87, 89–94, 106–10, 117–18, 121, 123–24, 127–29, 131, 136, 143–44, 147–49, 153, 155, 159, 160, 162, 164, 172, 183, 186, 190–91, 197–201, 203–4, 206–12, 216–17, 219, 221
relational power, 2–3, 35, 41, 50, 53, 59, 102, 106, 203, 206, 209, 216
resistance, 1 n. 1, 6, 9, 11, 13, 26, 29, 29 n. 17, 36–38, 40–41, 50–52, 54, 54 n. 11, 55, 55 n. 12, 56–57, 59–61, 64, 66 n. 5, 69, 87, 106–7, 109–14, 117–19, 120 n. 117, 121–22, 122 nn. 120 and 122, 123–25, 150–51, 160, 167, 172 n. 13, 173, 186, 190, 199, 208–12
scribes, 6, 67, 89, 93, 109, 111–14, 116 n. 105, 118, 120, 120 n. 116, 121, 121 n. 119, 124–26, 126 n. 124, 127, 134 n. 9, 150, 185, 198, 209, 211
silence, 13, 24, 33–34, 64, 91, 98, 103, 118 n. 108, 182, 186–88, 189 n. 70, 191, 194–201, 207, 210
sly civility, 5, 54–56, 59, 71, 197, 210
societal context, 2–3, 11, 15, 17, 20–26, 27 n. 14, 28–29, 34–36, 39–40, 47, 71, 77, 106, 123, 146–48, 182, 200, 204, 206–7
societal power, 4, 15, 43, 208
stereotype, 17–18, 29, 33, 36, 71, 90–92, 94, 98, 108
strategic, 5–6, 39, 43, 48, 51–53, 55, 59, 70, 84 n. 32, 105–6, 146, 150, 186
subaltern, 7–8, 7 n. 7, 49, 52 n. 6, 64, 68, 87, 100, 142, 154, 199–200, 209, 217, 221
supplemental agency, 5, 12–13, 54, 59, 131, 148–49, 203, 210–12
Syrophoenician woman, 12, 67, 149, 151, 153–55, 156, 157 n. 66, 158–65, 208, 214 n. 20
third space, 5, 53–58, 54 n. 11, 61, 211
trained reader, 8, 72, 72 n. 14, 73–75, 75 nn. 20–21, 76–77, 78 n. 24, 80, 85, 86, 94, 219–20

transformation, 5-6, 9, 11-12, 29, 37, 46, 50, 54, 57-58, 60-61, 70, 87, 106, 108-9, 124, 127-28, 147-48, 159, 160, 167-68, 169 n. 2, 172, 179, 182-83, 198-99, 201, 206-12, 215, 218

user-led movement, 205

woman with hemorrhages, 6, 12, 67, 129-30, 132-34, 134 n. 9, 135, 135 n. 10, 136 n. 11, 137, 137 nn. 12-13, 138, 138 nn. 16-17, 139, 139 nn. 19-20, 142-43, 145-46, 164-65, 200, 208, 216, 221

www.ingramcontent.com/pod-product-compliance
Lightning Source LLC
Chambersburg PA
CBHW021115300426
44113CB00006B/163